# Feminism and Antiracism

# Feminism and Antiracism

*International Struggles for Justice*

EDITED BY

*France Winddance Twine*
*and Kathleen M. Blee*

*New York University Press*

NEW YORK AND LONDON

NEW YORK UNIVERSITY PRESS
New York and London

Library of Congress Cataloging-in-Publication Data
Feminism and antiracism : international struggles for justice / edited
by France Winddance Twine and Kathleen M. Blee.
p. cm.
Includes index.
ISBN 0-8147-9854-3 (cloth : alk. paper) —
ISBN 0-8147-9855-1 (pbk. : alk. paper)
1. Feminist theory. 2. Feminism. 3. Racism. 4. Sex discrimination
against women. 5. Race discrimination. I. Blee, Kathleen M.
HQ1190 .F4189 2001
305.42—dc21 2001002007

New York University Press books are printed on acid-free paper,
and their binding materials are chosen for strength and durability.

Manufactured in the United States of America
10 9 8 7 6 5 4 3 2

*For Jonathan Warren*
FRANCE WINDDANCE TWINE

*For Pam, Eli, and Sophie*
KATHLEEN M. BLEE

# Contents

# Acknowledgments

We thank the contributors to this volume who responded to a Call for Papers that we issued in 1998. Their political and intellectual investments in social justice made this volume possible. We are also very grateful to all the feminist and antiracist scholars whose work has guided us, including but not limited to scholars in the following fields: gender and development studies, global feminisms, international feminisms, and transnational feminisms. Although we have met few of the feminists and antiracist scholars working in transnational feminisms we have been inspired and nurtured by their research and activism.

We received institutional support from the following during this project and thank our colleagues at the following institutions: Departments of Sociology at the University of California, Santa Barbara, the University of Pittsburgh, and the Henry M. Jackson School of International Studies at the University of Washington in Seattle. Winddance Twine would like to thank the Andrew Mellon Foundation and the participants in the 1999–2000 Sawyer Seminar at the University Center for International Studies at the University of North Carolina, Chapel Hill, which served as an intellectual home during the final editing of this volume. Winddance Twine also thanks the following colleagues and friends on both sides of the Atlantic for all the innumerable ways in which they continue to support her research (including the meals, rides to and from airports, lively debates, and unconditional friendship). In this vein Twine thanks (in England): Nelista Cuffy, Caroline Churchill, Amelia Dowdye, Rachel Hunte, Mary Hunte, Bernice Bennett, Owen Brown, Jane Brown, Mandy Burke, Gerry Burke, Sharon Dawkins, Janet Powell, and Cheryl Weathers; (in Ireland): Michael Smyth; (in South Africa): Julia Maxted and Abebe Zegeye; (in the United States): Ingrid Banks, William T. Bielby, Denise Bielby, Karen Brodkin, William Darity Jr., Troy Duster, Maria Franklin, Ruth Frankenberg, Arnell Hinkle, Kristin Luker, Mary Romero, Beth Schneider, Gay Seidman, Judy Taylor, Becky Thompson, Irma McClaurin,

Ruth Mostern, Kenneth Mostern, Pedro Noguera, Darrel Robinson, Kum-Kum Bhavnani, John Foran, Avery Gordon, Gail Hanlon, Ara Wilson, and John Wolfe.

Kathleen Blee thanks students in Feminist Theory and Gender, Race, Class seminars at the University of Pittsburgh as well as Lisa Brush, Kipp Dawson, Kathleen DeWalt, Patrick Doreian, Irene Frieze, Pam Goldman, Maurine Greenwald, Carol McAllister, Janet Montelaro, Marilyn Patete, Verta Taylor, Eileen VanSchaik, and Eileen Yacknin.

We would like to thank Despina Papazoglou Gimbel who, once again, worked diligently and with much patience and professionalism to keep this book on track. We owe Ms. Gimbel more gratitude than can be expressed here.

Finally Winddance Twine dedicates this book to her family who make the impossible possible for her each day: Mamie Lois Twine, Paul Christopher Twine, and Jonathan Warren. Kathleen dedicates it to Pam, Eli, and Sophie.

FRANCE WINDDANCE TWINE
*Santa Barbara, California*

and

KATHLEEN M. BLEE
*Pittsburgh, Pennsylvania*

October 2000

# Foreword

## *Mary Romero*

I read *Feminism and Antiracism: International Struggles for Justice* in the midst of the year 2000 U.S. election when the margin of victory was less than the margin of error. Internationally, the election debacle revealed some of the contradictions and hypocrisies of U.S. imperialist claims to be the guardian of democracy. Nationally we were confronted by strategists arguing the validity of charges lodged by diverse groups of disenfranchised citizens. It appears that standards requiring a recount are different for white middle-class retirees, for black Americans, and for mail-in ballots from overseas military personnel. Black Americans, Haitian Americans, and other citizens of color, largely ignored in the Supreme Court appeal, turned to the NAACP, the Rainbow Coalition, and other civil rights leaders to call for a federal investigation. Devices and maneuvers that disenfranchised Florida voters were as diverse as the groups affected: butterfly ballots, hanging chads, ballot tampering, destroyed ballots, voters turned away at the polls, racial profiling, and police harassment. The debates, lawsuits, and protests about U.S. electoral processes—and the important literature I was reading—focused my attention on the need for a feminist and antiracist struggle to make every vote count. The sixteen cases presented in this volume make us recognize risks and dangers, efforts, and strategies used to build real democratic institutions. Reflecting on the creation of a women's center in Italy; the struggles to organize immigrant women from Somalia, Eritrea, the Ivory Coast, Morocco, Kenya, Yugoslavia, Spain, Germany, and Tunisia; or the efforts of white and black South Africans in a rape crisis center—I pondered the rich possibilities for uniting Blacks, Haitians, Jews, Latinos, the elderly, women, the poor, and military personnel behind the struggle to change the electoral system and put an end to voter disenfranchisement.

*

France Winddance Twine and Kathleen Blee have edited an important scholarly work that moves the discussion of feminist and antiracist practices beyond theory and into the streets, schools, homes, shelters, clinics, campuses, broadcasting networks, courts, rape crisis centers, churches, and women's organizations. Kathleen and Winddance began this project by issuing a challenge to contributors to interrogate the concepts of feminism and antiracism by examining struggles within specific regional and national structures. They thus underscored the local limits and cultural constraints that shape antiracist practice. The resulting anthology offers focused cases of feminist activists who are committed to antiracist practices but must implement these practices for social justice in concrete and historical circumstances. Their work is grounded in specific local struggles throughout Africa, Asia, Europe, North America, the South Pacific, and the Middle East. Contributors explore successful and unsuccessful alliances across boundaries of gender, religion, class, caste, sexuality, ethnicity, generation, and nationalism. The analysis and personal reflection on coalition building in the struggles for social justice that takes place across multiple hierarchical axes helps move the twentieth century analysis of class solidarity and social change toward twenty-first century discourse on feminism and antiracism.

This volume challenges both scholars and activists to rethink binary models of organizing and embrace the complexities manifested in a global economy and the transnational circumstances created by colonialism and its legacies. Each case offers valuable lessons learned by activists and organizers laboring in the critical intersections framed by feminist and antiracist practice. The anthology also reveals the transformative potential behind feminist and antiracist organizing practices. It instructs us by allowing us to see both successful and not so successful processes of social change resulting from actual practices used by feminist and antiracist organizers in a variety of international settings, including: women's courts in India, immigrant women's centers in Italy, health care workers in Yemen, strippers in San Francisco nightclubs, and volunteers in rape crisis centers in South Africa and the United States. The authors carefully attend to practices and processes of feminism and antiracism and capture everyday challenges to hierarchical social structures and normative social relationships. In these accounts, tensions and transgressions suggest transformative potential and social justice beyond immediate needs and crises. Grounded struggles in feminism and antiracism challenge the existing hierarchical power structure and use both direct and indirect methods for reconstructing social relationships. For example, in her analysis of practices adopted by the *murshidat*, the women primary health care workers in Yemen, Delores Walters not only documents significant changes in maternal and infant mortality, but helps us understand the changing genealogical, racial, gender, and occupational social relations. Examining the "danger talk" occurring in staff meetings at a rape crisis center in South Africa, Michelle Rosenthal attends to tensions that push race, ethnicity, and class toward discussions of feminist empowerment and democracy. Yoshiko Nozaki's research on the inclusion of Comfort Women in Japanese history emphasizes how the process encourages teachers to confront their own racism and sexism.

Antiracist practice involves a process of changes introduced into the wide range of social relationships within multiple hierarchical axes. Struggles for maternal and child health care, religious freedom, immigrant women's rights, and better working conditions involve women and men in ongoing social transformations. In the various feminist spaces that serve as sites for antiracist practice, the transformative potential is revealed. Having read *Feminism and Antiracism: International Struggles for Justice*, I can now more easily imagine a coalition to challenge election practices in the United States, because it no longer seems an impossibility! The lessons offered by these feminist ethnographies are that social relations and power blocs seemingly set in stone are here for us to study, discuss, and change. This volume furthers transnational struggles for justice.

*Tempe, Arizona*
December 2000

# Contributors

*Michael P. Armato* is pursuing his Ph.D. in sociology at New York University. He earned his M.A. in sociology from the University of Florida in 1997. His research interests include gender, family, and social movements.

*Cathleen L. Armstead* teaches sociology as an Adjunct Professor at Valencia Community College in Orlando, Florida. As a sociologist she was trained in the interdisciplinary Social Relations program at the University of California at Irvine. She has been engaged in antiracist work as the Director of Research for Democracy Forum in Orlando, Florida (1998–99). Her work has been published in the *Encyclopedia of Sociology* (1992) and *Women's Studies International Forum* (1995).

*Paola Bacchetta* is an Associate Professor of Sociology based in the Department of Geography and Women's Studies at the University of Kentucky at Lexington. Bacchetta earned her Ph.D. in Sociology at the Sorbonne (Paris). She is the author of a book on Hindu nationalism entitled *The RSS and the Nation: Gendered Discourse/Gendered Action* (New Delhi: Kali for Women, forthcoming). She is the coeditor of *Right Wing Women across the Globe* (Routledge, forthcoming in 2001), which is a comparative, interdisciplinary volume that covers all regions of the world. She has been an activist in women's and lesbian networks and in antiracist movements in France, India, Italy, and the United States.

*Kathleen M. Blee* is Professor of Sociology and Director of Women's Studies at the University of Pittsburgh. She is the author of *Women of the Klan: Racism and Gender in the 1920s* (University of California Press, 1991) and *Inside Organized Racism: Women and Men in the Hate Movement* (University of California Press, 2001). She is the editor of *No Middle Ground: Radical Women and Protest* (New York University Press, 1998), and coauthor, with Dwight Billings, of *The Road to*

*Poverty: The Making of Wealth and Hardship in Appalachia* (Cambridge University Press, 2000).

*andrea breen* is a Tasmanian producer, composer, and designer of feminist sound installations whose activism has centered on the performance of feminist plays at national folk festivals, music festivals, and national radio broadcasts. As a producer of the CD *Improvisation-image-voice* (1998), breen has worked collectively with feminist and lesbian poets to counter racism and sexism in Australian public culture. breen completed an interdisciplinary feminist Ph.D. at the University of Tasmania, where she taught English studies, and has completed a Graduate degree in Creative Arts Therapies from the Melbourne Institute of Experimental and Creative Arts Therapies. She lives in Hobart with her two adult children.

*Siobhan Brooks* is pursuing a graduate degree in Sociology at the New School for Social Research in New York City. Her writings have been published in *Z Magazine, Third Force* magazine, *HUES* magazine, the anthology *Whores and Other Feminists*, and University of California, Berkeley's *Hasting Law Journal*. Between 1994 and 1999 she worked as a union organizer at the Lusty Lady exotic dance theater in San Francisco. She has lectured on race, sex work, and feminism at San Francisco State University, University of California, Berkeley, and Yale Divinity School.

*Ashwini Deshpande* is assistant professor of Economics at the Delhi School of Economics, India. This paper was written when she was a postdoctoral fellow at the Carolina Population Center, University of North Carolina, Chapel Hill, USA. Her publications have examined the international debt crisis of the 1970s and intergroup inequality in India with special emphasis on caste and gender. She teaches courses on the economics of discrimination, the history of international labor flows, and the international debt crisis. Email: *ashwini@cdedse.ernet.in* and *ashwini6@hotmail.com.*

*Jane Freedman* is Lecturer in the Department of Politics at the University of Southampton, United Kingdom. She earned her doctorate in political sociology from the University of Paris VII. Her research centers on issues of gender and politics in France and Europe. Her publications include *Femmes Politiques: Mythes et Symboles* (Paris: L'Harmattan, 1997) and *Women, Immigration and Identities in France* (Oxford: Berg,

2000). She has also published articles and chapters on issues of gender parity in French and European politics, and on gender and migration in France and Europe.

*Veronica Magar* is Regional Technical Advisor, Asia for CARE. She is responsible for designing, implementing, monitoring, and evaluating community-based reproductive health programs (including HIV/AIDS). She earned her doctoral degree in public health from the University of North Carolina at Chapel Hill in 2000. Her dissertation was titled *Reconceptualizing Domestic Violence in Delhi Slums: Multidimensional Factors and Empowerment Approaches.* Since the early 1980s, she has been involved with activism in international women's health and development and through labor organizing of nurses in the United States. Her social concerns emerged from her multicultural experiences which range from growing up Egyptian/German in America to working in low-income communities in Brazil, Egypt, India, and the United States. She can be reached at *magar@care.org.*

*Minelle Mahtani* is a Killam Postdoctoral Fellow at the University of British Columbia in the departments of Geography and Journalism, where she is exploring issues of identity among "mixed race" youth in Vancouver. She earned her degree in geography from University College, London. Between 1994 and 1999 she worked as a national television news producer for the Canadian Broadcasting Corporation in Toronto.

*Heather Merrill* is assistant professor of geography at Dickinson College. She earned her degree in 1999 from the University of California at Berkeley. She is a critical feminist geographer working on race, subalternity, and interethnic feminist politics. She is currently working on a manuscript entitled *Speaking Subjects: Remaking Feminisms and Race in the New Migrant Europe.*

*Yoshiko Nozaki* is Lecturer in the Department of Educational Leadership and Social Policy Studies at Massey University in New Zealand. Nozaki earned her Ph.D. in Educational Policy Studies at the University of Wisconsin-Madison in 2000. She earned her B.A. in Japanese history at Nagoya University and has taught in Australia, Japan, and the United States. Her recent articles have been published in *Anthropology and Education Quarterly* and *Urban Education.* Between 1979 and 1989 she taught geography and history to junior high school students in the Kasugai and the Nagoya public school systems in Japan.

*Eileen O'Brien* is Assistant Professor of Sociology at State University of New York at Brockport, where she teaches courses that contribute to the Women's Studies, African and African American Studies programs. She earned her M.A. in Sociology at Ohio State University and her Ph.D. in Sociology in 1999 at the University of Florida. She has written articles on white antiracist activists, as well as the issue of reparations for African Americans (with Joe Feagin) in *When Sorry Isn't Enough*. Her current research critically evaluates diversity training programs in the United States.

*Michelle Rosenthal* earned her Ph.D. in Anthropology from the University of California at Santa Cruz. She has studied at Yale University and the University of Sussex, England. Between 1994 and 1996 she conducted field research at a rape crisis center in Cape Town, South Africa.

*Ellen Kaye Scott* is an Assistant Professor of Sociology at Kent State University in Ohio. She earned her Ph.D. at the University of California, Davis, and her M.A. in political science from the New School for Social Research in New York. She is the author of the forthcoming book *Feminists Working across Racial Divides* and the codirector of a longitudinal ethnographic study on the impact of welfare reform on the lives of welfare recipients in Cleveland, Ohio. Scott's research is directly related to her engagement in battered women's movements and antipoverty initiatives in the United States.

*Carolyn Martin Shaw* is Professor of Anthropology and former Provost of Kresge College at the University of California at Santa Cruz. She is the author of *Colonial Inscriptions: Race, Class and Sex in Kenya* (University of Minnesota Press, 1995) which is based upon years of work in Kenya, as well as numerous articles. She first went to Zimbabwe in 1982. In 2000 she was declared an Honorary Trustee of the Women's Action Group, which she helped to found in 1983. She has been on the editorial board of feminist, anthropological, and gay/lesbian journals.

*Sohera Syeda* was born in Hyderabad, India, and raised in the United States. She earned her B.A. in Molecular Biology, Biochemistry, and Women's Studies at Wesleyan University in Middletown, Connecticut. She lives and works in Chicago, Illinois.

*Becky Thompson* teaches Sociology and African American Studies at Simmons College in Boston. She is the coeditor of two volumes and the author of *A Promise and a Way of Life: White Antiracist Activism* (University of Minnesota Press, forthcoming), *Mothering without a Compass: White Mother's Love, Black Son's Courage* (University of Minnesota Press, 2000), and *A Hunger So Wide and So Deep: A Multiracial View of Women's Eating Problems* (University of Minnesota, 1994). She is a member of Academics for Mumia Abu-Jamal.

*France Winddance Twine,* an enrolled member of the Creek Nation of Oklahoma, is Associate Professor of Sociology at the University of California, Santa Barbara, where she teaches feminist theory, critical race theory, antiracist studies, and field research methods. Twine is the author of *Racism in a Racial Democracy: The Maintenance of White Supremacy in Brazil* (1997) and *Bearing Blackness in Britain* (forthcoming). She is the coproducer of the documentary *Just Black? Multiracial Identity* (1991), and the coeditor of three volumes including *Racing Research, Researching Race: Methodological Dilemmas in Critical Race Studies* (New York University Press, 2000), and *Ideologies and Technologies of Motherhood: Race, Class Sexuality and Nationalism* (Routledge, 2000). Her recent articles have appeared in *Race & Class, Social Identities, Feminist Studies,* and *Meridians: feminism, race, transnationalism.* She is a member of the editorial collective that publishes *Feminist Studies* and a consulting editor for *American Sociological Review.*

*Delores M. Walters* earned her Ph.D. in Anthropology from New York University and her B.S. in Nursing from Columbia University. She is the Director of the ALANA (African, Latin, Asian, Native American) Cultural Center at Colgate University in Hamilton, New York. As an educator and administrator, she provides support for students of color while overseeing multicultural programs and activities that are inclusive of all students. She also teaches an anthropology course in which students are helping the medical staff in a nearby community to become more culturally sensitive to their diverse immigrant and refugee clientele. As a community organizer, she has coordinated various social, health, housing and educational self-help programs. Her doctoral research on African-identified Yemeni groups led to a documentary video entitled "*Murshidat:* Female Primary Health Care Workers Transforming Society in Yemen" (1999).

# Feminism and Antiracism

# Feminist Antiracist Maps
## *Transnational Contours*

## *Kathleen M. Blee and France Winddance Twine*

On March 9, 2000, in commemoration of International Women's Day eight thousand Mexican women, many of them Zapatista rebel sympathizers, peacefully took over a Chiapas radio station, to demonstrate for the rights of women and indigenous people (Indians) in Mexico. They stopped the programming for half an hour to call attention to their situation as women of indigenous ancestry who continue to suffer from discrimination and whose economic status is lower than that of lighter skinned women of mixed and European ancestry in Mexico.

The idea of International Women's Day arose at the turn of the twentieth century among women working in the clothing and textile factories in the United States. They staged a protest on March 8, 1857 in their fight against inhumane working conditions and low wages. Two years later these women formed their first labor union to protect themselves and gain some basic rights in the workplace. In March 1908, fifteen thousand women marched through New York City demanding shorter work hours, better pay, voting rights, and an end to child labor. They adopted the slogan "Bread and Roses," bread symbolizing economic security and roses a better quality of life. In May 1908, the Socialist Party of America designated the last Saturday in February National Women's Day. Following the declaration of the Socialist Party of America, the first Women's Day was celebrated in the United States on February 28, 1909. Women in the United States continued to celebrate the twenty-eighth of that month through 1913. In 1917 Russian women chose the last Sunday in February to strike for "bread and peace" in the aftermath of the death of 2 million Russian soldiers. Four days later, the Czar of Russia abdicated and the provisional government granted women the right to vote. That Sunday fell on February 23 on the Julian calendar then in use in Russia but coincided with March 8 on the Gregorian calendar used by many in other countries. Today International Women's Day is an international holiday observed around the globe.

## International Contours of This Book

In this volume feminist scholars and activists committed to feminist and antiracist struggles map the trajectories of several contemporary feminist and antiracist movements for social justice. This book builds upon the work of previous feminist volumes that considered postcolonial struggles, citizenship, and democracy.[1] However, in contrast to several feminist analyses of global feminisms, women and development, and transnational feminism, this book seeks to bridge feminist theorizing and transnational antiracist activism by bringing together empirically grounded studies of practices intended to explicitly challenge the intersections of racial, ethnic, and gender inequalities.

This volume includes sixteen chapters from scholars and activists trained in nine fields or professions, selected from those received in response to a Call for Papers distributed internationally via electronic mailing lists, advertisements in feminist journals, and newsletters. We asked the contributors to this volume to consider the following question: (1) How does gender and region/nation structure how feminists engage in antiracist practices? (2) How has the restructuring of the world economy affected feminist and antiracist practices? and (3) What are the actual practices of feminist and antiracist organizers?

While we[2] are aware that the terms "feminism" and "antiracism" must be problematized as they possess neither a fixed meaning nor a unitary history, we also recognize that practices that can be considered "feminist" and "antiracist" in intent or effect are refashioned and reworked by women to serve their interests in particular locales.[3] While the meaning of racism and antiracism is contested and mutable, for a number of the contributors who write from nations that have fought for independence against British imperial rule, the circulation of antiracist discourses has been facilitated by the struggle against British imperialism.[4] This volume covers ten countries in Africa, East and South Asia, Europe, North America, Oceania, the South Pacific, and the Middle East. With the exception of those chapters that address local movements in Western Europe and East Asia, the countries represented here were former colonies of the British empire.

Although they work in diverse national contexts, the contributors to this volume describe a number of recurring sites of transnational struggle against injustice. As women in particular local contexts with different legacies of colonialism and racism they may disagree about what constitutes a "feminist" or "antiracist" practice. Nevertheless, as we shall see, they draw on feminist discourses and form strategic coalitions in order to secure access to a wide range of services and rights. These include religious freedom, immigrant women's rights, access to maternal and child healthcare, access to trauma services, and nonracist labor conditions.

Contributors to *Feminism and Antiracism: International Struggles for Justice* map the struggles of women and men to establish viable communities and multiethnic coalitions in both women-controlled and male-dominated sites. We learn about organic struggles for travel rights in Zimbabwe (Shaw), access to healthcare services in Yemen and South Africa (Walters, Rosenthal), access to sexual trauma services in South Africa and the United States (Rosenthal, Scott), domestic violence services (Magar, Scott), and labor rights (Merrill, Brooks) as well as projects that counter nationalist and masculinist ideologies in India, Japan, and the United Sattes (Bacchetta, Nozaki, O'Brien and Armato), and national narratives and local practices that promote racialized exclusions in France, Italy, India, Japan, and the United States (Freedman, Merrill, Bacchetta, Nozaki, and Armstead).

## Feminist Spaces, Antiracist Maps

The first section of this volume is organized around an analysis of multiethnic feminist "spaces" where women working in four different national contexts (Italy, India, the United States, and Yemen) have achieved some success in organizing against racism and class inequalities. These chapters provide preliminary maps of organic sites of antiracist and feminist activism as practiced by women who occupy a range of national, migrant, occupational, caste, and citizenship categories. This section opens with Heather Merrill's analysis of *Alma Mater*, an antiracist women's center in Turin, an industrial city in northern Italy. Merrill's chapter describes the strategies employed by immigrant women to "rework" Italian feminism and thus generate a space from which they can launch a number of local antiracist projects with the goal of educating the Italian public (and Italian feminists) about cultural racism. Moreover they have found ways to work with Italian feminists on ventures that can empower them culturally and materially. Merrill, a geographer, charts the social and political activism of Italian feminists and immigrant women that has led both to the creation of a women's center, while also reproducing the socially divisive and exclusionary ideologies that they oppose. Merrill's analysis cautions feminists to consider conflicts that can emerge around differences of color, ethnicity, race, nation, and class and that can coincide with the establishment of organizations that bring women of diverse national and religious origins together.

In "Resisting Domestic Violence and Caste Inequality: All-Women Courts in India," Veronica Magar, a health activist, provides an analysis of Action India, a feminist nongovernmental organization (NGO) that has brought together women from different caste groups to challenge domestic violence and caste barriers. Magar provides a case study of what has become one of the most effective and efficient means of providing legal protection to lower-caste women living in Delhi's slums. She describes the work of mahila panchayats (all-women's courts in Hindi). These unofficial courts were created by women and are modeled after biradari panchayats (local caste brotherhoods). Magar argues that although they lack material privilege and literacy skills, lower-caste women living in the slums have successfully organized against domestic violence through all-women's courts that hold men accountable for domestic violence and neglect. Moreover the women have accomplished this while also being responsive to the needs of the men involved. It is a compelling account of nonelite women refashioning indigenous forms of social control to meet their own needs for social justice.

In "Exotic Dancing and Unionizing," Siobhan Brooks, a former exotic dancer, provides a rare analysis of union organizing among exotic dancers at the Lusty Lady, a woman-managed strip club in San Francisco. As a black feminist union organizer Brooks details the strategies employed by herself and other women of color to challenge the institutional racism operating within a strip club in San Francisco's Little Italy tourist district. As a former erotic dancer, Brooks describes in the first person her efforts as a U.S. black feminist to organize her colleagues into a collective to challenge racist labor practices that sustained a two-tier system of labor opportunities that economically privileged white women dancers and restricted the earnings of women of color.

This section concludes with "Women, Healthcare, and Social Reform in Yemen" by Delores Walters. This is a much needed analysis of a development project in the Middle East that places the legacy of slavery and ethnic domination at the center. By carefully considering the formerly enslaved African ethnic groups and centering antiracism, Delores Walters's analysis reframes the development literature and responds to a gap in earlier discussions of gender and development. We learn from Walters that in Yemen, where slavery was officially abolished only in 1970, there are social and economic divisions between Yemenis of slave ancestry and nonslave ancestry. Female health workers known as *murshidat* are effectively challenging these divisions through their work in a public health clinic by providing women who belong to formerly enslaved African ethnic groups access to health services and privileges that were previously denied to them. In this analysis of the first generation of women healthcare professionals (*murshidat*) in Yemen, Walters reframes development studies by considering how some women healthcare professionals challenge racialized hierarchies by entering the homes of and providing services to women who belong to formerly enslaved African groups and who were treated as "untouchable" until recently. By promoting social integration, Walters shows how African women who do not employ the terms "feminist" or "antiracist" are, nevertheless, engaged in practices that are having a transformative effect on one of the most important public institutions, the Maternal and Child Health Care Center. Centers such as this are becoming a model of the type of antiracist space that generates political possibilities for more egalitarian relationships between the descendants of slaves and nonslaves.

## Feminist Talk, Antiracist Dialogue

The chapters in the second section of this volume explore the dilemmas feminists encounter as they attempt to constitute feminist communities and antiracist language (and spaces) that enable women to engage in dialogue about race, racism, and power. The difficulties of generating multiethnic feminist spaces that promote antiracist dialogue between women and men who differ along axes of power (race, class, sexuality, immigrant status) are examined in four national contexts: Australia, Japan, South Africa, and the United States. This section begins with "Danger Talk: Race and Feminist Empowerment in the New South Africa." Michelle Rosenthal analyzes three acts of antiracist community building among the staff and volunteers working at a rape crisis center in Cape Town, South Africa. Rosenthal asks how South African women imagine and practice political empowerment in the "new" South Africa. She finds that the reconstruction of a feminist community in the postapartheid era in a multiethnic rape crisis center requires "danger talk," talk that involves accusations of racism by women of color. Rosenthal defines danger talk as "stories murmured alongside official accounts of conflict and reconciliation" as a significant form of *political* empowerment. We learn from Rosenthal's careful analysis that this "danger talk," which circulates among women working at the center, threatens parallel "narratives of sexual violence told by rape survivors" and that "narratives of conflict within this feminist organization break oppressive silences in their telling." Moreover, documenting sexual crimes and organizational racism is a narrative act aimed at *resolution* for the women. Ultimately Rosenthal provides insights into the way specific narratives are employed by women to generate new forms of political activism and reconfigure feminist communities organized against sexual violence in the postapartheid period.

This same theme of dangerous talk and "silence" is examined in a different national context by Ellen Kaye Scott. In "From Race Cognizance to Racism Awareness: Dilemmas in Antiracist Activism in California," Ellen Kaye Scott, a sociologist, examines practices that resemble racism awareness workshops in two women's centers: a rape crisis center and a battered women's center founded in the 1970s by feminists to assist women coping with male violence. Scott finds that complexities and contradictions emerge when multiethnic feminist organizations employ racism awareness workshops. Although racism awareness workshops are promoted as a vehicle for engaging in antiracist dialogue in a variety of organizational contexts, Scott asks whether such intentions are realized. Her analysis of two women's organizations in California suggests that antiracist workshops can reflect and perpetuate the notion that racism is a product of individual beliefs, ignorance, and misunderstanding, rather than a manifestation of racialized power relations. Scott found that a paradoxical "silence" prevailed even in feminist organizations that were self-conscious and had an institutional commitment to explicitly address racism because "they failed to challenge a culture of avoidance around racism." By mapping the obstacles to direct dialogue about the dynamics of interethnic and interracial relations between women, Scott cautions feminists to consider that racialized conflicts within organizations are not always manifested through the prism of white racism, but can involve hostilities among women of color who occupy varying national, sexual, citizenship, and ethnic positions.

Feminist theater and performance art is an important activist site for feminist and antiracist cultural work. In "Between the Covers: Feminist, Antiracist, and Queer Performance Art in Australia," andrea breen writes as a musician, composer, and sound installation artist to examine the use of poetry, music, and visual images as an activist site among lesbian feminist cultural workers. By providing a map of her collaborative work with Sue Moss, breen shows how lesbian and queer performance artists seek to provide a feminist and antiracist visual vocabulary and antiracist narratives to general and queer audiences in Australia. Queer performance artists strategically employ their work to generate feminist and antiracist spaces of experience and consciousness while challenging audiences to rethink their relationship to indigenous people, women, and national narratives of Australian history that do not consider the experiences of indigenous people (also referred to as Aboriginal), lesbians, women, and the land.

This section ends with Yoshiko Nozaki's analysis of Japanese national conflicts over how to understand and record the exploitation of Korean "comfort women" by the Japanese government during World War II. The issue of how to talk about routinized military sexual slavery is a critical one for feminists in Japan and South Korea. Nozaki, who has taught in Japanese high schools, explores the ways in which the Japanese imperial project rested on a myth of Japanese racial superiority over the Asians that they conquered and the ways in which feminists, particularly teachers, have engaged in a struggle over national memory. High school textbooks have become an important site in Japan for countering a masculinist Japanese nationalism and racism. Focusing upon the high school classroom, Nozaki examines the ways in which teachers have challenged a national silence about Korean women who have been constructed as racialized others within the Japanese national community. Thus, Nozaki points to the labor of teachers, who although they may not self-identify as feminists or antiracists, are engaged in intellectual projects that generate political possibilities for the constitution of a feminist and antiracist constituency among Japanese youth. Nozaki's analysis of the intellectual labor of high school teachers exemplifies initiatives by teachers to renovate the curriculum—thus countering Japanese racial mythologies and establishing fertile ground for transnational feminist and antiracist coalitions between Japanese and South Korean women.

## Coalitions at Work

Why is it crucial for feminists to build multiethnic coalitions to organize on behalf of women and men with whom they do not necessarily share religious beliefs, sexual orientations, cultural values, or even a commitment to feminist principles? The chapters in this section explore this theme within three national contexts. We begin with an analysis by Sohera Syeda, a South Asian, and Becky Thompson, a U.S. white woman, who were involved in coorganizing a successful campuswide rally in support of a new trial for Mumia Abu-Jamal, a U.S. black man on death row. In "Coalition Politics in Organizing for Mumia Abu-Jamal," Syeda and Thompson detail the specific strategies they employed to establish a multiethnic political coalition in support of justice in the punishment industry. In a provocative and compelling analysis, they explain why they decided not to designate their work on behalf of Abu-Jamal as "feminist." In their reflections upon how they forged a campus coalition that brought together women and men from diverse racial, ethnic, class, and religious backgrounds, they provide a number of instructive insights for feminists committed to organizing across racial, class, occupational, religious, and sexual lines. They describe for us the tools that they developed and employed to manage the conflicts that can emerge when working as part of a multiethnic coalition.

In another context in which women have established antiracist and what could be considered feminist alliances across caste, class, religious, and sexual lines in response to Hindu nationalism, Paola Bacchetta considers two forms of women's oppositional action and two specific incidents in which women organized across different positions in India. In her chapter, "Extraordinary Alliances in Crisis Situations: Women against Hindu Nationalism in India," Bacchetta analyzes the Ahmedabad riots among upper-caste Hindus in 1985 and the cinema trashings that occurred in response to the screening of Deepa Mehta's feature film *Fire* (1996). Bacchetta maps a shift in lesbian and gay political activism in India by carefully detailing the support that Indian lesbians have received from nonlesbian groups. The establishment of The Campaign for Lesbian Rights demonstrates how women in India can successfully organize across multiple axes of differences.

Writing from the perspective of a U.S. black feminist who has worked with West African feminists for two decades, Carolyn Martin Shaw, a Black anthropologist, considers how international feminists can support

African women. She reflects upon her own work in a women's organization in Zimbabwe called Women's Action Group (WAG) which formed in opposition to Operation Clean-Up, which resulted in the indiscriminate imprisonment of urban women in Zimbabwe in the 1980s by the government. Martin Shaw asks what it means to act as a socialist feminist, for Zimbabwean women nationals and for women outside the country. As a U.S. black woman she reflects upon what enabled her to forge and sustain a long-term relationship with Zimbabwean feminists. She discusses some of the dilemmas that emerged for the WAG because it was initially dominated by university-educated, middle-class white women and black women from Zimbabwe, Australia, Britain, and the United States. Although Martin Shaw cautions non-African women to consider "how" they should work with women in other countries, she concludes that international feminists have been and remain crucial in Zimbabwean women's struggles for social justice.

This section concludes with a comparative analysis of white antiracists and male profeminist groups in North America in "Building Connections between Antiracism and Feminism: Antiracist Women and Profeminist Men" by Eileen O'Brien and Michael Armato. O'Brien draws upon her interviews with two antiracist organizations, Antiracist Action (ARA) and the People's Institute (PI) for Survival and Beyond, while Armato draws upon his work with four profeminist men's groups, Men's Rape Prevention Project (MRPP), Men Stopping Violence (MSV), Men Stopping Rape (MS), and Men as Peacemakers (MP), based in four different cities in the United States. O'Brien and Armato offer insights for feminists concerned with building coalitions with men and women from racially dominant groups since they are looking at groups attempting to build antiracist and feminist cohorts among men and white women in Canada and the United States.

## Faith and Other Unfinished Feminisms

The final section highlights a number of dilemmas that challenge international antiracist feminists organizing for social justice. The first two chapters in this section center on religious traditions, faith-based imperatives, and feminist coalition building as they are negotiated in two different national contexts: France and the United States.

This section begins with Jane Freedman's analysis of the Islamic headscarf controversy in France. Freedman asks non-Muslim feminists who embrace different religious traditions and who are interested in supporting young Muslim women to avoid homogenizing them and to acknowledge the forms of agency they might employ as members of religious and ethnic minorities in France. Freedman examines the assumptions that French feminists make about the motivations of Muslim girls who choose to wear the headscarf to school in a national context in which they belong to a religious and ethnic minority. She identifies a number of problematics that emerge when French feminists fail to consider how French republicanism, nationalism, and liberalism operate in a neocolonial context in which women who have migrated from North African countries formerly colonized by France, attempt to negotiate racism and construct postmigratory identities that can accommodate their religious traditions.

In "Memorializing Racist Massacres: Faith versus Feminism in Florida" Cathleen Armstead analyzes the difficulties of forging effective and enduring religiously inspired feminist antiracist coalitions in the United States. She provides a sobering case study of an effort to engage in interracial "faith-based" organizing around a community history project to document a massacre that occurred in Florida in the 1920s. Armstead identifies the anti-intellectualism of some members of this coalition as one of the factors that led to the group's eventual failure. While Armstead sees the possibility of feminist antiracist work through faith-based coalitions that share common ideals of community building and universal recognition of human rights, she also warns of the pitfalls of such coalition politics, particularly when some members have antifeminist sentiments as well as radically divergent gender and racial agendas. Feminist antiracist politics, Armstead suggests, need to take into account the multiplicity of political strategies and goals that can be represented in coalition politics and to develop means by which these can be acknowledged and contested in ways that do not marginalize or silence members of particular racial groups while advancing their own agendas.

Feminist antiracist scholars need to develop sophisticated analytic tools to understand the rigidities and the points of fragility that constitute racial and gender orders, as well as deep and organic connections to collective movements for justice between genders, races, sexes, nations, and ethnicities. In "Casting Off Servitude: Assessing Caste and Gender Inequality in India," Ashwini Deshpande, an Indian economist, provides feminists with a means to measure multiple and intersecting forms of discrimination.

Deshpande suggests that it is possible to disentangle even complicated interactions such as those between caste status and gender status in postindependence India by reading quantitative estimates of women's status in conjunction with intensive qualitative case studies of women's lives in particular locations. Further, Deshpande moves us to carefully consider the relationship between scholarly excavations of caste and gender inequities and the social movements that challenge discriminatory practices toward women and members of low castes. It can be elusive to document the institutions and social practices in which gender and racial hierarchies are embedded, in part because these are altered constantly by the force of collective and individual acts of resistance and change.

This section concludes with Minelle Mahtani's "cautionary tale" about the recent history of women television broadcast journalists in Toronto, Canada. Despite the numerical gains that women have made in Canadian journalism, Mahtani, a former producer for the Canadian Broadcast Corporation (CBC), finds that what may appear to be a demographic success story for women is, instead, an example of an antifeminist milieu where there has been remarkably little change in the white and male-defined culture of the newsroom. The question that Mahtani poses—one on the agenda of many feminist antiracist activists in situations in which social change is more apparent than real—is, "Why do women remain marginalized symbolically when they are no longer marginalized numerically?" Mahtani's conclusion is sobering, but vital to feminist antiracist practice. She argues that women as individuals can embrace feminist or antiracist ideologies, and even incorporate feminism or antiracism into their self-identity, without a specific and thorough understanding of what these practices might entail. Only through organized and collective strategies can feminist antiracist actions, whether in the newsroom, the classroom, courtroom, or strip club, ultimately be effective in an international struggle for justice.

NOTES

1. See, for example, Bookman and Morgen 1988; Basu 1995; Alexander and Mohanty 1997; and Wing 2000.

2. We are two North Americans, both born in the United States, who have been engaged in feminist and antiracist work as activists and scholars. One of us (Blee) is a white feminist antiracist who has engaged in a number of antiracist, antipoverty, and social justice projects in the United States. The other (Twine) is

an American Indian and Black American who has been involved in antiracist projects in the United States, Brazil, and most recently in England. While we are both U.S.-based, we have worked with and are committed to building coalitions with and learning from feminist antiracists working in all regions of the world.

3. This book benefits from the insights of previous feminist volumes that theorized feminist activism in the United States and international context. See, for example, Bookman and Morgen 1988; Mohanty, Russo, and Torres 1991; and Cohen, Jones, and Tronto 1997.

4. See in particular the chapters by Michelle Rosenthal, Carolyn Martin Shaw, and Delores Walters which address South Africa, Zimbabwe, and Yemen respectively as nations that have struggled most recently against British imperial rule. The chapters by andrea breen on Australia and Minelle Mahtani on Canada reflect the struggles of indigenous people and non-European immigrants in Commonwealth countries whose citizens of European descent did not engage in collective struggles against imperial rule.

## REFERENCES

Alexander, Jacqui, and Chandra Mohanty. 1997. *Feminist Genealogies, Colonial Legacies, Democratic Futures*. New York: Routledge.

Basu, Amrita. 1992. *Two Faces of Protest: Contrasting Modes of Women's Activism in India*. Berkeley: University of California Press.

———. 1995. *The Challenge of Local Feminisms: Women's Movements in Global Perspective*. Boulder, Colo.: Westview Press.

Beccalli, Bianca. 1996. "The Modern Women's Movement in Italy." In *Mapping the Women's Movement: Feminist Politics and Social Transformation in the North*, ed. Monica Threlfall. London: Verso.

Bookman, Ann, and Sandra Morgen, eds. 1988. *Women and the Politics of Empowerment*. Philadelphia: Temple University Press.

Buckley, Sandra. 1997. *Broken Silence: Voices of Japanese Feminism*. Berkeley: University of California Press.

Cohen, Cathy J., Kathleen B. Jones, and Joan C. Tronto, eds., 1997. *Women Transforming Politics: An Alternative Reader*. New York: New York University Press.

*Feminist Review*. 1991. No. 39. Special issue. "Shifting Territories: Feminism and Europe." London.

Jaimes, M. Annette Guerrero. 1997. In *Feminist Genealogies, Colonial Legacies, Democratic Futures*, ed. Jacqui Alexander and Chandra Talpade Mohanty. New York: Routledge.

Kaplan, Caren, Normal Alarcón, and Minoo Moallem, eds. 1999. *Between Woman and Nation: Nationalism, Transnational Feminisms, and the State*. Durham and London: Duke University Press.

Kruks, Sonia, Rayna Rapp, and Marilyn B. Young, eds. 1989. *Promissory Notes: Women in the Transition to Socialism*. New York: Monthly Review Press.

Mohanty, Chandra Talpade, Ann Russo, and Lourdes Torres, eds. 1991. *Third World Women and the Politics of Feminism*. Bloomongton: Indiana University Press.

Ray, Raka. 1999. *Fields of Protest: Women's Movements in India*. Minneapolis: University of Minnesota Press.

Threlfall, Monica, ed. 1996. *Mapping the Women's Movement: Feminist Politics and Social Transformation in the North*. London: Verso.

Wing, Adrienne Katherine. 2000. *Global Critical Race Feminisms: An International Reader*. New York: New York University Press.

PART I

*Feminist Spaces, Antiracist Maps*

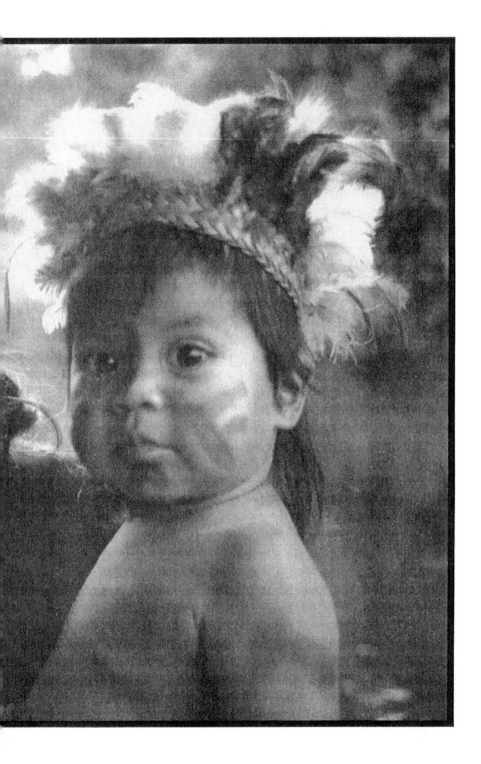

*Chapter 1*

# Making Space for Antiracist Feminism in Northern Italy

## Heather Merrill

### The New Immigration in Italy

On February 28, 1990 Italy passed the Martelli law (Law 39), an immigration bill drafted by the socialist Minister of Justice, Claudio Martelli. The Martelli law inaugurated the first comprehensive Italian immigration policy. It provided legal status and work permits for thousands of migrants already living and working illegally in Italy, but effectively prohibited the entry of new migrants. The law included provisions for self-employment and other forms of work and allowed clandestine migrants to regularize their status by presenting evidence that they had already entered Italy before December 31, 1989.[1] Although thousands of migrants applied for legal documents, the law also inaugurated an effort to "protect" the country's external borders and to crack down on the illegal presence of foreigners through intensified policing and advanced surveillance technologies.[2] Migrants continued to enter Italy in spite of increased border controls, but ideological boundaries were erected between those believed to belong to "Europe" and others who were classified as intruders.

The Martelli law was passed in the context of a concern by several European governments that Italy had become a "gateway" to Europe for Third World immigrants. As the national borders between European nations were breaking down, the ideological distance between those who "belonged to Europe" and those labeled as outsiders had grown. The Italian state was criticized for its apparent inability to address the "invasion of the Other" and pressured by the European Union to develop a strict immigration policy in compliance with the Schengan Agreement.

In contrast to other European countries such as France, Britain, and Germany the "new" immigrants to Italy had not come from countries formerly colonized by Italy. Between 1975 and 1990 thousands of immigrants—about half of whom were women and many of whom were from cities and had at least a secondary school diploma[3]—arrived in Italy from more than a hundred African, Middle Eastern, Asian, and Latin American countries. The greatest official concentrations of newcomers were from Senegal, Nigeria, Morocco, Somalia, Peru, the Philippines, Romania, and Albania.

Such international migration was new in Italy, and prior to 1990 the government had not established organizations to mediate the migrants' transition to the local community. For the most part, the newcomers were left to navigate their way on their own through migrant networks, ethnic associations, or with the help of Catholic voluntary associations. Many experienced considerable difficulty locating housing and access to healthcare. The majority had little knowledge of Italian, though a substantial number understood or spoke other European languages such as French, English, or Spanish. When the Martelli law was passed and thousands of migrants streamed to the Turin police headquarters to begin the process of acquiring legal documents, resident migrants and other volunteers had to be called upon to translate and explain bureaucratic procedures.

By 1989, these "new" immigrants had already been targeted for racial abuse across Italy. Immigrant lodgings were burned to the ground in more than one episode; youth gangs attacked and knifed Moroccans and Senegalese in Florence in 1989, and killed a South African refugee, Jerry Masslo, in Campania. Several newspapers introduced a new column entitled "La caccia al nero" (hunting down blacks) in which racist crimes were reported. Attacks on Senegalese and Moroccan peddlers and campaigns against them by Italian shopkeepers in several Italian cities made it clear that Italians could no longer be characterized as just *brava gente* (decent people), erstwhile victims of other people's racism.[4]

### Turin: Northern Industrial Italy

Turin is located in the northwestern province of Piedmont, and is one of three major cities in the Italian industrial triangle that includes Milan, Turin, and Genova. The Alps form a ring around the city, their snow-capped peaks often casting a luminous glow upon the muted colors of local buildings. For most of the twentieth century, Turin's political culture was rooted in industry, which revolved around the Fiat automobile company. Turin was once the center of one of the most intense and prolonged labor struggles in Italian and European history. This is where Antonio Gramsci conceived of the Italian Communist Party. Although Turin is a city with a pronounced worker culture, it is also the home of old Italian nobility and the House of Savoy.

In this Northern Italian city, a virulent fear of newcomers has resonated with antecedent forms of racism, giving rise to a popular disdain for immigrants.[5] During the early 1990s foreign populations from sub-Saharan Africa and North Africa, who represented some of the largest groups of immigrants, were also the most "racially" visible in Italian towns and cities.[6] These migrants were subsumed under the single nomenclature of "neri" or "blacks," and thought to be Muslim or to follow other strange, perhaps "animist" religious practices. There was little interest in acquiring detailed knowledge about migrant cultural and political backgrounds, and, as in other parts of Europe, a "new" brand of anti-immigrant and racist sentiment was often applied.[7] Fueled by mainstream and right-wing political discourses, this "cultural racism," as it is often called by European social scientists, suggests that cultural and religious differences are insurmountable.[8] Notions of cultural difference operate in subtle ways to justify the actual and metaphorical distance between Europeans and migrants from economically developing countries.

Popular representations of migrants intersected with changes in the local economy to portray Turin as a place where the poor migrant, pushed out of her country in search of employment, would simply be unable to find work. Unemployment rates hovered around 11 percent, quite high in a city that during the 1950s had attracted millions of southern Italian migrants to work as unskilled laborers for the Fiat automobile company. In the late 1970s, however, the Fiat company began to restructure and lay off thousands of workers. Today, Fiat continues to be Turin's major employer, but the stable, low-skilled jobs once readily available have all but disappeared. New workers are confronted with a series of short-term contracts, part-time employment, and demand for highly skilled work for which the majority of Turin dwellers are untrained—or no work at all.[9]

In spite of ongoing economic shifts, the popular idea of work scarcity in Italy is not entirely accurate. As in other parts of Europe, there is at the same time an expanded demand for low-skilled services and casual and temporary employment, often in the informal economic sector. Work in services for a rapidly growing elderly population has grown. In central and southern Italy, seasonal agricultural labor for extremely low wages has flourished, while in northern industrial areas such as Turin, there are an increasing number of jobs for men in construction or small industrial firms.[10] Moreover, with public services in short supply, many Italian families hire a burgeoning population of migrant women as domestic workers or child care workers. Part-time cleaning of market stalls or small businesses is often available to both men and women. There is also a growing market for prostitutes, recruited directly from Nigeria, Ghana, and more recently Albania.[11] Foreign prostitutes tend to be concentrated in major urban areas like Turin and Milan.

There has been considerable, albeit sometimes inconsistent, support for migrant rights among sectors of the Italian left, Catholic organizations, and Turin feminists. City residents show a high level of participation in the local political world. Trade unions appointed migrant delegates to represent new worker populations, and in the early 1990s the Office of Foreign Affairs (Ufficio di Strainieri) was directed by a Catholic priest who was a strong advocate for the fair treatment of newcomers. Many Catholic voluntary organizations sought to help migrants, sometimes providing spaces for them to sleep. A number of Italian feminists made an effort to meet migrant women, holding special meetings for the purpose of supporting female victims of the Gulf war or the war in Somalia.[12] However, the acceleration of international migration during the late 1980s coincided with the changing political climate in eastern Europe and the beginning of a prolonged Italian governmental crisis. The Italian socialist and communist parties fragmented and changed their names during this time and a number of popular protest parties appeared, including the right-wing separatist and anti-immigrant Northern and Lombard leagues.

### Alma Mater: An Immigrant Women's Center

In 1990, a group of migrant women proposed the creation of an antiracist women's center, as a way to oppose racialized work and social conditions for migrant women workers in Turin. Migrant women, they argued, were frequently exploited while working for Italian families and blocked from other avenues of gainful employment. Many women complained of being trapped in Italian households where they were not permitted to see family or friends, discouraged from learning Italian, and asked to perform duties not specified in their agreements or contacts. Others were unable to find work that applied their skills as hairstylists, seamstresses, artisans, or traders in foodstuffs, clothing, and jewelry. Many wished to engage in small-scale business practices. Numerous migrant women complained that they were racially, culturally, and sexually stigmatized, vulnerable to sexual harassment, and alienated. Many experienced Turin as an unwelcoming place which belittled them for everything from their use of the language to their style of physical adornment.

The Martelli law included a provision to fund initiatives for "accoglienza" or the reception of newcomers. A shelter had been established for migrant men, but there was nowhere for migrants to collectively promote social and economic initiatives. The migrant women proposed the use of an abandoned elementary girls' school for a place to receive the growing number of migrant women arriving in Turin. Migrant women, they argued, were dispersed throughout the city, and an interethnic center would bring them together and encourage cooperation and community formation. They further argued that such an organization could teach migrant women about local cultural geography, while developing their skills and talents through the establishment of small cooperative enterprises.

The women presented their arguments to the municipal government during a time of enormous political upheaval and a shuffle for power. Having lost a substantial portion of its working-class constituency, the Italian Communist Party (PCI) was split ideologically between an old labor wing and an intellectual left that wished to nurture a wide political base. At the same time, the former Christian Democratic Party had begun to splinter. As the traditional parties of the left were losing their base, emergent right-wing parties were gaining. The Lega Nord and Benito Mussolini's revived former Fascist party (MSI, Movimento Sociale Italiana) were developing anti-immigrant platforms. These political crises created a vacuum that was filled by some conservative forces, but also inspired the development of new initiatives among progressive politicians and activists.

The migrant women who sought to create the woman's center were from Somalia, Eritrea, the Ivory Coast, Morocco, Kenya, Yugoslavia, Spain, Germany, and Tunisia.[13] Although the group had no formal internal leadership structure, those with the most extensive knowledge of the Italian political world were at the forefront. All had lived in the city for at least one year and had some knowledge of Italian laws regarding the establishment of nongovernmental organizations (NGOs) or cooperatives. They were brought together through various channels, and included participants in local ethnic associations, migrants within the arc of the left-oriented political parties, and members of Catholic organizations. Many were part of intellectual networks organized around the university and trade unions. There was also an effort to include people only loosely affiliated with the intellectual migrants, the majority of whom had just arrived in Turin. These women were informally connected through associations and networks of friends or family, brought together by shared experiences, languages, and inter-African links.

The migrant women proposed a center that would be partially funded by the municipal and regional governments.[14] It was envisioned as an intercultural space to educate the Italian public about different cultures and encourage exchanges between people with myriad "differences." The organization would include various enclaves for migrant women to produce and sell goods representative of their countries of origin and a place where they might operate hairstyling salons and small restaurants, perform dances and other theatrical events, and engage in innovative productive or trade activities. These postcolonial women sought to reverse a pattern in which metropolitan countries exported European or North American social and economic practices to developing countries, so that through commodity exchanges those from less developed parts of the world might exert some influence on the most economically influential nations.

"We have imagined Alma Mater as a place where women could carry out work activities derived from their own cultures, which immigrants want to make known and appreciated, and other activities that would only have the function of responding to the work needs of women, and to the exigencies of the 'market.'"[15] Referring to themselves as "ignored soldiers," these migrant women argued that life in Turin was particularly difficult for women who were confronted with completely new cultural and religious practices. They also argued that in this European environment, migrant cultural diversity was either ignored or employed as a way to justify marginalization:

> This all occurs in a society that shuts its eyes to our own cultures, marginalizes us because of our diversity, because of origins, because of our color, and sees our diversity only from a negative point of view and never as a form of cultural enrichment.[16]

Among themselves, migrant women complained that the representation of foreigners as socially inferior "Others" was a form of racialization and that they intended to make the center an antiracist women's space. They believed it their right to demand fair treatment in Italian society. Many were also engaged in transnational struggles in their own countries of origin while others worked for a free press or for postwar economic reconstruction in their home countries.

When the proposal for the center went to the municipal government for a vote, it was approved by all the female council members. It had considerable support from members of the Democratic Party of the Left (PDS), the larger wing of the former Italian Communist Party, and was supported by the female president of the neighborhood in which the center would be located, a woman and former instructor at the school called "Alma Mater." The migrants decided to retain the name when they could not agree upon a term representative of all of the cultural groups that comprised their membership. They located Alma Mater in a working-class quarter on the outskirts of Turin in a large former elementary school in an old factory corridor, next to a Catholic church and across from a cemetery, a short tram ride away from the city's congested commercial zone.

To the considerable disappointment of the migrant women, the local government initially denied them the privilege of directing the center's finances. A legal stipulation requiring that an association be more than five years old obliged them to find a more established association to direct Alma Mater. They turned to the feminists of the Casa della Donna (Women's House), who rapidly became an integral part of the project.[17] The association, Produrre e Riprodurre (Production and Reproduction), and particularly its splinter group, Donne in Sviluppo (Women in Development), which was concerned with issues of women's work and development, was predisposed to taking on the Alma Mater project.[18] Several of these Italian feminists had been linked with the struggles of migrant women, helping to distribute ethnic meals through a catering service. Some had traveled to Africa, Asia, and Latin America to participate in projects aimed at invigorating women's independent work. Their support of Alma Mater took the form of material aid and time. A number mortgaged their own homes to support the project when government money was not forthcoming. Many retired feminists in their fifties and sixties volunteered their time. With the migrant women, they created a multiethnic women's alliance unparalleled in Italian history.

## Reworking Feminism in Turin

Italian historians have often ignored the legacy of women's social and political activism, but Italian feminists have made considerable contributions to local political culture. It was Turin feminists during the 1970s
who struggled as part of the labor movement to bring issues of inequality
out of the factory and into the domains of healthcare, schooling, and the
family. They fought to improve working conditions for women and for
the intellectual enrichment of workers who would take a series of courses
during working hours.[19] The women council members who voted for
Alma Mater were familiar with feminist contributions to local and national society and politics. In turn, Alma Mater exerted an influence on
the reformulation of progressive local and national politics, arguing for
an acknowledgment of immigrant populations as an important political
constituency.

The feminist interest in antiracist activities developed from the belief
that women are "universally" misrepresented, objectified, and exploited
on the basis of their gender, taught to subordinate themselves to their
male peers and authority structures, and rendered invisible. Through
Alma Mater, Italian feminists, in alliance with subaltern migrant women,
extended a feminist politics to oppose discrimination and forms of exclusion on the basis of ascribed "racial" or other differences and to create an
antiracist feminism forged in the context of a nascent, multiethnic political culture.

When Turin feminists assumed the financial directorship of Alma Mater,
many brought personal histories of prolonged participation in gendered
labor struggles. Most of the women in Produrre e Reprodurre had participated in left-wing or far left political organizations of the 1960s and 1970s,
and some of those most fully engaged in Alma Mater were former trade
union delegates. It is characteristic of Turin feminism to retain close connections with the local labor movement and trade unions.[20] Turin feminism
is deeply concerned with labor practices that impact women's family life,
mothering, sexuality and health. They have also struggled to promote abortion rights, day care centers, and to advance new forms of independent or
autonomous (autonomo) work for women.

When Italian women began to participate in the Alma Mater project,
some migrant women began to ask whether the center ought to be considered "feminist." Although Alma Mater was based on common migrant
experiences, the founders had never seen themselves as "Third World

feminists." Some migrant women reacted negatively to the prominence of Italian feminists in the organization, believing it to be an intrusion, an obstruction to migrant self-empowerment. Many equated the term "feminist" with "imperialism" or European power. And although most migrants in Alma Mater concurred that European societies are patriarchal, many did not believe that European feminist ideas could capture their experiences as women from developing countries. They feared that Italians would take over the organization, controlling its operations and undermining its goals.

Some migrant women argued that Italy, and Europe more generally, may need a feminist movement, but their own countries did not. One commented:

> There is no feminism in Somalia, because women are taught to be strong. It is the women who decide who their children are to marry. I was beaten by my mother if I didn't receive the highest marks in school. My mother believed that my success was more important than that of my brothers.[21]

And another argued,

> In Romania there has been an Equality Law since 1922. A king instituted it. That's why I don't understand feminism.[22]

Few migrants have taken an interest in European feminism, and some Italian women complain that while they would like to share their experiences and insights, migrant women are "only interested in improving their own situations, not in learning anything about Italian feminists or Italian feminism." Disagreements and power struggles obstruct the development of trust and the consolidation of a common vision.

Migrant and Italian women do not always agree on which power relations are the most critical to self-empowerment. An older generation of Italian feminists view unjustly distributed resources between men and women as the principal problem. Among working- and middle-class Italians, patriarchy is the crucial issue. In contrast, many subaltern migrant women locate their primary issues in "racist" European power structures that stereotype both women and men from developing countries, exploit their labor power and resources, and relegate them to the margins of employment and social status.

In spite of the different perspectives of members of Alma Mater, I would argue that Alma Mater represents a reworked form of Turin feminism. It is an interethnic organization concerned with improving the living, health, and working conditions of women in Turin. Alma Mater seeks to promote women's autonomous work and to raise popular consciousness about the productive activities of women from developing countries. It calls upon local feminists to redefine their social movements by incorporating the visions of migrant women from diverse national origins.

Alma Mater is also an inclusive space for women who experience daily life in Turin as socially and politically alienating. Women from Muslim countries whose cultures may not permit them to socialize with men can visit Alma Mater where they may exchange experiences and knowledge. Italian and migrant women attend meetings and cultural events and consume services on a daily basis at Alma Mater. The organization has popularized social exchange between migrants and Italian society, highly unusual in this local world.

However, the remarkable success of this organization in bringing together women of diverse national origins has not prevented conflicts around "racial," national, and class differences. In fact the center reproduces some of the socially divisive and exclusionary ideologies and practices that it so vehemently opposes. The scarcity of "good" jobs, unequal access to political and economic resources, and an ambiguous internal distribution of authority fuel resentments and competition among women. This organization exemplifies the challenges inherent in efforts to build feminist alliances between women with claims to diverse gender, "racial," and cultural identities.[23]

## Women Confronting Racism

In response to the absence of organized initiatives to defend migrant women against marginalization in the labor market and society, Alma Mater launched a number of antiracist projects. The women identified "cultural misunderstanding" as a root cause of Turin racism. Stereotypical ideas about cultural differences, or "cultural racism," had rapidly come to permeate every level of society from the halls of the European and Italian parliaments, to newspapers and television, public offices, schools, systems of transportation, open markets, and cafés. Popular stereotypes justified the relegation of many migrants to inferior positions within the labor force, fueling the treatment of migrants as "sexually loose," or prostitutes. A number of Alma Mater's initiatives were designed to educate the Italian public about the rich cultural backgrounds of migrants and to create alternative forms of employment representative of migrant talents and skills.

To contest these negative characteristics ascribed by Italian society, Alma Mater began to develop the practice of "cultural mediation"[24] whereby migrants act as formal cultural brokers between Italian state institutions and migrant populations in Turin. Between 1992 and 1993, Alma Mater directed several courses to train women as professional mediators, using the techniques of intercultural exchange, translation, and communication.[25] Alma Mater's Office of Cultural Mediation was frequently contacted by local schools, hospitals, the Office of Foreigners, and other public services and asked to help interpret and mediate problems concerning migrants that these organizations were unprepared to handle. To this end the municipal government awarded Alma Mater's Office of Cultural Mediation a modest amount of funding. A small number of migrant women procured employment as cultural mediators in the Office of Foreigners and the Saint Anna maternity hospital.

Alma Mater included two cooperatives, La Talea and Mediazione, in which women gathered to achieve common goals, sharing resources while pooling skills and expertise. Independent or autonomous work, and its collective form articulated in the cooperative, is a core symbol in Italian labor activism. The notion of "autonomo" is based on the romantic ideal of the precapitalist craftsman or artisan, who retained considerable control over the labor process, and is engaged in creative, nonalienating activity. This ideal has recently reemerged with vigor among some members of the contemporary Italian left who support social cooperatives as ethically sound and socially constructive forms of nongovernmental employment for a growing number of disenfranchised Italian youth. Alma Mater's cooperatives must be understood as part of this leftist tradition of promoting autonomous work through collective structures.

Alma Mater's cooperatives designed several projects intended to promote public interest in and knowledge of migrant cultures. A Turkish Bath was established in the Alma Mater building, intended as an intimate social space where migrant and Italian women might engage in intercultural exchanges. A set of large, padded, bedlike surfaces fill the room where women receive massages, drink tea, and talk about their lives. Ideally, the Turkish Bath was meant to encourage communication, solidarity, and the exchange of ideas. In 1996, it was directed and codirected by a Filipina and an Egyptian woman. The bath remains one of Alma Mater's most successful projects, attracting regular visitors from Turin's wealthy social classes, although elevated prices have prevented migrant women from participating and have limited intercultural exchange.

Another of Alma Mater's initiatives, the Almateatro or theater group, is widely recognized throughout Italy and parts of western Europe. Its works are shown in theaters filled to capacity with migrant and Italian audiences. Almateatro has produced several plays and a video for the purpose of teaching elementary schoolchildren about the effects of isolation and hatred. Members of the theater ensemble write, direct, and perform in productions. Although directed by Italians, the multiethnic ensemble collaborates on all aspects of production. Their play *Righbe* portrayed some of the physical and emotional hardships faced by migrant women in the daily struggle to survive in Italy. Another work, *Luna Nera*, expressed the passionate and conflictual relationships between daughters and mothers and the transmission of gender roles from one generation to the next. Recalling her mother's instructions on proper feminine behavior, one actress shouted: "Be Quiet! Don't get yourself dirty. Don't make noise while you're eating. Don't dress like a man. . . . Don't be lazy. Don't speak. Don't think. And don't exaggerate." *Luna Nera* and several other Almateatro productions were financially supported by La Commissione Pari Opportunita Donna-Uomo della Regione Piemonte (Regional Commission for Equal Opportunity between Women and Men) in which Italian feminists have served as board members, appointed by the regional government.

La Talea and Mediazione also frequently organize "ethnic dinners" by request of an Italian family or organization, preparing, for example, Senegalese or Moroccan food in a large room in the Alma Mater building. These dinners often include "ethnic" dances, music, or poetry readings. In order to raise money and awareness of Alma Mater, the cooperatives organize cultural dinners along the themes of particular countries or regions, such as West Africa. Advertising flyers are distributed throughout the city, stapled to lampposts, cork walls in public offices, near bus stops, and in train stations. Both migrants and Italians must pay to attend these generally festive events.

However, other practices at Alma Mater undermine and distort the organization's antiracist goals, contributing to the reproduction of unequal power relations. External forces such as global and local labor markets, traditional gender roles, emerging class relations, and "race" structure these internal practices. In spite of Alma Mater's goal of creating small-scale enterprises that afford women greater control over the labor process, migrant women continue to be recruited into forms of domestic service. Few manage to break through local barriers and obtain jobs that employ their artisanal skills. And even fewer succeed in constructing their own businesses. Some migrant women blame Alma Mater's Italian feminists for thwarting their efforts to become autonomous in business, and for subscribing to mainstream expectations that migrant women are newcomers of inferior rank who must care for and serve Italian families. An East African woman commented:

> In Alma Mater, all they do for foreigners is refer them to jobs as COLF (domestics), or help for the elderly, or cleaning. An original goal of Alma Mater was to help women obtain legal and other recognition for the training they received in their countries of origin, but this has not been met as a goal. This has not happened. So you have this dependency that exists.

In defense of their actions, Italian feminists have argued that, due to the exigencies of their local labour market, only domestic jobs were available to migrant women. Thus they had the choice of either helping migrant women obtain this employment or leaving them to fend for themselves without income, and possibly without housing. As one confessed, "I've given up living by ideals. In this context people are in need of basic things to survive, so that ideology has to measure itself against the reality of daily practices."

Nevertheless, domestic service is a highly gendered form of labor that tends to isolate migrant women in Italian homes, where they are frequently the objects of exploitation. Because much of this work is informal and undocumented, it leaves employers free to avoid the payment of healthcare and taxes associated with the maintenance of such workers. Without evidence of formal employment, migrants are unable to renew their permissions of stay in Italy and continually fear that they will be discovered and returned to their countries of origin.

Colorism, an aspect of racial ideologies, is a further axis of difference that has divided the Alma Mater membership. A year or so after the center was opened, members of the cooperative Mediazione weakened their relationship with Alma Mater, electing to hold meetings in private houses. Mediazione decided to admit only persons with very dark skin color, as opposed to lighter skin tones. Membership in the cooperative was to be based not upon national or ethnic origin, but rather on skin pigmentation. Crossing national boundaries, the group invited "black" Moroccans, Nigerians, Somalis, and Brazilians. Colorism represents a new system of color-based identity in Turin. Such distinctions, based on phenotype, threaten to rupture Alma Mater's delicate balance of alliance.

The often hidden complaint by migrant women that Italian feminists were "racist" toward migrants exerted a destabilizing effect on the daily workings of Alma Mater's administration and antiracist initiatives. In 1995 and 1996, migrant women contended that Italian feminists controlled Alma Mater. Some angrily argued that some of the center's initiatives, such as the Almateatro, were directed almost entirely by Italian women, excluding migrant women. Others complained that Italian feminists handled all the important administrative decisions without consulting migrants. It was often difficult for the migrant women to accept the fact that many of the Italian women were retired, which gave them a considerable amount of free time to devote to Alma Mater. The Italian women expressed their dedication to the organization and to the migrant women whose interests it was primarily designed to serve. However, there was an absence of direct communication between some of the migrant and Italian women, allowing feelings of animosity and distrust to fester.

A central problem in Alma Mater is that when Italian and migrant women depart from the center, their lives take them into entirely separate social orbits. Most Italian feminists have known each other for many years. They share long histories of local political struggle. The majority participate in the same social networks and informally continue their discussions when they leave the gates of Alma Mater. Italian feminists also regularly attend meetings at the Casa della Donna, to which migrant women are not invited.

## Situated Geographies

It is often taken for granted that postcolonial migrants in the metropole will have to struggle in uncomfortable, even relatively unwholesome conditions for at least a limited period of time. After all, it is suggested, it is the fact that they are from poor and economically underdeveloped countries that has compelled them to migrate. Even in Alma Mater, there is an expectation that many migrant women will live in marginal housing conditions. Assumptions about the manner in which migrants regularly occupy the spaces of their daily lives are embedded in ideologies of race, class, and other distinctions that concern social rights to certain kinds of knowledge and power. Often, the person who lives in economically poor circumstances will regard herself as somehow undeserving, and defer to others with greater economic and therefore social authority. Even within the safe walls of Alma Mater, the manner in which the migrant is symbolically construed as poor, in need of aid, and underprepared for the world of Europe—in sum, a social minor—is seldom, if ever, scrutinized.

The assumptions that migrants from developing countries are economically poor is extended to notions of mental impoverishment. Such ideas, part of a modern European model of progress, are produced and reproduced through different locally "situated geographies."[26] I employ this term to describe the material and ideological conditions in which various Turin residents, including both migrants and Italians, live their daily lives. Differently put, situated geographies refers to the geographical positioning of social actors, including real and imagined differences and their related practices that produce and reproduce social boundaries.

The members of Alma Mater are unified on the basis of gender, but this basic similarity is inflected by differences that stretch beyond the confines of the center. More significantly than differences of culture, religion, ethnic, or national origin, the participants occupy the material and ideological spaces of Turin in divergent ways. Outside Alma Mater, migrant and Italian women engage in different social and familial networks, occupations, and market exchanges. Some live in spacious, comfortable homes in secure neighborhoods, while others are crowded into dark, tiny rooms where they may not have access to a shower or a telephone.

While there is inequality between Italian feminists and the majority of migrant women, there are also differences among migrant women who, in spite of their racialization by Italians, by no means constitute a homogeneous social class. Although university-educated migrant women are usually unable to secure employment that corresponds to their training, they are typically in a better position than the less educated migrant women. If married, their spouses may be Italian or migrant men working in stable jobs or professional occupations. Some live in spacious homes with their immediate families. Those who have resided in Turin for a number of years may also have access to local political networks, although they remain excluded from Italian social or friendship networks. Other migrant women are political outsiders, but they live in modest, comfortable surroundings. However, even these migrant women complain that their achievements are ignored by most Italians, and that they are treated as social inferiors. Within Alma Mater, they are more likely than others to hold administrative positions and to secure work as cultural mediators.

The differential situations in which Alma Mater members live are reproduced through differential treatment within the organization. This generates constant tensions and frequent conflicts. Material conditions are mediated by ideologies and attitudes of social superiority or inferiority and Alma Mater accords insufficient attention to the ways in which such ideologies are reproduced by women in the center. This undermines feminist antiracist struggles. The few migrant women in leadership roles are in danger of nurturing their own authority, savoring the little power they may have acquired and have felt unable to possess. The desire to be somebody can be overwhelming, inspiring practices of self-aggrandizement, at the expense of the larger goal to improve the overall conditions of migrant women by helping them create and secure jobs.

Classification by "race," which the organization presumably contests, has come to assume an active role in Alma Mater. As I mentioned, one of the center's cooperatives does not admit light-skinned women. Migrants have appropriated popular Italian stereotypes, constructing divisions between "Arabs," with lighter skin, and "Africans."[27] Here racial classifications are employed to reverse or challenge "white" privilege by adopting a generic "dark" color of inclusion. It is "whiteness" that is marked as outside, dangerous, and complicit with racist practices.[28] This adoption of colorism operates in a number of postcolonial contexts, most notably in parts of the Caribbean, and may be considered an integral product of colonial systems of exclusion. As a manner of addressing the problem of racism, it may work to exclude the very groups that would otherwise support the challenge of exclusionary systems.

## Unfinished Feminism

For Alma Mater to become a more effective feminist antiracist organization, its members must expand and nuance their own understanding of who can be included in their antiracist struggle. They must confront the limits of the discursive structures that inform the meaning of antiracist and feminist practices. This will involve a process of rigorous dialogue and analysis of the ways in which racialization and racial discrimination are practiced in local communities as well as on a global scale. Moving beyond the dominant templates of black-white, First World–Third World requires the development of a shared language and trust, which takes considerable time and effort.[29]

Appearing at the juncture of significant global political and economic shifts that have prompted increasing numbers of people to migrate worldwide, Alma Mater may be seen as an organization that instructs us that "white" European feminists can form productive alliances with postcolonial and "black" women, extending the boundaries of local feminism into the international realm. As a feminist Italian once told me, "Alma Mater is an unfinished product, because it is so complex, including women from many parts of the world that together are changing, becoming something new." It is a reminder of what we are capable of, and what we are up against.

ACKNOWLEDGMENTS

Thanks to Allan Pred who encouraged me to write this essay; Ruth Wilson Gimore, whose comments inspired aspects of the analysis; France Winndance Twine and Kathleen Blee for their careful reading and perceptive editing; and Donald Martin Carter for his insightful comments and passionate discussions. This article is dedicated to William Shack, whose integrity and dedication to excellence has helped sustain my commitment to activist academic work.

NOTES

1. Vanessa Maher, "Immigration and Social Identities," in *Italian Cultural Studies: An Introduction*, ed. David Forgacs and Robert Lumley (Oxford: Oxford University Press, 1996), 163.

2. Umberto Melotti, "International Migration in Europe: Social Protests and Political Cultures," in *The Politics of Multiculturalism in the New Europe: Racism, Identity and Community*, ed. Tariq Modood and Pnina Werbner (London: Zed Books, 1997).

3. Maher, "Immigration," 164.

4. Maher, "Immigration," 163.

5. Donald Martin Carter, *States of Grace: Senegalese in Italy and the New European Immigration* (Minneapolis: University of Minnesota Press, 1997).

6. According to the Italian Statistics Center (ISTA), in 1991, approximately 706,750 foreigners had obtained regular stay and work permits. These estimates included 88,100 Moroccans, 46,575 Tunisians, 27,392 Senegalese, 13,358 Ethiopians, 11,599 Somalians, 12,632 Ghanaians, and 6,558 Nigerians. From Giovanna Campani, "Immigration and Racism in Southern Europe: The Italian Case," *Ethnic and Racial Studies* 16, no. 3 (July 1993).

7. Heather Merrill, "Speaking Subjects: Remaking Feminism and Race in the New Migrant Europe" (dissertation, University of California, Berkeley, 1999) and Allan Pred, *Even in Sweden: Racisms, Racialized Spaces and the Popular Geographical Image* (Berkeley: University of California Press, 2000).

8. See Pierre-Andre Taguieff, "The New Cultural Racism in France," *Telos,* no. 83, 1990, and Etienne Balibar, "Is there a Neo-Racism?" in Etienne Balibar and Immanuel Wallerstein, eds., *Race, Nation, Class: Ambiguous Identities* (London: Verso, 1991).

9. Arnaldo Bagnasco, *Torino: un profilo sociologico* (Torino: Einaudi, 1986); Giuseppe Dematteis and Anna Segre, "Da citta-fabbrica a citta-infrastructura," *Spazio e Societa,* Anno 11 (Aprile-Guigno, 1988), and IRES, Istituto Richerche Economico-Sociali del Piemonte, *Relazione sulla situazione economica sociale e territoriale del Piemonte 1995* (Torino: Rosenberg and Sellier, 1995).

10. Maria Immacolata Macioti and Enrico Pugliese, *Gli Immigrati in Italia* (Rome: Laterza, 1991), and Giovani Mottura, ed., *L'Arcipelago Immigrazione, Caretteristiche e modelli migratori dei lavoratori stranieri in Italia* (Rome: Ediesse, 1992).

11. IRES, Istituto Richerche Economico-Sociali del Piemonte, *Uguali e Diversi, Il mondo culturale, le reti di rapporti, I lavori degli immigrati non europei a Torino* (Torino: Rosenberg and Sellier, 1992).

12. Turin's history has been marked by activist struggles, from the labor movement to the student, feminist, and youth movements, to the current struggles over migration and racism. The city was once the center of some of the most intense and prolonged industrial labor struggles in Italian and European history. At all levels, a lively political culture is activated by debates between interest groups such as trade unions or voluntary organizations which are normally represented by the various political parties.

13. See Giovanna Zaldini, "Il Centro Interculturale Delle Donne Di Torino," *Alma Mater,* 1992.

14. In 1999, the Italian Ministry of Social Affairs allotted Alma Mater over 600 million lira in support of its initiatives, signaling that this organization has become a national beacon of collaboration between Italian-born and migrant women. Alma Mater sorely needed the money because initial funds from the European Union had been exhausted several years earlier and members had been struggling to keep the organization afloat.

15. Ibid., Zaldini 1992.

16. *Projetto per un Centro Di Donne Immigrate,* July 7, 1990.

17. As part of the general movement occurring in other Italian cities, Turin's Casa della Donna opened in 1979, after the occupation of a building previously used as a mental asylum. The Casa's opening made it possible for various strands of Turin feminism to organize and meet under a single roof. See Piera Zu-

maglino, *Femminismi a Torino: Pari e Dispari*, with contributions by A. Miglietti and A. Piccirillo. Introduction by I. Damilano (Milan: Franccangeli, 1996).

18. Produrre e Riprodurre was established during an international conference held in Turin in 1983. The topic was women and family in industrialized countries, and it brought together six hundred women from three continents. This movement represents the second phase of Turin feminism, in which women sought to understand what could be done to effect improved work and social conditions for women under post-Fordist economic and political conditions. The splinter group, Donne in Sviluppo, was generated out of a deepening concern for the living conditions of women in developing societies. The members of Donne in Sviluppo made a considerable effort to offer their assistance to migrant women in Turin. See Merrill, *Speaking Subjects*.

19. This was the hundred and fifty hours program, which gave workers permission to take a hundred and fifty hours of courses on a variety of subjects. Feminists from New Left groups designed some of the courses for Italian women on such issues as health education, women's history, and the history of women's work. Enrollment in the courses designed for women was unusually high. Participants included workers, housewives, students, and feminist intellectuals. See Joanne Barkan, *Visions of Emancipation: The Italian Workers' Movement since 1945* (New York: Praeger, 1984), and Robert Lumley, *States of Emergency: Cultures of Revolt in Italy from 1968 to 1978* (London: Verso, 1990).

20. Judith Adler Hellman, "Turin: Women's Struggles in a Worker's City," in *Journeys among Women: Feminism in Five Italian Cities*, ed. Judith Adler Hellman (New York: Oxford University Press, 1987).

21. Interview, Turin, 1996.

22. Transcript of interview conducted in Turin, 1996.

23. Chantal Mouffe, "Feminism, Citizenship, and Radical Democratic Politics," in *Feminists Theorize the Political*, ed. Judith Butler and Joan W. Scott (New York: Routledge, 1992).

24. Migrants were frequently called upon by local government officials to volunteer their services as informal mediators, but they were neither trained nor remunerated.

25. Anna Belpiede, "Le Politiche Locali sulla Mediazione Interculturale. Il caso Torino," *Seminaire sur la Mediazione Interculturelle*, Marseille (22/25 Mai 1995).

26. Geographies are produced through a series of processes, which are intertwined with taken-for-granted practices. Examples of such processes include urban politics, international economies, state policies, and mainstream ideologies.

27. Maher, "Immigration."

28. This may be a weak form of class consciousness, in that the object of derision (relatively light-skinned people) is identified by its relation to power, class

position, access to the job market, social privilege, and acceptance by the most privileged sectors of society. Dark-skinned groups are expected to have particular problems, including exclusion from certain types of jobs and social segregation. We may also note a contradiction at the level of ideology. Alma Mater was initiated and supported by left-oriented political parties. However, the political left has been highly critical of racial and other essentialist identifications, which are seen to undermine class solidarity.

29. See Susan Stanford Friedman, *Mappings: Feminism and the Cultural Geographies of Encounter* (Princeton: Princeton University Press, 1998).

# Chapter 2

# Resisting Domestic Violence and Caste Inequality

## *All-Women Courts in India*

### *Veronica Magar*

Action India began as a small, informal group consisting of part-time volunteers and became a large and significant feminist establishment in Delhi, India. In this chapter I describe how Action India successfully trained women from the slums to hold the perpetrators of domestic violence accountable through informal women's courts (mahila panchayat, in Hindi). Through this process, women activists have changed the way low-caste women in Delhi slums deal with male oppression inside their homes and have challenged two adverse conditions in the slums of Delhi—subjugation of women and the oppression of low-caste groups. Moreover, Action India has brought women from different caste groups together on one platform, empowering them as a new social force transcending caste barriers. In a deeply caste-ridden society like India, this is highly significant.

### *Action India*

India's contemporary violence against women movement began with two major issues in the late 1970s—rape and dowry. Individual cases were adopted by women's advocacy groups, then subsequently developed and amplified through the national media to mobilize for legal and social reform.[1] The emphasis on law, and thereby on the state, disappointed many organizations, as the laws were rarely enforced. Since the early 1990s India's feminist NGOs (nongovernmental organizations), like NGOs worldwide, have been shifting their focus from protest and antiestablishment rhetoric to the long-term empowerment of women as a new social force in a human rights framework. This is clear in the case of Action India.

Influenced by Black American social justice and freedom struggles during the 1960s in the United States, Action India began as a civil rights movement in 1976. Like other autonomous women's groups of its kind, Action India's orientation in the late 1970s was inspired by a core group of volunteer feminists, largely from upper-middle-class homes, who gathered in loosely structured fledgling organizations.[2] Their feminist identity was born in the late 1970s, when Action India's members began to address the needs of women encountering violence in Delhi. In describing how their goals were determined, a founding member elaborates: "We began working on rape and dowry. That's where we found our true work . . . with the women." Indeed, since its inception, Action India has applied its understanding of feminism at the grassroots level through women's experiences with violence, and by evolving ways to help women cope with it. One of Action India's earliest volunteers reports:

> We used the theories developed by feminist intellectuals and applied it to the work we do in the bastis (slums). We learned that consciousness raising had to happen on a mass scale, so we started working in the schools, with the girls. We saw a need for a crisis center for abused women who were poor and illiterate, so we developed one—Saheli. We needed a haven where women could be safe, so we founded a shelter—Shakti Shaleni, August 1987. We were all a part of this thinking. We were small, only a few of us, but we managed to do a lot.

Saheli (female friend), Action India's sister organization, represented an effort to put feminist concepts of sisterhood into practice as well as to redefine these concepts by basing them on traditionally accepted structures of friendship among women.[3] It was among the first to directly address issues of violence on an individual, case-by-case basis. With a focus on individual women, Saheli volunteers brought in lawyers, counselors, and educators to help their clients struggle through bureaucratic red tape, police harassment, and intrafamilial adversities. Saheli's "violence against women" program formed a prototype which many NGOs, including Action India, later followed. One of Action India's founders describes this period:

> Indira Gandhi was abusing her power. . . . That was really a time of public activism; there was a lot more protesting in the streets. We didn't have an

office, but went to the bastis (slums) every day. It was the greatest learning experience for me. When does a middle-class woman get the opportunity to see poor people, other than her servants? We saw how people lived and became very close to their issues. This was the beginning of Action India.

As funds were secured through the GTZ (German government), staff from the slums were hired to expand its programs, which eventually included offices in four slum localities, referred to as Sabla Sangh (organization of strong women). Since 1979 Action India has been counseling, advising, and helping women in Delhi's slums to resist male violence in their homes. Although volunteers played a critical role in providing support and counseling, health workers with little training managed the formal activities, including registering cases with the police and assisting women in obtaining medical examinations to build cases against their assaulters. These health workers provided advocacy, consciousness-raising activities, and social support to victims of domestic abuse until 1993, when trained caseworkers were hired. One caseworker, who married at fifteen years of age and lived in a community in which women remained veiled, describes what it meant for her to be able to work:

> I never even thought that I would be doing a job in my life, or even step outside the house, let alone do this kind of work. I'm not very educated. I studied only up until eighth [grade]. I stopped school because I got married. Moreover, I have lived in a society where women wear veils. Not even my hands were visible. After joining the Sabla Sangh, I changed a lot. I started coming out. . . . Nobody can obstruct me now.

## The National Context

Extensive evidence of the frequency of domestic violence in the Indian subcontinent has for the first time been demonstrated in the late 1990s. In a survey of 859 rural women in the north Indian state of Uttar Pradesh, 45 percent reported having been beaten by their husbands. Another survey of 6,700 husbands found that 30 percent acknowledged that they had physically beaten their wives and 22 percent acknowledged that they had forced their wives to have sexual relations. Although the literature suggests that scheduled and lower-caste women enjoy more freedoms and equality in marital relationships, recent studies reveal that women from scheduled and lower castes report more physical abuse than women from higher castes. Visaria's preliminary results, in rural Gujarat, reveal that although domestic violence occurs across caste and religious lines, compared to higher castes (38 percent), the most widespread violence was reported among women from low castes (75 percent). Furthermore, 35 percent of high-caste women in abused relationships mentioned that their husbands had threatened to expel them from the house, compared to 62 percent of lower-caste women. Not surprisingly, economic stress was the most commonly cited precipitating factor among low-caste women.

Thirty-six percent of India's population lives below the poverty level.[4] Scheduled castes and tribes are disproportionately represented among this lowest one-third of the population.[5] In a population of almost 9.5 million, Delhi is comprised of 19 percent scheduled castes and a negligible number of scheduled tribes. Its slums consist largely of individuals recognized as scheduled and lower castes, but it is important to note that not all the poor are scheduled and lower castes. There are also several upper castes who have fallen on "bad times," and live among the poor in Delhi slums. Since independence in 1947, when refugees displaced by India's partition arrived from Pakistan, Delhi has had a large and growing influx of migrants. Slum dwellers now consist mainly of first- and third-generation migrants with strong ties to their village roots.

A slum clearance program which began in 1976, during India's state of emergency (1975–77), uprooted and relocated 700,000 slum dwellers to approximately forty-seven resettlement colonies at the city's periphery.[6] The slum clearance program was spearheaded by prime minister Indira Gandhi's son, Sanjay Gandhi, who led the "Beautification of Delhi" initiative with the aim of improving Delhi's physical appearance and enabling politicians to showcase India's capital. Land was parceled off[7] for resettled families to build homes, on twenty-five-square-yard plots.[8]

Resettlement and squatter colonies now house the majority of these old and new migrants. Basic amenities such as electricity and public water are met in resettlement colonies, albeit very inadequately, but frequent government-imposed power cuts deny slum dwellers access to these minimal basic services. Often three stories high, their homes are made of semibrick and semicorrugated sheet iron walls with tile or sheet iron roofs. One or more families live in these units, built on twenty-five-square-yard plots. Some of the residents own the dwellings they live in. Most pay rent following a huge cash deposit obtained from moneylenders. Alongside and interspersed between the resettlement colonies lie a cruder kind of hutment called jhuggi jhompri, or squatter settlements, creating a "slums within slums" phenomenon. In contrast to the resettlement colonies, the squatter settlements are clusters of temporary dwellings crudely made of plastic, gunny bags, and cardboard. By 1991, resettlement colonies housed 214,000 families (approximately 2 million people); and approximately 259,000 households lived in squatter settlements.

In this essay I analyze the Sabla Sanghs based in four of Delhi's slum localities. There is considerable diversity among household inhabitants in terms of income levels, assets, skills, physical environment, language, and ethnic and caste identity. The majority are second- or third-generation north Indians from the neighboring states of Punjab, Haryana, Rajasthan, Uttar Pradesh, and Bihar. Another is dominated by Muslims, reflecting distinct foods, dress, music, and religious practices. Perhaps because it is closer to Delhi's center, the Muslim settlement is considered relatively affluent by slum standards, as it has somewhat greater access to resources, information, and attention from municipal authorities.

### Mahila Panchayats

All-women courts—mahila panchayats (in Hindi)—were created by women as one means of empowering and offering legal protection to women. These unofficial courts circumvent the official system of governance in favor of a more efficient and effective means of justice, capable of reaching close to people's lives. Each Sabla Sangh houses a mahila panchayat, which is convened by ten to twenty volunteer women who hold weekly hearings for women who need more than just legal advice and counseling. These are modeled after the traditional biradari panchayats, but their aim is to "determine justice for the woman who is tormented." One woman describes the mahila panchayats' evolution as follows:

> Law was made for justice . . . but, for us the law means nothing. We've seen that the law, when it is implemented, doesn't work for us. It actually works against us. But, we know what works. We have seen the traditional biradari panchayats work. They work, but are they fair? For the woman, there is no justice anywhere, whether it's the law or panchayat. So, we decided to form our own panchayat—the mahila panchayat.

In a Sabla Sangh office hangs a series of posters depicting a dejected-looking woman facing a traditional biradari panchayat,[9] a local caste brotherhood that predates the colonial period, convened to resolve conflicts or redress transgression.[10] The last poster in the series portrays a very different image, but with a similar scenario: a victorious and confident woman faces an all-woman panchayat. The posters' artist was forced to marry her depraved brother-in-law (shortly after her husband's untimely death), so that he could secure his family property through her. She describes how her experience inspired the posters she painted:

> They had arranged a [traditional, biradari] panchayat regarding my case. At that time I thought that if it has to do with her rights, a woman should be heard. People should help her, not point fingers. All those feelings that were buried in my heart [when I faced the biradari panchayat]. A woman can't express her feelings at all. Even when her face is covered with a veil, she is unable to express her feelings. How can she utter a word, if she is not permitted even to lift her head. When she must hide her hands and feet, it is hard for her to say anything. That is why I felt really happy when the mahila panchayats were formed. In the biradari panchayat, if you are rich, you will have members of the family in the panchayat. If you are poor, there is no chance of being heard, especially if you are a woman. In my case they forced me to marry my brother-in-law. I couldn't contest. Even then they said many bad things about me. "She is so shameless to make her brother-in-law ask her whether she wants to sit with [marry] him. It was she who caused her husband's death." And even after listening to those insults from men, I still respected them.

Unlike the biradari panchayats, the members of the mahila panchayats are intercaste and self-appointed. The only requirement for joining, besides being a woman, is a commitment to doing what is right. Because they are not part of the official panchayat system, members are not democratically elected, but rather appointed by senior members.[11] With more time available to them, participants tend to be mothers and mothers-in-law with adult children.

A striking feature of mahila panchayats is that by ascribing to the ideology of equality and fairness they transgress religious and caste lines. Unlike the biradari panchayat which consists of male elders from the same regional caste and subcaste groups, mahila panchayats have members from all the regional and subcaste groups present in their communities. Similarly, the major Indian religions represented in the slums, including Islam, Christianity, and Hinduism, are represented in the mahila panchayats.

At scheduled hearings both the woman and her husband describe their grievances, as mahila panchayat members who have been trained by caseworkers in annual workshops, weekly meetings, and special fora listen. A decision, or resolution statement, is developed according to agreed upon, documented pledges from both sides. A caseworker describes this process thus:

> They [the plaintiff and opponent] formulate the decisions themselves. . . . If we [mahila panchayat members] draft the decisions, if we tell them what we think, tell them what they should do, they will blame us if it doesn't work out. So, it's more meaningful when they write the decisions themselves. It is more likely to succeed. If it's what each side wants, we try to help them keep the family intact.

## *Caseworkers*

The Sabla Sangh's caseworkers are its greatest asset. An understanding of the caseworker's role helps us understand grassroots feminism as practiced by organizations like Action India. Caseworkers use interpersonal communication skills and a solid knowledge of the law, along with familiarity with the local idiom and sensibility of the women and their families. Given the sharp economic inequalities characterizing Indian society, and the incredibly multiethnic collage that is Indian culture, communication is often the key problem. The caseworker steps into this breach, with fearless strategies to apply the law, bring social pressure to bear on the perpetrators, and be treated with deference and respect by the police. In describing the qualities that a caseworker should possess, one caseworker remarks:

> She should be one who has suffered; then she feels she has gone through everything. She doesn't want others to suffer as she has. It's not necessary that she be educated.

To the women victims, what makes a caseworker acceptable as their representative is that she has lived through similar hardships. Like the mahila panchayat members and women who seek help, most of the caseworkers are poor, low-caste, and have suffered from hunger and abuse at the hands of their in-laws and husbands. One caseworker comments, "We fight against the wrong, and do not care about the woman's name. Only women who have gone through it [violence] can identify with her, in their hearts."

### Caseworkers and Law Enforcement

Women generally report that law enforcement officers either neglect or mishandle cases involving domestic abuse. It is not unusual for officers to secure bribes from the perpetrators—usually the husband and his family—thereby undermining a lawful course of action to protect victims and sanction perpetrators. Women report being treated inhumanly by the officers, which explains why they are generally afraid to use law enforcement services and why laws protecting women, such as the dowry laws, remain ineffective. However, in spite of law enforcement's mishandling of domestic violence cases, the mahila panchayats command the respect of the police. A lawyer who works for the NGO's legal literacy program for Muslim women described the caseworkers' interaction with law enforcement as follows:

> I know these caseworkers from the basti (slum). You can call them semiliterate. If they had not been organized, they would be like any other woman, terrified and intimidated to even go near a police constable. But, in truth I have seen with my own eyes. As soon as [someone from the Sabla Sangh] walks into the police station, the SHO (Station House Officer) stands up from his chair and invites her to come and sit. He actually calls her "madam," in a respectable manner—He brings her tea! And he will never turn her away. . . . He knows that even though she's illiterate, she is aware. She knows where to take the complaint. She knows the right channel and she's not afraid.

Contrary to the deferential posture assumed by low-caste women when engaging with a higher-caste male, women from the Sabla Sangh assume authority. According to one, they "forget their caste," and in doing so, they adopt an officious and brazen manner when advocating for the rights of abused women. By aligning themselves with others at the Sabla Sangh, they consciously raise their status in potentially formidable situations. A woman describes her first encounter with the police through the help of the Sabla Sangh as follows:

> Eight years ago when I was pregnant with my fourth child, my in-laws tried to kill me. They jumped on me, trampled on me. I was very hurt. The police refused to register my complaint unless I paid a bribe. The following day I returned with women from the Sabla Sangh. The SHO sarcastically responded, "Lots of madams here today." We began to shout claiming, "Are you humans? You will be responsible if anything happens to this woman and her children." We told him what we knew of the law and my rights.

Then the SHO apologized and sent police officers to my house. My brothers-in-law were arrested. The police beat them up with sticks. Then I felt very good. . . . After that my eldest brother-in-law apologized and touched my feet. He has never misbehaved with me again. To this day, he touches my feet.

## *Mahila Panchayat Members*

The mahila panchayat members are average slum dwellers who have either lived their life under a veil or worked in jobs such as construction labor, domestic service, gardening, sweeping, weaving, and rag picking. Their lack of formal education and low-caste status have rendered these women more vulnerable to poverty and abuse. Within a relatively short period, however, those who have joined the mahila panchayat begin to engage in a transformative process. In the two subsequent narratives, mahila panchayat members describe their experiences, illustrating their own personal transformations. Although she had no formal education, the first one impressed me with her adeptness at not only grasping complex topics quickly, but at accurately and thoughtfully critiquing Sabla Sangh deficiencies. According to caseworkers, the second informant had refrained from ever uttering a word during her initial months in the panchayat. Two years later she provided a daring account of her encounter with a law enforcement officer.

> I knew what life really was after I sat with these sisters four years ago. I was very ignorant. Most of us were. I got married at age thirteen. I lived with my husband's family. I remember, I must have been fourteen years old—was working in the house preparing food. . . . Something started to come out of my body. I didn't know what it was. It kept coming out. I kept trying to push it back up again. Eventually, it died. At the time I didn't know what it was. Then it happened again, for a second time. It died the second time also. You see, I was very ignorant! Now things are different. I learned many things from the sisters. If I had been with the sisters earlier, I would not have gotten married [a second time, after my first husband died]. I was alone and with my children so I married an eighty-year-old man. I wanted that he should support my children. I know now I didn't have to do that. There are other alternatives for women.

> Now I go out of my house and I'm not afraid. . . . Initially I used to be too shy to speak. I didn't know how to give an answer. I never said anything.

Now I can even talk to the police! I was always afraid of them. One day somebody put a small tree on fire. An old man said that my husband did it. The police came and initially we were very afraid. When they came to our home, I scolded them, "Why would my husband do such a thing? Don't you have any sense? Does he have an enmity with the tree?" I even scolded the dirty old man in front of the police. Then the policeman became quiet and went away. I surprised even my husband.

Through solidarity and critical consciousness, mahila panchayat participants gradually build self-esteem and gain skills that transform their lives. Many members have stepped out of their homes for reasons other than household duties or family affairs, for the first time ever. By claiming public space in which power and influence are collectively exercised, these women challenge traditional expectations of women's comportment in Indian society.

## Caste Relations in the Slums

Not unlike most groups who have been subordinated over generations, scheduled and lower-caste people also oppress each other. One often hears slum dwellers identify one another as scheduled caste and hurl caste-related slurs such as "bhangi" (SC, usually a scavenger) or "dirty caste," when referring to others. One illustrative encounter occurred between a newly enlisted mahila panchayat member and a woman soliciting the Sabla Sangh's help because her husband had been depleting family resources by buying lottery tickets. The woman's derogatory comments about scheduled caste people not only went unchallenged, but were echoed by the mahila panchayat member who, it was later determined, was a Valmiki (low-level SC) herself:

I am so troubled. Look at my four children. . . . We have no money to buy food. Again, last night my children went to bed with nothing to eat. . . . They wear clothes given to us by all kinds of offensive people—even harijans. Because I have nothing, they are forced to wear them [cries].

The slum is a juncture in which religions, castes, and subcastes from regions throughout north India converge. Women are often the victims of violence where these contrasting worlds intersect. One such example is the aftermath of intercaste marriage, a phenomenon which is increasing as younger girls are opting for "love" marriages instead of "arranged" ones. Although marriage alliances are still negotiated by a girl's family and subcaste community, reflecting a family's relative status, with little say from the girl herself, self-arranged alliances are taking place more frequently. Undermining both parental control and caste divisions, this pushes the boundaries that have upheld social stratification for centuries. In the cases that follow, it is the girl who is targeted by her family and society for transgressions against societal norms. As in many instances throughout a woman's life, a girl's premarital comportment, not the boy's, is seen as responsible for the family's loss of status and honor.

An elderly-looking widow provided an account of her son's romantic relationship with a neighbor. Her son's secret girl friend of six years had suddenly disappeared. The girl's family had been brutally beating her since the liaison was discovered a few years earlier. Upon determining that she was eight months' pregnant, she was reported missing. The boy's mother reported:

> *Boy's mother:* The girl is missing and I don't want to be blamed if something happens [to her]. Many people in her community agree that she should marry my son. After all, her life is ruined as it is. Who would want to marry her?
>
> *Caseworker 1:* Tell us about her. How much has she studied in school?
>
> *Boy's mother:* Only up to the first or second year. Her family is very poor. They cook food only once a day because there is hardly enough to eat. . . . We are also poor, but we have enough food.
>
> *Caseworker 1:* What is your caste?
>
> *Boy's mother:* We are Valmikis [SCs]. Why should I hide it or be ashamed?
>
> *Boy's aunt:* Her family refuses to let her get married to my nephew. . . . Now she is missing. They have taken her. God knows what they'll do with the baby. Will they kill it; throw it away?
>
> *Caseworker 2:* Getting them married isn't a problem. If she is an adult, they can have a court marriage. We can stand as her witness if her family is unwilling.

Caste divisions are maintained through union between a bride and groom of the same caste and subcaste. In much of north India, these are arranged by the parents and biradari. Because an alternative for couples who object to this custom is virtually nonexistent, caseworkers play the role traditionally played by the parents. They cleverly pride themselves on their incongruous role, which is to "arrange" "love" marriages—a kind of oxymoron in the traditional Indian context. Because love matches are spontaneous and motivated by romance, they usually occur between individuals of different castes.

The caseworker plays the role of witness, legal counselor, and parent. She replaces the parents as the girl's alter-family, even if this undermines strong cultural tenets supported by the girl's family and biradari. As these cases reflect, gender and caste lines are not easily severed through marriage, even by the prospect of greater economic prosperity. Nonetheless, the caste system is regularly challenged by young girls themselves through self-arranged alliances, subsequently made visible and institutionalized by the activities of grassroots feminist NGOs such as Action India.

This point was made particularly poignantly by one caseworker whose daughter had become romantically involved with a boy from an allegedly lower subcaste than her own. Her family of three children and an unemployed husband were relatively poor. While she and her family were weavers and considered scheduled caste, they had a higher rank in terms of social practice and beliefs than several other scheduled castes. Although the boy's family was financially visibly better off, the girl's family vehemently opposed the alliance. In the excerpt from the interview that follows, the caseworker describes how, through extreme opposition and difficulty, she struggled to support her daughter in her marriage to a "Harijan 18":

My mind is always under tension because of what people say about my daughter. My husband's brothers and sister have broken all ties with us. They say that they are no longer related to me. . . . The problem is that the boy is a Christian. . . . They say that only harijans become Christians. We are kolis [weaver caste]. Kolis are very proud. . . . My biradari said that I should have nothing more to do with my daughter. . . . I told them that I would leave them, but never my daughter. And God willing, if I ever have money, I'll give her a share of it. For my daughter's happiness, I'm ready to die.

This caseworker revealed the extent to which caste distinctions prevail in the slums. Her enlightened perspective, which compelled her to action on her daughter's behalf, runs counter to the predominant patriarchal and caste-specific social norms in her community. The Sabla Sangh offers an alternative space in which intercaste realities can take a progressive course. Unlike institutions outside the Sabla Sangh, women's suffering in the context of marriage is not taken for granted.

## *Mahila Panchayat Hearings*

Unlike the biradari panchayats, the mahila panchayats in the study do not stand alone. Once they reach a formal decision in the hearing, caseworkers carry out their ruling through frequent interchange with family members, police, and neighbors. The caseworker's initial obligation is to collect information from the husband and relevant family members involved in the dispute to obtain each side's view and to get a first-hand sense of the home situation. If both sides agree, the husband and wife sign a mutually agreed-upon contract at the closing of the mahila panchayat hearing.

The most common grievances handled by the caseworkers are those related to lack of household resources. Because most women depend on their husbands for maintenance and do not work outside the home, they are inclined to become destitute if their husbands' income is not forthcoming.[12] Many women report that their wage-earning husbands squander their limited earnings on alcohol and/or drugs. Such women often report dual scenarios of an alcoholic husband and one who plays the lottery excessively. A husband's excessive jealousy is not uncommon. Still other husbands become romantically involved with a second or third woman. Although it is not legally recognized, many men attempt to legalize their illicit relationship(s) by undergoing ritual marriage rites. In most such cases, husbands spend their income on the maintenance of the "preferred" wife/woman. Such scenarios are marked by an escalation of battering when the woman protests about the lack of money or from the time the illicit affair begins.

The most serious cases brought to the Sabla Sangh are those related to insufficient dowry or property inherited by a young widow. These women report threats and abuse of the most extreme nature. Extreme forms of physical abuse, often leading to death, are one way in which power and control are used to extort money or property from a woman.

What follows are descriptions of the kinds of cases handled by the Sabla Sangh. Accounts of specific cases discussed by the mahila panchayat provide a first-hand view of their potential force. The first is an excerpt of an interview, which preceded a mahila panchayat hearing, conducted several hours after a woman (Saira) had reported two grievances—that her husband (Meer) was not providing financial support for her and her children, and that he was forcing her to have sex against her will. Meer holds two jobs as a wage laborer. Although Saira does "piecework" at home, it is insufficient to make ends meet. All four children appeared stunted and malnourished. The interview took place at Saira's residence, a small dusty room where she and her four children live:

*Caseworker 1:* [to Saira] Why don't you speak?

*Saira:* Yes, Didi (sister), I will tell you everything . . . he goes away for fifteen to twenty days without telling me. He leaves no money. He just goes and comes, then goes away again. We still have to pay Rs. 42,000 [debt] for this place we are staying. This [small bag of rice] is our only ration.

*Caseworker 2:* [to Meer] What do you do with your money? Look at her. Don't you have any responsibility toward this family here?

*Saira:* I have been through such a bad condition. My children and I have hardly any clothes or food.

*Caseworker 2:* [to Meer] Why haven't you paid the rent?

*Meer:* I will.

*Saira:* He says that I am vain over the fact that I have sons and that I believe they will take care of me when they are older. So he threatens to take away my sons. I will never know where they are. He will leave the girls with me.

*Caseworker 2:* [to Meer] Where do you go to for fifteen–twenty days?

*Caseworker 1:* [to Meer] Is there some other woman? Where is the money going?

*Meer:* I have a job.

*Caseworker 2:* [to Meer] Why don't you give her money for the house expenditures?

*Caseworker 1:* [to Meer] You wait and see, we will go to the place where you work and garnish your wages.

*Meer:* [shouts] Yes you can! I'll give you the address! I'm a painter at the Hyatt hotel. . . . Now you listen to me, she is the one who got her father here for a fight. It's not my fault.

*Caseworker 1:* [points to youngest girl] Look at the faces of these poor children. Do they deserve to go to bed hungry? Look at your daughter. She is five and looks no older than two years.

*Saira:* After all this, he still fights with me the entire night [to have sex]. What will I do with another one? I can't have any more children . . .

*Meer:* She also poured kerosene oil over herself. Just ask her.

*Saira:* Yes, Didi, I will not lie. I did it.

*Caseworker 1:* [shouts at Meer] It's not her fault, you are the one who drives her to this. Why don't you give her money for the family?

Husbands who squander family resources put their family's economic and physical viability on a declining spiral. Whether it is related to alcohol, lottery, or a second woman, if the wife is not working, the lack of a husband's economic contribution renders a family destitute. In the above example, the caseworkers were particularly harsh on the husband, in part because he had denied the accusations throughout the encounter. Generally, if a husband shows signs of remorse, the caseworkers support his efforts to change. In the ideal scenario, the husband agrees to stop maltreating his wife and gives her an allowance from his wages. Often, however, as in this case, the husband plays the lottery and gambles, leaving no money for his family's basic needs. With the help of her brothers and occasional handouts from sympathetic neighbors, Saira and her four children had been able to survive, albeit marginally. Although this was unclear at the beginning, Saira's main reason for soliciting help from the caseworkers was that she wanted her husband to stop forcing her to have intercourse. Once this was accomplished, the case was dropped, as Saira was disinclined to pursue it further.

The extent to which power and control is used against women is especially clear in cases involving dowry. This is seen when husbands attempt to "excuse" their abusive behavior. Violent episodes are often triggered by incidents and circumstances such as ill-prepared meals, the untimely preparation of tea, or a lack of financial resources; such a response is considered justifiable behavior by husbands, by their family members, and by the culture more generally. This attitude explains in part why it is practically impossible for a woman to leave her abusive husband unless she has secured the support of her family in doing so. Contrary to traditional practice where low-caste women, abused by their husbands, were generally welcomed home, today those who find life with their husbands intolerable do not readily return home.[13] The following is an example of the no-escape situation in which women often find themselves:

*Ruchira:* His family locks up the latrine. . . . Where should I go to relieve myself—the jungle? He wants more money from my father. My father is poor. He beats me very hard. Once my face was bleeding very bad. They tried to burn me once.

*Mahila panchayat member 1:* [to Sunil] Now we'll give a decision and if you don't obey, the mahila panchayat will punish you.

*Sunil:* And punish her if she's wrong.

*Mahila panchayat member 2:* Ruchira, what do you want?

*Ruchira:* Only that he shouldn't beat and harass me, and abuse me.

*Caseworker 1:* Everyone uses the same latrine, why can't she? I don't get it?

*Mahila panchayat member 3:* It's so shameful that she has to go outside.

*Caseworker 1:* [to Ruchira] You have to have a latrine of your own.

*Sunil:* OK, but it will take time: three–four months. I need money for it.

*Caseworker 1:* See we are not biased.

*Caseworker 2:* Don't abuse her. No taunting her after going back from here
. . . that she came to the mahila panchayat and stuff like that.

*Sunil:* She should also listen to me if I obey her.

*Mahila panchayat member 1:* She wants 300 rupees for her child's medicines, tonics etc. no abusing from now on. Bury the past.

[caseworker documents the decision]

*Sunil:* Her brothers threaten me on the streets.

*Mahila panchayat member 3:* [angry] Why will they do it if you take care of
their sister? Don't you get it—she would fight with them over you if you
treated her properly.

*Mahila panchayat member 4:* [to Ruchira] Don't be worried any more. We
will not let anything happen to you or your daughter.

Caseworkers and mahila panchayat members strike a balance between
being hard on men who justify their abusive behavior and providing supportive counsel to the couple or family. Anxious about her marital situation, Ruchira required more than merely a decision by the mahila panchayat. Frequent home visits and reassurance assuaged Ruchira's concerns and eventually enabled her to return to her husband's family—with
a list of provisions stipulated by the mahila panchayat in hand. Building
the latrine did not have practical implications alone. It symbolized the
collective strength behind Ruchira who, like most women in her situation, had neither her family nor her biradari backing her. Once "out" and
in the hands of the mahila panchayat, even when the case is closed, a
woman's husband and in-laws would unlikely risk attempting foul play.

Unlike Sunil, the husband in the next case was well received by the
mahila panchayat. Complemented by a well-finessed case-management
response, the following is an example of how a successful final decision
was secured by the mahila panchayat. The dramatic account began when
Anjali, a newly married woman, frantically entered a Sabla Sangh soaked
in kerosene oil. She implored the caseworkers to save her from Naren, her
husband, and her in-laws who she accused of attempting to set her on
fire. During the interrogation at the police station, the husband and in-
laws denied criminal activity. After privately probing and counseling her,
the caseworkers determined that Anjali had poured the kerosene over
herself. She also revealed that her in-laws harassed and beat her endlessly;

that her mother-in-law was attached to Anjali's son but rejected her daughter and had been demanding that Anjali and her infant daughter move out. The caseworkers also determined that as an orphan, Anjali had no social support. Consequently, the police report was dropped. The mahila panchayat had held a hearing for them, two months earlier, at which time they had reached an interim decision. At the second hearing, when the final decision was to be reached, both Anjali and Naren appeared with their two children. Naren seemed unusually delighted as he waited to be heard at the mahila panchayat hearing:

> *Caseworker:* What was the interim decision in this case?
>
> *Mahila panchayat member 1:* Naren agreed that if anything happened to his wife, he would be fully responsible. He agreed to move out of his parents' home and find a place for himself, Anjali, and the two children.
>
> *Mahila panchayat member 2:* How are things working out since the last hearing?
>
> *Naren:* [grinning] Ask my wife if she's happy.
>
> *Mahila panchayat member 2:* No, we want to hear from you. We will ask her later.
>
> *Naren:* [grinning] Yes, I am very happy. I am happy only if my wife is happy.
>
> *Caseworker:* What have you learned?
>
> *Naren:* My job is very difficult. I drive an auto rickshaw ten hours a day. By the time I arrive home, I am completely fatigued, mentally. I couldn't handle the fighting from inside the family—with my wife, my brothers, and mother. My wife and mother do not speak, but I'm sure that will change.
>
> *Mahila panchayat:* We are very happy that you found a solution.
>
> *Naren:* I am entirely responsible for my wife and family and am very happy that she is happy now.
>
> *Caseworker:* And you, Anjali?
>
> *Anjali:* [subdued] Now, I'm okay. I am living with my husband and children separately. My husband takes the children to meet his mother and I don't go. Now there is no more trouble.
>
> *Caseworker:* Who will write the final decision?

Naren's delighted expression signified his relief and gratification that the mahila panchayat had solved his case. Husbands often feel torn between loyalty to their parental families and commitment to their wives who are tormented at the hands of his family. While the mahila panchayat supports women who are unjustly treated in these circumstances, husbands receive equal benefit.

Unfortunately, not all cases end as agreeably. Many cases are complicated by social problems resulting from chronic alcohol use, playing the lottery, and unemployment. Generally, long-term reconciliation is not possible in the most severe cases. Ideally other NGO programs, such as the microsavings project, the education program, or some other NGO project can absorb the needs of these women to help them acquire skills and resources to become self-dependent. Unfortunately, however, there are many such women and many find no help.

An outsider may find it curious that men oblige the mahila panchayat. There are several reasons why an accused not only appears at his hearing but subsequently fulfills the mahila panchayat's demands after a decision is made. First, if the accused does not show up, a registered letter indicating the new hearing date is sent. The closing line of the letter usually reads, "If you do not attend the hearing, further legal or police action will be taken." Slum dwellers are generally terrified of police intervention, which often involves brutality at the hands of the police. Generally, after the registered letter is sent, the accused appears at the hearing. Second, traditional panchayats have a long history and a prominent place in the lives of slum dwellers. Resembling the structure of a traditional community council, the mahila panchayat commands authority and respect in the locality. When the parties appear at the hearing, they assume the appropriate roles of opponent and defendant. Third, by the time a case reaches the mahila panchayat, the details of the case have been exposed, with many individuals becoming involved in resolving it. The extended family, neighbors, and sometimes even local politicians begin to intervene in cases. It seems clear that social pressure plays a critical role in male compliance. Fourth, the caseworkers know the law and how to work the system. They are not afraid to carry the case beyond the scope of the mahila panchayat, even if it means involving lawyers who are available at Action India's headquarters on a part-time basis. Fifth, unlike the traditional systems of jurisprudence through the biradari panchayat or the judicial-legal system, the mahila panchayat is a new urban force which is close to the community. Mahila panchayat members and caseworkers interact regularly with abusers, their families, and neighbors even after the case has been resolved. This active participation close to people's lives lends credibility and respect to this grassroots initiative.

## Conclusion

By overlaying equitable notions of jurisprudence and women's rights upon an efficient patriarchal one, the Sabla Sanghs have developed a way to defy abusers and deter violent behavior. Through their collective initiative, case-workers and mahila panchayat members exemplify a powerful way of being in the world, not otherwise apparent for many women living in the slums. Indeed, mahila panchayats challenge women's traditional comportment in the community both through their rulings which stand for women's rights and by their strong personal example, made visible through hearings as well as in day-to-day encounters with authority, such as the police. Unlike institutions traditionally considered women's guardian—such as the family, bi-radari panchayat, or the judicial-legal system—mahila panchayats do not tolerate a husband's "justification" of abusive behavior as his "right." In contrast, their decisions reflect a feminist sentiment: namely, that actions which trigger violent episodes do not *cause* abuse or justify abuse, nor are they the victim's fault. Instead, abusers are implicated, held responsible, and hence culpable for abusive behavior.

Indian society's hierarchical caste system is assumed to be entrenched and unchangeable. The caseworkers and mahila panchayat hearings have proven this notion wrong. Within the Sabla Sangh framework all sub-caste groups and religions are represented, creating a democratic space for its members to talk, sing, deliberate, and share meals side by side. This last collective activity is particularly significant because—as for blacks under the Jim Crow southern United States—who one eats with has long been a key indicator of one's caste in the Indian system. But this is only the beginning, as one change leads to another. Lower-caste women in mahila panchayats deliberate on cases involving higher-caste families, something which would have been unthinkable before the Sabla Sanghs came into existence.

Instead of looking to Europe or the United States for models of domestic violence intervention, this NGO has utilized an indigenous approach. By establishing a feminist variant on a traditional Indian male-dominated method of self-governance, the mahila panchayats have taken the first step in institutionalizing radical social change in India's poorest communities. Believed by many to be entrenched and impervious to change, rigidly held beliefs sustaining the caste system are now bending as a result of Sabla Sangh forces. Similarly, Sabla Sangh strategies push the boundaries of acceptable behavior for women in their communities toward greater freedom and individual choice. Their strengths, however, have not yet been fully realized on a mass scale. Perhaps the most important factor guaranteeing continued social change through the mahila panchayats are the women themselves and their increased self-awareness and collective self-esteem. As one caseworker commented:

> [I would like] our mahila panchayat to become so powerful that men realize it as a strong identity—that people learn to respect it and improve their attitudes toward women—that women know and understand their rights—and, that they have the courage to demand it. She should be able to do something for herself and others. A woman should have a sense of herself. These are my personal views.

### ACKNOWLEDGMENTS

I thank Ashwini Deshpande and France Winddance Twine for their readings and very helpful suggestions. I also thank Minelle Mahtani and Narendra Panjwani for invaluable insights and critiques. My heartfelt thanks to Prena Rahuri for her endurance and kindness. I am grateful to the women of Action India who shared their stories and wisdom, which have helped enlighten me in the course of doing this research.

### NOTES

1. See Nandita Gandhi and Shah Nandita, *The Issues at Stake* (New Delhi: Kali for Women, 1991).

2. Most contemporary Indian feminist ideas emerged out of the far left. Groups opted for autonomy, which they defined as separate, women-only groups without any party affiliation or conventional structures considered "patriarchal." Awareness of women's problems and rights was accumulated and expressed through women's campaigns (such as dowry and rape) which later defined Indian feminism. Unlike many Western countries, feminism in the Indian context has been largely influenced by an awareness of women's oppression and exploitation within the family as well as in society from a social class and caste perspective.

3. Radha Kumar, "From Chipko to Sati: The Contemporary Indian Women's Movement," in *The Challenges of Local Feminism: Women's Movements in Global Perspective*, ed. Amrita Basu (Boulder, Colo.: Westview Press, 1995).

4. Poverty level is defined as individuals living below subsistence, calculated at an income able to purchase 2,200 calories per person in a family.

5. Scheduled castes (SC) refers to those specifically recognized as "castes" by the Indian constitution—for the purposes of affirmative action benefits—which otherwise prohibits caste distinctions. Scheduled castes, formerly referred to as untouchables, are sweepers, leather workers, cobblers, hide processors, and those who handle and sell beef, pork, and meat in general. In the Brahminic Hindu purity-pollution culture, these people perform the most "impure" tasks and lead the most "impure" lives. Thus they are untouchables. Gandhi coined the term Harijan, a "child of God," a phrase considered patronizing. It has since been replaced by Dalit, "the oppressed."

6. Municipal Corporation of Delhi (MCD), "Action Plan Affidavit to Tackle Slum Problems through the Delhi High Court" (Delhi: Slum and JJ (Jhuggie Jhopri) Department, Municipal Corporation of Delhi, Policy Planning and Monitoring Division, 1999).

7. In a scheme to both reduce Delhi's population and displace squatter families, men received a small plot of land where they would relocate in exchange for proof of sterilization. During this period, thousands of men were vasectomized at camps. Police roundups for compulsory vasectomies resulted in violent riots. The singular focus on male sterilization is thought to have sparked protests that brought about the eventual collapse of the ruling party in 1977. Since that time, the government sterilization policy has targeted only women, but it is now being eliminated.

8. Sabir Ali, *Environmental Scenario of Delhi Slums*, ed. Planning Commission Council for Social Development (Delhi: Gyan Sagar Publications, 1998).

9. Although they originated in villages, biradari panchayats are influential and culturally accepted entities with the capacity to wield power over the lives of slum dwellers in Delhi. Like their village counterparts, biradari panchayats are caste-based, organized by regional caste groups.

10. David Mandelbaum, *Society in India: Community and Change* (2 vols.), vol. 1 (Berkeley: University of California Press, 1970).

11. The mahila panchayats referred to in this study are unofficial entities modeled after traditional all-male panchayats. Members of these mahila panchayats are not elected, nor do they hold fiscal or locally sanctioned decision-making powers. Officially recognized mahila panchayats have existed at the village level since independence. For an interesting study of all-women panchayats in Maharashta, see *"And Who Will Make the Chapatis?" A Study of All-Women Panchayats in Maharasha*, ed. Bishakra Datta (Calcutta: Shree, 1998).

12. The majority of women seeking help at the Sabla Sangh are scheduled and lower castes. As described in Deshpande's chapter in this volume, it is unclear whether the reason behind the objection to women working is due to tradition or a desire to emulate higher castes, who strictly limit women's mobility outside the home.

13. It is unclear why women are less inclined to leave an abusive husband.

One may speculate that this shift may be a result of the following: (1) women's labor in the home is no longer an economic asset as it once was in the village context; (2) lower-caste families have been gradually adopting the practices of upper-caste women, who object to divorce or separation; (3) a larger proportion of a family's resources are invested in the marriage of daughters than ever before.

# Chapter 3

# Exotic Dancing and Unionizing
## *The Challenges of Feminist and Antiracist Organizing at the Lusty Lady Theater*

### *Siobhan Brooks*

On August 30, 1996 the Lusty Lady theater in San Francisco made history by becoming the only women-managed strip club in the United States to successfully unionize. Dancers at the Lusty Lady joined Local 790 of the SEIU (Service Employee International Union) to protest racist hiring practices, customers videotaping women via one-way mirrored glass without their consent, an inconsistent disciplinary policy, lack of health benefits, and an overall dearth of job security.[1] Despite this big victory, problems of racism remained at the Lusty Lady.

In this chapter I discuss my involvement with the Lusty Lady union and its lessons for a feminist, antiracist praxis that places issues affecting sex workers of color at the forefront. To understand the events that took place at the Lusty Lady, it is important to view them in the context of the setting in which they occurred. San Francisco, a predominantly middle-class city in northern California with a racially diverse population that includes significant numbers of Asian Americans and Asians, Black Americans, Latina/os, Mexican Americans, and whites has a history of ac-tivist struggles over race, class, and gender issues and politically active gay, lesbian, bisexual, and transgendered communities. Its North Beach neighborhood, where the Lusty Lady is located, is a tourist area, with many Italian restaurants and strip clubs. Since North Beach also borders Chinatown and the financial district, the Lusty Lady attracted white busi-nessmen from the financial district, Asian men from Chinatown, and Japanese and European male tourists. Its patrons varied from men in their fifties and sixties during the week to a younger, more racially mixed, and rowdier crowd on weekends. The racial and union struggles of the Lusty Lady reflect both the racial demographics of its workers and customers and its location in a city with a long history of organizing among queer communities.

## History of Racism at the Lusty Lady

I began working at the Lusty Lady while I was a twenty-two-year-old Women Studies major at San Francisco State University. Like many college students, I was having financial difficulties. I knew a few women who were stripping to supplement their income. They told me about the Lusty Lady peep show, a female-managed strip club that had started in Seattle, a major city in the U.S. Northwest, in 1979 and expanded to San Francisco in 1982. I auditioned and was hired by Josephine, the only Black show director at the time. Dancers were paid $11 to $24 an hour, and didn't have to pay stage fees or hustle tips. Shifts were four to five hours long with a ten-minute break every half-hour.

Dancing at the Lusty Lady was very surreal, like dancing in a neon fish tank with its sultry red and green lights. The dance stage was small, with four or five women on stage at a time. Men (and occasionally women) would go into a booth, drop in quarters, and a glass window would rise up revealing a dancer, quite similar to a video arcade. The men usually masturbated in the booth. There was also a so-called "Private Pleasures booth," where dancers charged customers five dollars (now ten) for three-minute shows. These shows were more intimate but also separated by glass. The Private Pleasures booth was more lucrative for dancers, who could make sixty dollars an hour in this way.

The managers of Lusty Lady, themselves former dancers, were pleasant. They encouraged open communication and provided snacks for us in the dressing room. Because we danced behind glass and did not have physical contact with customers, it was relatively safe. The male support staff did a good job of ensuring our safety, escorting us to our cars during late-night shifts. We never had to worry about them sexually harassing us, unlike many women who work in strip clubs. In this way, I felt that the Lusty Lady lived up to its reputation for being a safe, feminist strip club. Within a few months, however, I noticed covert forms of racism by my white coworkers and management. This took several forms.

First, there were few women of color at the theater. Out of seventy dancers, only ten were women of color. Of these, five were Black, most light-skinned, one was part Chinese and Japanese, one was Korean, one was from Argentina, one was part Native American and European, and one was part Indian and French. Yet nonwhite women rarely worked with others of the same race. For example, if a Black woman came on stage she would replace the current Black woman on stage; the same for Asian dancers, Latinas, and so on. But white women (usually busty and blond) were allowed to work together.

Second, Black dancers rarely performed in the Private Pleasures booth.[2] Like the other Black dancers, I was trained to work in booth, but was hardly ever scheduled there. One day I asked Josephine why Black women didn't work the Private Pleasures booth. She told me that Black women made the company lose money, that white customers would rather pay a quarter than five dollars to see a Black woman. I did notice that some white customers would lose interest in my show and walk out in the middle of it, or wave me out of view. I had also heard from other dancers that when Josephine was a dancer and booth performer, a group of young white customers yelled through the glass that she looked like a monkey in a cage. Although racist comments like that were rare, they reflect one of many psychological risks that women of color take when doing sex work for white men. However, in spite of some negative encounters with white men, I also knew that other white men enjoyed my show and asked whether I was going to do booth. I had also heard from various male support staff that white customers would ask them why Black women and other women of color did not perform in booth.

In general, the younger, racially mixed weekend crowd at the Lusty Lady preferred to see women of color as well as white women, while the white and Asian businessmen preferred to see white women. The management assumed that the latter group had more money and placed their desires first. When I asked the general manager (a white male) to provide an estimate of how much money the company made and the economic risk of having Black women and other women of color in booth, he refused to answer, perhaps because he did not want to venture information that would make him liable for a race-based lawsuit. It is hard to obtain exact figures as to what owners of strip clubs and porn video shops make per year. However, according to a U.S. bankruptcy court against the San Francisco-based Bijou Group, Inc., Bijou made over $5 million per year between 1992 and 1994.[3]

A few months after my meeting with Josephine, a white Jewish coworker wrote a petition stating that dancers who worked booth should receive a higher commission (at that time dancers kept 30 percent of their wages, while the club kept 70). She directed the petition to the general show director, June, and posted the petition in the dressing room. A number of dancers (most of whom were white) instantly agreed that they were being exploited and signed her petition. I felt angered by her petition because if it were to pass, it would only further widen the wage gap between the Black dancers, the few nonwhite booth performers, and the white women. At that time, several incidents had occurred in the dressing room in which white dancers had talked about how economically well or poorly they were doing in booth in the presence of a Black dancer. When Black dancers complained about not being scheduled in booth, the white dancers were sympathetic, some angry, but most saw the situation as *our* problem. Unfortunately, because of the systematic economic positioning of white women within a white supremacist, patriarchal, capitalist structure in which they shared racial privileges with white men, they could not see that their struggle to acquire a higher percentage of their booth wages was directly related to the exclusion of Black dancers in booth and in the workplace.

To rectify this situation, I decided to write my own petition, also directed to June, stating that it was unfair that Black dancers were not regularly performing in booth. I posted my petition in the dressing room, and many dancers signed it. Within a few days Josephine called me into her office and asked about my petition; I told her it was pretty self-explanatory. She wanted to arrange a meeting between the other Black dancers and myself and June. During the meeting Josephine and June accused me of jumping to conclusions about their being racist; they asked me why I hadn't just asked to be scheduled in booth if I wanted to work it so bad. I replied that it wasn't a matter of how "bad" I wanted to work booth, but that other dancers didn't have to ask to work booth, other dancers weren't discriminated against in this way. I and the other dancers then demanded to see documentation proving that Black dancers in booth would hurt business, but no such documentation was produced. Further, we asked to see the Private Pleasures incomes of the Black dancers in Seattle and found that Black dancers there did pretty well. One of the Black dancers suggested that we try rotating Black women in booth once a week. This was done, but in retaliation for this concession, management called a general meeting about the "misunderstandings" of my petition and prohibited the posting of any political literature (especially dealing with the workplace) in the dressing room. Only postings about shift trades and parties were allowed. However, in spite of this regulation, I was pleased with the outcome.

## Issues Leading to Unionization

The main issue that led women at the Lusty Lady to unionize was the videotaping of dancers by customers without their consent, a situation that the management would not change. In response, women at the Lusty Lady teamed up with the Exotic Dancer's Alliance (EDA), a nonprofit organization started at the Market Street Cinema in 1992 in response to payment of stage fees by dancers, substandard working conditions, and health and safety issues in the exotic dance industry. Through several court battles, EDA tried to get exotic dancers recognized as employees rather than independent contractors, so they would no longer be forced to pay stage fees, but this is still a site of struggle. Unfortunately, owners of the Market Street Cinema and other clubs filed bankruptcy to avoid paying their dancers back wages due under this judgment.

During the union organizing effort, the issues that led most white women to unionize were not a high priority for most women of color. For example, I was concerned with increasing the number of women of color, wage increases, and instituting a fair disciplinary policy. These issues were less central to the white women involved in the unionization effort. Their priorities were the one-way windows and, later, the problems of wages and disciplinary policies, but not race. Moreover, the names and organizations of people of color were hardly mentioned in the mainstream media coverage. Organizations and people of color such as Center for Third World Organizing, Rhodessa Jones (director and founder of the MEDEA Project), Theater for Incarcerated Women, Angela Y. Davis, and police commissioner Pat Norman were not mentioned in the press, while sex-positive white activists like Carol Queen and Annie Sprinkle did appear. For example, a *Los Angeles Times* article addressed issues affecting dancers at the Lusty Lady without mentioning anything about race. Although the reporter interviewed me, what she wrote did not reflect my political views on the racism at the theater:

> Naomi [my stage name at the time of the interview], 24 and a union supporter, said she doesn't want to be treated as a sexual object when she walks

down the street. "But in there it's OK to be an object of someone's desire," she said. "Actually I think it's fun. It's kind of a spiritual relief to come here and dance with other women, and have men looking at me."

In contrast, when the same reporter interviewed a white dancer, also a union organizer, she focused on the politics of the one-way window:

> "We had been complaining vocally for months," said a dancer who calls herself Jane. "Can you put in a metal detector? Can you take out the one-way windows?" She [the general manager, June] said "no way."[4]

In 1996, I filed a racial discrimination complaint with the Department of Fair and Equal Housing to put pressure on the company to hire more women of color. After an investigation, the management of Lusty Lady did hire more women of color, most of whom, initially, were Black. But I was still the only woman of color who served on the union bargaining committee and worked as a shop steward. I found this very frustrating because I felt pressured to represent all women of color, and felt like a token. The other women of color said they did not have time to serve on the bargaining committee, which did consume a lot of time and energy, but I wondered whether they felt that their presence would not make a difference.

After six months of long, tedious negotiations we voted in our first contract. We received four paid sick days, basic contract language regarding sexual harassment and racial discrimination policies, wage increase, free shift trades,[5] and a grievance procedure. Even male support staff who originally felt uncertain about having a union, voted for the union to support the dancers.

Unfortunately, this organizing success did not inspire the dancers in Seattle to follow suit. Unlike the dancers in San Francisco, the Seattle Lusty Lady dancers were not interested in unionizing. Historically, the dancers in Seattle had viewed management as friends and family and, as its first location, the Seattle management was willing to meet more of the dancers' needs. Moreover, although Seattle has a long history of resistance and a large number of women in electoral politics, San Francisco may have a stronger culture of sexual politics, especially among the queer community. Thus when dancers at the Lusty Lady in Seattle tried to unionize, they did so over some personal misunderstandings with management rather than over working conditions, and the union drive failed.

### Postunionization Challenges

After my racial discrimination complaint, the number of Black dancers and other dancers of color increased, but this presented new challenges. As a union shop steward, my job was to bring new dancers into the union. We had a cross between an open shop and an agency shop, which meant that dancers did not have to join the union to work and could enjoy union benefits without being members. Fortunately, most dancers did join the union and, whenever there was a new dancer of color, I went out of my way to explain the reasons why we had unionized, stressing the race issue.

For the first four months following the contract vote, the theater had more Black dancers than ever before in its seventeen-year history. I loved dancing with the other Black women on stage. The jukebox now had more of a musical cornucopia (in addition to rock, punk, and country we had hip-hop and gangsta rap), and, with a variety of beautiful women on stage, I did not feel so racially isolated. The customers also loved the racial diversity, especially customers of color. However, some subtle problems emerged in the interpersonal relationships between the new Black dancers and white dancers.

One problem arose due to white dancers' discomfort when they were outnumbered on stage by women of color. In the middle of a shift, white dancers would comment about being the only white woman on stage in the presence of women of color, or would block a customer's view of a woman of color dancing, sure that the customer only wanted to look at white women. We would respond that these comments were crass, racist, and disrespectful, and that we were outnumbered by white women all the time. But this would make the white women assert their racial privilege even more strongly and insist they were not racist.

Another problem had to do with the way white dancers treated customers of color. An example of this occurred when customers of color who did not speak English went into a booth without closing or locking the door behind them. Sometimes the white dancers would yell at them to close and lock the door in a very derogatory manner or would ask them if they spoke English. To eliminate this form of racism, we demanded that management install signs on the windows in English, Mandarin, and Spanish telling customers to be respectful to dancers and to close and lock their door. Some white dancers were also reluctant to dance for Black men. At times when a window went up to reveal a Black man, white dancers took their time moving to that window, or ignored him altogether. I found this unnerving and would dance for Black men myself when this occurred. To my dismay, some Black men did not want to look at a Black woman dancer and would look around me to the white women who were ignoring him.

The jukebox was another site of racism. Dancers were paid forty dollars to create a jukebox of fifty to one hundred songs, and the jukebox was played the following week. When a Black dancer created a jukebox it would include R and B and gangsta rap, as well as modern rock. When the jukebox created by a Black dancer was playing, white dancers complained that they could not dance to the music, or that the music was too violent. Although I understand feminist concerns about violence in gangsta rap, the violence of rap artists like Tupac Shakur is about the legal system or the street; it is not misogynist. These complaints were voiced in the presence of Black dancers, who, not wanting to deal with further racial harassment, remained silent.

More covert forms of racism included comments that some Black dancers wore too much hair oil and that it smeared the mirrors on stage. Many times a white dancer took a bottle of rubbing alcohol (used to clean the stage) and wipe the mirrors or the pole where a Black dancer was standing even though other women of color and myself told white dancers that to clean up directly after a Black dancer's presence could be interpreted as suggesting that she was dirty. White dancers also complained that Black dancers wore too much perfume and that it irritated white dancers who had environmental illness. After four months, I noticed that many Black dancers had left the Lusty Lady. I asked them why they had left and their response was that the Lusty Lady was just "too white" and that they were working at other clubs that were more "down to earth." I respected their choice to leave, but I was hurt because the Lusty Lady has the best working conditions of any strip club in the country. The alternative was to work at clubs like the Market Street Cinema that had a higher percentage of women of color, but also horrific working conditions such as stage fees and, reportedly, coerced prostitution.

The final factor that pushed Black and other dancers of color out of the Lusty Lady was the institutional racism of the management. When a dancer was fired, if she felt that her termination was unfair she was permitted to file a grievance with the shop steward. A few times, I and other shop stewards noticed that a Black dancer was no longer at the theater and assumed she had quit, only to find out from other dancers of color that she had been terminated. For example, two Black women who were close friends worked at the theater for more than a year. They were both tall, friendly, and beautiful. Everyone loved them. At some point, I did not see them any more and thought they had quit. I learned later that they were fired for calling in sick too many times. Other shop stewards and I were angry that no one had told us earlier and that they did not come to us. When I called them, they told me that when they were fired management told them there was nothing the shop stewards could do to get their jobs back. We then met with management to make sure that women of color had equal access to shop steward representation and were given fair treatment. We also insisted on a program of cultural competency training at the theater to deal with the problem of racist interpersonal relationships between white dancers and dancers of color and to make sure that all dancers got equal access to union benefits.

## Implementing an Antiracist and Feminist Agenda

In addition to my work as a union organizer at the Lusty Lady Theater, I am a Board Member of the Exotic Dancer's Alliance. I joined the Exotic Dancer's Alliance because it is a nonprofit organization geared to help dancers with legal grievances such as filing wage and hour claims, taxes, and filing suits against club owners. It is one of few sex-worker organizations to help sex workers win legal cases and fight for their rights. EDA also works with the prostitutes' advocacy group COYOTE (Call Off Your Old Tired Ethics). EDA also assists Asian women working in massage parlors to insure that they get work permits from the health department. This protects them from the possibility of police arrest, and having their money taken away, especially in the case of young Asian women who don't speak much English. This kind of abusive police procedure also exists in the strip clubs where immigrant women of color are arrested on suspicion of prostitution and robbed of their money.

Like many sex worker organizations, the EDA is predominately white.[6] Besides me, there are only two active women of color in the group: Dawn Passar, a cofounder of EDA who is an immigrant from Thailand and a former sex worker who works with Asian women in massage parlors,[7] and Gina Gold who is a Black former sex worker. At one time, there were five active women of color in EDA, including Hima B, an Indian filmmaker and *decadence?*

exotic dancer, and Isis Rodriguez, a Latina artist and former dancer. But these women left the group.

There are aspects of EDA that makes it difficult for women of color to participate, particularly the fact that other than Dawn no woman of color has a real leadership position. Additionally, women of color may be alienated by the lack of cultural specificity at EDA. After I brought this up at a board meeting, we created language in EDA brochures stating that EDA makes an effort to be racially, culturally, and sexually inclusive. We also discussed providing child care for women to make it easier for women with children to attend meetings and workshops.

In spite of these efforts, it is mainly middle-class and working-class white women who attend EDA's meetings and workshops. A few women of color have occasionally attended meetings, but most stop coming. To change this, I have started to work with organizations for communities of color, such as Center for Third World Organizing and Wages for Housework. Because I had attended a training session at the Center for Third World Organizing, and had published in their magazine, *Third Force*, I knew they were supportive of sex-worker issues. I became aware of Wages for Housework at a symposium at UC Hastings College of the Law entitled "Economic Justice for Sex Workers." There I met Margaret Prescott, a founder of Wages for Housework who worked with Black prostitutes in Los Angeles, and was really impressed by her work. I felt that somehow I could merge these groups with EDA, but I was wrong. One of the white women in EDA felt that these two groups were good at organizing, but did not agree with their stance on prostitution and did not want to work with them.[8]

## Conclusion

It is dangerous to separate issues of race, gender, and class from issues of sex work. As an exotic dancer, I have observed that most workers in the sex industry are poor or working-class women of color or white women. This is especially true in sex clubs with poor working and health conditions. Moreover, the stereotypes that whites hold about people of color—for example that Blacks and Latinas, especially light-skinned mixed-race women, are sexually desirable and domineering, that Asians and Native Americans are passive, and that Middle Eastern women are exotic—do not enhance our economic status in the sex industry, but rather serve to justify the economic exploitation of women of color. We are still seen as "Other" compared to white women, while white women are perceived as "Real" women.[9] For these reasons, it is perilous for feminists to take an unqualified position against sex work. White middle-class radical feminists like Catharine MacKinnon and Andrea Dworkin fail to see sex work as a labor issue and an issue of choice. Certainly, some women, especially poor women of color, are economically coerced into sex work. But seeing sex work as a form of sexual slavery makes it impossible to recognize the positive struggle by sex workers to change their working conditions and unfairly reproduces the dichotomy between "good" and "bad" female sexuality.[10]

It is important that people of color take on the issue of sex work. More than half of sex workers are people of color from Third World countries and the United States, who face particular problems because of conservative views about sex work. Women of color in the United States now make up a huge percentage of those imprisoned in the prison-industrial complex because of crackdowns on street prostitution. Women of color in Third World countries have skyrocketing rates of HIV infection and AIDS, as do U.S. women of color who face poor working conditions and racist management practices in strip clubs and the sex industry. Many women of color in the U.S. sex industry are immigrants, scared to seek legal advice for fear they will be deported from the country.

The situation faced by women of color in the sex industry has a profound effect on the health status, immigration situation, child rearing practices, and future of all communities of color in the United States. It is up to those of us who identify as feminists to take part in the sex-workers' movement. White sex-worker activists need to challenge racism and white supremacy within the sex-worker movement, while activists of color need to challenge sex phobia and sex-worker phobia within movements of people of color. Coalitions between sex-worker activists across the racial divide are a necessary, but difficult, aspect of the struggle.

ACKNOWLEDGMENTS

My thanks to Angela Y. Davis, Rhodessa Jones, Gloria Locket (COYOTE), Gina Gold, Dawn Passar, Johanna Breyer, Hima B., Ahimsa Timoteo Bodhran, Marshall Trammell, Michael Ulrich, Scott Rector, Chuck, Randen Kane, Robert Stewart, Julia Query, Teresa Ellis, the late Stephine Kulick aka "Honeysuckle," Stephine Baty (Union Representative for SEIU Local 790), Margaret Prescott (Black

Women for Wages for Housework), France Winddance Twine, Demetrius Semien, and [stage names] Miss Mary Ann/Jane, Summer, Honey, Sunny, Stealth, Sybil, and Velvet.

## NOTES

1. For more information about the unionization process at the Lusty Lady, see Siobhan Brooks, "Organizing from Behind the Glass: Exotic Dancers Ready to Unionize," *Z Magazine* (January 1997): 11–14.

2. Employers tend to view non-Black people of color as less threatening to white people, as opposed to Black people. This is one of the many unique ways Black women are discriminated against in the workplace and pitted against other people of color. In the sex industry this is even more evident.

3. Case no. 95–3–3389–TC.

4. *Los Angeles Times*, August 29, 1996.

5. Prior to unionization, dancers had to find a dancer of their own race and body type to trade shifts with. This policy was eradicated, making it easier for all dancers to pick up shifts and give them away.

6. As I write this essay I realize that I did not exercise every possibility of making EDA more culturally appropriate for women of color. I am only writing about the actions that interested me at the time because I do not think it is the job of women of color to consistently provide white women with ways to further diversify organizations that are supposed to be racially diverse already. While coalitions are necessary, they are only short-term goals when the main focus of these predominately white organizations is not the enhancement of people of color. Organizing is more effective when people of color work in our communities, and white allies work in theirs to educate other whites about issues of race.

7. For a more detailed analysis from Dawn Passar of the situation of women in Thailand in relation to the military industrial complex, see the Exotic Dancer's Alliance web page where I interview Dawn Passar at <http://www/bayswan. Org/siobintvw.html>.

8. Since the writing of this essay, that woman has been asked to leave the Board of EDA because of complaints about her rude behavior from people of color within the community.

9. Patricia Hill Collins, *Black Feminist Thought: Knowledge, Consciousness, and the Politics of Empowerment* (New York: Routledge, 1991); Angela Y. Davis, *Women, Race, and Class* (New York: Random House, 1981).

10. Gail Pheterson, *Sex Work Writing by Women in the Sex Industry*, ed. Priscilla Alexander and Frédérique Delacoste (San Francisco: Cleis Press, 1987).

# Chapter 4

# Women, Healthcare, and Social Reform in Yemen

## *Delores M. Walters*

Politically, women's participation in the emerging democracy of Yemen is being recognized, but legally, women's rights remain limited. In Yemen's 1997 parliamentary elections, the presence of women—as campaigners, monitors, and voters (25 percent out of a total of 4.6 million eligible voters)—was impressive.[1] In fact, women educated other women on their voting rights. Yet fewer than twenty women ran for office out of a total of more than two thousand persons of both sexes for three hundred and one open seats. Women candidates were fielded only in the former South Yemen but not by either of the two major political parties. Most women candidates were independents, and only two of them won seats.[2] Thus, the growing commitment to improving women's political status, and their socioeconomic conditions as well, does not mean an unfettered advance, especially at the government level. And women who are considered too outspoken on women's rights can expect severe reprisals.[3]

The Republic of Yemen is comprised of North and South Yemen, the former Yemen Arab Republic (YAR) and the Peoples' Democratic Republic of Yemen (PDRY), respectively. The national liberation Forces of South Yemen gained independence from Britain in 1967 and established a socialist regime.[4] North Yemen emerged as a modern state during the 1970s, following the 1962 overthrow of the thousand-year-rule of the conservative imams and a subsequent civil war. Relative stabilization of tribal opposition was finally achieved in 1978 under Colonel 'Ali Abdallah Salih, the president of the republic. Thus while colonization in South Yemen was externally imposed, in North Yemen restrictive policies were maintained by indigenous monarchs. Despite the discovery of oil in both

Yemens, and the remittances of over a billion dollars sent home from labor migrants during the 1980s, the two countries remained amongst the poorest in the world at the time of reunification in 1990.[5]

The joint government unifying the two struggling economies opposed the United States and its ally Saudi Arabia during the Persian Gulf war, resulting in the expulsion of Yemeni migrants from Saudi Arabia and other countries of the Arabian peninsula. Unresolved ideological divisions between the North and South were exacerbated by the multiparty, popular parliamentary elections in 1993. Civil war, which erupted in 1994 and lasted two months, ended when Northern Yemeni forces seized control. A significant outcome of these events was the strengthening of the Yemeni Congregation for Reform (Islah) Party—a coalition of conservative tribal and Islamist interests. Ultimately, Islah aligned with 'Ali Abdallah Salih's General Peoples' Party (GPC) against the Yemeni Socialist Party (YSP). The considerable gains made by Islah in 1993 were not maintained relative to the GPC, which won two-thirds of the seats in the parliamentary elections held in April 1997.[6] Domination by conservative Northern ideologies means to a certain extent the reinstatement of social as well as gender inequalities.

In 1999, the population in united Yemen was approaching 17 million.[7] Yemen's annual population growth rate of 3.8 percent (in 1997) makes it one of the fastest growing countries in the world. Yemen is also characterized by a high fertility rate (7.4 children per woman, 8.2 rural); low life expectancy (51 years); low literacy (45.5 percent); and low per capita GNP ($527).[8] Undoubtedly, the development of adequate health services cannot be expected to meet the demand in the near future. In rural areas, where the majority of Yemenis still reside, sanitation and knowledge of basic hygiene are limited or virtually nonexistent. Most Yemenis, who live in hamlets and villages scattered throughout an extremely varied terrain, lack ready access to disease supervision and health monitoring systems. The high incidence of infant and child mortality in Yemen are directly attributed to the absence of nationwide medical and sanitation delivery as well as lack of awareness regarding health matters.

In light of the urgent need to improve basic human conditions, advocates for women's socioecoomic or political parity with men are the exception rather than the rule in Yemeni society. Still, many Yemenis, including men, have long advocated for a democracy that permits women's full participation. Similarly, Yemenis, both women and men, recognize the advantages of educational and employment opportunities for women. Comparatively few Yemenis would term themselves feminists, however. Rather, the goals of women's activism in Yemen typically center on improving the standards of living for one's family and community.[9] As Margot Badran so succinctly observes: "In Yemen, women practise feminism. They do not label it."[10] Her statement refers to women's political pragmatism, especially as it pertains to gender equality.[11] Yet, such pragmatic activism also applies to Yemeni women's family-oriented social change involving work that traditionally is female.

Yemeni society also would not be characterized by many as racist. Despite constitutional and Islamic egalitarian ideals, Yemen's rigid social hierarchy is based on birth and occupational status rather than race. However, implicit in the categories that Yemenis use to identify themselves and others are racial and ethnic ideologies. Yemenis with known African ancestry, former slaves (*'abid*), and Yemenis with reputed African origins (*akhdam*) are relegated to the bottom of the social scale. Moreover, Yemeni servant groups with no known or presumed African ancestors (*khaddam*) are considered black and thereby racialized.

While the terms feminist and racist do not fit precisely in the Yemeni context, the female primary healthcare workers, known in Arabic as *murshidat*, are not only effectively delivering health services, but are also helping stigmatized African-identified groups gain access to rights and privileges that previously were denied. In so doing, they are promoting social integration and reducing the barriers that have long divided Yemenis of different social status. In this essay, I examine the *murshidat*'s pivotal roles in alleviating Yemen's disabling economic conditions and social divisions, especially Yemen's cultural, racial, and gender hierarchies. My analysis also includes the ways in which patriarchal authorities within the State and within the home gradually are endorsing these efforts.

I conducted field research in Yemen between 1982 and 1984, in Wadi Dabab, a farming village in the midlands, just south of Ta'izz, and in 'Abs, a town north of the port city of Hudaydah. Both Dabab and 'Abs are located in what was then North Yemen. My visits to Dabab and 'Abs, between 1994 and 1998, after an absence of ten years, revealed that women's involvement in the processes of inclusive socioeconomic development is both varied and complex. In 'Abs, women are establishing themselves as activists in promoting healthcare and social integration, while in Dabab, women's utilization of new educational opportunites appears less certain. As devout Muslims, women in both communities must negotiate ambiguous boundaries between modern and traditional values in a conservative, but transitional, political economy. The *murshidat* in 'Abs are ameliorating social and economic differences among fellow Muslims. But how has this momentous reformation occurred?

## Constitutional Reforms in the Two Yemens

The Constitutions of both North and South Yemen declared the equality of their Yemeni citizens, thereby officially abolishing all social categories, including slavery—though neither document specifically names the categorical labels and the social hierarchy to which they refer. Accordingly, the 1970 Constitution of YAR (North Yemen) stipulates that "[t]he State has no right to impose distinction in human rights due to religion or color or sex or language or natural origin or profession." The 1970 Constitution of the PDRY (South Yemen) states that "[a]ll citizens are equal in their rights and duties irrespective of their race, ethnic origin, religious faith, language, level of education or social status. All are equal in the eye of the law."[12] Proclaiming also that the State will do "all it can to realize this equality through providing equal political, economic, social and educational opportunities,"[13] the PDRY government took a more proactive stance than the North in promoting the inclusion of its most oppressed citizens. As a result, the South was more effective in eliminating the demeaning social label "akhdam" from popular use. Education was encouraged and members of the group were hired in both rural and urban settings in civil service jobs, and as soldiers, police, and teachers.[14]

Similarly, the PDRY Constitution states that "[t]he State shall guarantee equal rights for men and women in all fields of political, economic and social scope and shall provide in a progressive manner the conditions necessary for realizing that reality." This contrasts with the YAR's "[w]omen are the sisters of men. They have their mandatory rights and obligations as stipulated in the Shari'ah and in accordance with the law."[15] Although incomplete, policies aimed at equal participation for women were more advanced in the South than in the North.[16] Provision was made in the South for equalizing women's status through education and through employment, both within and outside the home, while subsequent legal reforms also included advances toward equal rights within marriage.[17]

Currently, however, the conservative Islamic influences in the government resulting from the Northern victory in the 1994 civil war threaten to reverse gains made by progressive authorities in the socialist South, especially with regard to improving the status of women and social outcasts.[18] According to some scholars, for example, the Personal Status Law of 1992 in reunified Yemen is a reenactment of the Family Law in the YAR (North Yemen) which exposes women, in both North and South, to the prospect of polygynous marriages, and restores male dominance over female family members.[19] Therefore, women's advance toward professional roles in the public sphere has been curtailed.

### Slavery and Social Hierarchies

To a certain extent, domination by conservative North Yemeni ideologies means that social as well as gender inequities have been reinstated. Yemenis, especially in the North, still adhere to a system of intricate, ranked, ascriptive categories to define social relations—despite being banned.[20] Most Yemenis identify themselves as tribespersons (*qaba'il*), especially in the highlands; or as farmers (*ra'iya*) in the southern midlands; or as "people" (*nas*) in the southern portions of the coastal plains (Tihamah).[21] The important common element is the ability to trace one's origins to a respected, named ancestor. For most individuals, including members of servant groups, to be Yemeni means that one is an Arab.

The highest rank is reserved for elites who are known as *quda* (sg. *qadi*), or as *sada* (sg. *sayyid*) in the highlands. The latter claim descent from the Prophet Muhammad. Members of these groups typically serve as tribal mediators, Islamic scholars, and village administrators. They share these functions with *shaykhs* (or sheiks, as they are commonly known in English), who are the main tribal leaders of *qaba'il* status.[22]

The lowest-ranking category consists of several servant groups who perform tasks considered too demeaning for those in respected social categories. Included in the servant category are *khaddam* or *muzayyin* who possess neither a recognized tribal affiliation nor an African ancestry, as well as the African-identified *'abid* and *akhdam*.[23] All are deprived of a tribal ancestral genealogy. Unlike repected groups, the genealogies of Yemenis in the servant categories are not acknowledged either by other Yemenis or by schoalrs. Nevertheless, servant affiliations with territorial or tribal domains have persisted for generations. Economic survival for many in servant groups often necessitates continuing their relationships of servitude.

Discrimination against the 'abid and akhdam is not primarily a matter of skin color or race, but involves one's inability to claim an honorable lineage which others acknowledge. While 'abid (former slaves) may be able to specify their East African country of origin, akhdam can neither confirm nor deny the accuracy of popular belief in their pre-Islamic origins in Yemen.[24] Both groups are considered Yemeni, but are denied the benefits of respectability in their society. Members of the three servant groups often work as craftspersons, but they are also obliged to perform as musicians and ritual specialists at weddings and other occasions. The akhdam who are relegated to the occupation of street sweeping are assigned a position even lower than slaves who formerly were the personal militia and commercial agents for prominent families.

In poorer villages such as Dabab, labor migration in the recent past usually involved males in respected social groups. It is likely, however, that substantial numbers of akhdam men chose outmigration as one of the few means of escaping their degrading social position.[25] Particularly 'Absi residents who live close to the Saudi border could avoid costly exit visas merely by "walking." Therefore, it is difficult, if not impossible, to quantify the actual numbers of akhdam among migrants, or in the overall population. Indicative of the status assigned the group is the admission by town officials that akhdam were excluded from the regional census as late as 1975.[26] Furthermore, it is unlikely that the percentage of the population which was formerly enslaved, 'abid or akhdam, will be documented as such. To enumerate the population according to social category or ethnic group would stir controversy since status terminology is illegal despite its persistence in everyday practice.

As a coastal plains (Tihamah) town, 'Abs is situated at a crossroads of Arab-African cultural exchanges. Contacts between Southern Arabia (present-day Yemen) and East Africa, dating to antiquity, are evidenced by the thatch-roofed dwellings found on both sides of the Red Sea—and in the physical appearance of 'Absi residents.[27] Aesthetically, Yemenis prefer lighter skin, but that ideal is less attainable for Tihamah residents than for Yemenis living in the mid- and highlands. Skin color is a prominent marker of one's identity in 'Abs, especially for the 'abid whose sub-Saharan slave origins are more recent and more readily identifiable. The tendency for the 'abid to be taller, darker-skinned, and heavier than fellow Yemenis (including the akhdam) and for elite group members to be lighter skinned, especially if they reside in, or have emigrated from the mountains is particularly noticeable in the coastal regions.[28]

In Yemen, skin color and ethnicity do not correspond precisely to social status. Yemenis, however, often perceive each other in racial terms.
Accordingly, the tendency to label members of all servant categories, regardless of their ancestry or skin color (which ranges from the extremes
of light and dark brown) as "black" (*aswad*) was previously noted. Regional factors also play a role in how Yemenis identify themselves and
others. For example, non-Tihamah residents denigrate all Tihamis as
"black." Furthermore, as if to confirm such popular perceptions, 'Absi
residents in the *qaba'il* category readily report having legendary Ethiopian ancestors. In reality, the Tihamah's proximity to East Africa has resulted in intermarriages and other sexual unions.[29] Still, Arab identity su-
percedes real and imagined Arab/African interrelations. Therefore, the
correlation between race and social status is imprecise. There is no question, however, that sub-Saharan Africans were targeted for enslavement
in Yemen and elsewhere on the Arabian Peninsula.[30] Particularly in the
Tihamah which was a center of the slave trade[31] race, then, is a more overt
factor in 'Absi women's assumption of their professional roles.

## Socioeconomic Status of Women in Two Communities

Girls throughout the social hierarchy in Yemen have greater access to education in the 1990s than they did a decade ago.[32] Yet men have been the
main beneficiaries of advances in the educational system.[33] In the early
1980s, no girls were attending school in Dabab or the rural districts of
'Abs, and relatively few were going to school in the town itself. And, despite the greater availability of education, village women's expectations
about their futures remain virtually unchanged. In Dabab, a high school
student from the former outcast *akhdam* group whom I remembered as a
toddler aspired to college and a professional degree. Yet, like the other
young village women I encountered, she expected to assume the same domestic and agricultural roles as her mother and grandmother once she
married.

Moreover, in Dabab, women's transition from informal labor markets
as petty vendors of homemade goods to the formal wage-earning economy matched the slow pace of daily life in the village itself. Despite the
greater availability of schooling for girls, women remain the mainstays of
agricultural production. Furthermore, in the mid-1990s, basic necessi-
ties—thermoses for tea, food items, dresses [*qumsan*], land, bride-price

[*maher*], etc.—had to be acquired with drastically depreciated riyals. Thus, women are maintaining their households at a higher cost relative to earlier times. Although village women spend less time hauling water, firewood, and fodder, women's persistent workloads have not permitted them to take full advantage of recent trends in the economy or in educational opportunities.

## Women Primary Healthcare Workers: The Murshidat

Changes occurring in the community of 'Abs are the result of the accomplishments of the female primary healthcare workers, or *murshidat*. In the early 1980s, despite the efforts of an international British health team, 'Absi residents rarely used the healthcare facility in the town. The health team sent to 'Abs by the organization now known as the International Cooperation for Development (ICD),[34] consisted of doctors, midwives, nurses, and an anthropologist. Yet, babies were routinely born at home and often died of dehydration within their first year. Mothers with severe anemia went untreated. Persistent high maternal as well as infant mortality was the norm.[35] Residents assumed, often correctly, that fees, especially for medication, would be required at the health facility even though it is run under government auspices. Most people, especially the marginalized *akhdam*, were unable to afford such payments.

Further, the spatial configuration of houses in 'Abs reflected the social, ethnic, and occupational demarcations of prerevolutionary society. The main division was the market (*suq*) where the *akhdam* live, and the town (*medina*) inhabited by most persons who claimed tribal (*qabilah*) or former slave ('*abid*) ancestors. Today, due to the growth in population, these sections are less distinct. A surge in new housing construction has supplanted the airy compounds and wide roadways of the past. Nevertheless, while various groups are interspersed within the *medina*, only the *akhdam* live in the *suq*.

On my return to Yemen in the mid-1990s, I found the health facility bustling with members of an entire community engaged in pursuing health services. At the center of this remarkable activity were the *murshidat*—nineteen women, all but one of whom was assuming a professional public role for the first time.[36] Women from the '*abid* category and *akhdam* women had been trained as well. The transition in the once dormant facility was directly attributable to the *murshidat*'s outreach in the town, including the *akhdam* quarter (*suq*) and the neighboring villages. The several hundred clients that were seen weekly by the *murshidat* at the Maternal and Child Health Center were, therefore, a representative cross section of the community. Essentially, the *murshidat* provided wellness and preventive health services to mothers and children, including prenatal care, routine deliveries, well baby examinations, vaccinations, and treatment of common ailments. Interactions between those of higher social status and those who had been excluded within the society were now part of the *murshidat*'s work routine.

Was it possible to reconcile the activist approach of the *murshidat* in 'Abs with the more conservative stance of their counterparts in Dabab? How could such divergent, but contemporaneous, female agendas be explained? Gender identities in Yemen, as in other Muslim societies, are mediated through a shared understanding of religious and moral observances. However, Yemeni women's identities are also mediated through prevailing genealogical, racial, gender, and occupational distinctions. Thus, some (though not all) of the *murshidat* were entering the homes of individuals they previously considered untouchable. Others were going even further by initiating self-improvement projects among women from the rejected group. Clearly, female gender identities in Yemen defied monolithic categorization.

It is not surprising that women assumed responsibility for implementing a program that has had such an impact on women and children. Establishing health programs in Yemen, however, has required international support. In 1962, the first health center was built with the assistance of the Egyptian army, which backed the Republicans during North Yemen's civil war (1962–70). During the mid-1980s, the Maternal and Child Health (MCH) extension was built. Constructed according to Yemen's cultural imperative of sex-segregated domains, the MCH Center was designed by the American Peace Corps and funded by the British and Canadian embassies as well as the Yemeni local and central governments. In 1985–86, the first training program for the *murshidat* took place at the new MCH Center. In conjunction with the Yemeni government and foreign aid organizations, the program was financed by ICD.

## Impact of the Gulf War

The changes occurring in 'Absi women's lives and in the community at large are a result of these women's accomplishments. Yet, the increased demand for health services in 'Abs during the 1991 Gulf war played a part. 'Abs was already a rapidly growing town when up to a million Yemeni migrant workers were expelled mainly from Saudi Arabia during the Gulf war. As a result of this massive relocation, the population of the town of 'Abs, which is only 72 miles (116 kms.) from the Saudi border (along the Hudaydah-Jizan Road) more than doubled between 1986 and 1994. Likewise, the larger rural areas in the district of 'Abs which the Health Center also serves experienced a similar expansion over the same period.[37]

The increased demand for services at the health facility in 'Abs can be attributed, at least in part, to population growth. Furthermore, the transformation in health consciousness in 'Abs is also explained by the influx of a more sophisticated returnee population. The returnees were accustomed to social, educational, and health services which were still very rudimentary in Yemen. To a certain extent, therefore, familiarity with these services, healthcare in particular, accounts for the dramatic rise in use of the mostly outpatient hospital in 'Abs.

The returnee camps were also a fertile source of recruits for *murshidat* training. Sabah's story is typical of several of the women now working at the Maternal and Child Health Center. One morning when I accompanied two of the *murshidat* on a home health visit to one of the returnee camps outside 'Abs, Sabah (not her real name)[38] told me that she used to live there. Although her father was originally from 'Abs, Sabah was born in Saudi Arabia and received a primary education there before relocating to the camp prior to the onset of the Gulf war. She compared facilities for girls' education in Saudi Arabia favorably to those in Yemen: In Saudi Arabia, unlike in 'Abs, all the teachers for girls are women; school supplies, including books, were provided; furnishings in the schools were properly maintained. Sabah further explained that the school facility was appropriately designed with an enclosed yard (*hawsh*) which allowed students to remove their face coverings to eat, for example.

Sabah, now in her twenties, is married and has one child. When the couple first relocated from Saudi Arabia, her husband was unable to find work, and he is still only minimally employed. She learned about the work of the *murshidat* at the MCH Center through neighbors and friends. Eventually, her salary of 5,600 Yemeni *riyals* per month (approximately $43),[39] paid by the Yemeni government, enabled the couple to move from the camp into the town proper.

## An Essential Resource

Although the increase in demand for health services by a more informed returnee population was a factor in the transition which took place at the 'Abs health facility during the mid- to late 1980s, the *murshidat*'s health outreach was the decisive turning point. The conspicuous rise in health awareness in 'Abs is obviously due to the impact of the *murshidat*. Like their clients at the health center, the women are residents of the town and surrounding villages. Five of the women, including Sabah, came to the *murshidat* training program at the 'Abs facility from a returnee camp; one of the *murshidat* still lives there. Everyone knows them by name. The women actively encourage members of the community to take responsibility for their own health and welfare. Although outside developers, including medical staff, are involved in the training process, the key to the facility's success is the fact that members of the community are establishing a health-centered dialogue with their neighbors, friends, and relatives. Consequently, the messages and information imparted to the community are well received and responded to. Clearly, they are considered an invaluable resource in the community.

Between 1986 and 1998, four classes of young women with at least a sixth grade education graduated from a one-year training program. Throughout the program, the primary trainers have been Sudanese women who are certified midwives. The *murshidat* trainees have been instructed in basic hygiene, nutrition, physiology and anatomy, oral rehydration therapy, immunization, promotion of breast-feeding, monitoring infant growth using weight charts, assessing and prescribing appropriate birth control methods, midwifery, and monitoring pre- and postnatal women through blood pressure measurements, and urine and blood tests.

The first class of *murshidat* trainees consisted of nine women from the town of 'Abs and neighboring villages. Among the members of this first class were two sisters from a nearby market town that is largely populated by *akhdam*, the lowest status group. Both women returned to their hometown to work after completing their training. Despite the closing of their health station, one of the sisters is currently enrolled in a three-year midwifery course to advance her skills. Among the trainees in subsequent classes have been women from the *'abid* category, including returnees, as well as women of prominent *qabili* status. Women from these various social groups are currently working at the MCH Center in 'Abs. The last class of *murshidat* trainees in 'Abs consisted of fourteen young women, all from the countryside.[40]

### Seamless Boundaries between the Household and Health Center

Invariably, the women's household and clinic responsibilities coincide. The workday totally integrates the two domains. Healthcare visits often take place during off-duty hours, for example. Hence most of the women have established flexible boundaries between their roles in establishing healthy families and establishing a healthy community. On a typical workday, the *murshidat* who have not been on duty during the night arrive at the MCH Center around 8 A.M. to begin their duties. Those with school-age children or who live out of town arrive an hour later. One of the women petitioned district health officials for approval of the later arrival time. (Nevertheless, this mother, lacking other alternatives, must bring her preschool-aged child to work with her.) The women may drink tea and share breakfast foods they have made or bought from female vendors after they change into their work attire. Typically, the women replace their black coatlike garment, called a *balto*, face veil (*lithma*), and scarf (*sitara*) with a white or tinted full-length smock and headscarf. Amid the greetings and discussions, often quite lively, the *murshidat* supervisor adjusts the work schedule to accommodate absences. Often, one or as many as six, of the *murshidat* or members of their household are suffering from the fevers of malaria or typhoid.

The supervisor assigns two women on a two-week rotation to the various clinics which the women call "rooms" (*qurafat*). While the women go to their assignments to meet patients—who start arriving by 9 A.M.—another pair leaves to make home visits. One of the women, also on a rotation basis, collects money (20 Y.R. per day) for the midmorning meal which she also prepares. Ingredients may include any of the following: eggs, tomatoes, bread (*ruti*), salted, dried fish, or beans (*ful*). These are purchased from the market in town by one of the center's cleaning persons or a child. The meal is eaten quickly at around eleven and then work resumes. Also sharing the meal may be the mother of one of the *murshidat* who has just been treated at the health center, or a young child who is waiting to go home from school with an older *murshidat* sister. If one of the *murshidat* has a child to breast-feed, she may go home for a short time or the grandmother may bring the baby to the center for a feeding.

On an average day:

- 15 women are checked in the prenatal clinic
- 30–50 immunizations are given, mostly to children, but also to mothers for tetanus
- 50 children are weighed
- 30 mothers (and often fathers) are given nutrition instruction on adding solid foods to the child's diet
- 20–25 women and children are treated for malaria, usually by intramuscular or intravenous injection
- 3–5 women are seen in the family planning clinic
- 3–5 babies are weighed during home visits
- 3–5 pregnant women are checked during home visits and advised to come to the hospital for regular prenatal check-ups
- Babies are delivered by the *murshidat* throughout the day; it is not uncommon for as many as three babies to be born on the night shift

At one o'clock, the workday at the MCH Center ends for all but the two or three *murshidat* who will stay at the center overnight. Some of the women leave together to attend middle or high school; others have to return home promptly to prepare lunch.

## Impact on Social Relations

The *murshidat* are making an impact both on attitudes to health and on attitudes toward social hierarchies. Some women are overcoming their reluctance to serve those they consider social inferiors, particularly on home visits. Others, however, continue to resist visiting in the market area (*suq*) where the *akhdam* live. They are neither advocates for nor against change. For most of the women it has been less than ten years since they abandoned a home-based existence. As one of the *murshidat* explained, it will take time before her reluctant colleagues feel comfortable entering the homes of people they so recently considered beneath themselves.

The most visible architect of social reform is Fatimah, one of the *murshidat*, who is helping women in the *suq* to organize a cooperative cleanup of the roadways surrounding their homes. Fatimah agreed to oversee the venture. She successfully approached municipal authorities about using the sanitation truck to conduct a thorough trash removal and providing a trash bin which residents could then use. Afterward, Fatimah personally encouraged *suq* families to help maintain the area themselves. She remained hopeful that town officials would continue to comply with anticipated requests.

The *murshidat*, in collaboration with the most neglected members of society, are demonstrating how some social barriers might be overcome. By virtue of such initiatives, the *murshidat* are having a profound impact not only on healthcare, but on social relations as well. A phenomenal reversal of the social order is underway as *murshidat* from high-status groups begin to view former servants not as pariahs but as legitimate beneficiaries of their care.

## Impact on Women's Self-Perceptions

Women in 'Abs as elsewhere in the country have long contributed to the financial support of their families by working in the informal economy. However, the *murshidat* are making the transition from work in the informal sector to work as salaried professionals. In the process, subtle changes are occurring in these women's self-perceptions. Their new public role requires certain behavioral and attitudinal adjustments. In the 1980s, most women in 'Abs wore the loose fitting, colorful dresses known as *qumsan*. Now, women who work outside the home or go to school wear the all-black *balto* even in this sweltering climate. As one of the *murshidat* explained when I asked about the change, "Before, we were ignorant in our understanding of Islam." Changes in the *murshidat*'s identities as Muslim women may be influenced by increasingly conservative Islamic influences. However, another woman explained that 'Abs was no longer a small town. Now houses are very close together and there are many more people, especially men from outside. Veiling in 'Abs, as in Cairo, allows women to undertake new roles and responsibilities in the public sphere.[41] Finally, ready-made outfits worn by some women and girls under the *balto* may simply be more accessible and are sometimes preferred over homemade clothing.

In certain instances, personal circumstances combined with the decline in demand for older fashions have resulted in a reassessment of economic options. In the early 1980s, respectable work for women, particularly those of high status, included sewing the traditional dresses that 'Absi women wore for every occasion. Through agents, these women successfully conducted their home-based businesses without having to enter the public marketplace. Nabila, whom I had met during my first stay in 'Abs, had worked with her sisters and a former slave making dresses in what I described elsewhere as a home factory.[42] Nabila decided to become a *murshidah* (sg.) when faced with the prospect of raising her young son after her husband and father died, as her brother could not provide financial support.

Virtually all the *murshidat* said that their lives had improved as a result of the opportunity to acquire an education. At the same time, most are aware that many girls cannot attend school for financial reasons. 'Arwa, who was the first woman to earn a high school certificate in 'Abs in the early 1980s, is in her thirties, and unmarried. Yet she expressed the sentiment of her colleagues when she stated that she did not want to just "sit" at home after she completed her education. Initially, she had been an elementary schoolteacher and a registrar at the health facility, but became a *murshidah* because it offered the possibility of advancement.

## Sustainability

A difficulty faced by outside donors in Yemen and elsewhere is the transfer of leadership to people who will continue the development project. One of the women at the MCH Center in 'Abs has completed an additional year of training and is the *murshidat* supervisor (in her words, she is "responsible," as this terminology is less threatening to male authority). Yet she has been prevented from exercising her ability and training to recruit and teach future *murshidat*. Thus far, all trainees have been instructed by a trainer-midwife who is not a Yemeni. While readily acknowledging the role that foreign medical personnel have played in implementing the healthcare program in 'Abs, the *murshidat* must also negotiate their positions with respect to these advisors.

Not only must the women establish their extant jurisdiction over wellness for mothers and children in conjunction with non-Yemenis, but they must also contend with antagonism from other healthcare providers who are Yemeni. For instance, the women reported persistent attempts by male Yemeni doctors to take over the Maternal and Child Health Center or incidents in which the doctors had been critical of *murshidat* services to potential clients. Thus, the women are also defining their roles as healthcare providers in the context of constant efforts to undermine their authority by male doctors. Recently, however, as a result of the appointment of a new health center director, the *murshidat* now feel that they have a male ally ("he cooperates with us and we cooperate with him"). Since the local district health officials tend to be supportive, the government's long-range plans for a more decentralized healthcare delivery system may also help the *murshidat* realize their objectives toward greater leadership.

Women also seek support, both materially and professionally, for conducting their day-to-day responsibilities. Home visiting, an essential service provided by the *murshidat*, is now restricted to areas within walking distance of the health center because the women do not have access to transportation. In the past, the *murshidat* made visits in outlying areas in vehicles driven by foreign staff. Most of the women stated without hesitation that they would learn to drive if a vehicle were made available to them.

Other supplies such as medicines, which are urgently needed, must be made available to clients at low or no cost. Despite the substantial numbers of children seen in the immunization room, vaccines for DPT (diphtheria, pertussis, tetanus) and polio were sometimes lacking for months at a time.[43] Drugs for malaria that are manufactured in Yemen were completely lacking at the MCH Center during my visits. Indeed, the *murshidat* often seemed resigned to a routine of house calls to the families of various adults and children who had died from malaria. Until antimalarial chemicals were sprayed in the center between 1997 and 1998, making the night shift somewhat less hazardous, the women were in greater danger of contracting malaria at the MCH Center than in their own homes. Finally, the young children of the *murshidat* are at risk of injury, particularly from discarded syringes when they are brought to the health center while their mothers are working. Thus the *murshidat* often mention the need for child care if they are to continue working.

The *murshidat* in ‘Abs recognize that their knowledge of healthcare is limited and most express a strong desire to continue their education. Yet, an in-service training program which members of the first class of trainees remember fondly as an occasion for both social interaction and educational learning, has yet to be reinstated.[44] Furthermore, while the women share a close working and social relationship, they also describe differences among themselves with regard to commitment to their jobs. Those in the first class of trainees see themselves as more committed to their work than their successors. Members of the first class believe that salary is uppermost in the minds of the later trainees. Indeed, these deeply dedicated *murshidat* are more often on call than others and available to assist residents in the town, surrounding communities, or their colleagues on duty at the MCH Center itself.

Recently, a women's organization (*gama'iyya al nisawiyah al ijtima'iyah*) including some of the *murshidat* was formed in 'Abs. It is likely that the organization will facilitate *murshidat* demands for scholarships, in-service training, and child care. Significantly, the women's organization has attracted women from different backgrounds to implement common goals, especially increasing access to education and income generation for women. It is also likely to have a positive impact on particular *murshidat* initiatives such as promoting a nondiscriminatory outlook in the town. Toward this end, Oxfam is providing both material support and an express commitment to alleviating *akhdam* exclusion in 'Abs and elsewhere in Yemen.

## Conclusion: Modeling the Murshidat

While the terms "feminist" and "antiracist" are not employed by Yemeni women themselves, as female primary healthcare workers the *murshidat* are not only delivering health services, but also promoting social integration and reducing barriers that have long divided social groups. The emergence of the stigmatized *akhdam* from the margins of society is a particularly remarkable attempt at equalizing economic and social relations between various categories of Yemenis. The *murshidat*, therefore, play a pivotal role in challenging Yemen's social divisions, especially Yemen's cultural, racial, and gender hierarchies.

The work of the *murshidat* at the MCH Center in 'Abs exemplifies Yemeni women's integration of various roles—as health workers, as students, and as homemakers, both in rural and urbanized environments. By establishing strong working and social ties with clients at the MCH Center, the *murshidat* are extending healthcare to areas where there was previously little consciousness about health, hygiene, and sanitation. Furthermore, the women are helping to remove social prejudices that hitherto prevented broad-scale access to employment and educational opportunities to members of different social groups, especially to persons of African descent. Many of the *murshidat* are not only empowering themselves, but their entire community as well.

Yet they are not unique. The *murshidat's* success in 'Abs is being repeated in several parts of the country under the auspices of various non-governmental organizations, such as Oxfam. NGO training programs, especially those in Sana'a, also focus on women from Yemen's disadvantaged groups, including returning migrants. Similarly, women in the Islah party sponsor numerous activities focused especially on educational, health, and social services involving women and children in the poorest and lowest social groups. The diverse roles that women play in promoting parity between members of different groups in this transition tend to be overlooked. Clearly, inclusive socioeconomic development, particularly women's involvement in the process, is a multifaceted endeavor.

It is evident that the *murshidat's* efforts have value beyond the economic needs of individual families. Yet, despite their impact on changing health and social consciousness, it is questionable whether the significance of their work is fully recognized. In a male-dominated society which is also struggling economically, the *murshidat's* contributions may not be viewed beyond their monetary benefit for individual families. Since the work of a *murshidah* provides the primary support for entire families, fathers demand that their daughters be recruited and trained as *murshidat*, regardless of the girls' interest or ability, because they will earn a salary upon certification. Ironically, however, the *murshidat's* success is largely based on the tacit understanding that their efforts are not driven by personal gain. Clients visiting the Maternal and Child Health Center trust that no additional fees for service will be required.[45]

At the end of 1998 when I left Yemen, the Ministry of Public Health invited the government, NGOs, and the donor community to participate in the systematic improvement in healthcare for all Yemenis. Yet while the ministry remains committed to primary healthcare,[46] plans for establishing programs to train *murshidat* in areas where they do not presently exist (such as Wadi Dabab) have not been clearly articulated.[47] Women such as the *murshidat* in 'Abs demonstrate how Muslim women negotiate their dual responsibilities as mothers and professionals. Despite constraints that exist in their society, Yemeni women are successfully challenging certain gender prescriptions and social boundaries. Women from Yemen's formerly enslaved and elite classes are generating new social spaces. Their work requires the support of foreign and local program officials who seek fundamental change in the building of Yemeni communities.

ACKNOWLEDGMENTS

Parts of this paper were delivered at the 1996 Middle Eastern Studies Association (MESA) conference in Providence, Rhode Island. I gratefully acknowledge support for my field research provided by the American Institute for Yemeni Studies (AIYS) and Fulbright-Hays Fellowships. I am also grateful to Huda Seif, Robert Burrows, Barbara Michael, Najwa Adra, and Paula C. Johnson.

NOTES

1. Confidence in women's previous experience in decision-making roles in Aden apparently allowed the women's candidacy there (Barbara Croken, personal communication). The major parties avoided backing women candidates either because they did not believe it was appropriate for women to run or they did not think that female candidates could win, according to Bob Burrowes, one of the international observers. Other observers included Ambassador William Rugh and John Duke Anthony. Also see John Lancaster, "Women Take to the Polls in Male-Dominated Yemen," in *Washington Post Foreign Service*, April 26, 1997, A01 (Web address: www.clark.net/pub/alkebsi/news.html).

2. Uluf Bakhuba'ir from the Hadramawt, and Awras Sultan, a medical doctor from Aden, were the two women elected. In December 1999, the Deputy Minister of Information, Amat al-Aleem As-Suswa, the highest female appointee in the Yemeni government, was named Ambassador to Holland. She becomes the first Yemeni woman in modern times to be appointed to an ambassadorship.

3. Dr. Raufa Hassan, long a vociferous crusader for Yemeni women's rights, was dismissed as director of the Empirical Research and Women's Studies Center at Sana'a University in November 1999. The center was ordered closed by the government, then reinstated with another woman appointed as director. Ironically, these events were reported in the same issue of *The Yemen Times* (December 6, 1999, p. 1), which devoted extensive coverage to a symposium on Human Rights in Yemen.

4. The two Yemens are not easily characterized by the labels "socialist" and "capitalist," as Sheila Carapico discusses in "The Economic Dimension of Yemeni Unity," *Middle East Report*, no. 184 (1993): 9–14.

5. See Charles Dunbar, "The Unification of Yemen: Process, Politics, and Prospects," in *Middle East Journal*, vol. 46, no. 3 (1992): 456–76; Fred Halliday, "The Third Inter-Yemeni War and Its Consequences," *Asian Affairs*, vol. 26, part 2 (1995): 131–40.

6. The president's GPC Party won 187 seats, and Islah 53 seats. The Yemeni Socialist Party (YSP) either boycotted the 1997 elections or its members, who ran as independents, took 54 seats. The five remaining seats (plus two undisclosed) went to two other parties. See "Yemeni President Rules Out New Coalition Government," Reuters, May 7, 1997 (www.clark.net/pub/alkebsi/news.html). In 1993, Islah

dominated key government ministries, including the Ministry of Health, but due to the landslide victory of the president's party in 1997, it has lost its former strength in the policy-making ministries (Bob Borrowes, personal communication).

7. 17.3 million according to the Population Reference Bureau (PRB), a U.S. statistical source located in Washington, D.C., www.prb.org/pubs/wpds99.htm; 16.8 million according to *World Population 1998* published by the UN Population Infrmation Network (POPIN), www.//undp.org/popin/wdtrends.htm.

8. UNICEF, *The State of the World's Children* (Oxford: Oxford University Press, 1997), 88; and Amat al-Aleem As-Suswa, *Yemeni Women in Figures* (Sana'a: UNICEF, 1996), 13–14.

9. For example, Islamist women in the Islah political party focus primarily on improving healthcare and alleviating poverty and illiteracy. See Janine Clark, "Women and Islamic Activism in Yemen," paper delivered at Middle East Studies Association, 1996.

10. Margot Badran, "Unifying Women: Feminist Pasts and Presents in Yemen," in *Gender and History*, special issue: Feminisms and Internationalism, ed. Mrinalini Sinha, Donna J. Guy, and Angela Woollacott (Oxford, U.K.: Blackwell, 1998), 511.

11. Ibid, Badran, "Unifying Women," 499–518. Elsewhere, Badran also uses the phrase "gender activism" to describe the pro-feminist behaviors of Egyptian women. See "Gender Activism: Feminists and Islamists in Egypt," in *Identity, Politics and Women*, ed. Valentine M. Moghadam (Boulder: Westview Press, 1994), 202–27.

12. Article 43 of the YAR Constitution (English version); Article 34 of the PDRY Constitution (English version).

13. Article 34 of the PDRY Constitution (English version).

14. More data, albeit incomplete, exists pertaining to the gender composition of the urban labor force than about the social status of newly educated workers. In general, service and low-skilled jobs have more women than occupations associated with higher education. See Helen Lackner, "Women and Development in the Republic of Yemen," in *Gender and Development in the Arab World*, ed. Nabil F. Khoury and Valentine M. Moghadam (Tokyo: United Nations University Press, 1995), 86–89. Also, Mouna Hashem, "Patterns and Processes of Social Exclusion in the Republic of Yemen," in *Social Exclusion: Rhetoric, Reality, Responses*, ed. Gerry Rodgers, Charles Gore, and Jose Figueiredo (International Institute for Labor Studies, United Nations Development Programme, 1995), 174–86.

15. Article 36 of the PDRY Constitution and Article 34 of the YAR Constitution.

16. See Maxine Molyneux, "Legal Reform and Socialist Revolution in South Yemen: Women and the Family," in *Promissory Notes: Women in the Transition to Socialism*, ed. Sonia Kruks, Rayna Rapp, and Marilyn B. Young (New York: Monthly Review Press, 1989), 193–214.

17. Ibid., Molyneux, "Legal Reform," 204–7.

18. For PDRY vs. YAR policies with respect to women, see Lackner, "Women and Development in the Republic of Yemen."

19. Lackner, "Women and Development," 81–82.

20. Conversely, transition from a subsistence-based to a cash-based economy has reduced certain occupational distinctions. For example, members of the tribal social category were likely to engage only in certain occupations, like farming, and only in cultivating certain crops, like grains. As a result of the extremely limited job market back home, labor migrants have become barbers (albeit in their own shops) in the 1990s—a livelihood that was formerly considered low status.

21. See Anne Meneley, *Tournaments of Value: Sociability and Hierarchy in a Yemen Town* (Toronto: University of Toronto Press, 1996).

22. The words "tribe" and "tribesperson" are direct translations of the Arabic *qabilah* and *qabili* (m.); *qabiliyyah* (f.), terms commonly used by Yemenis especially in the Central Highlands (or "Upper Yemen," located in the area south of the Yemeni capital, Sana'a), and extending northward to the Saudi border. In Yemen, being tribal connotes a territorial affiliation with a recognized and respected social group. Notably, Yemen differs, therefore, from Africa and the Americas where persons to whom such terminology was applied were deemed inferiors, according to colonial perspectives.

23. The words *khaddam* and *akhdam* both come from the triliteral Arabic root, kh-d-m, for the word meaning to serve.

24. According to popular belief, *akhdam* origins date back to Ethiopians who arrived in Southern Arabia in the sixth century. Historians attribute *'abid* ancestry to possible Ethiopian "slave" dynasties who arrived in the Tihamah during the eleventh and twelfth centuries, although pre-Islamic forebears cannot be ruled out. Overlapping histories and intermarriage has meant that distinctions between the two groups have not always been maintained.

25. See Delores M. Walters, "Perceptions of Social Inequality in the Yemen Arab Republic," Ph.D. dissertation, New York University, 1987, 243–48; and Thomas B. Stevenson, "Yemeni Workers Come Home: Reabsorbing One Million Migrants," *Middle East Report*, no. 181, vol. 23, no. 2 (1993): 15–20.

26. A survey conducted by Oxfam revealed that the population of four shantytown communities in Sana'a is 2,345 inhabitants—all of whom are thought to be *akhdam*. Afrah Ahmadi and Sharon Beatty, *Participatory Socio-Economic Needs Survey of the Sana'a Urban Settlement Dwellers with Special Reference to Women* (Sana'a: Oxfam, 1997). The populations of three other shantytown settlements in the capital city, which has a population of approximately 1 million, have not been documented. However, Basmah al Qubayti, director of the Social Organization for Family Development (SOFD), states that one out of the three communities alone contains 2,000 residents. She then concludes that there are 1 million *akhdam* in the country as a whole, based on the fact that between 70 and 80

percent of Yemenis generally continue to live in rural areas (*Yemen Times*, February 20, 1994, 7). Although these observation serve as a gauge, the actual number of African-identified persons in the overall population is still incomplete.

27. The sharing of cultural traditions between Yemen and Ethiopia dates back at least to the legend of the Queen of Sheba, called Bilqis in Arabic and by other names in Ethiopian languages. Her visit to King Solomon (around 950 B.C.) coincides with the existence of Southern Arabia's Sabaean kingdom.

28. Protecting oneself from the tanning effects of the sun is an ideal more easily achieved by women from elite, more prominent families who also usually have the advantage of living at the country's higher elevation. Comparatively, few women, however, have reached a standard of living that precludes them from farm and household labor.

29. Whether Yemenis of dual parentage (*muwalladin*), who are mainly individuals whose mothers are from East Africa, should be recognized as full citizens remains an unresolved debate. See, for example, "A New Form of Yemeni Discrimination in the Making," in *Yemen Times*, vol. iv, no. 47, November 28, 1994.

30. Even until the nineteenth and early twentieth centuries, most slaves from Ethiopia were imported onto the Arabian peninsula via Jiddah (Saudi Arabia) at the rate of between 1,400 and 5,000 annually depending on the European source consulted, according to Richard Pankhurst, *Economic History of Ethiopia 1800–1935* (Addis Ababa: Haile Sellassie University Press, 1968), 124.

31. See Bernard Lewis, *Race and Color in Islam* (New York: Harper and Row, 1970), 40; and Walters, "Perceptions of Social Inequality," 222, for other references to the slave trade in the Yemeni Tihamah.

32. Literacy for girls in urban areas was 54 percent vs. 84 percent for males in the 1990s. The literacy rate in the rural areas was 15.4 percent for females vs. 64.7 percent for males, according to UNICEF, *The State of the World's Children*, 88; and *Yemeni Women in Figures*, 13–14.

33. These developments are similar to the labor migration movement of the 1970s and 1980s, which mainly mobilized males for social and economic opportunities. While men labored outside of Yemen, women continued to engage in every aspect of agricultural production.

34. Formerly known as the British Organization for Community Development (BOCD), the ICD is the overseas department of the Catholic Institute for International Relations founded in 1940, with headquarters in London and one of its regional offices in Sana'a.

35. In *The Human Development Report for 1999*, published by UNDP, these rates remained high; the infant mortality rate stood at 78 per 1,000 (in 1997) and the maternal mortality rate was 1,400 per 100,000 (in 1990).

36. Exceptions included a woman who served as the health facility's registrar in the early 1980s.

37. According to the Central Statistical Organization, Ministry of Planning

and Development, in Sana'a, the population of the town of 'Abs increased from 4,197 in 1986 to 11,237 in 1994. The population of 'Abs district grew from 38,883 to 85,602 over the same period.

38. Generally, the names of people mentioned in this article are pseudonyms.

39. The exchange rate was 130 riyals to the dollar, with minimal fluctuations between 1996 and 1998.

40. As of 1998, ICD had, for various reasons, discontinued the *murshidat* training program in 'Abs and was focusing on health projects in other parts of the country and the world.

41. See Arlene Howe Macleod, *Accommodating Protest: Working Women and the New Veiling and Change in Cairo* (New York: Columbia University Press, 1991).

42. See Delores M. Walters, "Invisible Survivors: Women and Diversity in the Transitional Economy of Yemen," in *Middle Eastern Women and the Invisible Economy*, ed. Richard Lobban (Gainesville: University Press of Florida, 1998).

43. Nationally, the number of children immunized against these six diseases (DPT, polio, measles, and TB) has been dropping steadily. The percentage of Yemeni children who are immunized against the six diseases fell from 90 percent in 1989 to 50 percent in 1991 and to 30 percent in 1994 according to the *Yemen Times*, March 1996, as reported by the American Institute for Yemeni Studies, *Update*, 1996, no. 38.

44. The women speculated that a video that I directed in collaboration with them would be a valuable resource in helping to improve their skills as health workers. Completed in March 1999, the thirty-five-minute documentary video entitled "*Murshidat*: Female Primary Health Care Workers Transforming Society in Yemen," will be used by the *murshidat* to promote their work to others in the community, including new recruits and health officials.

45. An early program to train male health workers at the center failed mainly because the men, once they were trained, invariably set themselves up as "doctors" who charged fees to their clients. See Timothy Morris, *The Despairing Developer: Diary of an Aid Worker in the Middle East* (London: I. B. Tauris, 1991).

46. A stated objective of the Ministry of Planning and Development, in *Central Statistical Organization, Population and Health in the Republic of Yemen*, "Proceedings of the First National Population Policy Conference," October 26–29, 1991, 112–13, 149.

47. See Health Sector Reform in the Republic of Yemen, vol. 1: *Strategy for Reform*, October 1998.

PART II

*Feminist Talk, Antiracist Dialogues*

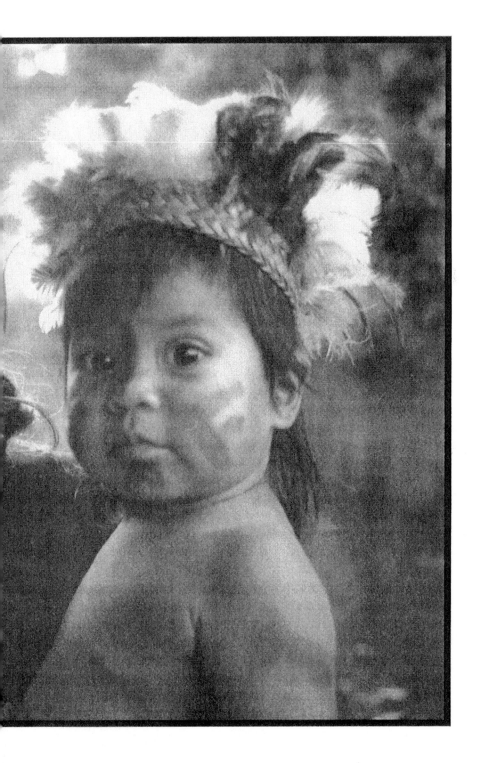

# Chapter 5

# Danger Talk

*Race and Feminist Empowerment in the
New South Africa*

## Michelle Rosenthal

South Africa's first democratic elections, on April 26, 1994, technically marked the beginning of a nonracial democracy headed by the Government of National Unity. For many women who had been active in the antiapartheid movement both at home in South Africa and abroad in exile, national liberation was no longer the primary basis on which to organize.[1] In the postapartheid democratic transition, many feminist activists argued that gender inequalities could now be addressed in their own right without jeopardizing nationalist goals.[2] Democracy in South Africa is a contested and ongoing everyday practice of "becoming" politically empowered whereby new citizens work to build postapartheid equality in their local communities and nation-state from within and across civil society and state institutions.

Citizens' memories of apartheid state violence are intimately tied to everyday notions of democracy in the new South Africa. The Population Registration Act of 1950, as amended, categorized all South Africans into one of four racial groups defined as: White; Indian; Coloured; and Native (later to be Bantu and then Black).[3] The goal of apartheid (literally meaning separation) policies like this one under the National Party government elected in 1948 was to ensure White, Afrikaner supremacy, further entrenching racial divisions in the country.[4] Resources were disproportionately allocated according to a racial hierarchy in which Whites received the best land, jobs, medical care, and education followed by Indians, then Coloureds, and finally Blacks.[5] Black women have eloquently articulated the difference that gender makes in experiences of racial inequality under apartheid and in the antiapartheid movement.[6] Many Black women argued that they had more in common with other Black men, based on race and class experiences, than they did with White women during the apartheid era.[7] The uneven legacy of apartheid's racial policies poses challenges for feminist organizations seeking to build multiracial coalitions in the new democracy.

Activists and scholars have begun to analyze the historical significance of gender politics for the democratization process.[8] Women's equality became an important issue on the political agenda and activists began to discuss the importance of voicing "women's concerns" in the transition toward creating a more equitable democracy with regard to race and gender.[9] Significantly, feminist activists shifted their political position in the democratic transition from one of resistance to the state to one of engagement with the state.

This chapter is based on research conducted in 1994 and 1995 with the members of South Africa's first rape crisis center. Rape Crisis (RC) is a feminist, nongovernmental organization in the Western Cape Province of South Africa whose members struggle to end sexual violence against women with the goal of ensuring gender equality and freedom from gender-based violence.[10] I offer an analysis of how these activists imagine and practice feminist political empowerment as newly democratic citizens. "Danger talk" reveals contested meanings of political participation and empowerment within Rape Crisis and requires us to consider how these differences are related to the legacy of apartheid inequalities. When we listen closely to members' danger talk, we begin to see how seemingly neutral values such as feminist empowerment are often racialized in practice. Ultimately, members' danger talk articulates what is exclusionary about their political process in an attempt to make political participation more inclusive and empowering for all.

## Rape Crisis

Rape Crisis was the first organization in South Africa to provide support services for women survivors of rape. In 1976 a group of five women in the Western Cape, organized by Anne Mayne, advertised their services in the *Cape Times*, offering to listen to women who had been raped. The response was overwhelming; their phone rang continuously for three days.[11] The South African antirape movement had begun and with it a forum for the discussion of rape as an identifiable form of violence against women.

From the beginning, RC was linked to a transnational network of women, sometimes identified as feminists, organizing to end violence against women. In an interview with South African feminist Diana Russell, Mayne credits her travels to Mexico to attend the 1975 United Nations International Year of the Woman Conference as pivotal to the further development of her feminist consciousness about the injustice of violence against women and its connection to broader patriarchal ideologies. Her story is similar to many others told by RC members, in that her activism was born out of a search to reconcile past experiences of violence. Almost twenty years later, the organization continues to be a vitally important resource for women in the Western Cape.

Rape Crisis is located in a racially, ethnically, and religiously mixed working-class residential neighborhood. From the outside it looks like any other house on the street, as anonymity is crucial for the protection of its clients. Geographically, it lies between the city center of Cape Town and a major university. It is walking distance from both the nearest train station and the main road on which "black taxis"[12] travel regularly. As a result it is relatively accessible to clients living in Cape Town, though this does not necessarily apply to Black and Coloured women living in the surrounding township and squatter communities located on the borders of Cape Town proper (that is, the borders that appear on official maps of Cape Town).

The primary aim of Rape Crisis is to provide essential services for sexual assault survivors in Cape Town. More than this, RC also works to prevent violence against women. The stated goals of Rape Crisis were:

> to fight violence against women by supporting survivors of rape; to educate the general public on issues pertaining to violence against women; and to actively influence the nation-state's agenda regarding women's rights.[13]

In general, activities are divided into two main sectors within RC: counseling and public education. Political beliefs and values associated with gender equality and democracy are not only held by individual members, but are reflected in the organizational structures of the center itself. One of the most important ways it does this is by involving the community.

The majority of members are volunteers who go through an internal training course. In addition, there is a staff made up of six full-time workers who are hired by a committee made up of volunteers and workers.

Hence, volunteers are the core of RC's organizational structure. While this may in part be due to funding restrictions, the situation has resulted in creating a feeling of community involvement. Still, while the organization has benefited from the membership of Black, Coloured, and Indian women since its beginning in 1976, it remains a mostly White, middle-class organization. Thus, one of the central challenges facing Rape Crisis in the new democracy is how to better serve the diversity of women living in communities that continue to be segregated with regard to race, ethnicity, and class outside the city center and how to extend their membership base to include more of the women living in these communities.

## Danger Talk

I can still hear the murmur of "danger talk" as a low but continuous sound from my fieldwork in Cape Town. Though at times indistinct, its message lingered as the actors and events grew into a cacophony of half-suppressed and potentially transgressive stories. These were the stories murmured alongside official accounts of past violations under apartheid, next to newspaper coverage of crime and ethnic conflict, and behind current attempts at reconciliation. As an ethnographer interested in the quotidian experience of the transition to democracy, I felt compelled to listen. Danger talk is one way that postapartheid citizens talk back to official discourses on nonracial nationalism, democratic equality, and political empowerment. Hence, listening closely to the murmurings of danger talk allows one to learn about the contested stakes and requirements of equal belonging as citizens work to build a better future out of the rubble of apartheid's uneven legacy.

Danger talk is practiced by members as they work to construct a postapartheid, antiracist, feminist culture in their organization. I examine the process of "becoming" politically empowered through an analysis of three acts of democratic process and community building undertaken by Rape Crisis—the Values Retreat, the Township Satellite Project, and Nomsa's Review—whereby members evaluate cherished tenets of Rape Crisis. In each act, danger talk is audible and I argue that it provides important clues as to the unofficial practices of belonging to RC. Ultimately, empowerment as practiced by RC members is not equally liberating for everyone involved. Rather than being a universal experience of political power for these women, it remains fractured along racial fault lines.[14]

Discussions of political empowerment in the postapartheid democratic transition are fraught with questions of how to reconcile apartheid's racial inequalities. Rape Crisis members consider internal organizational practices and seek to develop new projects in this context.

Violence figures in this article as a gendered force that feminist activists organize against. Experiences of sexual assault and/or battering in South Africa's patriarchal society deeply inform Rape Crisis's attempts to construct an equal and supportive environment.[15] Importantly, feminist activists at the local, regional, and national levels in organizations like Rape Crisis as well as in the National Women's Coalition insist that women's rights to freedom from violence are a *human* right in the new democracy and should be protected as such in the new constitution.[16]

## The Values Retreat

The Values Retreat was born out of a workshop organized to discuss and mend a growing divide between members over the future mission of Rape Crisis. The debate at this workshop revolved around one central question: was Rape Crisis a home or a professional organization? The divide roughly fell along lines of seniority and type of membership (volunteer or worker) in the organization, with older volunteers being more invested in Rape Crisis as a "home away from home," a haven where they could come for solidarity and understanding in an otherwise hostile society that did not respect women. Many of the senior volunteers, members since the late 1970s, reminded others in the workshop that this was the only space where they had been able to freely express their real political beliefs and sexual orientations under apartheid. Some of these volunteers further charged that newer members were trying to change the very nature of the organization and that they felt betrayed after all their hard work over the years to establish a safe home space for women in Cape Town. Thus, Rape Crisis had become an invaluable source of community over the years, allowing them a sense of belonging and a vehicle for dealing with sexual violence and thus improving the lives of women in Cape Town.

Newer members, comprised of both workers and volunteers, argued that the organization would have to restructure itself substantially in order to become a better service provider to the racially diverse population of women in the Cape Town environs. As a nongovernmental organization mainly dependent on overseas donors for funding and survival, the treasurer reminded the members of the need to move forward in the New South Africa. Though the goals of a "good home" and "good service" were not mutually exclusive, there remained a struggle over where the power would lie. Would Rape Crisis continue to be controlled by volunteers or by the workers that the volunteers had hired because they were professionally trained as counselors, lawyers, social workers, and educators? Some senior members were suspicious as to how restructuring or "professionalism" would affect the consensus style of the organization's decision-making process. They argued that Rape Crisis was essentially a volunteer organization and that was where the decision-making power must remain—with volunteers.

Lingering on the edge of all discussions in that initial workshop were accusations of racism. Such accusations were a significant kind of danger talk, in that they questioned ideas of sisterly solidarity based on common oppression espoused in many feminist narratives. Further, a number of young, Black, Coloured, Indian, and White workers questioned the appropriateness of service provided to "the community" when they identified issues of access to all racial ethnic communities.

The consultant hired to mediate this initial discussion over values had clout as a past member of Rape Crisis. She began by narrating a history of the organization and then described the current danger talk around issues of racism and power as a gender-specific crisis caused by the very high expectations women have of one another. Together, in the workshop members voiced their fears about past events in an attempt to deal with the past once and for all. Some of the fears were: "Things are going downhill"; "If I do x, then I will be labeled as racist or as unprofessional"; and "This doesn't feel like a home anymore."

The consultant urged members not to engage in extended "rehashing," but to focus their energies instead on what needed to be accomplished right now. She recommended a program of "strategic forgetting for the good of the whole." Interestingly, this process of strategic forgetting mirrored national discussions of community building and reconciliation in an emphasis on future rather than past reconstruction once the "truth" was told. In order to accomplish this "reconciliation" and plan for the future of the organization, a retreat was planned for a weekend away along the Cape Coast. It was called the Values Retreat.

We are thirteen women seated around a large picnic table; together we represent a range of racial and ethnic groups, educational levels, ages, and sexual orientations. All six employees, members of the Steering Committee, and interested volunteers are present. The following is an excerpt from our first meeting, which took place in English:[17]

*Margaret:* Working on issues of violence is tough work. It is draining and there is a high rate of burnout. It sounds like we all can agree that the goal is to stop rape and other kinds of violence against women. The challenge is how to best accomplish that. Would you agree?

*Faith:* This is not about us feeling good. It's about helping women cope with the trauma of rape . . . about serving women out there in all of Cape Town's communities including the Coloured community.

*Margaret:* But this becomes impossible if we aren't feeling empowered ourselves.

*Melanie:* That's right! I have been here longer than almost anyone else. Volunteers have always been the core of our organization, but now the workers are trying to turn this into a business with professionals and it just isn't going to work . . . this place is about women helping women.

*Sarah:* Things weren't really working anyway, Melanie. We have to reach more women, not just White women like us, but women in townships. In the last year since I have been here, I've seen many Black women slip through the cracks because we aren't organized enough. We hold meeting after meeting trying to come to a decision and it is impossible to get anything done. We just sit around and argue wasting precious time and energy. Meanwhile a woman is being raped every 83 seconds.

*Silence.*

*Faith:* As a feminist, I care about having a voice in decision making, but not if it takes away from providing services to the women who need it.

*Nomsa:* We are supposed to be in the New South Africa and look at us. . . . I am very worried. We still don't have enough volunteers for the new satellite office. Why not? We want more Black women to know about our services, but the main office isn't giving me the support I need to do this project. You don't have to speak Xhosa to volunteer.

*Melanie:* We are spreading ourselves too thin . . .

*Faith:* No, we must follow through with our commitment to diversify our client services. We will have to change our way of doing things. I want us to feel good about being here and the work we do, Melanie. I also think volunteers should remain at the heart of this organization. What we are ignoring are the accusations of racism leveled against us by women that have left. They didn't feel empowered in this feminist community.

*Margaret:* Does empowering ourselves mean we can't address the real challenges facing our organization during this time of transition, that we can't take internal criticism and assessment?

*Sarah:* It would seem that way for some of us.

*Margaret:* I want to remind all of you of something. You aren't really equal. You may all be citizens, but you aren't belonging equally.

The Values Retreat was a conscious attempt by members of Rape Crisis to create a safe space in which to articulate and deal with danger talk that had been circulating in the organization around issues of racism and feminist empowerment. It is a productive place for me to begin an analysis of democratic political participation because it is a moment when the volume of danger talk temporarily gets turned up. It also allows me to approach citizenship from a perspective often made invisible by an analysis of rights that is an either/or model—either you have them or you don't. In other words, if we start with a framework suggested by the above quote that acknowledges inequality despite universal citizenship ("You aren't really equal. You may all be citizens, but you aren't belonging equally"), we begin to operate in the more shadowy terrain where unofficial practices of national belonging are enacted and negotiated daily.

Following political theorists concerned with the fate of institutionalized freedom,[18] I understand democracy to be an everyday practice that must be exercised rather than an achieved state. This approach requires a close examination of everyday political participation for what makes democracy in the New South Africa. I use danger talk narrated by members of Rape Crisis to think through the meaning of democratic political participation. Ultimately, I identify a central point of tension between two discourses of equality vital to Rape Crisis members—feminism and democracy—for what it suggests about the formation of a distinct women's political identity in the New South Africa.

Employing the term cultural citizenship, anthropologists Renato Rosaldo and Aihwa Ong have called attention to the ways in which marginalized citizens in the United States, including ethnic minorities and immigrants, have struggled for representation in what counts as a national "we."[19] However, South Africa has a different history, in that it was the majority of the population—Black Africans—who had to fight for rights as citizens. Still, Ong's definition of cultural citizenship as "a dual process of self-making and being—made within webs of power linked to the nation-state and civil society,"[20] provides a useful framework for thinking through Rape Crisis's struggle to reconstruct both its feminist community as well as the nation-state's agenda regarding women's rights by foregrounding the tension between agency and constraint experienced by its feminist activists. I utilize the concept of cultural citizenship as a way of underscoring the contested nature of constructing narratives of "we-ness" and the unofficial practices of belonging that are not always captured in conventional analyses of citizenship and nationalism. Thus, *cultural* citizenship captures the process of "becoming" citizens in the new democracy whereby Rape Crisis members at once negotiate and redefine existing political identities and rights.

Danger talk is an unofficial practice of belonging, and while its presence is not normally captured in conventional analyses of citizenship and nationalism, its very existence urges us to reimagine what counts as politics. Anthropologist Donald Brenneis draws on two forms of conflict narratives told in Bhatgaon, Fiji, to argue that narratives of conflict become powerful not so much on account of what they tell, as in their telling. For him, such narratives are never merely reflections of sociopolitical realities, but importantly they *create opportunities* for political action with the ability to transform social relations.[21] Brenneis' concept of "Telling Troubles" captures the double work of danger talk as practiced by members of Rape Crisis during their Values Retreat. Like narratives of sexual violence told by rape survivors to members of Rape Crisis, narratives of conflict within this feminist organization break oppressive silences in their telling. More than this, documenting sexual crimes and organizational racism is a narrative act aimed at *resolution* for these women. Thus, opportunities for resolution become available through talk that not only utters conflict, but also demands new political possibilities for both the narrator and her audience.

Margaret's claim about the limits of democracy—"You aren't really equal. You may all be citizens, but you aren't belonging equally"—can be read on two levels for what it tells us about democratic political participation. In the context of the Values Retreat, her assessment challenges members' beliefs that feminism automatically ensures equal representation. She enacts practices of democratic political participation with her danger talk that at once threatens the assumed coherence of this feminist community while simultaneously having the potential to renew its members' sense of empowerment. Further, this danger talk reveals an important and productive discrepancy between national promises of equality and the lived experiences of difference both inside and outside the organization. In the context of nationalist community-building efforts and an interim constitution that constructs nonracial citizens, she reminds us that we should look beyond newly acquired, formal citizenship status. Thus, the Values Retreat was a rich site for mining democratic sentiment.

Danger talk urges us to reimagine what counts as politics because it captures a crucial aspect of political participation—that moment when *taken-for-granted values shift and demand reconsideration*. Community values of empowerment for all and equal representation emerged in the context of two debates played out at the Values Retreat. The first debate revolved around the purpose of the organization itself: was it a home or a professional place? The second debate confronted the issue of race and the structural ways in which race was or was not being addressed by the organization. Questions of how best to facilitate empowerment for both workers and clients at Rape Crisis revealed a contested process of creating narratives of community that often excluded the very women they were trying to help. When Nomsa said, "We want more Black women to know about our services, but the main office isn't giving me the support I need to do this project," she pointed to structural ways in which stated values about racial diversity had not yet been implemented. As it stood, the separateness of the township project was problematic because it marginalized Blacks in a space outside the organization, literally a place that had to be reached with outreach services. Such racial geographies are telling for the ways in which notions of empowerment become racialized. If outreach is performed for Black communities, it sets White communities up at the center of client services.

Though this danger talk threatens to rip Rape Crisis apart at the seams, it is actually central to what counts as democracy in a feminist politics of participation. These fights over values make obvious the limitations of categories of identification like "women" when they show the operation of divergent stakes and agendas. Here empowerment, like democracy, is a practice that must be exercised and negotiated rather than assumed. Danger talk is one important, if unofficial, way in which Rape Crisis members make democracy. Telling troubles within the organization identifies what remains to be done in their struggle for empowerment. Hence narratives of conflict, though potentially dangerous to their shared sense of community, are not, in fact, a destructive force but rather a constructive one aimed at reimagining a more equal way of belonging both as "citizens" of Rape Crisis and as citizens of the New South Africa.

### The Township Satellite Project

In this section, I suggest that murmurs of danger talk are one way in which these women, as cultural citizens, constructed community because they articulated stories that might otherwise be submerged in feminist narratives of sisterhood and equality. The following narrative was told to me in low tones and alongside Rape Crisis's "feminist" rhetoric on coalition building. My goal in retelling one woman's murmurings of danger talk is to illuminate contested practices of belonging and to identify one way in which empowerment becomes racialized. This woman, whom I call Nomsa, was deeply engaged in the process of becoming empowered both as a worker within the organization and as a service provider to women in her township community.

I noticed Nomsa at the onset of my participation in Women's Crisis Support. Out of six full-time workers, she was the only Black woman employed full-time by the organization. As I sat in on meeting after meeting I observed that she participated minimally in group discussions, though her sighs, muffled comments, and rolling eyes spoke volumes or at least seemed to communicate frustration. This continued until there were days where she arrived late or not at all. Not surprisingly, Nomsa's so-called "attitude" did not go over well with the other workers and many of the volunteers who had also encountered similar behavior during the general meetings. Now when I came into Rape Crisis in the morning for work I heard murmurings of danger talk about Nomsa and her upcoming review. "Was she qualified?" "Should she be fired?" "What about the need to represent Black women in the community?" And yet none of these comments were made audible publicly. Instead they lingered in the background, building tension. What was dangerous about these murmurings was their ability to cast a shadow of doubt over one of their "sisters" and in the process threaten the success of Rape Crisis's feminist community.

Of course this tension was not lost on Nomsa. Her murmurs were indeed dangerous in their transgressive potential; they dared to call into question standard operating procedure while they challenged Rape Crisis's internal politics with regard to democratic participation. Issues of race fractured an assumed feminist sisterhood that some members based on White experience in the main office. Hence Nomsa's murmurs of danger talk are evidence of the requirements of constructing community within this feminist organization. Though I heard murmurings of danger talk everywhere at Rape Crisis, some murmurs were more dangerous than others. Nomsa's half-suppressed murmurs were dangerous because they registered as discordant with the organization's official discourse regarding feminist agendas for social change and internal assumptions about "women's needs."

The events preceding Nomsa's review are critical for understanding the process of constructing feminist narratives of "we-ness" and marking the unofficial practices of belonging to RC. It reminds us that belonging is never simply a matter of legal or experiential qualifications. Rather, there are a set of unofficial cultural practices that are continuously being defined and redefined, which mark individuals as either members or outsiders. Cultural citizenship, as defined above, pays attention to contested practices of belonging as a citizen to the nation-state. Here, I suggest that a similar process takes place within Rape Crisis—there are actually contests over the cultural practices that come to define feminist politics within the organization.

Rape Crisis wanted to redefine the community in which it provided services and by extension broaden its multiracial, feminist coalition. Since the cost and time required for transportation was so often an issue for poorer Black clients living in townships, RC's solution was to set up a satellite office in the township. It was to be headed by both a member of the township community and Rape Crisis. This woman was Nomsa. Nomsa and I developed a relationship as we worked together in the public education program and the satellite project in the nearby township where she was the project director. I started interviewing her regularly at the beginning of 1995 as the township project was just getting under way. So it was here behind closed doors, away from the general membership, and without a tape recorder[22] that Nomsa spoke of her frustrations regarding her job and the politics of building a women's community in the township and at Rape Crisis.

The dialectic between self-making and being made was one that Nomsa negotiated daily in her attempts to both construct community in the township satellite and reconstruct community at Rape Crisis. She had the difficult task of being a cultural intermediary between two worlds. "It is very different there than this side," she stated, emphasizing the difference in clients' needs at the main office in Cape Town compared to the township clinic. Indeed, many women in the township did not recognize counseling as a service they required as they were unfamiliar with the cultural practice of confiding in strangers about their personal business (even if those strangers were from the township). Further, they did not want to be seen visiting the local clinic by their neighbors for fear of the potential repercussions such a visit might incur. As a result, Nomsa was forced to rethink Rape Crisis's original goal for the satellite project and focus on public education as a space for opening up conversations about violence against women. In addition, Nomsa insisted that leading work-shops required rethinking styles and techniques used at Rape Crisis. For example, many clients spoke isiXhosa, some English, and at times Afrikaans, but did not read or write any of these languages. She realized she would have to change the whole format of the training she had received and practiced as a worker at the Cape Town office, training that depended upon a considerable amount of education and literacy.

Nomsa had her work cut out for her. Eager to exercise her leadership skills by setting up a much needed clinic, she told me she hoped to stage a discussion among women regarding violence that had yet to be openly discussed in her township community. Her desire to help construct a space of belonging for women (based on their identity as potential victims and survivors of violence) where there had been none, now met with considerable opposition from male community members who were suspicious of her role as director of the project. According to Nomsa, "traditional" Xhosa values and expectations around age, gender, and sexuality made it difficult for her to assume her role as project director in the ways that were expected of her by Rape Crisis. Her status as a young, unmarried woman without children did not give her any claims to authority as a mother, wife, or elder.

Cultural constructions of empowerment are worth considering here, as the stakes of belonging were raised considerably when Nomsa felt she had to strategically "forget" aspects of her experience and community in order to belong unproblematically to the Rape Crisis feminist community. Though all members of Rape Crisis seemed to agree on the need for the satellite project, few participated. In conversations with me, Nomsa wondered aloud: "Was this project merely a gesture toward a more inclusive community of feminists?" In her danger talk, she argued that this was all it could be, at least until the different needs and experiences of Black women from the township were recognized more fully. During interviews she confided that Rape Crisis's program to help rape survivors often did not translate well for the township satellite office and its clients, nor for the demands of her job as its director. One important example was that women in the township told Nomsa that they wanted to "do it themselves" and use her as a one-time consultant rather than as a permanent service provider. Nomsa and I found that to these women, empowerment meant getting the necessary services and then taking care of themselves. Occupying an identity as a rape survivor who needed outside help was not an empowering subject position for them to inhabit on more than a very temporary basis.

Agency is a slippery issue in discussions of violence, especially those that focus on violence against women. Violence named as domestic is analytically problematic in that it maintains a false dichotomy between the public where men appear (read political), and the private where women reside (read domestic). Too often, analyses of women's experiences of violence become disconnected from larger political processes where women are represented as something other than full-fledged political subjects. In this equation women are depicted as victims, the recipients of violence, and in need of protection. In such scenarios the role of victim reproduces unproductive dichotomies between the powerful and powerless, making it virtually impossible to imagine agency.

Rape Crisis members see themselves as potent actors capable of fighting terror in their communities. They name violence against women as a political rather than a private matter. Bookman and Morgen's definition of empowerment as "a *process* aimed at consolidating, maintaining, or changing the nature and distribution of power in a particular cultural context" emphasizes the inherently dynamic and contested nature of empowerment.[23] What remains unexplained is how particular cultural constructions of empowerment are racialized in exclusionary ways.

The concept of "whiteness" as a marker of race and belonging is central to my analysis of the RC community. Ruth Frankenberg critically examines White women's descriptions of their cultural identities in the United States and insists on the need to analyze "the social and political contexts in which, like race privilege, white cultural practices mark out a normative space and set of identities" (p. 192). She draws attention to the complex intersections between race and nation in her discussion of whiteness and North Americanness. From her interviews with White women, she finds that "Whites are the nondefined definers of other people. Or to put it another way, whiteness comes to be an unmarked or neutral category, whereas other cultures are specifically marked as "cultural" (p. 197). Frankenberg later concludes "whiteness and Americanness both [stand] as normative and exclusive categories in relation to which other cultures [are] identified and marginalized."[24]

Though many feminist activists during my fieldwork openly discussed the problem of oppression as greatest for Black women, little discussion of racism within the women's movement in South Africa has been published.[25] I am not claiming that whiteness in South Africa is the same as that experienced by White women in the United States. Certainly, ethnic differences between Afrikaner and British Whites were openly discussed within the organization and reflect the particular colonial history of South Africa. However, Frankenberg identifies a useful model for examining the often invisible work of establishing normative standards. This set of operations, I believe, is applicable to Rape Crisis in the transition. It could be argued that historically a mostly White membership had established a "commonsense" notion of feminist empowerment, which in the context of the township satellite project has begun to be questioned.

In moments of danger talk, when the tide of daily business-as-usual recedes, the normative space and attendant identities delineated above by Frankenberg emerged more readily within RC. Danger talk makes it apparent that Nomsa's participation fit uneasily into a framework of empowerment made up of White cultural practices. Frankenberg also makes the important point that the categories of race and nation collapse with regard to whiteness for her informants, so that whiteness is unremarked upon as setting the standard whereby others are marked by cultural difference. In this case, Nomsa and "township culture" (read Black) were marked as special, as outside the regular client services provided in the main office in town. Put another way, the logic of this normative move positions Nomsa (intimately linked to the township satellite project) as marginal to the practice of feminist political empowerment in the organization. To what extent is whiteness then collapsed here with South Africanness or South African feminism as it operates within the organization?

The township satellite project and its uneasy inclusion in the agenda of the main office calls into question what counts as empowerment and to whom. What began to emerge was a hegemonic pathway to healing and reconciliation advocated by most RC members. Consciousness raising around issues of violence against women and gender discrimination was part of the program. Township residents and satellite workers did not always enact this program for empowerment in visibly obvious ways for other members based in the main office. Hence danger talk makes visible the link between the unofficial cultural practices of belonging and the ways in which such practices carve out a way to belong that is in fact determined by temporarily visible White standards of participation. Here, the meanings attached to "good" empowerment are collapsed with whiteness, while practices of participation associated with blackness fall outside expected performance standards.[26]

The translation work required in order to travel between the main office and the satellite took a toll on Nomsa and she told me repeatedly that she felt frustrated by the lack of support from Rape Crisis workers and volunteers. For example, members did not volunteer to participate in the satellite project on the grounds that they could not speak isiXhosa. Nomsa insisted that not speaking isiXhosa in the organization was not relevant, that they "put language as a barrier, but anyone can help." According to Nomsa, this was the wrong way to approach the project, for it continually emphasized the satellite's differences rather than redrawing Rape Crisis's notion of community to include it.

## Assessing Empowerment

Meetings are a prominent cultural practice of democracy in constructing this feminist community. As a volunteer in the public education program and a participant-observer, I often felt the meetings were endless; weekly meetings were standard operating procedure, while daily meetings were common. RC meetings can be divided into four main types: volunteer meetings; worker meetings; Steering Committee meetings (made up mainly of volunteers and a worker representative); and general membership meetings. Worker assessments are performed publicly in general membership meetings after a volunteer representative has researched a worker's performance by interviewing other volunteers and workers. The transparency of the assessment process and its public discussion by the entire membership are crucial to maintaining a sense that RC is run in an egalitarian way. Meetings are often lengthy and emotionally charged as members voice their opinions, debate the issues, and jockey for power within the organization. I now turn my attention to one of the general membership meetings called for the purpose of an employee assessment.

Nomsa was worried about her upcoming assessment. This would be her final assessment and it would determine whether RC would keep her on as director of the township satellite project. She confided in an interview, the day before the meeting, that her last assessment had been devastating. Accounts from other members confirmed this. Earlier, the general membership had determined that she was unqualified for the counseling position that she was originally hired for and that she might be better positioned within the public education program of the organization. Nomsa also admitted to me that she did not feel comfortable in counseling and that she preferred working in public education overall. Eventually, the organization targeted her as the perfect candidate for the township satellite program as she herself was a resident and would perhaps feel more confident and "at home" there. Nomsa agreed to take the project on.

The general meeting at which Nomsa's final assessment would occur was well attended. Women crowded into the main meeting room of the house/office that evening and sat in a circle along the perimeter of the room. The regulars were all there and even a few women whom I had not seen since my volunteer work had begun. I surveyed the scene, looking for Nomsa, and made eye contact. Then I picked up the report written by a volunteer, entitled "Nomsa's Final Assessment," and sat down next to a colleague named Moena from public education. This was my first assessment meeting and I was eager to see how the event would unfold.

After the tea had been poured and cigarettes extinguished, a volunteer named Sue called the meeting to order. She announced her job, reading from the first page of the report:

> In order to prepare for this assessment, I interviewed everyone that I could get hold of that has worked with [Nomsa] within the [Rape Crisis] environment. Basically, workers and volunteers were asked to comment on [Nomsa's] contribution to [Rape Crisis] under three headings: Positive, Concerns, and Suggestions. From the onset of this task, it became clear that while these headings were useful, the fact that a large proportion of [Nomsa's] work has been done outside of the office places a strain on this form of assessment. It is unfortunate that I was not able to speak to anyone from outside [Rape Crisis] who has encountered [Nomsa] as a worker for our organization.[27]

Immediately, the purview of this volunteer is remarked upon. She could not assess the work done by Nomsa in the township satellite. The boundaries of "the Rape Crisis environment" were in question here. First, Sue said she interviewed everyone she could within that environment. Then, she admitted that these interviews were limited to the main office. Did this literally mean that Rape Crisis was limited to what happened at the Cape Town office or that RC had not yet adjusted its assessment practices for its newest venue? Earlier, it was suggested that Nomsa would feel more "at home" as director of the township satellite project. Here, we can

begin to see why. If Nomsa could set the standards and operating procedures in the satellite, she had a greater opportunity to reformulate what
counted as empowerment in terms of her daily work habits, her agenda in
the township for education, and the means by which this change could be
structured in accordance with community members. However, the problem of how best to assess her work arose once Nomsa and her work were
reincorporated into the main office.

No one seemed to explore the reasons why Nomsa was not comfortable
in the main office. Clearly she was useful to the organization for her ability
to link racial communities. But to what extent did she feel like a real member of RC? Upon facing serious challenges in community meetings—such
as her inability to wrest authoritative control from vocal, senior, male members of the township who doubted the need for a rape crisis center in their
community—Nomsa had little support and models from the membership.
With the exception of two Black sociology interns from the university and
myself, volunteers were nowhere to be found for the project from the main
office. It would seem that although RC had a strong desire as a whole to re-
constitute its diverse racial membership, it lacked the models for how to
best accomplish this without reinscribing remnants of racial separateness.
Hence, the interiority of the solution—have a Black woman head a Black
satellite. Ultimately, Nomsa had to take charge of the satellite and to perform translation work for other members who were either unwilling or unable to change the racialized structures and practices that made whiteness
the normalized center of the RC community.

Sue then proceeded to read through the comments made under the three
headings and opened the floor for comments and questions from the general membership. The following assessments were listed under "Positive":

- perceptive
- confidence on a one-to-one basis
- keen to learn [Rape Crisis] skills/techniques
- warm and easy to get along with; nice to work with
- growing motivation
- beginning to feel more comfortable asking for assistance
- Xhosa speaking; opens up new facet of counseling service
- sense of trust between [Nomsa] and other workers being established
- supervision with [Moena] getting off to a good start[28]

The picture these comments paint is one of potential and tentative beginnings. Notice the words and phrases used to assess Nomsa: *keen* to

learn; *growing* motivation; *beginning* to feel more comfortable (not in the organization as a member, but more comfortable asking for assistance); sense of trust *being* established; and supervision with the director of public education (Moena) *getting off to a good start.* Taken together, these evaluations suggest that Nomsa was learning to negotiate her way within the organization. Interestingly, the very first positive descriptor commented on her ability to be perceptive. The question remains: to whom? Was she being described as perceptive to her clients or to other RC members? The remark that Nomsa was confident on a one-on-one basis seemed to imply that she was insecure working in larger groups or the organization as a whole. And yet, she was also described as "warm and easy to get along with." Finally, her cultural capital—Xhosa speaking—was identified as significant to the organization. Nomsa importantly "opened up" RC's client services to include "Xhosa-speaking" women in previously hard-to-reach areas like Cape Town townships.

Compare these comments with the assessments listed under "Concerns":

- insecurity in position; difficulty with self-motivation
- unaccountability re: her progress and day-to-day activities in the same way as other workers
- inability to "throw her weight around" when necessary—to nag/remind other workers of needs/voice concerns
- lack of supervision for the [township] project
- lack of planning skills/task follow-through
- concern re: commitment to organization
- not in office when arranged re: meetings/messages
- too many personal phone calls[29]

To begin with, I want to point out the slippage between the first two "concerns." The first assessment appeared to be more of an observation about Nomsa personally while the second assessment is more a concern with her place in the organization as a whole. One member asked Nomsa during the discussion, "How do you feel about being the only Black employee?" Nomsa answered, "You just feel that you are alone."

The concern listed as her "inability to 'throw her weight around' when necessary—to nag/remind other workers of needs/voice concerns" brings us back to the issue of empowerment. It would appear from the quote here (taken from interview material that Sue compiled for her assessment report) that Nomsa was not seen as being in charge and assertive enough with her colleagues. How was Nomsa expected to practice empowerment within the organization and why was she not willing or unable to do this?

The summary part of the report addressed this later:

> it did become glaringly apparent that the most central concerns were rooted in the fact that [Nomsa] appears to feel insecure in her role within the organization. This insecurity appears to be rooted in both a lack of appropriate training/skills and in a lack of effective structure surrounding [Nomsa's] employment as a whole.[30]

Concerns regarding lack of planning skills, missed appointments, and personal phone calls served to question Nomsa's professionalism. In fact, I had witnessed all these "concerns" myself while working with her and admittedly I was frustrated at times. And yet all staff members received personal phone calls despite the fact that they had a phone at home to use while Nomsa did not (phones were not easily available to township residents). Still, many members during the meeting that night echoed these concerns and said that they worried about exactly what was going on in a satellite office that they could not easily monitor. Perhaps the most disturbing assessment here was the one that questioned her commitment to the organization. This seemed like a summary assessment that meant that if one put all the "positives" and "concerns" regarding Nomsa and her work together, the result was an unconvincing performance of dedication.

Finally, the group turned to the "suggestions" made at the end of the assessment report:

- skills training:
- [Nomsa] completes counseling section of upcoming training course
- training in out-reach structuring
- job description: broad/vague
- incorporates elements of all other workers' jobs
- possibility of hiring another worker to assist with project?
- need better feedback mechanisms, not just [Nomsa's] work report
- more [Rape Crisis] structural support: integrate [township] into organization and create more concrete support for [Nomsa]
- progress/issues should go to Pub Ed meetings—need to establish an interest group within the organization
- necessary to link up with other community structures[31]

Three out of the five "suggestions" made in this part of the assessment were the responsibility of RC as an organization, rather than Nomsa as an individual worker. Hence, Nomsa's assessment, in many ways, was an assessment of RC and its ability to successfully incorporate the Township Satellite Project into the organization. Nomsa had already requested further skills training, so there was no issue in the meeting with that particular suggestion. Where the meeting started to erupt with danger talk was around the question of greater structural support for the satellite. Nomsa was required to perform and manage all the duties currently divided into four different job descriptions for the main office (that is, counseling, public education, managing the office, and workers). She was also the least experienced employee within the organization and yet was expected to perform every facet of a worker's duties with the added challenge of being geographically removed from the nexus of structural support.

Nomsa's assessment and the danger talk murmured around it was not only about Nomsa but also provided a critical space in which other previously existing tensions, normally suppressed, could be discussed—such as the disagreement over the current mission of Rape Crisis and the role of the satellite project. At least part of the tension that had built up over the past week had been in anticipation of such heated exchanges. It became impossible for members to express their concerns and make suggestions about Nomsa without addressing the larger issues facing the organization, such as how best to transition the organization into the New South Africa. The feminist belief that "the personal is the political" as previously practiced by RC members was now being challenged to accommodate race, ethnicity, and class in a way never considered before the transition to democracy. It was no longer enough to create a safe haven from apartheid and from male violence in a separate world. It became clear that RC was no longer the "home" it had once been and that assumed notions of sisterhood could not adequately speak to the diversity of experience among its members and clients. What counted as political empowerment for members of RC was not as transparent in Nomsa's personal experiences as they expected. As the room heated up with grievances during the meeting, a coworker told Nomsa that "this is our problem, not yours."

## Conclusion

This essay is an attempt to think through the politics of race in the democratic transition as it pertains to issues of political empowerment within an urban feminist nongovernmental organization in the Western Cape of South Africa. This case study of Rape Crisis offers us the following lessons in our consideration of the politics of race among feminist activists in postapartheid South Africa. First, the democratic transition is a potent moment for reflection regarding values that may normally be taken for granted. In this case, "feminist empowerment" is reexamined in the context of a new project in a Cape Town township. What becomes clear is that race, ethnicity, and culture are all key factors worthy of consideration for the success of this new satellite project. Of course, Rape Crisis members know this. But what becomes clearer as time goes on is the extent to which their feminist values and notions of empowerment are complicated by examining the racialized mechanisms through which their politics are practiced. What is specific to Rape Crisis in this case study is the way danger talk allows members to articulate what is wrong with the political process in an attempt to ultimately make it more inclusive.

Furthermore, many feminist activists in South Africa, including members of Rape Crisis, are engaged in vital discussions over the meanings of feminism(s) as they challenge postapartheid legacies of racial and gendered inequality in areas such as education, health, employment, and political participation. Many of the socioeconomic problems facing South African women today such as equal wages, violence against women, or the alarming rate of HIV infection demand an analysis of race and its unequal effects among and between women specifically rather than a desire to gloss over the differences for the sake of a "common women's identity." Though potentially divisive, discussions of racism and its ongoing effects, such as those addressed by Rape Crisis members as well as other regional and national feminist activists, illustrate the importance of an analysis of race within South African feminisms.

I have also sought to rupture what has at times become an emblematic representation of South African women in North America by foregrounding differences among and between feminists within the organization. Black African women have often been represented as a homogeneous group of oppressed victims under apartheid, albeit capable of considerable resistance to the state. A binary model of power wherein either you lack it (as a victim) or you have it (as a resistor) cannot adequately explain the position and actions of Nomsa discussed above. She traffics between differences as she performs the translation work necessary to do her job both in the main office and in the satellite. As the director of the township satellite, Nomsa occupies a complicated position in relationship to both these communities as she navigates *within* the continuing constraints of apartheid's legacy.[32] By marking the racial identity Coloured, I attempt to identify the differences among Black women in the Western Cape where Coloured women have often enjoyed differential access to privilege under apartheid when compared to Black African women. In this essay I have also considered the differences among White Rape Crisis members according to political generation and programs for postapartheid cross-racial coalition building within the organization.[33]

Finally, I offer my perspective as a White, North American, antiracist activist, teacher, and researcher.[34] As an outsider without a long history in their organization, I offer this discussion of the activities of Rape Crisis members in the transition as a partial account of the complex scene of gender politics that continues to unfold in South Africa. It is only one story nestled among many others being told by South African feminist activists and scholars (including Fester 1997; Meintjes 1998). I have attempted in my writing here to enact the danger talk that I identified within Rape Crisis. In other words, I utter the organization's internal conflicts not to "air dirty laundry" or worse, to cast the organization as racist. Rather, my aim is to illuminate one of the challenges facing multiracial feminist organizations that attempt to empower women in South Africa's postapartheid democracy. I suggest that the danger talk of Rape Crisis members is key to the reconsideration of supposedly neutral democratic values for many feminists in South Africa during the democratic transition. If feminism and democracy, as discourses of equality, share a nonracial subject in theory, to what extent can everyday practices of feminism and democracy be empowering for South Africa's postapartheid citizens? Thus, in the end, Rape Crisis activists offer us a model for a feminist politics that continues to have its ear to the ground, always listening for danger talk and its liberating possibilities.

### ACKNOWLEDGMENTS

I wish to thank Lisa Rofel and Don Brenneis for encouraging me to pay attention to danger talk. I also appreciate the valuable input of Carolyn Martin Shaw, Wendy Brown, Lena Sawyer, Scott Morgensen, and Deborah Mindry at critical junctures. Research for this essay was funded by USIA Fulbright. France Winddance Twine worked hard to shepherd this essay into publication and had numerous conversations with me about the stakes of feminist and antiracist scholarship for which I am very grateful. Brian Bennett made finishing this project possible. My greatest debt is to the activists who worked tirelessly on issues of violence against women in Cape Town, South Africa. I especially want to thank the women at Rape Crisis for their hard work, vision, and generosity as they build a New South Africa that guarantees better lives for all women. Though members and clients remain anonymous, their willingness to work with me does not go unappreciated.

### NOTES

1. National women's organizations like the Federation of South African Women (FSAW) clearly identified the need for women's rights in their historic 1956 "Women's Charter," though the goal of national liberation remained the priority. Thus, like other women engaged in nationalist struggles around the world, South African women's equality often took a political backseat to national liberation politics for the sake of strategy and the overall struggle. See Cherryl Walker, *Women and Resistance in South Africa* (New York: Monthly Review Press, 1982).

2. I use the term "feminist" to describe the political position and identity of the majority of activists I conducted fieldwork with in the Western Cape Province of South Africa. Though I was told by one member of Rape Crisis when I began fieldwork that "feminism is an okay word around here," not all activists working to end violence against women and to ensure greater women's rights identified with this political identity in the same way or at all. Importantly, many South African feminists argue for the historical specificity of this political identity in the context of the South African women's movement, refusing the charge that it is merely an imported Western concept.

3. See Laurine Platzky and Cherryl Walker, *The Surplus People: Forced Removals in South Africa* (Johannesburg: Raven Press, 1985), xiii.

4. These racial divisions have origins in Dutch and British colonial histories.

5. I capitalize all racial markers of identity to highlight the culturally constructed process of racialization whereby meaning is assigned to an individual based on historically situated and therefore changing notions of what counts as race. In every instance, I view racialized identities as politically contested. Put another way, I do not consider "race" as fixed, despite legislation intended to do just that. Rather, I want to mark a process of racialization whereby individuals are constructed as raced subjects, with often devastating consequences, at the same time as they navigate these constructions in strategic and often unintended ways.

The Black Consciousness movement begun in 1969 and led by Steve Biko is illustrative of the struggle over racial definitions and political identity. He advocated that black Africans join ranks with other so-called non-White peoples in an attempt to redefine what counts as Black to include Indians and Coloureds. In opposition to a National Party "divide and conquer" strategy that allocated limited political rights based on apartheid's racial hierarchy, Biko sought to organize around a commonality of discrimination based on a shared non-White identity. At the same time, he insisted on the importance of a Black consciousness that draws on the strength of traditional African community practices as a way of decolonizing the mind from colonial values and standards. See Steve Biko, *I Write What I Like*, ed. Aelred Stubbs C. R. (San Francisco: Harper and Row, 1978).

The problem with using the term Black analytically is that it works to occlude the differences between Indians, Coloureds, and Africans within this category and the continued inequalities in postapartheid South Africa. In the Western Cape Province, Coloureds were given preferential treatment under apartheid legislation like the Coloured Labour Preference Act. This points to the importance of marking differences within the racial category of Black due to regional histories in discussions of racial identity. Finally, this issue is further complicated by my consultants' use of race in everyday language. At times, Black was used as an inclusive non-White marker of identity. Alternately, they used the term Black to refer specifically to Africans. This is complicated further still by Whites in the transition, who insisted on their African identity.

6. For example, see Ellen Kuzwayo, *Call Me Woman* (San Francisco: Spinsters Ink, 1995); Mamphela Ramphele, *A Life* (Cape Town: David Philip, 1995).

7. For a discussion of this, see Fidela Fouche, "Overcoming the Sisterhood Myth," *Transformation* 23 (1994): 78–95.

8. See Gertrude Fester, "Closing the Gap—Activism and Academia in South Africa: Towards a Women's Movement," in *Sisterhood, Feminisms and Power: From Africa to the Diaspora*, ed. Obioma Nnaemeka (Trenton, N.J.: African World Press, 1998); Sandra Liebenberg, ed., *The Constitution of South Africa from a Gender Perspective* (Cape Town: David Philip, 1995); Shelia Meintjes, "Gender, Nationalism, and Transformation: Difference and Commonality in South Africa's Past and Present," in *Women, Ethnicity, and Nationalism*, ed. R. Wilford and R. L. Miller (New York: Routledge, 1998), 62–86; Gay W. Seidman, "Gendered Citizenship: South Africa's Democratic Transition and the Construction of a Gendered State," *Gender and Society*, vol. 13, no. 3 (1999): 286–307.

9. I regard the "transition" to democracy as an incomplete process rather than a finished chapter of history. In 1989 Nelson Mandela of the African National Congress (ANC) entered into talks and negotiations from prison with the then president, P. W. Botha, of the National Party (NP). In February 1990, president De Klerk of the National Party unbanned the ANC, the South African Communist Party (SACP), the Pan-African Congress (PAC) as well as other previously banned political organizations. Nelson Mandela was also released from prison after twenty-seven years in February 1990. The new multiparty government with Nelson Mandela as president was the result of four years of transition from White minority rule. The new government's commitment to freedom from all

forms of discrimination included women's oppression explicitly. For example, in 1996 a national Commission on Gender Equality was established and ten out of the twelve commissioners appointed were women.

10. Fieldwork for this piece was conducted as part of a larger dissertation project on violence, gender, and citizenship in Cape Town, South Africa, in January to April 1994 and again in December 1994 to July 1995. Though beyond the scope of this chapter, I locate the "translation work" of local and regional feminist activists in South Africa within a transnational web of feminisms whereby conceptions of human rights, democracy, and justice are being communicated, borrowed, and redefined.

11. Diana Russell, *Lives of Courage: Women for a New South Africa* (London: Virago, 1989).

12. Black taxis, often the only kind of transportation available to Blacks living outside the city center in townships, were a form of nonregulated transportation. These "taxis" are minibus vans usually operated by Black men that charge a comparably small fee to transport passengers into the city center from outlying areas. They are also a quick method of transportation along the main roads of Cape Town and I often rode them around town while conducting fieldwork.

13. Unpublished papers.

14. For the purposes of clarity of argument, I identify race as one significant strand among others such as generation, educational level, class, ethnicity, etc., in the constitution of identity and experience of power in the context of feminist politics. The history of apartheid and the resulting racial policies which structured the day-to-day experiences, opportunities, and worldviews of all South Africans were frequently invoked in explanations given to me regarding the spatial mapping of race onto segregated communities.

15. In 1993, the National Institute for Crime Prevention and the Rehabilitation of Offenders (NICRO) estimated that one rape occurs every 83 seconds. During the time of my fieldwork, Rape Crisis estimated that a woman was raped every 34 seconds. This estimate attempted to include unreported rapes.

16. The Women's Charter for Effective Equality, a 1994 document that reflected the findings of the National Women's Coalition, names violence against women as "one of the most widespread and endemic aspects of the experience of all women in South Africa." *The Charter*, 1994: 7, as quoted in Meintjes, "Gender, Nationalism, and Transformation," 81. This charter was an important political document in the transition since it documented the diversity of South African women's needs and was used strategically to inform the shape of the new constitution with regard to the equality clause.

17. I have changed all proper names to ensure greater confidentiality.

18. Hannah Arendt, *Between Past and Future* (New York: Viking Press, 1968); Wendy Brown, *States of Injury: Power and Freedom in Late Modernity* (Princeton: Princeton University Press, 1995); Michel Foucault, "Space, Knowledge and

Power," in *The Foucault Reader*, ed. Paul Rabinow (New York: Pantheon, 1984); Mahmood Mamdani, *Citizen and Subject: Contemporary Africa and the Legacy of Late Colonialism* (Princeton: Princeton University Press, 1996).

19. Aihwa Ong, "Cultural Citizenship as Subject Making: Immigrants Negotiate Racial and Cultural Boundaries in the United States," in *Race, Citizenship, and Identity*, ed. Rodolfo D. Torres, Louis F. Mirón, and Jonathan Xavier Inda (London: Blackwell, 1999), 262–93; Renato Rosaldo, "Cultural Citizenship and Educational Democracy," *Cultural Anthropology*, vol. 9, no. 3 (1994): 402–11.

20. Ong, 264.

21. Donald Brenneis, "Telling Troubles: Narrative, Conflict and Experience," in *Disorderly Discourse*, ed. C. Briggs (New York: Oxford University Press, 1996), 41–52.

22. Due to the sensitive nature of information in the history of state repression under apartheid, many of my consultants were understandably uncomfortable with the presence of a tape recorder. I respected all requests for nonrecorded interviews so as to protect informants' privacy and ensure maximum confidentiality. Alternative methods of recording were developed as a result. In addition, Rape Crisis considers confidentiality to be of paramount importance with regard to its clients and activities. Finally, an appreciation of Nomsa's tenuous position within this organization as outlined above further complicates the issue of protection of information and confidentiality. This is precisely why danger talk is a cultural practice worth paying attention to.

23. Ann Bookman and Sandra Morgen, eds., *Women and the Politics of Empowerment* (Philadelphia: Temple University Press, 1988), 4.

24. Ruth Frankenberg, *White Women, Race Matters: The Social Construction of Whiteness* (Minneapolis: University of Minnesota Press, 1989), 192, 197, 198.

25. An important exception is Fester, "Closing the Gap."

26. Analytically, it is not productive to collapse the differences between race (Black), ethnicity (Xhosa), and space (township). However, it is worth remarking that each were used interchangeably by members. Contextualizing these practices within a history of apartheid that emphasized cultural differences based on ethnicity and race which then corresponded with spaces for living, education, and medical care (among others) is the beginning of an explanation.

27. Rape Crisis, "Assessment" (unpublished paper, 1995), 1.

28. Moena's job was to supervise all community education outreach projects in public education. Hence, she was responsible for supervising the Township Satellite Project. Moena traveled to the Satellite Project at least once a week and it was on these trips that I was permitted to volunteer at the Satellite Project. I was the only White volunteer with any Xhosa skills (due to the privilege of my North American graduate education and the peculiarity of the anthropological project). Since personal safety was an issue, especially for the White, uninitiated outsider, I was required to be accompanied by either Moena, a Coloured woman,

who knew her way around the labyrinth of unmarked roads and buildings based on prior activism in the township, or Nomsa, who was a local.

29. Rape Crisis, "Assessment" (unpublished paper, 1995), 4.

30. Rape Crisis, "Assessment" (unpublished paper, 1995), 4.

31. Rape Crisis, "Assessment" (unpublished paper, 1995), 4.

32. See Iris Lopez's instructive discussion of Puerto Rican women's agency in "Agency and Constraint: Sterilization and Reproductive Freedom among Puerto Rican Women in New York City," in *Situated Lives: Gender and Culture in Everyday Life*, ed. Louise Lamphere, Helena Ragone, and Patricia Zavella (New York: Routledge, 1997), 157–71.

33. While there are significant differences among White women based on colonial heritage and ethnic affiliation between Afrikaner and British Whites, this did not seem to be the basis on which White women within the organization were distinguishing themselves. Rather, the main difference was constructed around political generations and subsequent differences in programs for political action. Anthropologist Lisa Rofel offers an excellent analysis of three cohorts of Chinese factory women who form their identities in relationship to their differential experiences and memories of the socialist revolution, the Cultural Revolution, and post-Mao reforms. See her ethnography, *Other Modernities: Gendered Yearnings in China after Socialism* (Berkeley: University of California Press, 1999). Apartheid violence and these RC activists' experiences of it as a significant collective memory inform their differential approaches to the mission of Rape Crisis in the New South Africa.

34. The goals of my work were threefold: First, I wanted to work alongside Rape Crisis members as a volunteer by providing community education on the issue of prevention of violence against women. I had previous experience in this area from the United States and wondered how issues of violence against women were being addressed in the context of national attention to human rights abuses under apartheid as later discussed in the Truth and Reconciliation Commission. Second, I wanted to learn more about the activities of Rape Crisis as the first Rape Crisis organization in the country. Finally, I cared about the issue of political empowerment as it was practiced by feminists in the democratic transition and wondered how cross-racial coalition building was taking place nationally in movements like the National Women's Coalition, and on the local level in organizations like Rape Crisis.

# Chapter 6

# From Race Cognizance to Racism Cognizance
## Dilemmas in Antiracist Activism in California

## Ellen Kaye Scott

Racism awareness workshops are one of the most popular mechanisms in the United States for addressing racism in organizational settings. They date to the late 1960s when they were used by the U.S. Army to facilitate the racial integration of the armed forces[1] and became widespread by the 1970s in a range of settings from police departments to social service agencies and social movement organizations.[2] One premise of antiracist workshops in the United States is that it is the responsibility of white people to understand and take action against racism. Typically, these workshops take place over a weekend or a series of three- to eight-hour sessions in which participants explore their personal identities (usually racial, but sometimes also issues, such as gender and sexuality) and the social relations of power in which they as individuals are embedded in American society. In these settings, participants are asked to engage in a series of exercises designed to help them become more aware of their own role in oppressive social relations and thereby change their behaviors. The hope in these racism awareness workshops is that by changing individual behavior we can change the world.

In this chapter, I examine practices that resemble racism awareness workshops in two organizations in California that employ racism awareness workshops.[3] Both the rape crisis center, which I call West Coast Women Fighting Rape, and the battered women's shelter, which I call El Refugio de la Paz, were founded in the early 1970s by feminists seeking to assist victims of male violence and hoping to end violence against women. From the outset, the activists involved in these organizations also expressed an explicit concern about understanding and addressing differences among women within the organization, as well as in the communities they were serving. In the twenty years since the organizations were founded, members have expressed the greatest and most consistent concern with racial diversity and racism, believing that white-dominated organizations could not provide services to the local racially diverse communities. They developed explicit strategies for confronting racism within the organizations. In both cases, the focus on race and racism appeared to obscure the politics of class, sexuality, language, national origin, and ability/disability.[4]

Despite their shared intention of openly addressing racism, a silence about these topics prevailed in both organizations. Antiracist discourses in the United States help create this silence about everyday racism. In antiracist political discourses, individuals occupy one of two subject positions: victim or perpetrator.[5] This discourse of agency in racial politics paralyzes action. Activists tend to vie for membership in the victim category and attach a great deal of shame to belonging to the perpetrator category. In his analysis of the British context, Paul Gilroy argues that the construction of two oppositional subject positions, the victim and the perpetrator, causes paralysis in the practice of antiracist politics. In order to build alliances and coalitions, other subject positions must be created, according to Gilroy. Until this happens, silence is the logical alternative. In West Coast Women Fighting Rape and El Refugio de la Paz, this construction of subjectivity explains part of the fear that predominated in both settings when women thought about confronting everyday racism. Their failure to follow through with dialogue, despite their intentions, constituted a form of paralysis.

Open discussions about race and racism in the everyday practices of feminist organizations require a new framework for naming and countering racism, one that breaks from this dichotomous construction of people as victims or perpetrators, and one that departs from the common tendency in the United States to invoke an individual analysis of dominance and subordination. In West Coast Women, some white women expressed considerable fear of openly acknowledging racism. They feared being attacked, as they put it, ridiculed, or condemned. Similarly, in El Refugio white women also felt that the workshops did not offer them the space to discuss racial dynamics and racism without fear of being silenced at the very least, and humiliated at the worst. If being condemned as the perpetrators of racism is the logical outcome of white women's active participation in examining the manifestations of racism in organizational contexts, they have little incentive to do so. Some women of color also judged these forums to be unconstructive opportunities for white women to be attacked.

Women of color, like the white women, also expressed a fear of discussing conflicts and racial dynamics among themselves, quite aside from white racism. In urban centers in California women of color do not share the same racialized positions. Instead, they must negotiate different racialized identities, immigration histories, class inequality, vocabularies of race and racism, sexuality, and prestige hierarchies among them that generate obstacles to the open discussion of the tensions that divide them. The women of color I interviewed, like the white women, have difficulty confronting interethnic hostilities, particularly as ethnic differences intersect with other axes of difference. In both feminist organizations conflicts involving racial and ethnic differences were as painful for women of color to confront as they were for white women. Like the structures available to confront white racism in interpersonal relationships, those available to confront the racial dynamics among women of color often provided opportunities for attack rather than dialogue. Instead of confronting those tensions directly, many women acknowledged that it was easier to simply avoid such conversations. In so doing, they failed to challenge a culture of avoidance around racism. Consequently silence prevailed even in organizations as self-conscious as El Refugio and West Coast Women about addressing racial difference in the delivery of social services. Although members argued that racism was palpable in their organizations, they had difficulty finding ways to respond to it.[6]

### *West Coast Women Fighting Rape and El Refugio de la Paz: Racial Histories in a Sketch*

West Coast Women Fighting Rape was founded in 1973. This small organization was initially run exclusively by volunteers until 1980 when they began to establish paid staff members. Throughout the 1980s, West Coast Women had a staff of two to three women. In 1993 the staff increased to four and by 1995 there were five paid staff positions. The main service offered by this organization, a crisis counseling phone hotline, was provided by approximately twenty-five volunteers. The paid staff coordinated the crisis services and did extensive prevention and education work, especially within the public school system. Members of West Coast Women also provided short-term, in-person counseling to rape survivors, as well as advocacy in the healthcare and legal systems.

Until 1994, the staff and volunteers of West Coast Women were predominantly white women from a range of class backgrounds.[7] Between 1984 and 1988, there were two staff members, a white woman and a U.S. black woman who was replaced by a Filipina. From 1988 until 1993, there were three staff members—two white women and a Latina who had immigrated from South America, who was replaced by a South Asian woman, who in turn was replaced by a Japanese American woman. During this period, a woman of color[8] always occupied the position of volunteer/outreach coordinator. The white women coordinated services and administration. In 1993 the racial composition of the organization began to shift. The staff and board instituted mechanisms for addressing racism in their day-to-day work, recruited a number of women of color to the board of directors, hired two women of color into staff positions simultaneously, and initiated volunteer training sessions exclusively for women of color. These combined strategies effectively turned around a legacy of white dominance, and throughout the 1990s the organization has succeeded in sustaining a majority membership of women of color.[9]

El Refugio de la Paz was founded in 1974, although the shelter was not established until 1976. Established initially by an ad hoc group of Latina community activists and white feminist activists, El Refugio was racially diverse from its beginnings and quickly incorporated women from other racial and ethnic backgrounds.[10] Like West Coast Women, the members of El Refugio were from a range of class backgrounds. El Refugio provided a variety of services to battered women, including overnight shelter, support groups, advocacy in the legal and welfare systems, child advocacy, drop-in counseling, hotline counseling and referrals, as well as violence prevention and public education. Because of the range of services provided by El Refugio, including the very demanding twenty-four-hour shelter, the staff has always been significantly larger than that of West Coast Women. In 1994–95, there were twenty-one paid full-time staff members. A number of women also worked as relief staff, doing the graveyard shift at the shelter and filling in when staff were absent, and a group of about twenty volunteers worked primarily on the hotline. Funding for this comparatively large feminist organization came from city, state, federal, and private philanthropic sources.

Until the 1990s the direct service staff was typically fairly racially mixed, including Asian American, Black, Latina, and white women. For example, one member described the staff in the late 1980s as being comprised of a Latina program director, 1 Latina, 2 Black, and 2 white women's advocates, and 1 Latina, 1 Black, and 1 white children's advocate. Frequently, Asian American and Asian immigrant women (of many different national backgrounds) were also on the staff. During this period and throughout the history of El Refugio, the management positions and the board of directors were occupied almost exclusively by white women. After a severe crisis erupted over race and bad fiscal management in the early 1990s, two key players in the organization undertook the task of hiring women of color into leadership positions in the organization. They succeeded, and finally El Refugio became racially diverse at all levels, including staff, management, and board of directors. In 1994, the executive director was a Chinese Indonesian woman, and the associate director was a Puerto Rican woman raised in New York. Together, they persisted in hiring an increasingly racially diverse staff and board of directors. Only the volunteer pool remained predominantly white when I was involved in the organization.[11]

## Feminists Fighting Racism and Shifting the Racial Demographics

Both West Coast Women and El Refugio faced the task of increasing their racial diversity in order to become more representative of the communities they served. However, their strategies for doing so were not identical. They were both committed to an affirmative action approach to hiring new staff members, this being a critical part of their success in transforming the racial composition of their organizations. However, in these sites of feminist activism women had different approaches to addressing racism in their day-to-day work and their personal interactions.

West Coast Women, historically a predominantly white organization, instituted mechanisms for addressing racism or racist incidents in the daily interactions between organization members and even between members and women using the services. One mechanism was the "Antiracism Discussion Group" (ARDGs), an approach that resembles racism awareness workshops. Two years prior to my participant-observation in the organization, the staff and board instituted a policy requiring white women to attend one antiracism discussion group each month.

Women of color were not required to attend the ARDGs, and they never did so. The ARDGs were intended for white women. Members of West Coast Women perceived the ARDGs as a central mechanism for addressing racism which they felt was the primary obstacle to attracting and retaining women of color staff and volunteer members.

El Refugio, historically racially diverse at the direct service staff level, though not management, established what they called "Everyone against Racism" meetings. Also modeled after racism awareness workshops, the EAR meetings involved both white women and women of color and were not conducted on a regular basis. Indeed, while I was involved in the organization the leadership rarely held and even objected to the EAR meetings as a method of addressing everyday racism. The deliberate decision of this organization's leaders not to implement such a strategy offers insightful critique into some of the problems inherent in this approach to racial politics.

The ARDGs of West Coast Women and the EAR meetings of El Refugio have common ideological origins, although these origins were not necessarily articulated by the members of either organization. The implicit and underlying assumption that grounds their methods—versions of racism awareness workshops—is the notion that racism is a product of individual attitudes and beliefs that can be eradicated through education. This understanding of racism derives in part from a prejudice model of racism. It is also a product of the complex way in which racism operates in interpersonal interactions and day-to-day work.

According to the prejudice model, racism is generated by ignorant misunderstandings of minority groups.[12] In this social-psychological approach, racism is seen as the product of negative attitudes derived from wrong beliefs, falsely generalized and expressed about individuals and groups. Prejudice and racism, in this model, are generally perceived to be irrational, unattached to the defense of interests or what Blumer called "group position."[13] There is no theory of power and conflict of interests in this approach to race relations. Prejudice models hold that through contact and education, members of dominant groups can have the opportunity to learn the "truth" about minority groups and thereby dispel false beliefs and eliminate racism. The problem of racism is fundamentally an individual one; to change individual attitudes is to end racism.

This model has been the dominant paradigm of racism in the United States since the early part of the twentieth century. It is composed of taken-for-granted beliefs and has become folk wisdom, or what Gramsci refers to as commonsense meanings.[14] In the media, public policy debates, and social science paradigms the prejudice model has historically dominated other perspectives and understandings of racism. Thus it makes sense that the prejudice model so profoundly influenced the practices of these organizations. While their understanding of racism could not be reduced to the prejudice model, this model nonetheless shaped their definition of racism in their day-to-day work so that racism was seen in part as a product of individual attitudes that could be eradicated through education and dialogue.

Philomena Essed has examined the complexity of everyday racism in the Netherlands. Essed argues that

> Race relations . . . are a process present in and activated at the everyday level as well as pre-structured in a way that transcends the control of individual subjects. Everyday racism is the integration of racism into everyday situations through practices that activate underlying power relations. This process must be seen as a continuum through which the integration of racism into everyday practices becomes part of the expected, of the unquestionable, and of what is seen as normal by the dominant group.[15]

Further, "Everyday racism cannot be reduced to incidents or specific events. Everyday racism is the process of the system working through multiple relations and situations."[16] In Essed's analysis, everyday racism is a system of power much larger than any individual, yet articulated and normalized through daily life processes and events. At this level, racism as a system, a set of institutions and social meanings and practices, is obscured and can be misconstrued as simply individual attitudes and behaviors. Thus it was easy for the activists in West Coast Women and El Refugio to construe racism in the daily life of the organization as a problem of individual beliefs, although in other aspects of their organizational discourse and action they clearly articulated a structural analysis of racism.

## Race-Cognizant White Women

The impetus for the antiracism discussion groups in West Coast Women was clear: between 1973 and 1990 the women of color involved in the organization numbered very few and they argued that in order to attract more women of color, white women had to "deal with their racism." Robin, a white board member, told me:

> When the antiracism groups first formed, I think it was very clearly feel-ings from the women of color who were in the organization, "Look, if you want us to stay, and if you want other women of color to be coming into this organization, you need to do some work."

Conceived as forums in which white women could learn about racism without placing the burden of education on women of color, the ARDGs were grounded in the philosophical tenets of racism awareness training. White members of West Coast Women were required to attend one ARDG each month for the duration of their involvement in the organiza-tion. Sometimes the discussions were structured by common readings or a set of questions posed to the group; sometimes they were unstructured conversations about the reflections or experiences of the white women in attendance. The main idea was that the ARDGs were peer groups, no one was the expert, and all white women had a responsibility to learn from and teach one another about racism and antiracist activism.

While the members of West Coast Women were not entirely uncritical of the ARDGs, they expressed considerable appreciation for this institu-tionalized mechanism for talking about race. Women of color in the or-ganization generally agreed that the ARDGs reassured them that the or-ganization was committed to putting racism at the top of its political agenda. Emily, a Japanese American former staff member, said:

> I think as a woman of color [the ARDGs] would give you more confidence to walk into an organization that . . . historically was very, very white. Giv-ing the confidence that people really are trying to do some work, really are committed. Practically, it really helped to change the atmosphere of the organization.

Anita, a Chilean staff member, remarked:

> I thought [the ARDGs were] a really good idea. That was actually one of the big things that made me think really positively about taking this job because I was like, "Okay. They don't just talk bullshit. They actually do the shit."

Yumi, a Japanese American volunteer, remarked,

> I was definitely drawn to the agency because of its stance on racism, and definitely feeling like having antiracism discussion groups was an amazing

thing. . . . I do not have white privilege. I've been confronted with racism all of my life, and it's something that I don't have a choice as to whether or not I think about it. And that's not true for all white women. . . . But I think that that is like one really big difference, making the choice to take it on, to deal with this issue.

For women of color board members, volunteers, and staff these policies indicated a particular political intention and practice that encouraged them to take the risk of joining what was at the time a white-dominated organization.

White women who worked to establish these policies, as well as many of those who joined West Coast Women after the ARDGs were established, tended to be what Ruth Frankenberg has called "race cognizant."[17] They articulated a discourse of racial consciousness that acknowledged that "race makes a difference in people's lives and that racism is a significant factor in shaping contemporary U.S. society." Through race-cognizant discourses, people express their recognition that racism includes institutional, social, and structural factors, as well as individual prejudice and discrimination. However, for the women Frankenberg calls race cognizant, to be race cognizant is to be aware of having a racial identity and to recognize that identity as a relationship of power, with others defined racially. After West Coast Women had instituted various antiracist practices by the early 1990s, the organization was able to attract and retain white women who were race cognizant and willingly reckoned with the burden of responsibility for the racism implicit in whiteness.

White women agreed that the demonstrated commitment to antiracist activism was positive. They were appreciative of a structure that required them to think about racism. In the words of Suzanne, a white staff member:

> I think one thing they do for me is like every month I sit and read and talk about racism explicitly. And with white people . . . I don't think that white people sit around with other white people and talk about racism very often. . . . That's pretty unique actually that that happens on a structured regular basis. I don't know if there's any other organization that does that every month. I think to me that speaks—that speaks to commitment.

A white volunteer said,

> I think that the ARDGs are excellent because they—The number one thing that has changed—Not changed, but influenced how I view it is just that I think about [race]. Like I have—I'm not going to say that I never used to think about it before, but [now] there is a very structured time in which

> dialogue takes place around the issue. There is outside information
> brought in in the form of readings and so I think that in that way [the
> ARDGs] are positive.

White women repeatedly said to me that they valued a structure that required them to talk about race and racism, since they were not the targets
of racism and they were not confident that they would initiate these types
of discussions on their own.

Members of West Coast Women also felt that the required ARDGs
functioned to "weed out" those who were less committed to this aspect of
the organizational ideology and thus they forged a greater collective identity among the remaining members. The white executive director informed me:

> A lot of [potential] board members and volunteers have [said], "I'm ac-
> tively antiracist," but yet when it becomes clear that they'd have to attend a
> monthly meeting, they don't want to do that. . . . It's a good way for us to be
> clear that our philosophy is that white women need to educate ourselves
> around racism, and that you would be amazed at how many people don't
> agree with that. So from the get, you're aware that either you're going to
> have to come to an agreement with us about this, or it's not going to work
> for you in the organization.

Nonetheless, observing the ARDGs over a period of almost two years
revealed one of the limitations of race cognizance for an antiracist
agenda: race cognizance is not the same as racism cognizance. That is,
while white women could problematize their white racial identity, they
had a great deal of difficulty identifying manifestations of racism and the
ways in which they perpetuated racism. In other words, while some white
women could recognize racial hierarchies and racial privilege they were
unable to identify its immediate effects.

## Problematic Practices: Limitations within the Antiracism
## Discussion Groups

I found that the women who participated in the ARDGs during my field
research were comfortable identifying their white racial identity as historically problematic because it is bound irrevocably to a history of colonialism and racism. Although they assumed their complicity in a system
stratified by race, the structure of the ARDGs presumed they would be

able to identify racism in their daily lives and to understand their own agency in it in order to work to eliminate racism. However, I found that beyond recognizing their racial privileges and their white identity, their ability to move from race cognizance to racism cognizance was not easy. The problems inherent in the self-education approach of the ARDGs were multiple.

One, it is often very difficult for white people to identify and name racism. For example, in the antiracism discussion groups, white women were asked to discuss specific incidents with which they had been involved or which they had witnessed that they felt involved a racist interaction or comment. This proved to be very difficult for them. In the year that I participated in these meetings, they rarely discussed a specific event. Rather, I observed their tendency to deflect the issue when asked to reflect on their own experiences of racism within West Coast Women. For example, in one meeting, someone first reflected that she found it difficult to introduce the issue of race into rape counseling, saying that if a rape survivor didn't raise the issue herself she didn't know how to do so. Several women said that they "feel blank about this," or "I can't think of instances" of racism in West Coast Women. After a moment of silence while the group reflected, another participant launched into a long story about helping a distressed woman on the street, and this volunteer's rage at the lack of services to help apparently mentally or emotionally ill people. Rather than ground the discussion in a concrete examination of the politics of race in social service agencies like the rape crisis center, the conversation meandered around a debate about what exactly the rape crisis center could or couldn't do for a woman in such circumstances. This was in part a product of both the difficulty of identifying specific manifestations of racism and a structure that lacked a group leader or facilitator.

Participants also tended to deflect the discussion by talking about racism in the abstract or giving examples from outside West Coast Women. This shift away from the context of the rape crisis center resembled the spatial and temporal shifts France Winddance Twine found in her study of racial discourses in Brazil.[18] For example, women would describe a discussion that occurred in a class they had taken, or someone might reflect on her experiences growing up, or people would comment on situations in staff meetings or confrontations with bosses in other organizations. Typically these reflections were about situations in which participants in the ARDGs were in the position of confronting the racism of others.

One discussion exemplifying a spatial shift which focused the conversation outside the rape crisis center also revealed in interesting ways one manifestation of racism. A young, fairly new member of West Coast Women talked about her outrage that white people assume a bond with other white people based on a shared politics of race. To illustrate, she told a story about being at a party at which a white man was saying offensive things to her about their Latino neighbors, assuming she would agree with him. She concluded by saying, "People assume that we can bond on white racism. Why is it okay to say that shit to me? How do I let them know that we won't bond on this?" Her point about the assumption of white alliances based on racism was a good one which stirred fruitful discussion. However, in this instance, as in most of the discussions in these groups, this volunteer did not reflect upon her own participation in such assumptions. Rather, she implicitly encouraged discussion about how to confront the racism of others.

Confronting the racism of others was the most common conversation occurring in the groups. The women were most concerned about when and how it was appropriate to address remarks made by people who had called the hotline. This was the source of much confusion, as hotline volunteers at West Coast Women were required to interrupt racist comments even during a crisis call. But exactly how to go about doing so was not always very clear. The women were not sure they were capable of determining when a comment was indeed racist. Invariably, these conversations took place in the absence of concrete examples from the hotline, but the women often pondered whether it was racist to name racial identity. Besides the question as to what was racist, they wanted to know how to confront a remark they had perceived to be racist. A white staff member said,

> If someone is in extreme crisis, when is the appropriate time to call someone on racism on the crisis line? How would you do that? This is important in terms of the client, but it is also important for building an organization where we trust one another to represent the organization in a certain way and build trust within the organization between women of color and white women. So I feel it is really important to do that in an appropriate way. We are supposed to be there for rape survivors, and we are supposed to be there to challenge racism, and I'm not sure if those two things fit together sometimes. How do we do that?

Another limitation of this self-education approach of the ARDGs is the problem of fear. White people are afraid to talk about their own agency and responsibility in a system of white domination. Beyond the potential contradiction of agreeing to confront and dismantle a system from which one benefits, problems also arise because of the dichotomous way in which racism has been constructed in progressive circles in the United States and elsewhere. White women, the ostensible agents of racism, engage in a variety of strategies to negotiate this subject position. In the groups I observed, women deployed three strategies: (1) the attack, in which one woman can establish herself as better than, or less racist than, another; (2) the plea for a safe space in which to discuss these issues without fear of being attacked; and (3) the confession of guilt. While I witnessed no instances of the attacks white women so feared, many West Coast Women talked about a time in the organization when this had occurred in the ARDGs. Stacy, a white volunteer who came to the organization in 1992, shortly after the ARDGS were established, said to me:

> I feel like with racism, people all have the capacity, I think, or the chance to say something offensive without meaning to, no matter how learned you are, and I have felt like it would be nice if people felt like those environments were supportive instead of policelike. And I haven't felt it lately, but I certainly have seen it with some people, almost like waiting to catch someone doing something wrong. And I think that energy stinks because I think then people are afraid to really air their ideas, and I think that's the kind of place where you would really learn about things. . . . I haven't felt it lately, but I certainly have felt it before, that people would be afraid that they would be jumped on so they would be quiet.

Another member remarked that the ARDGs had been a forum for "proving how wonderfully antiracist you really are" by viciously attacking other women.

The fear that this would again be the climate lingered. In many of my interviews and in many of the discussions within the ARDGs, women talked about this as an obstacle to their being willing to be open and discuss racism directly. In one discussion about this problem one member said, "I feel scared because there is such a high level of suspicion. I feel scrutinized, if anything can be interpreted as racism it will be." Another member responded, "It's good to be scrutinized. It keeps us on our toes." The first retorted, "And it makes me feel like shit."

Because of this fear of being attacked, some women said that they wished the ARDGs could be what they called a "safe space" to discuss race and racism. By a "safe space," they meant a place free of criticism and perhaps even emotions like anger or frustration—a protected space for women to make mistakes and say racist things without fear of condemnation. Other members questioned the notion of a safe space for the dominant group, saying this claim was only legitimate for those who were subordinated; some women were critical of the desire for a safe space in which racism was not challenged. "Safe space for whom?" they asked. A white woman said, "There's all this stuff about needing to feel safe. Do we need to feel safe? A woman of color once said, 'I never feel safe, and I do this work anyway.'" Others argued that the issue was how racism gets challenged, and whether the groups were being true to the mission of creating a place for white women to learn from one another about racism and their culpability.

Finally, white women sometimes provided examples that resembled confessions but seemed to reveal what they defined as their own racism. These examples were usually tied to stories they told of being threatened or attacked by Black men. The few women who talked of such events told the group that they experienced a generalized fear of Black men, accompanied by stereotyped images they would struggle to resist, unsuccessfully. In these moments, participants confessed to something they felt was racist—the generalized fear of Black men. This indicates their consciousness of the pervasive racist images and stereotypes that become internalized by many living in the United States. However, they also framed these generalized feelings of fear in ways that justified them. Group discussions of these events were typically quite sympathetic to the feelings of fear and hostility while also acknowledging the politics behind the host of feelings evoked by such an event. These rare moments of actually attempting to examine the manifestation of racism in their psyches and thought processes were cloaked in guilt, but were also usually accompanied by what seemed to me to be a legitimation for the feelings: stories of violation.

Whether the discourse was one of attack, safety, or guilt and confession, this structure did not lend itself to the original goal of providing a forum in which white women took responsibility for teaching one another about racism and antiracist activism. One member noted in a discussion about confronting people about racism that "It's hardest to challenge friends, and not strangers." This was true for the women participating in these groups as well. Their friendships, or at least their familiarity with one another, as well as the victim-perpetrator subject positions in discourses of race, made it very difficult for them to find a way to honestly and openly address the racial politics in which they were embedded in the daily life of the organization. In spite of their best intentions, they lacked adequate tools to fully examine their participation in the system they hoped to resist.

### Talking about Racism across Racial and Ethnic Divides

After being a white-dominated organization for twenty years since its inception, West Coast Women became a majority woman of color organization—75 to 80 percent women of color at the board, staff, and volunteer levels. In this context, many women asked if they should not conduct groups about a range of oppressions, especially about class politics, but also about the politics of sexuality. Both white women and women of color asked if the changing racial composition warranted organization-wide discussions about racism, rather than just white women's discussions about racism. As West Coast Women became more racially diverse, both white women and women of color raised the question of whether the ARDGs should be interracial discussion groups, or whether there should be a comparable group established for women of color in the organization. This did not get implemented while I was involved in West Coast Women. In fact, members said that outside the ARDGs they "almost never" discussed racism within the organization even when they intended to. They could not seem to get to it, I was told. Some of the experiences and reflections of women working in El Refugio de la Paz offer some insight into the obstacles to structured cross-racial dialogue about race and racism.

Historically much more racially mixed than West Coast Women, El Refugio had instituted its own version of the ARDGs, the EAR or Everyone against Racism meetings, during a time of particularly intense conflict over racial politics. Through this organizational mechanism for confronting racism and dealing with interpersonal racial dynamics, the staff were expected to openly discuss particular events or personal attitudes with one another. Either a staff member would facilitate these meetings or an outside facilitator would come in and conduct a daylong antioppression or antiracism workshop for the entire staff. If an outside facilitator conducted the workshop, she typically asked the staff to do a series of exercises on identity and oppression, and did not initiate discussions about the particular organizational issues that had led to their bringing in the facilitator. If a staff member conducted the EAR meeting, she typically created a forum for the staff to discuss with one another some conflict identified as racial, in the hope that the dialogue could lead to greater understanding and resolution. However, this approach to addressing racism was rarely employed. Both the leadership and staff of El Refugio argued that this approach was ineffective.

When I first became involved with El Refugio, they held a staff retreat to address racism. They hired outside facilitators and spent a day together off the premises. As a new member of the organization, I was not allowed to attend this retreat. I asked Giney, a staff member of Filipino and Honduran descent, how she felt about the retreat. She responded that it had not been particularly helpful because the same thing always got talked about in such sessions—"basic stuff about stratification in society. . . . I don't see it getting really deeper . . . [or to] more specific things." Giney found it strange that this "process-oriented staff" was willing to learn how to address difficult issues with clients but not with one another. Wendy, a white staff member, told me that the retreat was typical of this organization's manner of addressing racism. They could not seem to move past the most basic level of awareness about racism. She wanted to move on. However that, she said, would require a level of trust that did not exist in the organization.

Another concern expressed by both white women and some women of color was that these forums provided an opportunity for the expression of anger, often in a rather harsh manner, but little constructive dialogue beyond the venting of anger. The most recent example of this followed an incident that had occurred before I joined El Refugio but was still a frequent topic of conversation in my interviews. During the period of transition from a white-dominated staff and management to a racially diverse organization at all levels, El Refugio prioritized both the hiring of women of color and the increased visibility of non-Anglo cultural practices. According to staff present at the time, Patty, a white woman who had been with the organization for a number of years, expressed her fear that because she was white she would no longer have a place in the organization; she called the priority given to women of color "reverse discrimination." Patty objected that white-skinned women were being wrongly lumped together as all white, saying, "We have cultures too." Staff reported that in Patty's opinion, El Refugio failed to recognize the diversity of cultures among white people, such as Italian and Irish, and in fact actively refused to include those ethnic groups in their celebration of diversity. She said that for El Refugio, ethnic diversity meant non-European American ethnicities.

The women remembered a range of reactions to Patty's position. They remembered women of color being angry at this leveling of experience that denied the specific history of racism against, and exclusion of, people of color in the United States which the policies and priorities of El Refugio sought to address. They also recalled that both white women and women of color had little sympathy for Patty. Instead, they were frustrated that, as Kate, a white volunteer, said, "Patty was definitely kind of backlashing [against] women of color, and feeling like 'Oh, I'm not being included here,' and not looking at her white-skinned privilege." And Virginia, a Puerto Rican staff member, said,

> I think she was one of those people who's here but not into the way the organization was going. And should we stop, and explain to people where we're going? Isn't it obvious that these are the priorities? Just look at who's coming in through the door.[19]

Those who disagreed with Patty disliked what they saw as her attitude or her failure to understand the situation. This was, in their opinion, racism, and they expressed a good deal of anger at Patty's challenge to the organization.

The organization's leaders decided to call an EAR meeting in order to provide staff members the opportunity to discuss the conflict this had stirred in the organization. Various staff members reported that this strategy had proved largely ineffective, in part because of the harshness with which Patty was addressed during the EAR meeting. Wendy, a white staff member, reported that the problem was that women had "no ability to talk about racism.... It was like Patty was wrong, and she needed to be like put back in her place, or something. I felt like Marta [a Puerto Rican staff member] was really lecturing at her." While Wendy disagreed with Patty, she felt that there was a lot to learn about race and racism, but El Refugio was not the place for that, and this was very disappointing to her. In her opinion, the EAR meetings "never really worked.... There was not the ability to ... have the honesty of 'Okay, we disagree, and this is how I feel, and this is how you feel, and we're going to try to listen to each other.' No, it was like, 'You *have* to get this.'"

Virginia said that from time to time her staff asked for EAR meetings, but that she did not institute them on a regular basis. In her opinion,

> It's not something that I even see as constructive.... I think that it actually puts white women on the spot and lets other people sort of interpret it as they wish without them also being accountable. I guess what I'm saying is I think that it's more than just race and racism. I think it's internalized

oppression. . . . So I think some people want to automatically jump to race as an issue, and not like look at the other variables. And then there are those people who never want race to be an issue. And finding that balance and that safety to discuss it at the same time challenging it is I think something that we still haven't worked on successfully.

Virginia said that after her experience in the EAR meeting when Patty felt attacked by fellow staff members and felt "so devastated," Virginia "decided that the EAR meetings were not successful." Because members of El Refugio questioned the effectiveness of this approach to addressing racial dynamics within the organization, they held EAR meetings and antioppression workshops very infrequently.

Women of color also said they had little desire to expend their energy interacting with white women in this manner. They said they had "been there, done that." Nita, the Chinese Indonesian executive director said to me,

> We can dig up our consciousness raising groups, and we can hope for the best, and we can deal with problems as they come up. . . . Well, quite frankly, I left long ago. And the reason I left that long ago is because it takes so very much out of us in the way of mutual support and education. . . . I generally speaking will not—This is definitely a generalization, but I generally won't engage on a personal level where I invest myself personally in working with white women around racism.

Both Nita and Virginia expressed an interest in white women, and other women, making an individual commitment to introspection and accountability that would, in their minds, relieve the group of responsibility for addressing some of the everyday racism inherent in their day-to-day work. At the heart of the critique was an exhaustion brought on by the confrontations over racism. Despite their exhaustion, to their credit they retained their vision and commitment to work in a racially mixed setting and engage in the struggles that such a context entails.

This exhaustion among women of color was an old one. In 1981, in *This Bridge Called My Back*, Audre Lorde published a letter to Mary Daly stating her intent to once again pursue a dialogue with white women about racism. She said,

> This history of white women who are unable to hear black women's words, or to maintain dialogue with us, is long and discouraging. . . . I had decided never again to speak to white women about racism. I felt it was wasted energy, because of their destructive guilt and defensiveness, and because whatever I had to say might better be said by white women to one another,

at far less emotional cost to the speaker, and probably with a better hearing. This letter attempts to break this silence.[20]

Because of experiences such as the one described by Lorde, Chrystos wrote, "I left the women's movement utterly drained."[21] The exhaustion and frustration of women of color remains a significant factor in the lack of sustained, open dialogue between white women and women of color in feminist organizations.

Women of color were also reluctant to discuss the racial and ethnic divisions that existed among them. It was often too painful and too complicated. When I asked members of El Refugio about interracial relations among staff members, frequently they would tell me about incidents involving conflict between women of color. Some even thought this was more significant at that point in the organization's history than conflict with white women. For example, several staff members talked about the conflict between Black women and Latinas in the shelter. A Black staff member remarked,

> One of the important conflicts here that we need to see is the Latina/Black thing. I'm not as concerned about a white/Black or white/Latina thing. I'm more concerned with the Latina/Black thing because that's the conflict that I see happening here more.

Staff members who shared this perspective told me that this conflict appeared over preferences in hiring as well as what they believed was preferential treatment of Latina residents in the shelter.

The question of whether Latinas were given preferential treatment in this organization was debated under the surface of things—individuals discussed this with one another, and many women referred to this conflict in my interviews. Some women were convinced of the inequity in decision making with regard to U.S. Black and Latina women and said that this was a matter of who held power in the organization, and who was in the majority on the staff. There were no Black women in any of the leadership positions in El Refugio and only a few on staff. Latinas both outnumbered and outranked Black women.[22] Others argued that this inconsistency in decision making did not exist, but the additional services provided to Spanish-speaking women gave an appearance of special treatment and higher priority. Whatever the "truth" of the matter might have been, the point here is that this conflict simmered just below the surface of interaction and dialogue; staff members did not talk about it directly in the organization.

Other conflicts were also said to occur between women of color in the organization. However, in this racially mixed setting it was very difficult to address those clashes directly because women of color experienced confrontations among themselves as even more risky and frightening than those with white women. When I asked Nita, the director, if it was common for them to talk about race and racism in El Refugio, she replied:

> No. It's not a common experience. It's a different flavor [in a majority women of color organization]—The dichotomy of whites and people of color was so much more clear [in another organization] and it's not necessarily clear here. It's unique that we would have so many people in leadership be people of color, and that's sort of when we get into the spectrum of sort of cross-racial hostilities, and that has happened.

In an organization as racially diverse as El Refugio, in which white women no longer constitute the majority, power dynamics and disagreements between women of color can displace white racism so it is no longer at the center of racial conflict. When cross-racial hostilities that were essentially about race and ethnicity emerged among women of color, they told me that this felt more threatening than white racism. When asked to provide examples, Nita replied that it was difficult to talk to me about this because, in her words:

> It's hard because several of them have to do with cross-racial hostilities. Some have to do with internalized oppression. And this is definitely the issue of airing dirty laundry. This is definitely the issue of talking to a white woman about what people of color engage in that's very painful amongst ourselves. And how much that for me is about potentially giving ammunition to white people to not work on their own stuff, you know?[23] Having said that, there are sometimes underlying and sometimes very overt pressures around who is of color enough. So whether it's a person—We had one staff member accuse another staff person, both Latinas, of not knowing your heritage enough. "You're not Latina enough for me or for your clients." We have issues certainly as they pertain to language. Who speaks Spanish, and at what level, and what kind of Spanish. We have accusations that So and So isn't black enough.

When I asked why she thought those issues were not talked about, Nita said to me,

> There is a level of fear. And I'm speaking for myself, too. Sometimes it's fear. Other times, perhaps, it's laziness. Laziness in that we can easily use our diversity as a crutch to not engage. It's once again right now that we're

all here and we're diverse, are we actually going to do the hard work in terms of the dialoguing amongst ourselves? So, once again, the commitment is really there in recruitment, but once recruitment happens, and people are on the staff, do we invest in keeping people here?

Repeatedly in my interviews, women mentioned the fear and pain of confronting interracial hostility between people of color. In this organization, there was little formal or structured dialogue about racial dynamics and racism between white women and women of color, or between women of color.

Nita went on to say that discussing cross-racial hostility among women of color was further complicated by the intersection of other identities. As a lesbian, Nita said that the homophobia of other women of color in the organization was very painful to her. In my observations this source of tension lay distinctly below the surface, scarcely visible, whereas the racial tensions were openly acknowledged in the daily life of the organization—even if imperfectly or incompletely so. While El Refugio institutionalized the practice of confronting the politics of race, differences of sexual orientation, immigrant status, and ethnicity were not openly talked about.

## Conclusion: The Pervasiveness of Silence amidst Antiracist Talk

In both West Coast Women Fighting Rape and El Refugio de la Paz, I found that despite their intention to openly address racism and the politics of race in their organizations, a pervasive silence existed both among women of color and between white women and women of color. While these organizations consistently adhered to affirmative action hiring policies and shared a collective consciousness about providing services to a racially diverse community, it was enormously difficult for their staffs to talk directly about the racial dynamics of interpersonal relations. The silence that resulted was a consequence of the significant obstacles to open dialogue about racial politics in the United States, even in progressive organizations that want to disrupt the status quo of white dominance and address the racial dynamics within. As El Refugio de la Paz and West Coast Women demonstrate, even explicit and institutionalized organizational commitment does not guarantee the ability to adequately confront everyday racism.

ARDGs and EAR meetings were symbolically important to the demographic shifts in these organizations. However, the leap from race cognizance to racism cognizance remained difficult. Race cognizance, or acknowledging the centrality of race in shaping the lives and privileges of white women, is a crucial yet insufficient step in antiracist activism. Identifying individual agency within a system of racial domination and subordination proved very difficult for these women, despite their willingness to recognize their own white racial identity as a political position. The experiences of the white women, particularly in the ARDGs, suggest that dominant groups have limited ability to educate themselves and take action to challenge the very systems of power from which they benefit. While the race cognizance of the members of these organizations was impressive, racism cognizance was more elusive.

While in certain contexts and in certain historical moments, white racism may be the most significant divide among women in interracial organizations, it is critical to remember that this is not always the case, particularly outside the United States, Canada, and Europe. Even in white-dominated nations, as the demographics and even the structure and internal politics of organizations change, so too can the salience of other divisions exceed that of white racism. In order to build strong working relationships and political alliances, feminists working in multiethnic contexts both inside and outside the United States must commit to cross-racial dialogue about multiple and intersecting politics of oppression. The willingness to engage in this kind of dialogue demands a frame for racism and oppression that no longer emphasizes an individual analysis of the problem. Rather, individual action must be located in institutionalized ideologies and practices of domination in local cultures, and in social and economic structures.

Further, given their unique willingness to acknowledge multiple sources of power inequalities between women, feminist activists are in an excellent position to forge new and more complex subjectivities from which to create cross-racial alliances and take political action. These new subject positions must move beyond antiracist discursive constructions that position individuals as either the victims or the perpetrators of oppression. Instead, they must accommodate women's shifting relations to one another as lesbian and straight women, women of different class backgrounds, multiple racial and ethnic backgrounds, diverse immigration histories, various religions, and varying abilities and disabilities, for example. When we foreground the complexity of these multiple sites of potential inequality, as well as potential shared experience, and presume neither unresolvable conflict nor automatic alliance,[24] perhaps we can hope to diminish the fear the activists in West Coast Women and El Refugio expressed and thereby open the lines of communication about the structure and experience of oppression.

NOTES

1. Peter G. Nordlie, "The Evolution of Race Relations Training in the U.S. Army," in *Strategies for Improving Race Relations: The Anglo American Experience*, ed. John W. Shaw, Peter G. Nordlie, and Richard M. Shapiro (Manchester, U.K.: Manchester University Press, 1987), 71–88.

2. See Judith Katz, *White Awareness: Handbook for Anti-Racism* (Norman, Okla.: University of Oklahoma Press, 1978), and John W. Shaw, Peter G. Nordlie, and Richard M. Shapiro, eds., *Strategies for Improving Race Relations: The Anglo American Experience* (Manchester, U.K.: Manchester University Press, 1987).

3. My analysis of antiracism workshops derives from an ethnographic study of two feminist antiviolence organizations located in a racially diverse and politically progressive city. Both organizations were, for the U.S. context, unusually race conscious and racially diverse. I conducted this study in 1994–95. Census data for 1990 reported that the racial composition of the city was 46.6 percent white, 13.9 percent Latino, 10.5 percent African American, 28.4 percent Asian, 0.3 percent Native American, and 0.3 percent classified as "other" or "unknown." Thus, this urban center offered the feminist activists in these organizations both the opportunity to create racially diverse organizations and the imperative to do so if they were to provide services to the women residing in that city. In both organizations, I worked as a volunteer on the hotlines, participated in organizational meetings, and conducted interviews with past and present members. However, all members knew I was there to study the politics of race. These executive directors, board members, staff, and volunteers gave generously of their time and deserve much credit for their willingness to talk openly about racial dynamics.

4. During the period in which I did my fieldwork in West Coast Women and El Refugio, this appeared to be shifting. As the organizations became more racially diverse at all organizational levels, so too did there appear to be an increased focus on other axes of difference between the women working there, particularly class, sexuality, and immigration status. However, these sites of difference were still not the source of overt conflict among the members of the organizations. Rather, they seemed to simmer below the surface, increasingly apparent in the context of ever-greater racial diversity. I discuss this later in this paper and elsewhere. See Ellen Scott, "Feminists Working across Racial Divides: The Politics of Race in a Battered Women's Shelter and a Rape Crisis Center," Ph.D. dissertation, University of California, Davis, 1997.

5. Alastair Bonnett, *Radicalism, Antiracism, and Representation* (London: Routledge, 1996); Paul Gilroy, *"There Ain't No Black in the Union Jack": The Cultural Politics of Race and Nation* (Chicago, Ill.: University of Chicago Press, 1987).

6. When conducting these interviews, I was aware that relations of power structured both by the relationship between researcher and subject of research, as well as by the racial dynamics between myself and my respondents, would affect who would say what to me, and what questions I would ask. I began my interviews by acknowledging our racial positions and inviting respondents to talk about the racial dynamics and the potential for racism in the interview context. Rarely did the women interviewed engage in a full discussion about the potential dynamics between us. However, they often acknowledged their fears. Many also thanked me for acknowledging how difficult it is to discuss race. White women tended to thank me for recognizing their fears in discussing race and racism, and women of color did so for recognizing the power differences between us and the potential misuses of information.

7. The class backgrounds of the women involved when I studied West Coast Women ranged from poor to upper-middle class. However, the majority of members were from working- or middle-class family backgrounds, with about equal numbers from each.

8. I recognize that the term "women of color" is a problematic category of identity unique to the U.S. context. Though this term simplistically implies a unified category that often obscures the racial, ethnic, national, religious, class, and sexual diversity of the women who include themselves in this category, it also signifies the solidarity felt by those who are the targets of white racial oppression and discrimination. Further, the term was frequently deployed by the women in the settings I studied. The context of white dominance in this rape crisis center and battered women's shelter, as well as in the society at large, provided salience to the category "women of color." I sometimes use the term "women of color" as shorthand for a group of women with very different racial and ethnic identities.

9. The explanation for how and why the racial composition of the organization changed is long and complicated. For a more detailed analysis of this particular aspect of organizational history, see Ellen Scott, "Creating Partnerships for Change: Alliances and Betrayals in the Racial Politics of Two Feminist Organizations," *Gender and Society*, vol. 12, no. 4 (1998): 400–423, and Scott, "Feminists Working across Racial Divides."

10. From reports of past and present members, it seems that the Latinas involved with the organization have been South and Central American, Mexican, Puerto Rican, and also U.S.-born Latinas. This was the case when I worked in El Refugio—hence my use of the category "Latina."

11. For more detailed analysis of this transformation, see Scott, "Feminists Working across Racial Divides," and Scott, "Creating Partnerships for Change."

12. Gordon Allport, *The Nature of Prejudice* (Cambridge, Mass.: Addison

Wesley, 1954); Thomas F. Pettigrew, "Prejudice," in *Prejudice*, ed. Thomas F. Pettigrew, George Fredrickson, Dale T. Knobel, Nathan Glazer, and Reed Ueda (Cambridge, Mass.: Belknap Press, 1982).

13. Herbert Blumer, "Race Prejudice as a Sense of Group Position," *Pacific Sociological Review*, vol. 1, no. 1 (1958): 3–7.

14. Stuart Hall, "Gramsci's Relevance for the Study of Race and Ethnicity," *Journal of Communication Inquiry*, vol. 10, no. 2 (1986): 5–27.

15. Philomena Essed, *Understanding Everyday Racism* (Newbury Park, Calif.: Sage, 1991), 50.

16. Essed, *Understanding Everyday Racism*, 51.

17. Ruth Frankenberg, *White Women, Race Matters: The Social Construction of Whiteness* (Minneapolis, Minn.: University of Minnesota Press, 1993).

18. France Winddance Twine, *Racism in a Racial Democracy: The Maintenance of White Supremacy in Brazil* (New Brunswick: Rutgers University Press, 1993).

19. Here, Virginia was referring to the racial composition of the women using the services. White women were a distinct minority.

20. Audre Lorde, "An Open Letter to Mary Daly," in *This Bridge Called My Back*, ed. Cherrie Moraga and Gloria Anzaldua (New York: Kitchen Table Women of Color Press, 1983), 95–97.

21. Chrystos, "I Don't Understand Those Who Have Turned Away from Me," in *This Bridge Called My Back*, ed. Cherrie Moraga and Gloria Anzaldua (New York: Kitchen Table Women of Color Press, 1983), 69.

22. None of the Latinas in the organization were of African descent.

23. This part of Nita's quote, which I felt was important to preserve in this article, refers to the beginning of our interview when we talked about the politics of race embedded in the very interview I was conducting. I, a white woman and a "researcher," would be asking her, a woman of color, to talk to me about the politics of race, a historically vulnerable and risky thing for her to do. She was reminding me that she was concerned about how I would use the knowledge I gained through these interviews. She also implicitly reminded me that the conversations in such interviews might have been very different had a woman of color conducted the interview, though that would of course be complicated by the very fear she acknowledged in this interview. See Scott, "Creating Partnerships for Change," for further discussion.

24. See Scott (1998) for further discussion of alliances and betrayals in multiethnic feminist organizations.

# Chapter 7

# Between the Covers

## *Feminist, Antiracist, and Queer Performance Art in Australia*

### *andrea breen*

### *Tasmania: The Legacy of Colonialism*

Tasmania was settled as a penal colony in 1803, fifteen years after the first fleet of convicts and free settlers from Britain sailed into Botany Bay where Sydney now stands. Because Tasmania was isolated from the rest of the Australian continent it was perceived as an appropriate location for a penal settlement. With a climate similar to that of England, it also quickly gained popularity as a "pastoral" space in which free settlers and convicts who had served their time could begin a new life in the colonies. An island state that includes several small islands, Tasmania lies two hundred miles off the southeast coast of mainland Australia. It is known for its dramatic landscapes, indented and beautiful coastline, temperate climate, clean air, and relaxed lifestyle. Among its population of 470,000, there are 13,000 residents who self-identify as Indigenous.[1]

Tasmania is as indelibly marked by the injustices of invasion two hundred years ago as it is by its stunning topography. Tasmania has a racial history that many conservative white inhabitants would rather forget or ignore. In contrast, broad-minded Tasmanians are often so constricted by guilt about this narrative that they have lost a clear sense of their own destiny and identity. Originally called Van Diemans' Land by Dutch explorers, the perception of the land as "terra nullius" (empty land) that pervaded the discourses of conquest throughout mainland Australia was echoed in Tasmania.[2] Indigenous peoples living on the "empty" island were severely displaced within a very short time by white occupation.

They were pushed from their hunting grounds, solicited or forced into sexual and "diplomatic" relations, killed in barbaric acts, and imprisoned under the white man's law. Many succumbed to European diseases against which they had no immunity. A peaceful people, by the late 1820s Tasmanian Aborigines had developed strategies of defense against the inundation. In what has been called the "Black War" they fought to defend themselves and their diminishing lands against the push by white settlers for agricultural expansion.[3]

In the public imagination of white Australians (called "Numera" by Indigenous Tasmanians facing the invasion), and until very recently in school history books, Tasmanian Aborigines (Palawa)[4] were believed to have died out with the death of the last tribal woman, Trukanini, in 1876. To continue to cleanse the island of what was considered its "nuisance" element[5] after the Black War, Aborigines were rounded up over a period of five and a half years by their government "protector" George Augustus Robinson and resettled in Victoria and then on the islands of Bass Strait to the north of mainland Tasmania. After seventeen years they were again relocated to the south, to a former convict station, Oyster Cove, within sight of Trukanini's tribal homelands. Their numbers continued to decline rapidly. Trukanini, who outlived the rest of the group by forty years, found favor with the governor and was mythologized as a princess by the settler population. At her death she was considered to be the "last" of seven thousand tribal Aborigines.[6]

While this perception of "extinction" is based on the reality that partial genocide had been committed, it fails to affirm the survival of the race by other means. The perception that this small group of survivors was the "last" of Tasmania's Aborigines does not acknowledge the continuation of the race by children produced through rape or seduction of Indigenous women into relations with settlers and itinerant sealers on outlying islands, nor the voluntary intermarrying that took place between Aborigines and often Irish immigrants in the South of Tasmania who had integrated into white society to hide their identity. As historian and activist Henry Reynolds suggests, naive assumptions of eradication inherently brand Aborigines as too ignorant and unskilled to put up a fight, and support the widespread myth that they were unable to make their own decisions about their welfare. Indeed not only did they fight back (often with European weapons) but they took action when the conditions agreed upon in the settlement camps were not fulfilled.[7] Aboriginal representative Walter Arthur was one of the party of fifty-four remaining tribal Aborigines relocated to Flinders Island in Bass Strait under Robinson's leadership with agreement from the Aborigines to surrender their lands in exchange for provision of care. Arthur and his wife Mary Anne Arthur became known for their activism on behalf of the group. They organized a petition to Queen Victoria in 1847 for a more sympathetic supervisor to replace the one supplied by the governor. As historian Cassandra Pybus puts it, this "extraordinary document is probably the very first land rights claim in Australian History."[8]

Given this history it is little wonder that the Tasmanian Aboriginal population today—a strong, politically active community—is divided over cultural issues. As Palawa writer Greg Lehman suggests,

> [there] was a cost . . . of having to revive an indigenous Tasmanian identity from the very brink of extinction. With Palawa law and ceremony almost obliterated, we have to conjure new meaning by reinterpreting a history written by others.[9]

The deeply regretted loss of tribal knowledge, language, family ties, and land are the legacies of displacement and genocide that can never be atoned for. A more insidious bequest, however, is the suspicion many white Tasmanians have of fair-skinned Aboriginal Tasmanians because they do not "look" Aboriginal and the conflict that arises within the Palawa community when non-Palawas pretend to have Indigenous ancestry. As those who identify as Aboriginal in Australia are entitled to funding for a variety of activities, racist attitudes are often rooted in jealousy and misunderstanding about the dissemination of financial support. The current conflicts of identity bear some similarities with the assimilation policies legislated through the Aboriginal Protection Acts from the 1940s to the 1960s when thousands of Australian, including Tasmanian, children who were considered "half-caste" were forcibly removed from their parents and placed in foster homes, orphanages, and domestic service where many endured sexual, physical, and mental abuse.[10] It is not surprising, then, that the fabric of Australian society is crosshatched with guilt, arrogance, confusion, and a preoccupation with the assessment of racial stereotypes.

As the call for reconciliation and the recognition of self-determination gains momentum and acceptance, the fight for land rights continues to generate action by Indigenous groups throughout Australia. Since 1995 and after more than two hundred years of struggle and protest, the Tasmanian government has handed back twenty-one sites to the Aboriginal community for management in a gesture of reconciliation.[11] Denial of access for the wider community to some sites of sacred significance, while minimal, has resulted in protests against handback by white locals, who believe they have valid rights to these lands for recreation on the basis of their recent possession or traditions of leisure or work activities. The perceptions of the "body," which, like "land," has been objectified as article-artifact by colonists and their descendants, continues to cause ripples in both the black and white communities in Tasmania. Despite the return, after years of pleading by the Palawa community, of tribal ancestral remains of Aborigines that were taken to British and European museums ostensibly for scientific and archeological purposes, there have been disputes within the Aboriginal community over the most appropriate housing in which to honor these remains.[12]

In the context of marginalization and postcoloniality, the "colored" and "other" body and places of belonging are still not free from the injustices of the past. In Tasmania, gays and lesbians have experienced their own war of difference, intensifying mutual support within the queer community and generating affirmative action from without on its behalf. Until 1998, it was illegal for consenting adults to practice homosexual acts in Tasmania.[13] For ten years the Gay and Lesbian Rights Group mobilized to fight this law until it was finally repealed. In 1998 the Tasmanian government also passed an Anti-Discrimination Act that is considered to be Australia's most comprehensive. As a result of this act, Dr Jocelyn Scutt, a highly regarded woman lawyer, was appointed Anti-Discrimination Commissioner in 1999, breaking new ground in the area of human rights in this country.

## Speaking for the Arts

While inroads are being made at the legislative level, inequalities still exist. In the field of artistic endeavor, musical composition remains the last bastion of sex discrimination in Australia, with only 1 percent of "art-music" compositions by women composers performed or broadcast on the public broadcaster[14] although at least 18 percent of composers in this country are women.[15] In Australia, the arts are an affirming space from which to speak to the experiences of difference and marginalization. With financial assistance from the Australia Council and state arts bodies, marginalized groups have been increasingly able to establish their own publishing houses, to have works published with mainstream companies, and to bring the visual, performing, and "hybrid" arts into the broad arena. For queers and Indigenous artists there is now more acceptance and outspokenness within the arts, reflecting the core concern of artistic endeavor that it support the expression of feelings and experience, and demonstrating that it is a relatively safe environment in which to voice and affirm difference.[16]

As feminist historian Marilyn Lake suggests, "the recognition that nation-building rested on the dispossession of Aborigines and the violent destruction of their communities" has generated such shame and concern in the Australian community that many ordinary Anglo-Celtic citizens have lost confidence in their perceptions of themselves as Australians. As Aborigines, lesbians, gays, bisexuals, and migrants stand taller and speak with more assurance, ordinary "Aussies," women in particular, need reassurance, confidence, and a loosening of the knots of disgrace and responsibility for reconciliation. How do we do this? How will the women of the suburbs and the factories find a voice in the wilderness? How will they be heard? It is not surprising that feminist concerns in Australia have a paler profile than they had in the 1970s and 1980s although, in reality, white women, black women, and lesbians are fighting the same power wars. As Lake puts it:

> Feminism *is* historically embedded in white/Western/liberal culture. Recognizing that the relationship between Anglo and Aboriginal women is a matter not just of benign "difference," but also of power, historically and structurally entrenched, is to recognize, as Ien Ang has said, that "complicity" is a structural inevitability. Feminism has empowered white women, but its gains were not reserved for white women.[17]

### The Working Woman Artist in Tasmania

Despite the frustrations of isolation from other centers, many artists, feminists included, prefer to live and work from a space with a small population, cheaper living costs, clean air, and stunning scenery rather than eking out an existence in a large mainland city. This climate-of-inspiration has been particularly favorable to poets and writers, many of whom live in rural locations and write out of a sense of place and landscape. Musicians and visual artists too are increasingly finding that Tasmania's lifestyle and vibrant arts scene pay dividends in terms of survival and that visiting, rather than relocating to, larger centers is sustenance enough.

The sense of community in Tasmania often generates collaboration between artists of differing genres. As a musician and composer, I have been privileged to work with dancers, poets, and visual artists, and most recently my performance work has been with the lesbian and feminist poet Sue Moss. In this paper I explore that collaborative relationship, looking particularly at concerns of performance in relation to issues of feminism and race relations.[18]

Born in Melbourne in 1945, Sue Moss trained as a secondary school-teacher and later completed an honors degree in dance and aesthetics in the United Kingdom. Moss changed careers in the early 1980s when she moved into work that assisted women toward self-agency: setting up a Neighborhood House for disadvantaged women in a broad acre estate; lobbying for and establishing centers of women's refuge and affordable cooperative housing; teaching Welfare Studies; supporting older women in literacy and education; and creating programs for women's health education.

Moss began her writing career as a lyricist for musicians in 1988 and then began writing poetry. Her first public reading was a gay law reform fund-raising benefit concert in 1989. Moss has been closely involved with lesbian, feminist, and gay rights in Tasmania, particularly in the ten-year battle to change discriminatory legislation. Much of her work is also informed by her choice, like my own, in the 1970s, to move from Melbourne to Tasmania for environmental benefits. Her oeuvre straddles the discourses of feminism, ecofeminism, queer theory, antiracism, and morphology in sexualities. In an interview for the Tasmanian arts journal *Island*, Moss said:

> Inevitably my politics inform my writing. I've always been very self-conscious of not being a polemicist, although a piece like *Mary Wollstonecraft's Rap* was written intentionally as a full-on polemic. It's in the context of a music theatre piece called *May I Have This Dance Miss Stein?* and reflects my perception of Mary Wollstonecraft as a strong stroppy[19] woman. She'd be a polemicist if she were around today. Yes my politics inform the work, with the result that the themes I choose could be interpreted as coming from a politically informed woman's perspective. If you present work that isn't choked by polemic you can make a political point through humor and irony.[20]

As Hélène Cixous reminds us, the theater provides a way to explore and create the space between the "I" and the other, where we rewrite the "ancient and eternal truths" through a "new image" and "a new way of saying."[21] For Cixous, "changing genres" enables her to bring together poetry and politics, to speak against violence and marginalization. Sue Moss's turn to theater, including performance poetry, in recent years, reflects the same intention: to use a medium of expression where poems can be acted out, lived through the performing body as it is in "everyday" experience, so that the "I" is physically present. Its presence punctuates the text, in the moment of reception, and "humor and irony" enhance the representation, making it more than a fixed political text.

Moss's poetry in performance is popular in feminist and queer circles but also with general audiences, because of her courage and determination to speak to acts of injustice and because she confronts and entertains audiences with issues of difference, diversity, and the space of the new. By bringing her work to these audiences, Moss helps to break down the barriers to acceptance of difference and diversity. As a "hybrid" art form, our collaborative associations that merge spoken word and musical gesture extend even further the parameters set by the performance poetry event.

At any time and place, writing poetry to be performed is a risky occupation, more so if in performance the poet sheds the security of books and papers and allows the moment of word-making to enlarge or reduce the compass of the words contained in form. A woman performing in this improvised way risks loss of memorized fragments and dignity and possible rejection by an audience long conditioned to expect structure. In taking risks with the poetic impulse (creativity) and meaning (interpretation) by being open to nuance and change in the moment of performance, the work dances to a new dimension, both for the performer and the audience. The addition of an improvising musician to the performance event pushes the event to an even more tenuous interactive space in which sound and word "cross-dress" to become a new text, something with a morphology created in hybridity.[22]

Feminist collaborative improvisations in sound and word can honor the moment-of-being from which the creative act comes, and serve as political acts. Whether in recording or performance, they can act as channels for feminist activism. I believe that the deepest understanding in creativity comes from expressing the richness of personal experience. Sue Moss and I explore this kind of expression in our collaborations in performance and recording. Our collaborative efforts illustrate how collaboration and improvisation can be sites for the exploration of experience and transformation: transformation in space and time during performance, transformation for the audience through confrontation in the event, and the possibility of transformation through performance-collaboration-improvisation that represents and enacts intertextuality and genre-in-process.

In 1995 I began working with Sue Moss when I was invited to provide a sound installation for a collaborative feminist exhibition entitled *Will the Real Australia Please Stand Up . . . a Travelogue*, the result of travels north and west through mainland Australia by three women. My composition *Sonic Arc* was constructed in the studio from improvised events and word fragments provided by the participants to fit in with the exhibition's themes of unframing the location of landscape in the Australian collective psyche (a frame of conquest and domination) and deconstructing tourism and (Euro-Australian) male myths of the land.

While traveling through remote areas of Australia, Moss, Cath Barcan (a photographer), and Julie Hunt (a multimedia artist) were constantly reminded of the quest for objectification of landscapes, domination of space by boundaries, possessive ownership, ecological degradation, and loss of "country" by Indigenous people. The resulting exhibition emerged as a palimpsest of evolving parts with juxtaposed "sites" of interpretation (parodies of tourist markers), poems, photographs, magnifying tools, an enlarged score of the sound installation *Sonic Arc* (as a one-page chart), and two prerecorded sound installations. All these interacting elements provided comment from a feminist perspective on the inescapable hierarchy of the binaries of colonization. Gallery visitors and tourists had to construct their own journey-text and to confront antiracist and feminist concerns about power and possession. Participants moved along a pathway of visual markers while the thirty-minute looped sound installation made random comment on the themes, depending on the moment a person chose for viewing and listening.

Both *Sonic Arc's* score and the sounds it loosely maps use footsteps as a unifying motif because, as a composer, I felt that travel is experienced through mud-mapping, or sensory experience, rather than just as topography interpreted through a tourist map and traditions of the explorer's panoptical gaze. Monotonal humming by a woman's voice weaves through the piece as a possible symbol of a creation myth; it might be understood as the ever-present female voice. Other signs include musical fragments for improvisation by viola, piano, and prepared piano, signs from the nonhuman environment such as bird calls, frogs, and wind, and lines from poems and diary entries (by Sue Moss and Julie Hunt written during their journey).[23] Central to the piece both visually (in the score) and aurally is the labyrinth, symbol of the journey of death and rebirth, represented as an image on the score as a spiral and acoustically by female voices singing a repeating round intersected by the sounds of a footstep.

The sounds and images selected hint at a continuum of experiences rather than fixed, closed tropes associated with Post-Enlightenment musical and visual imagery. Moments of reflection, listening to bird sounds and walking the ground, suggest a personal narrative of engagement with the land which loops back and forth in space and time, provoking questions of representation, exploration, and exploitation. Gestures of dissonance and frenzy signify the tension and hurry of the early stages of the journey while pentatonic harmony and silence, or space for deep listening later in the piece suggest unity, attunement to nature, self-knowledge, openness, and regeneration. The piece is not meant to represent "the Feminine" in an essentialist sense, but to hint at the possibilities for diversity, interconnectedness, and nonclosure that women may embody. In poststructuralist terms, *Sonic Arc*, through its fragments and vulnerability to meaning-responses, opens up and "becomes" a new text.[24]

In the catalog essay for this exhibition, traveler-collaborator Sue Moss describes the phenomenological core of the journey that generated the making of her textual artifacts:

> Starting at Lake Mungo, we read around the campfire, cadences spilling, disappearing into darkness. We're journeying across far western NSW [New South Wales] reading Evelyn Crawford's *Over My Tracks*, through Brewarrina, Bourke, Yantabulla, and on to Yowah. We can't stop. Here there is no fragment of horizon, no allotment of stars. We're in the red country, the red road unraveling . . . cockatoos flashing pink and feeding on rotund clumps of bitter melon. "Come to me my melancholy baby . . ."

> Three women, each a decade apart, the generation Xer [Barcan], the 70's anarchist [Hunt] and the clapped out baby boomer [Moss]. Day after day, separated by a handspan, on a Kingswood bench seat. "What ya drivin girls?" We see the Pajero or Subaru [four-wheel drive] expectancy glaze their eyes. "An HZ wagon." And they're off, telling stories about shearers, suspension, floods, and Holden Kingswoods. Our fragile authenticity. Their iconography.

> At Brewarrina the Aboriginal kids say "Mirrigunah." Their eyes wide. Camping at Four Mile Reserve, Mirrigunah, spirit dog, wakes me howling across the river's loop. At Ubirr, a thylacine[25] in ochre, high on a rock overhang. The rationalists talk ladders. The locals talk story. We keep reading aloud. Stories have replaced our speech. Written story, untold story, wind

story, palms erasing the story-in-sand-story. On return I can't tell the story. Unspoken words boom through my hollow core.

This exhibition provides a glimmer of fragmented, piss-take, eye-weep story. *My eye is still dasseled. My tong still burns.*[26] I dream in red and I can't stop.

The exhibition, through collaboration (both in the journey to collect material and collating it later for the gallery) and improvisation (in the recording studio, at the opening performance, and in the multiple readings by gallery visitors), demonstrated that texts are slippery sites, as this extract from a display "site" in the exhibition shows:

> Do not allow potent hues to seduce mind's defended territory. Know thy territory. Defend thy territory with poisoned flour and gun. . . . This is my land won by other men following the path of demise. . . . Crows tore the landscape clean.[27]

Meaning is unstable. Yet for women patriarchy closes meanings, silencing experience and story. We need to make new texts, intertexts where our own narratives can be read and encoded and where the diversity and difference, within biological sameness, can free us from the limiting frame of essentialism. Both the land, as a feminized space, and women have suffered from exploitation and domination: as victims of the gaze we share the suffering.

One of Moss's poems, *Red Hunger*, was prerecorded as a collaborative piece for use in a listening-station installation for the exhibition.[28] The poem sings of the reciprocity between the land and the female body in the experience of Indigenous belonging to place, while referring obliquely to the torrid context of colonization in which both female and land were conflated and abused. To use the word "universal" would be to negate the richness of experience, yet we have, as sisters (like the land that has been feminized), universally endured a projected sameness by androcentric narratives. My improvisation was intuitive as I allowed myself to be affected by the poem's songlike quality (as a villanelle), by Moss's sonorous reading voice, and by identification with Indigenous experience in the moment of recording. The gestures were simple and repetitive, using a didjeridu-like drone on viola and an overlaid vocal chant, creating, in tandem with Moss's reading of the poem, a merged, blurred construct: a "mantra" open to a multiplicity of meaning-responses.

*Red Hunger*

The body, hungering for red
she gathers sand in slender vials.
Some women eat this earth it's said

replenished by a story read:
old voices carried on blood shift
the body hungering for red.

Urban exiles sent envoys instead
to swing on earth's magnetic thrum.
Some women eat this earth it's said

to ease new life's travails, the head's
onward rush through water into light.
The body hungering for red.

Rigid road-kill tugs the eye. Fire fed
by mulga[29] we sleep aligned to stars.
Some women eat this earth it's said

We offer mantras to river beds.
Rain hints, begins, the night turns mud.
Our bodies hungering for red.
Some women eat this earth it's said.[30]

## New Space for Configuring Texts

Sue Moss and I used this poem, and several others from the travelogue collection together with a new poem, *Space*, as scaffolding for a twenty-minute improvised piece for live broadcast when we took performance collaborations further into the field of spontaneous word-sound improvisation. The broadcast was part of the ABC's "Improvisatory Music Awards" held from April to August 1999. The aim of this award was to tease out innovative "art-music" collaborations that explored improvisatory practice. The participants were selected on the basis of written applications and previous experience in performance and recording.

Moss and I began our process of preparation for the award by using poems about space (from the exhibition and more recently written texts) as contours on which to relocate deferred meaning through extemporization. From one rehearsal to the next, as we tried to respond intuitively to each other in the moment, we could not predict which words would be cut, extended, sung, or spoken, whether phrases or syllables would be emphasized or where and how sound gestures would interact with selected words. Over several weeks of rehearsal we moved from a structured set of poems and precomposed sound gestures to an improvisation that was like a skyscape theater, as we shunted meaning and denied closure on the material. Every word and phrase became a site for substitution and contiguity, both sonically and linguistically. At the outset of the process we felt so constrained by the poems and our enforced intimacy that we could improvise for no more than five minutes; as the performance event approached we became more and more liberated into metamorphosis: the poems became springboards of suggestion and the weaving of sound and syllable synonymous with a growing collaboration.

*Space*, originally a song composed by Moss and appropriated in part to bring the improvisation event to a moment of conclusion, captures simply, I think, the sentiments that both Moss and I believe to be central to the collaborative improvisatory process. Word-sound improvisation is an interactive, movable space in which words and sound can be deconstructed and recreated, and where women can, through their own performativity, resignify themselves away from constructions of androcentric conformity (desire fulfilled through closure) and projected essentialist prefigurations.[31]

> *Space*
>
> We meet in the space
> The space between you and me
> Between the earth, between the sky
> Lives a possibility
>
> In the space. In the space
> We don't know where we are
> Stepping from the here to there
> We could fall between the stars
>
> Between, between, between
> We are the space between
> The space is where it happens
> Beyond our wildest dreams
>
> In the space, in the space,
> We don't know where we are
> Stepping from the here to there
> Borders are sabotaged

It's the space between an idea
The space between a song
The space between each night and day
We know as dusk and dawn

It's a naming and un-naming
Both a circle and an edge
Words dissolve, the world unfurls
Both beginning and an end[32]

## Exploring the Space Between

Much of Moss's writing explores between and becoming states and sites, and so embodies the core impulses of improvisation and collaboration I have been describing. Her poems prompt the reader/listener to ask questions beyond sameness and difference toward diversity and nonteleological presuppositions, to a space that is "always coming home," to use Ursula Le Guin's phrase. As Carol Bigwood writes, "home is a nomadic place but a belonging place nevertheless"[33] and the space where we "become" is the deep well of mythopoesis, the home-hearth, womb, phenomenal self enriched through sharing with another but never rigid in stasis.

Drawing on images of the French performance artist Orlan, Moss's theater piece *Speech Acts under a Cosmetic Surgeon's Scalpel* confronts the bleak territory of rigid binary oppositions which patriarchy forces women to inhabit, denying them the choice to generate their own mode of being. Moss (reading Orlan's performance practice) renders a body that is emerging and intertextual, resisting the standards of unblemished youthfulness determined by patriarchal stereotypes (exemplified by plastic surgery and the fashion industry).

*Speech Acts under a Cosmetic Surgeon's Scalpel*

Here is my face shaped like a promise.
I am utterance beneath the scalpel,
redeeming old silences and talking you through
your deliberate act of effacement . . .
The mask flapped back reveals emptiness; sinew, skin,
and suction's incessant hiss.
I am the space where meaning is lost.
Hear my voice, an unfaltering ostinato

beneath staunched seepage.
This meld of blood and word disturbs
your masterful silence, my tongue
refuses to rest mute and suppressed.
A voice exists. Know that I wait
watchful, renewed and will scream
to disclaim any false move.

Orlan's performance is a defiant act, yet at the same time a collaborative improvisation between her invited medical staff, film crew, and herself. There is a script (which she, in a sense, parodies by reading selected textual excerpts during the operation) but it unfurls in the moment, like her skin as it is pared away from behind the ear, beneath the lip. Who is this woman, what is this body, this disembodied voice, this gender? She recreates herself as she directs others to deconstruct her face, the signature-self. No one can feel comfortable with such defacement, with a woman taking the power to herself for her undoing and redoing, just as she wants to be, for now.

### *Performance Space as a Site for Transformation*

To be willing to unmake oneself publicly in order to remake oneself can result in misunderstanding, ridicule, and possible failure. Sue Moss and I are sometimes criticized for attempting collaborative sound-word improvisations that have no generic model, and we encounter something akin to disregard from many men and patriarchal women who choose to find little point of contact in the skin of words and sound that we cut, paste, and reinvent. As Moss often says, "It challenges their Mozartian comfort zones," and clearly the performances are unsettling to the point of pushing participants into a spectrum of responses. There are moments of "beautiful sound" but not enough for the audience to be completely immersed. There is wordplay but not enough for uproarious comedy, and there is story but not enough for plot and closure. The collaboration falls between genre descriptions and signifies and expresses the self becoming organic in the moment of creation, even though the use of prefigured structures is necessary to production.

Moss observed to me that it was not until she began to improvise with her poems that she realized the constant unfolding of meaning open to her. In a similar fashion I have noticed when developing musical gestures that if I remain fixed within classical expectations of viola playing and singing that represent and mirror words only through contiguous extension, my improvisations quickly become clichéd. These gestures have very little association with the changing shape of the meanings in the wordplay or my feelings and thoughts in the moment of experiencing. While I need a skeletal shape from which to move, I do not want to be reduced to the bare bones of through-composed formalist structures.

Performativity, the making of markers for self-description, joins performance through corporeality. Lived experience comes to, and "becomes" in, the theater, as the speaking, moving, singing, playing subject breaks with prior contexts of being in the process of resignifying languages, bodies, and texts-contexts. As Judith Butler observes:

> We do things with language, produce effects with language, but language is also the thing that we do. Language is the name for our doing: both "what" we do (the name for the action that we characteristically perform) and that which we effect, the act and its consequences.[34]

Naming—that is, actions, objects, concepts, and thoughts—becomes a transformative process, I would suggest, in the event of collaborative improvisation because, as women enacting being through performance, we reconstruct ourselves and our emplacement by deconstructing the language that reduces us through violent iterative acts. We unhinge the door to meaning, understanding incrementally that each moment in the process breaks up language still more until we begin to build an interface unscripted by our own or others' expectations and histories. And it is interactivity that assists the process: repeating phrases, words, and gestures opens up a space for change, for deepened, shifting responses that bring the *habitus* into the performativity of performance.[35]

As our improvisations evolved in resonating interactivity, Sue Moss and I intuitively sought out repetition and found that the subtlety of timbre changes led to shifts in the creative imagination. In this way, repeating fragments preempt new refrains and beckon the audience to stay committed to listening for slippages.

In this essay I have suggested that for women performance is strengthened by improvised collaboration and that the theater can be a site for transformation, a space in which "cross-dressing" to new forms of expression can take place. Word-sound "intertexts" that confront our "comfort zones" act as vehicles for the transformative process through which participants can come to terms with an (implicit or explicit) agenda of necessary change. While meaning may be deferred, unstable and constantly changing at such events, the underlying intention in these works is to shift the consciousness of the listener toward thought and action that honor diversity and difference. In feminist terms, performances such as these operate primarily as tools for the artist-activist to speak from the personal experience of marginalization and/or to inform local audiences about injustices in the wider national community. By merging political intention with performance craft, the "message" intensifies the urgency for action and finds a way into sectors of the community than may not necessarily be open to overt forms of activism and discussion.

Sue Moss's poems have also reached a wider audience through the printed text. Her work is a cutting-edge contribution to feminist writing in her home state of Tasmania as well as in the wider Australian context.[36] Moss's work moves feminist, queer, and antiracist sentiments into new territory. The most salient feature of her oeuvre, whether performance poetry, collaboration, or written text is her determination to open cracks in the genre, conservative art practice, and political institutions that harbor injustice. This description of the presentation and reception of a hybrid art form that attempts to speak for political and social change applies to the collaborations that have taken place between Sue Moss as spoken word artist and myself as composer-improviser and to other solo and collaborative events in our careers as performers. Moss's poems are written for performance and laced with surprises, ambiguous wordplay, and themes that unsettle. Her theatrical style of presentation deconstructs the tradition of "poetry readings," insisting on more active responses from the audience.

ACKNOWLEDGMENTS

My thanks to Sue Moss for her assistance with this article, permission to use her poems, and for the opportunities she has created for our joint performance efforts. Thanks also to Julie Hunt, Cath Barcan, and curator Christl Berg for their enthusiastic collaboration that made "Will the Real Australia Please Stand Up" a reality.

NOTES

1. The number of those identifying as Aboriginal has increased in recent years. As reported in the 1996 federal government census, 10.2 percent of Tasmanians

were born in more than one hundred forty countries other than Australia. Population growth in Tasmania, at 0.45 percent, has fallen below the national average which is 0.64 percent. The main reason for this decline is the "youth drain" to mainland city centers for employment. ABS Catalogue 1301.6, Year 2000.

2. Native title was not recognized because Aborigines were "held incapable of intelligent transactions with respect to land." D. P. O'Connell, quoted in Henry Reynolds, *Why Weren't We Told* (Ringwood: Penguin, 1999), 186.

3. The "Black War" took place between 1824 and 1830. As Henry Reynolds points out, "the colonists realized . . . that they were engaged in a particular species of warfare [for which] the term 'guerilla' . . . [was] perhaps for the first time [used] in Australia." Henry Reynolds, *Fate of a Free People: A Radical Re-Examination of the Tasmanian Wars* (Ringwood: Penguin 1995), 66.

4. The Tasmanian Aboriginal term for the white invaders was "Numera," meaning "ghosts of the ancestors." "Palawa" (and its dialectic versions) was used by many Tasmanian tribes before invasion as the collective noun for "Aborigines." Greg Lehman, *Island*, no. 79 (1999), 19.

5. The surviving Aboriginal people who had not been assimilated into colonial society after the Black War were increasingly considered a hazard and a nuisance to expanding settlement when they acted in self-defense and retaliation for loss of land and lives.

6. The determination of Aboriginal people, women in particular, to survive in Tasmania is exemplified by one of the few surviving Aboriginal traditions. "Maireener," a custom of making shell necklaces by women, particularly on the Bass Strait Islands, is described by Aboriginal writer Greg Lehman as "a sacred practice, a ceremony unbroken by the invaders." Lehman, *Island*, no. 79, 13.

7. See Reynolds, *Fate of a Free People*, 7–9.

8. See Cassandra Pybus, *Community of Thieves* (Port Melbourne, Australia: William Heineman, 1991). Despite the political influence of humanitarian and missionary organizations to recognize Aboriginal land rights, in Australia in general and Tasmania in particular there has never been a land treaty between Indigenes and colonizing forces. See Henry Reynolds, *The Law of the Land* (Ringwood: Penguin, 1996), 97–99. *The Draft Document for Reconciliation* that is under discussion with a view to including it in the changes to the national constitution as part of the Federation Celebrations in January 2001, will be the first "treaty" to be incorporated as an official document in Australia. This document is being drafted through nationwide consultation meetings by Aboriginal and white citizens "to help heal the wounds of our past so that all Australians can go forward together." Evelyn Scott, [Aboriginal] Chairperson of the Council for Reconciliation, foreword to *Finding Common Ground: Towards a Document for Reconciliation*, Council for Aboriginal Reconciliation, July 1999.

9. Lehman, *Island*, no. 79, 11.

10. In May 1997 the "Bringing Them Home Report" of the Stolen Generation

shocked the nation when it was released by the Human Rights and Equal Opportunity Commission. In response, many thousands of Australians have sent messages of sorrow and apology to the Stolen Generation and pledged to work for reconciliation and justice. All but two state parliaments (Queensland and the Northern Territory) have formally voiced an apology. Despite continued pressure on the Prime Minister, John Howard, the federal government has expressed "regret" but not apologized. But as third-generation Stolen Generation victim, feminist, and writer Sally Morgan says, "For my grandmother, [an apology] would be a meaningless gesture because the loss was too great. When I wrote *My Place*, we thought Nan had only one child. We've since found out that she had at least six children and they were all taken away. So I think for people like my grandmother there's nothing that could compensate for that scale of loss." Sally Morgan, *Weekend Australian*, October 23–24, 1999, 25; *My Place* (Fremantle: Fremantle Arts Center Press, 1987). See also Peter Read, *A Rape of the Soul So Profound: The Return of the Stolen Generations* (St. Leonards: Allen and Unwin, 1999).

11. The fight to have the land handed back has been long and difficult. In the words of Palawa elder Ida West: "All I wanted to do was fight for the right to be there with the people and care for the spirits and the land." Ida West, *Island*, no. 79 (1999), 46. See also Robyn Friend, *We Who Are Not Here: Aboriginal People of the Huon and Channel Today* (Huon Municipal Association, 1992).

12. On November 20, 1999, the Hobart daily newspaper *The Mercury* carried this caption: "Remains grabbed as black war explodes," and continued: "Tasmania's inter-community 'black war' took a new turn yesterday when an Aborigine opposing the Tasmanian Aboriginal Center confessed to breaking into a sacred keeping place and taking tribal remains."

13. See Miranda Morris, *The Pink Triangle: The Gay and Lesbian Reform Debate in Tasmania* (Sydney: University of New South Wales Press, 1995).

14. The Australian Broadcasting Commission (ABC).

15. See Sally Macarthur, "Feminist Aesthetics in Music: Politics and Practices in Australia." Ph.D. thesis, University of Sydney, 1997.

16. The international biannual arts festival held in Adelaide (South Australia) has sustained a strong reputation over forty years as a festival that endorses difference, diversity, new Australian works, and an internationally recognized standard of excellence.

17. Marilyn Lake, "Nation Gazing," *Australians' Review of Books*, October 1999; see also Marilyn Lake, *Getting Equal: The History of Australian Feminism* (St. Leonards: Allen and Unwin, 1999), 275.

18. In 1998 four Tasmanian women poets and I collaborated to make a CD of poems of landscape with improvisations. *Improvisation-image-voice*, robin records, P.O. Box 706, Sandy Bay, Tasmania, 7006.

19. Stroppy in this context means feisty and assertive.

20. Interview with Lyn Reeves in *Island*, no. 67 (Winter 1996).

21. Hélène Cixous, "Conversations," *Writing Differences: Readings from the Seminar of Hélène Cixous*, ed. Susan Sellers (London: Open University Press, 1988).

22. Performance poet Hazel Smith has coined this term for her own word-sound events which are splicings of her prefigured poems and "applied" improvisations in collaboration with hypermedia technology manipulated by improviser Roger Dean. See Hazel Smith and Roger Dean, *Improvisation, Hypermedia and the Arts* (London: Harwood, 1997); see also Hazel Smith, "Sonic Writing and Cross-Dressing: Gender, Language, Voice and Technology," in *Music and Feminisms*, ed. Sally Macarthur and Cate Poynton (Sydney: Australian Music Center, 1999).

23. *Will the Real Australia Please Stand Up . . . a Travelogue* was commissioned after Moss, Barcan, and Hunt (who had all at some time been residents of Tasmania) agreed to make an extensive journey together to remote areas of mainland Australia to collect material for the creative enterprise. The exhibition was first shown at the University of Tasmania Gallery (Launceston) in August 1996, followed by a repeat at the Contemporary Art Space of Tasmania (CAST) Gallery in Hobart in March 1997.

24. I have appropriated the term "becoming" from the writing of Deleuze and Guattari. I deploy "becomes" here as a signifier for process: an artefact that is not closed to interpretation. While I have reservations about Deleuze and Guattari's term "becoming woman," I believe they have given poststructuralist feminists some terms to help divulge their own. See G. Deleuze and F. A. Guattari, *Thousand Plateaus: Capitalism and Schizophrenia* (Minneapolis: University of Minnesota Press, 1987).

25. The thylacine, or Tasmanian tiger, was once widespread on the Australian mainland as recently as four thousand five hundred years ago. The thylacine survived in Tasmania until 1936 when it became extinct due to the imposition of a bounty by European settlers. Sarah Dawson, ed., *The Australian Encyclopedia* (Ringwood: Penguin, 1990).

26. These words, collected on the journey, came from the "last words scratched onto the empty canteen of a squatter called Coulthard" in 1858.

27. From "Cautionary Tales," published following the exhibition in *Tinfish*, no. 4 (1996), University of Hawai'i.

28. Here the listener could, through headphones, experience a sampling (parody of souvenirs) of poems with viola improvisations. The sounds of footsteps linked the readings of the poems.

29. Mulga (*Acacia aneura*) is the small tree dominant in the 125–250mm rainfall zone of mainland Australia. Dawson, *Australian Encyclopedia*.

30. Also published in *Australian Women's Book Review*, vol. 8, no. 2 (June 1996).

31. Feminist musicologist Susan McClary suggests that most music of the canon is constructed around masculine narratives. That is, gender marking is ev-

ident at many levels but particularly through the conventions of buildup (desire) and climax (closure). Second (less important?) movements of sonatas, concertos, and symphonies that are not as climactic and quieter, cadences that are "unfinished," and gestures such as ostinati (repeating patterns) have been named "feminine" within the canon. My point here is that music by women that is improvised (or "through-composed" without loss of the improvising intention) defies, parodies, and redefines these conventions, demonstrating, through nonclosure and collaboration, that diversity in women's creativity abounds. See Susan McClary, *Feminine Endings: Music, Gender and Sexuality* (Minneapolis: University of Minnesota Press, 1991), and andrea breen, "Creating a Place: Women, Land and Improvisation," Ph.D. thesis, University of Tasmania, 2000.

32. Unpublished poem used with permission from the author Sue Moss.

33. See Carol Bigwood, *Earth Muse: Feminism, Nature and Art* (Philadelphia: Temple University Press, 1993).

34. Judith Butler, */Excitable Speech/ A Politics of the Performative* (New York: Routledge, 1997), 8. As Butler suggests,

> The name one is called both subordinates and enables, producing a scene of agency from ambivalence, a set of effects that exceed the animating intentions of the call. To take up the name that one is called is no simple submission to prior authority, for the name is already unmoored from prior context, and entered into the labor of self-definition. The word that wounds becomes an instrument of resistance in the redeployment that destroys the prior territory of operation. Such a redeployment means speaking words without prior authorization and putting into risk the security of linguistic life, the sense of one's place in language as it calls into question the linguistic survival of the one addressed. Insurrectionary speech becomes the necessary response to injurious language, a risk taken in response to being put at risk, a repetition in language that forces change.

Butler, */Excitable Speech/*, 162.

35. According to Pierre Bourdieu, life's experiences "are internalised as second nature and so forgotten as history [that the habitus is] the active presence of the whole part of which it is a product." In other words, the subject is formed through an accumulation of tacit and conscious moments; we embody our experiences. (Habitus comes from the Latin, meaning "bodily constitution.") See Pierre Bourdieu, *The Field of Cultural Production: Essays on Art and Literature* (Cambridge: Polity Press/Basil Blackwell, 1993).

36. As one reviewer of the performance text suggests, "Plundered M/others provides thought-provoking material, which on many levels provides readers with opportunities to practice lateral reading skills." Janis Laming, *Australian Women's Book Review* (December 1996). Sue Moss, *Motherlode* (Melbourne: Sybylla Feminist Press, 1996).

# Chapter 8

# Feminism, Nationalism, and the Japanese Textbook Controversy over "Comfort Women"

## *Yoshiko Nozaki*

In 1993, "women's human rights" were recognized at the World Conference on Human Rights in Vienna, resulting in the "Declaration of the Elimination of Violence against Women." In 1994, the International Conference on Population and Development in Cairo recognized the reproductive rights of women, and the 1995 World Conference on Women in Beijing included the issue of sexual rights of women in its report. At these UN conferences, the wartime rape and abuse of women was viewed as constituting (sexual) war crimes. The participants of these conferences were well aware of what was happening in places such as Bosnia and Rwanda, and it was in that connection that the issue of "comfort women" became a constant focus of discussion.[1]

The existence of comfort facilities and comfort women during the Asia-Pacific War (1931–1945) has not been a secret. In fact, at the end of the war the Allied Forces, led by the United States, took many comfort women into custody as POWs. However, although the Allied Forces knew that many of the women had been forced to work in the comfort facilities, they did not view the matter as a war crime requiring the prosecution of the Japanese involved. (Except for two cases—one involving Dutch women in Indonesia, and the other Guam female residents, no further investigation was conducted.)[2] The issue remained by and large unrecognized in postwar Japan, in spite of a hard-fought struggle over the national memory—in particular, "the official wartime history" as taught to Japanese schoolchildren—for many years.[3]

Many Japanese writings on war memories referred to comfort women, known as *ianfu* in Japanese. They were Japanese and non-Japanese women who "comforted" Japanese officers and soldiers on the front as well as in occupied territories during the Asia-Pacific War. Some comfort facilities were privately run (and supervised by the military), others built and directly managed by the military.[4] In his memoirs, Japan's former prime minister Yasuhiro Nakasone, a political ally of Ronald Reagan, mentioned his involvement in building comfort facilities in Borneo when he was a young navy officer. He wrote about it rather proudly:

> [The troop I commanded was] a big one consisting of three thousand men. Soon [after the occupation of the island it turned out that] there were some who raped the native women and some who indulged in gambling. In some cases I built comfort facilities for these men, with considerable effort.[5]

In the 1990s the Japanese military comfort women system came to be seen as one of Japan's major war crimes. The issue became a major site of political as well as educational struggle, as feminists and progressives put the question of Japanese imperialism, particularly as expressed in the military's sexual slavery, on the national and international agenda. In this chapter I examine how South Korean and Japanese feminists as well as teachers engaged in peace and justice education (who did not necessarily self-identify as feminists) challenged nationalist narratives of the nation.[6]

## *The Emergence of a New Meaning of Comfort Women*

South Korean feminist activism was one of the major forces that helped to place the issue of military comfort women on the international human rights map. In the struggle for democracy that took place in the 1980s in South Korea, the women's movement gained considerable strength. Having successfully protested against police sexual abuse of women political prisoners, and having developed a network to support the women raped or abused, South Korean feminists gradually moved on to direct their attention to the issue of comfort women. In 1990, Yun Chung-ok, a Professor at Ewha Womans University, published a series of reports in a major South Korean newspaper based on her interviews with surviving former comfort women living in Japan, Thailand, and Papua New Guinea.[7] The timing coincided with the issue of women's human rights, including the wartime violation of those rights then being raised by the international women's movement.[8]

In May 1990, the planned visit of Roh Tae-woo, then President of South Korea, triggered intense South Korean public debate regarding Japan's accountability for its colonial rule of Korea. Those who had lost their family members in the war voiced their opposition to the president's visit to Japan. In their view, a visit by Roh would be appropriate only if the Japanese government first apologized and paid compensation for war damages. This strong opposition indicated that ordinary people in South Korea felt that the issue of war and colonialism was still unresolved.[9] A number of women's organizations also requested that Japan apologize and pay compensation for the comfort women. The issue of military comfort women showed signs of becoming a "national" issue— rather than a "women's" issue—for South Korea.[10]

In June 1990 an event took place in Japan that further enraged South Koreans. During a session of the House of Councilors' budget committee, the administration headed by Prime Minister Toshiki Kaifu, who was then a member of the Liberal Democratic Party (hereafter LDP, Japan's ruling party since 1955), dismissed a request for an investigation of the comfort women issue made by a Diet member of the Japan Socialist Party (hereafter SP), then the major opposition party. In its response, the administration stated that private business (traders) had been the perpetrators, suggesting that there had been no involvement by the state and its military during wartime.

Upon receiving the news, in November the South Korean women's organizations sent an open letter to Prime Minister Kaifu, demanding Japan's recognition of the facts, an apology, compensation, and the development of appropriate history education in its schools. They soon formed the Korean Council for the Women Drafted for Sexual Military Slavery by Japan (with Yun Chung-ok as the chair), a group specifically focused on the issue. In August 1991, Kim Hak-soon came forward to give her name as one of the comfort women—making her the first Korean former comfort woman residing in either North or South Korea to reveal herself as such in public.[11] On December 6, 1991, joined by three others, Kim filed a lawsuit against the Japanese government with the Tokyo District Court, asking for an apology and compensation.[12]

A number of feminist groups, such as Military Comfort Women Issue Uriyosong Network, were formed in Japan around the time to support Kim's lawsuit (and forthcoming cases). Some existing women's organizations, such as the Asian Women's Association (Ajia no Onnatachi no Kai, an organization founded by feminist journalist Yayori Matsui), also began to work on the issue.[13] At that point, the Japanese government, still in denial of the military and the state's involvement, refused to begin any investigation.

The Japanese media responded to Kim's coming out by criticizing the government for not confronting the issue. The media response included TV coverage featuring Kim and her accounts of being forced to become a comfort woman. Yoshiaki Yoshimi, a specialist in Japanese wartime history, was among those who were moved by Kim's testimony. He recalled that he had once come across official documents that could prove the involvement of the Japanese state and its military in the establishment of comfort women facilities. Yoshimi then returned to the archives in the library of the Defense Department and found the wartime official notification issued by the military that clearly showed the Imperial Army was involved in setting up the comfort women facilities and recruiting the women (though the kind of involvement and its extent were still in need of further study).

Yoshimi's findings were reported in *Asahi Shinbun*, a major Japanese newspaper, in early January 1992. The Japanese government then had no choice but to admit to military involvement (but not to the point that the women had been "taken by force"). Prime Minister Kiichi Miyazawa (of the LDP) apologized to South Korea when he visited there later that month. In 1993, the Japanese government conducted a hearing of testimonies given by fifteen Korean former comfort women in Seoul. This hearing was conducted without the partnership of the Korean Council for the Women Drafted for Sexual Military Slavery by Japan.[14] Nonetheless, it yielded sufficiently compelling evidence for the government to admit that many women had been taken and made to work in the system involuntarily.

On August 4, 1993, Yohei Kono, then chief secretary of the Cabinet, in a government statement published as an informal talk, spoke of the "direct and indirect involvement" of the (Imperial) Japanese Force in the establishment and administration of comfort facilities. He proceeded to describe the various kinds of "coercion" (*kyosei*) the women faced:

> [I]t became clear that the recruitment of the comfort women was done primarily by traders meeting the requests of the military. Even so, there were a number of cases in which the women were gathered involuntarily against their will, through the use of honeyed words and coercion. Moreover, in some cases, government authorities were directly involved in the matter.[15]

Kono proceeded to state that "the lives [of the women] in the comfort facilities, being held in those forced conditions, were heart-rending." He referred to the government's "feeling of apology and reflection" for comfort women "who received physical and mental injuries that cannot heal," and expressed "Japan's firm determination" to remember the historical facts of Japan's wrongdoing during the war, in order not to repeat them. As he put it:

> We would like to look straight at this kind of historical truth as a lesson of history rather than to avoid it. Through historical research and education, we keep remembrance of these issues for the ages, and will never repeat the same faults.[16]

The Kono statement, while constituting a step toward the recognition of Japan's violation of women's human rights during the war, was contradictory at best, and in several key points. First, it still suggested that "traders" were the main perpetrators (the implication being that state involvement was largely "indirect"). Second, it represented the ethnic and national backgrounds of the non-Japanese comfort women as being primarily Korean, even though "the feeling of apology" was expressed for "the comfort women of any origin" (e.g., Chinese, Taiwanese, and Indonesian). In fact, no hearings had been conducted to hear all voices across Asia and no plan had been formed. Third, it "express[ed] a feeling of apology and reflection," but it fell far short of specifying governmental policies that would follow. It did not, for example, refer to any further investigation. Nor did it recognize the matter as a war crime, which would have required plans for compensation. It laid out no plans for future preventive measures. None of this was coincidental, since the government's use of the phrase "a feeling of apology" had sometimes been used as a euphemism to avoid accepting legal and political responsibility.[17]

In subsequent years, the contradictions, in particular those concerning government responsibility, became more sharply divisive and contested, as the Japanese, feminist, and international struggles for compensation for the women progressed. In July 1995, the government proposed to "support" the lives of former comfort women through a foundation called the Asian Women's Friendship and Peace Foundation (hereafter the Asia Women's Fund). The foundation would take "moral responsibility" (but not officially compensate the victims) by raising funds and presenting money to the former comfort women of certain countries.

While the proposal met with considerable criticism, the Asia Women's Fund was soon established. To date, however, it has created more confusion than resolution. For example, it used the government's budget of approximately 500 million yen to cover costs such as advertising, while raising 460 million yen of private money.[18] Though the Japanese government continues to take a firm position against compensation for individual civilian victims, whether Japanese or non-Japanese, it has been increasingly involved in the operation of the foundation, including financing the foundation's health service programs Asia Women's Fund for the former comfort women. Thus, the foundation has been criticized both by nationalists for paying "compensation in practice," and by leftists for not paying "official compensation." Importantly, most of the former comfort women, in particular those who live in South Korea, have refused to take such "private charity money."

The Kono statement, while problematic, provided the basis upon which the issue could be addressed in education. For example, twenty-two (out of twenty-three) senior high Japanese history textbooks that included the topic of military comfort women passed the 1992–93 [and 1993–94] government textbook screenings and the textbooks of other social studies subjects taught at senior high level (for example, geography, world history, and contemporary society) followed the trend. All seven junior high history textbooks included the topic and passed the 1995–96 screening. By 1997, eighty textbooks in the senior high social studies subject areas (almost all the textbooks in these areas) included the subject.

Some textbooks read as follows:

> In order to supply the shortage of labor power, approximately 700,000 Koreans and 40,000 Chinese were forced to come to Japan and to engage in heavy labor in places such as coal mines. . . . [M]any women, such as Korean women, were sent to the front as war comfort women.[19]

> The violence against women by the Japanese soldiers became a problem, and the military came to establish comfort facilities. By inducing women— most of them Korean women—by various pretenses, or by taking [them] by force, it forced [them] to become war comfort women.[20]

The descriptions of senior high textbooks have generally been more concrete and detailed, though the reference to the number of women remains vague—a "great many" or an "enormous number." This is in part because the exact number has been unknown, and in part because the government asks the authors to write based on "proven facts."

## The Struggle over Textbooks in a Changing Political Landscape

In 1993 Japanese political parties entered a tumultuous period, in which the issue of comfort women and school textbooks became highly politicized. A series of corruption scandals involving many LDP members had been brought to light in the late 1980s and early 1990s. In the 1993 election, the LDP, the ruling party for four decades, was finally unable to hold a majority in the House.[21] On August 9, a coalition government was formed by seven parties, including the new parties of former LDP members and leftist parties such as the SP, on an anti-LDP platform. (Even though the SP thereby lost a large number of seats, it became a party in power.) Morihiro Hosokawa of the Japan New Party became the new prime minister. Immediately upon assuming the position, he said of the Asia-Pacific War: "I personally recognize it as a war of aggression, a wrong war."

In the face of this political change, the LDP's nationalist wing became more visible and vocal. The Kono statement of 1993, which was issued in the last days of sole LDP rule, had never been supported unanimously by its members. In the process of the LDP split, before the 1993 election some nationalists left the party to join the new parties, but those most vocal remained, forming a study group called the (LDP) Committee for the Examination of History. In its first meeting in October, committee members discussed launching a campaign to criticize school textbooks, as well as channeling financial assistance to right-wing scholars in order to disseminate a view of history that evaluated "The Great Asia War" (the Japanese term for the Asia-Pacific War used during the war) in a positive light. In their view, the comfort women issue was Japan's national issue.

In April 1994, despite his popularity, Prime Minister Hosokawa resigned because of suspicions of corruption. The new administration was headed by Tsutomu Hada. Hada was a former LDP member, and around the time of his succession to power, some parties, including the SP, left the coalition. This eventually resulted in the resignation of his administration en masse. On June 29, a new coalition government was formed by the LDP, the SP, and the Sakigake (another new party of former LDP members). Tomiichi Murayama of the SP headed the administration, but the real power was seized by the LDP (that is, the LDP returned to power). Murayama soon announced that the SP was abandoning its progressive positions on major postwar Japanese political issues, such as the U.S.–Japan Security Treaty, the constitutionality of Japan's Self-Defense

Force, and the national flag and national anthem. At the end of the year, through further breakups and consolidation, two large new parties emerged, both of which were "oppositional" (in the sense that they were out of power), while holding a more or less conservative platform.

In the redrawing of the political map, it appeared that what was really disappearing was the Japanese progressive political bloc, which had been in the opposition since the late 1950s. What was reemerging was the nationalist tide inside and outside the LDP. When the LDP returned to power in 1994, for example, the nationalist tide within the party seemed stronger than before. In the Murayama administration, several ministers repeatedly delivered speeches refuting the view of the Asia-Pacific War as a war of aggression, and some were fired for what they said. Moreover, some members of the new conservative opposition parties created a nationalist group called the "Coalition of Diet Members for the Dissemination of Accurate History."

In 1994–95, the Diet entered into negotiations on a Diet Resolution, to be issued as part of the commemoration of the fiftieth anniversary of "the end of the war" in apology for Japan's past aggression and colonialism against other Asian countries. Nationalist groups in the Diet worked together across party lines to block it, and right-wing (lobbyist) organizations, including the Japanese Association of Bereaved Families, collected 4,560,000 signatures to support their efforts. When it became clear that the resolution would succeed, the nationalist groups pressured the administration not to include in the resolution phrases such as Japan's "acts of aggression" and its "colonial rules." When the resolution was finally passed, it was self-contradictory, like the Kono statement (or worse), and left both leftists and nationalists unhappy.[22] The Asia Women's Fund, as described above, also exemplified the contradictions and compromises of the time.

The nationalist tide also became a presence in the general public discourse, in which "education" became a major battlefield. For example, in 1995 Nobukatsu Fujioka, a professor of education at the University of Tokyo, began to write a series of articles in a social studies education journal in which he argued for the "reform" of history education. Fujioka, who also established a group called the Liberal-View-of-History Study Group,[23] maintained that history education in postwar Japan had focused on Japan's "dark side" (such as the war atrocities Japan had committed in Asia), that it was "self-tormenting," and that it had thus hindered the development of a positive identity as Japanese in the younger generation. In essence, he attacked history education as taught from the peace and justice perspectives common among progressive teachers, and recommended that it be taught from the perspective of the "liberal view of history," which evaluated Japan's past conduct, such as its invasions of China and other Asian countries, in a more positive light.

In 1996, the public learned that all seven junior high history textbooks that included the topic of military comfort women had passed the textbook screening process. In response, Fujioka and others intensified their attacks on peace and justice education, and some publishers were willing to publish their arguments. For example, *SAPIO*, a popular magazine, published a special issue featuring "A Recommendation for War Education." Among the contributors to that issue was Yoshinori Kobayashi, a popular cartoonist who joined Fujioka's group. Kobayashi asserted that "comfort women were [doing their] business, and not taken by force," and he commended for their silence the Japanese women raped by Soviet soldiers who invaded northern China at the end of the war:

> [The Japanese women] were raped by Soviet soldiers in front of their husbands and families, which was a picture of hell, with agonies and cries. . . . Some women got pregnant and then were "self determined" [that is, they committed suicide], and some had abortions in the camps. . . . However, these Japanese women thereafter shut their mouths like shellfish, never talked about it and kept the matter only to themselves. Now it appears as if there were no such facts. Japanese women are amazing. I am proud of Japanese women like these.[24]

Kobayashi's nationalism was intended to silence the voices of the non-Japanese former comfort women by promoting the silence of Japanese women with similar experiences. It seems that such arguments succeeded in silencing Japanese women as well (and it is perhaps no coincidence that very few Japanese former comfort women have come out).

The LDP nationalists also criticized the textbooks and the textbook screening process of the Ministry of Education. The criticisms expressed by high-ranking LDP leaders included: "The comfort women were [conducting their] business. There was no case of women being taken by force"; "[The textbooks] include, as if they were historical facts, things that were not truths of history"; and "Too much emphasis is placed on the bad side of Japan." Later that year, Tadashi Itagaki, one of the most vocal nationalists among the LDP Diet members, took up the issue of school textbooks in a session of the budget committee of the House of Councils. Citing the article written by Fujioka, he requested that the Minister of Education order the removal of the description of comfort women from school textbooks. The minister refused to take such an action, insisting on the legitimacy of the existing textbook screening system.[25]

So far, despite repeated requests from some nationalist LDP Diet members, the Ministry of Education has maintained its position, and some LDP members have kept their distance from the nationalists (as of May 1998).[26] Kono, for example, has regarded the recent nationalist tide as the result of "extreme conservatives coming to have a feeling of crisis because the current of [politics] as a whole has . . . changed." In his view, "It would be the most appropriate [for us] to teach history correctly and make [our] way, confirming directly with ourselves that [we will] never repeat those wrongs again."[27] He has also addressed the younger Diet members on the need for men to "understand women's dignity, claims, and will," in order to build a gender-equal society, a "graceful nation."[28]

## Gender and Japan's Peace and Justice Education

Since the early 1990s, a number of books and education journals have featured the reports of progressive teachers from a range of backgrounds who have attempted to include the issue of comfort women in their classrooms. A major group that has taken up the issue has been that of progressive social studies teachers. For example, a 1992 issue of *Rekishi Chiri Kyoiku* (History-Geography Education), a journal published by the (Japanese) Association of History Educators, featured a report by a high school teacher on his curriculum development and his teaching of the issue.[29] The journal has continued to cover the topic, resulting in more than twenty articles, including ten reports from teachers (as of December 1998). National and regional study meetings regularly held by the association, as well as other occasions (for example, teachers' union study meetings), have provided further opportunities for concerned teachers to voice their views.

Before confronting the issue of comfort women, progressive teachers as a collective had already had long experience teaching about the Asia-Pacific War from peace and justice perspectives. In particular, since the 1970s, they had stressed the importance of teaching the role of Japan as perpetrator and wrongdoer in the history of the war. In so doing, they had sought to overcome the previous paradigm of wartime history teaching, which had tended to focus on the sufferings of ordinary Japanese citizens. Subsequently, they had developed several approaches to teach Japan's wartime history, including one which viewed the people(s) of Asia as having agency and as having actively resisted Japanese colonialism and aggression.

Interestingly, even among these teachers, there were some initial reservations regarding the need to include the issue of comfort women in their curriculum. Social studies teaching has been a male-dominated profession in Japan and the leaders of various study groups have more often than not been men.[30] While progressive in terms of race and ethnicity, they have been rather conservative with respect to gender. For example, when Kiyoko Ihara, a junior high social studies teacher, reported her teaching about the issue in 1993 at a regional study meeting, she received largely negative comments, including statements such as "[The comfort women issue] brings up the issue of sex [and sexual relations], which is difficult to deal with" and "The feeling of a woman teacher is not sufficient reason for venturing to include the topic.[31]

Male teachers have been more reluctant to address the issue of sex—perhaps because it forces them to confront an issue that would inevitably question their own sexism. Fumiko Kawada, a feminist writer who has written extensively on the comfort women issue, recalls her experience of joining a teachers' study group:

> After two junior high social studies teachers presented their reports on wrestling with [the issue of] "comfort women" in their classrooms, the participants were asked to give their thoughts and opinions in turn. [One of the male teachers said,] "My school is a boys' school, so . . ." [What he meant was] he was reluctant to deal with the issue of "comfort women" in his classes. . . . Why is there resistance to addressing the issue of "comfort women" [among teachers] in a boys' school? . . . That male teacher must be a conscientious teacher, since he joined the voluntary group for the study of teaching. Even so, though, he does not directly face up to the issues concerning sex, but seals them in a dark place, and leaves them there.[32]

This attitude has begun to change as the right-wing attack on textbooks has intensified. More and more teachers, both men and women, have begun to consider this subject an important step in their decades-long effort to address Japanese colonialism and war crimes. They have come to feel the need to overcome their reluctance and address the issue of sex and sexism, in order to promote peace and justice education.[33] By the mid-1990s, teaching about military sexual slavery had become not only legitimate, but was considered an ideal approach to peace and justice education.

For example, Mikiko Katsuji, a junior high social studies teacher, states her reason for including the topic in her curriculum as follows:

> To plan and teach about wartime military sexual slavery plays a major role in getting students to understand "war," not only from the perspectives of national interest or economic aspects, but also in concrete terms, from the positions of both wrongdoing and suffering.[34]

Katsuji also argues that learning that "the [comfort] women were deceived, taken by force, and raped by the Japanese military when they were at the same age [as the students are]" helps students to see "the [wartime] human rights violation of the women as a war crime."

Teachers of other subject areas have taken slightly different paths on their way to realizing the importance of addressing the issue of comfort women in their classrooms. Sumie Tsuzuki, for example, has been teaching the issue of comfort women in her health education class since 1992. When she first encountered the issue in a book on the topic twenty years ago, she recalls she was somewhat indifferent, thinking, "Japan did a terrible thing. But it was a thing of the old days, about which I can do nothing."[35] Her subsequent experience teaching students of diverse backgrounds caused her to be concerned with the issue of social justice, and brought her eventually to recognize the importance of looking at the issue of comfort women from a peace and human rights perspective. She believes the issue cannot be avoided in health education, in which learning the subjects such as the "human body" and "life" is crucial. So she includes it in the unit on sex education offered at the end of ninth grade health education.

Rumiko Harada, a junior high science teacher, learned of the issue in the late 1980s, when she saw a play representing the lives of Korean comfort women (in which her close friend played the role of a comfort woman). Moved to tears, she began to study the issue by reading several books she could find on the subject (as she recalls, she had not herself been taught about it in school). She soon came to recognize the need to teach the next generation about it, and took up the issue in her homeroom classes (which are generally nonacademic, geared toward dealing with various issues related to student lives, school-related or otherwise).

Harada also learned that some of her female students were raped during what is called "support dating" (*enjyo kosai*). Support dating, which has become a large social issue in recent years in Japan, occurs when men, usually of middle age, ask young girls, usually teenagers, to a date in exchange for some "support" (euphemism for money), and rape them.[36] Harada states:

On the point [that we have] a culture of sex in which men treat women as the objects of their sexual desire and violate women's human rights, it is not an exaggeration to say that nothing has changed in the value system concerning sex since the prewar period. Contemporary junior high school students live in that environment.[37]

Harada hopes that teaching about comfort women will allow her students to understand rape and other kinds of sexual abuse and exploitation as violations of their sexual rights. So far the students in her classes have been very receptive to the issue.

## Classroom Approaches and Student Responses

Curriculum planning is the selection of knowledge. Teachers, with little official support, usually develop their own curriculum and materials when teaching about comfort women. Their materials may consist of excerpts from books, slides, or videos. However, some teachers go beyond that. For example, when Tsuzuki, a teacher discussed above, began to teach about the issue, she used excerpts of Kim Hak-soon's testimony in newspapers and books. But as she taught her classes, she kept asking herself questions such as, "How did the former comfort women feel when they were coming out?" "What do they think of Japan now?" and "What are their lives like now?" She decided to visit and hear them directly. Since then she has visited former comfort women in South Korea several times, and has gradually come to feel closer to them, and has found them to be more and more important to her. She uses her first-hand knowledge of being with them in her classes.[38] Although Tsuzuki's case is perhaps unique, it is not uncommon among teachers with this level of commitment to participate in study meetings and tours, to which some former comfort women are invited.

The inclusion of a new topic inevitably requires the modification of the existing curriculum. Tsuzuki views the issue of comfort women as one that needs to be examined at least in terms of ethnic and gender relations. Ideally, she states, the topic should be taught in different classes: in social studies, in relation to the Asia-Pacific War and Japan's war crimes; in health education, in relation to sex education; and in homeroom classes, in relation to human rights and peace education. In her view, it is extremely important for teachers to accumulate a sufficient variety of teacher-planned curricula examples. The health education curriculum she has developed (with other teachers) for grades seven through nine includes sex education in each grade. The curriculum includes topics such as the development of the body, sex and reproduction, pregnancy and delivery, abortion and contraception, sexual diseases, AIDS, sexual relationships and abuse, the commodification of sex, and sexual violence in war. Her students spend two hours on the last topic, examining it through the experience(s) of comfort women.[39]

Curriculum decision making also involves the allocation of time. When social studies teachers attempt to teach about comfort women, they usually find little room for the subject in the existing curriculum. Tadaaki Suzuki, a junior high social studies teacher, sees the existing curriculum as failing to meet the demands of his students, who wish to know Japan's wartime history in greater depth. The curriculum of his school (drawn up in accordance with the *Instructional Guidelines* written and published by the Ministry of Education) suggests that eight hours of teaching be allocated to the history from the 1930s to 1945, including the economic depression, Japan's invasion of China, and events leading up to World War II. Suzuki has developed his own plan, which allows him to use twenty hours for the entire unit, by reducing the allocation of hours here and there in other units. In particular, his plan enables him to spend four hours on the war atrocities Japan committed in China and other Asian countries, including the Nanjing Massacre, Unit 731, the massacre of the Chinese population in Singapore, forced labor, and comfort women.[40]

Nontraditional instructional methods are also used. Takuji Yoshida, a high school politics and economics teacher, supplements his traditional mass teaching methods with a theme-learning approach in which he lists fifteen themes, from which he asks his twelfth-grade students to choose one. Within the theme of their choice students are expected to find a specific topic to study and present to their class. Every year, in Yoshida's experience, students who choose the theme of "Japan and Asia" present the comfort women issue in about half the classes he teaches (another topic that appears often is the Nanjing Massacre). Presentations are followed by a discussion session. Presenters usually come prepared with answers to questions they anticipate will be raised.[41]

In terms of their students' responses, teachers for the most part have reported good results. Their reports indicate that some common reactions and views have emerged among students working through the issue: first, the students were greatly shocked by the stories and testimony of comfort women and by the fact that the perpetrators were the wartime Japanese government and military (and in a broader sense Japanese soldiers, that is, ordinary Japanese). Second, they soon came to understand the issue as one that remains unresolved, and for that reason an important contemporary matter about which they have to think. After five hours of classes on the subject, for example, a sixth-grader in Masao Yamada's class stated:

> I had thought that we [the younger generation] were not involved, since the people of the old days were the ones who did it, but [after the class] I thought we were involved since we [belonged to] the same [group], Japanese.[42]

Many students also recognize the need for an apology and compensation from the Japanese government, and further, they feel the issue needs to be included in school textbooks, wishing to know more about the facts. For example, a junior high school student in Suzuki's class (discussed above) stated:

> What the Japanese government should do now is first to disclose all the data and sources concerning the war comfort women, and then apologize. . . . Japan has given economic aid and so on [to Asian countries], but I want it to do this [the disclosure and apology] first. The other day, there was a minister who said "there was no Nanjing Massacre." [This] is very disappointing to me.[43]

In a survey Suzuki conducted after implementing his lesson plan, many of his students singled out Japan's war atrocities as the topic about which they desired to learn more.

## Conclusion

The Japanese imperial project involved a myth of Japanese racial superiority over the Asians they colonized. To this extent, education remains central to overcoming of racialist and masculinist narratives of the Japanese nation. While some Japanese teachers initially resisted including the topic of comfort women in teaching their courses, the nationalist attacks on peace and justice education and school textbooks motivated reluctant teachers to confront their own sexism, and to transform the school curriculum by teaching wartime history that sometimes centered on the experiences of Korean women suffering under Japanese imperialism. The struggle over Japanese national narratives exemplifies one way that feminist and nonfeminist teachers can be included in projects that can be considered feminist and antiracist in their objectives.

In the 1990s, the appearance and voice(s) of former comfort women shot through the imaginary national unity of both South Korea and Japan and led us to inevitable intersections of nationalism and feminism. A new meaning associated with the issue of comfort women—which represented the matter as one of many Japanese war crimes and human rights violations during the war years—clearly pointed to the gendered and ethnicized construction of "nation." As its new significance came to gain some legitimacy, however, Japanese right-wing nationalists, including politicians, journalists, and scholars, launched a series of counteroffensives. What Joan Wallach Scott calls the "politics of history"—that is, the play of forces involved in the construction and implementation of meaning associated with past events—has intensified.[44]

Japanese politics and policies of the 1990s on unresolved issues of the war have been the products of compromise, and therefore remain contradictory at best. How one evaluates the politics and policies of the period depends on how one assesses such compromise and contradiction. Interestingly, those at both ends of the political spectrum—nationalists and critical leftists (including many feminists) who did not move to the center—have been the most incisive critics of the current policies. Although the critical left has a valid point in my view when it contends that the important principles underlying Japan's war responsibility and official compensation should not be sacrificed to practical political compromise, it is also clear that the nationalists have been taking advantage of the confusing situation. Japanese feminists—activists or academics—need to find ways to participate fully in the process of compromise, while honoring our commitment to bringing justice to the unresolved issues of war, including the issue of comfort women.

Despite the great advances made by teachers in the 1990s concerning the subject of comfort women, the major problem they face has remained—the Japanese government's lack of real interest in teaching about the issue. While maintaining its position for the inclusion of the topic in history textbooks, the government has done very little to promote and support the kinds of teaching efforts discussed above. For example, had it been serious, the government could have suggested several substantial changes in the existing preservice and in-service teacher training programs, and in the existing social studies and history education curricula. However, almost no such suggestion has been made in either area (or in the related areas of educational and curriculum policy).

The majority of new teachers, including social studies teachers, enter the field without sufficient training to confront unresolved issues of war, including that of military sexual slavery. For those who are already in the profession and wish to include these issues in classrooms, their school districts typically offer no in-service training, or if they do, such training sometimes adopts a nationalist or militarist perspective. Moreover, the existing curricula are already packed and leave little room for the incorporation of new topics of any kind. Many concerned teachers have revised their courses in order to include the subject of comfort women (and other war-related topics), even though schools and school districts do not always welcome the modification of traditional curricula.

### ACKNOWLEDGMENTS

I am grateful to France Winddance Twine, Kathleen Blee, Michael Apple, Eri Fujieda, Yuki Tanaka, Hiro Inokuchi, Judith Perkins, and Sylvan Esh for their encouragement, criticisms, and editorial assistance.

### NOTES

1. The term "sexual slavery" would be more accurate than "comfort women." In this paper, however, I generally employ the latter term because it has been the one most often used. The terminology has been controversial in Japan. The term *jugun-ianfu* ("war comfort women") was once used commonly, but recently the term *gun-ianfu* ("military comfort women") has come to be seen as more suitable. These terms also appear in this chapter, depending on the context.

2. Toshiyuki Tanaka, "Naze Beigun wa Jugun Ianfu Mondai o Mushi Shitanoka" (Why Did the U.S. Forces Ignore the Issue of War Comfort Women?), *Sekai*, no. 627 (1996): 174–83, and no. 628 (1996): 270–79.

3. Yoshiko Nozaki and Hiromitsu Inokuchi, "Japanese Education, Nationalism, and Ienaga Saburo's Court Challenges," *Bulletin of Concerned Asian Scholars*, vol. 30, no. 2 (1998): 37–46. See also Yoshiko Nozaki, "Textbook Controversy and the Production of Public Truth: Japanese Education, Nationalism, and Saburo Ienaga's Court Challenges." Ph.D. dissertation, University of Wisconsin, 2000.

4. Some women were paid, others were not. A clear distinction between the two is problematic, however, since in either case women experienced severe gender and sexual oppression.

5. Yasuhiro Nakasone, "Nijusansai de Sanzen'nin no Soshikikan" (The General Commander of Three Thousand Men at the Age of Twenty-Three), in Takanori Matsuura, *Owarinaki Kaigun* (The Navy That Never Ends) (Tokyo: Bunkahoso Kaihatsu Senta, 1978), 98.

6. This chapter can only refer to a few of the great number of volumes and articles on the subject. See the *Bulletin of Concerned Asian Scholars*, vol. 36, no. 4 (1994), for a list of publications dealing with this topic and the featured article, Kazuko Watanabe, "Militarism, Colonialism, and the Trafficking of Women: 'Comfort Women' Forced into Sexual Labor for Japanese Soldiers." See also *positions east asia cultural critique*, vol. 5, no. 1 (1997), which is a special issue entitled "The Comfort Women: Colonialism, War, and Sex." Recent significant publications include: Laura Hein, "Savage Irony: The Imaginative Power of the Military Comfort Women in the 1990s," *Gender and History*, vol. 11, no. 2 (1999): 336–72; Maria Henson, *Comfort Woman* (Lanham: Rowman and Littlefield, 1999); Yuki Tanaka, *Comfort Women: What Our Fathers Did Not Tell Us* (New York: Routledge, forthcoming); and Yoshiaki Yoshimi, *Military Comfort Women*, trans. Suzanne O'Brien (New York: Columbia University Press, forthcoming).

7. The Korean names in this chapter follow Korean name order.

8. For further discussion, see, for example, Yayori Matsui, *Onna-tachi ga Tsukuru Ajia* (The Asia That Is Built by Women) (Tokyo: Iwanamishoten, 1993), 194–205.

9. In 1965 South Korea and Japan had concluded an agreement in which, in essence, South Korea had renounced its claim to compensation in exchange for Japan's economic aid. South Korea, at that time governed by a dictatorship, ratified the agreement despite strong opposition from across its population, including students.

10. This "nationalist" development had certain consequences, including less concern among South Koreans about unequal gender relations in South Korea. See Yeong-ae Yamashita, "Kankoku Joseigaku to Minzoku: Nihongun 'Ianfu' Mondai o Meguru 'Minzoku' Giron o Chushinni" (South Korean Women's Studies and Nation: On the Discussion of "Nation" in the Issue of Japanese Military "Comfort Women"), *Jyoseigaku* 4 (1996): 35–58.

11. In the next few years, approximately two hundred Korean former comfort women followed in Kim's steps. To be sure, there were a few Korean former comfort women who had come out before Kim, but they did not have a strong impact either because of the timing of their statements, or because they chose to remain anonymous.

12. As of January 1999, a total of six suits had been filed in Japanese court. See *Pacific Rim Law and Policy Journal*, vol. 8, no. 1 (1999), which features Etsuo Totsuka, "Commentary on a Victory for 'Comfort Women': Japan's Judicial Recognition of Military Sexual Slavery," and Taihei Okada, "The 'Comfort Women' Case: Judgment of April 27, 1998, Shimonoseki Branch, Yamaguchi Prefectural Court, Japan."

13. For a list of organizations, see the *Bulletin of Concerned Asian Scholars*, vol. 36, no. 4 (1994): 16.

14. Because of the Japanese government's desire to end the investigation once and for all, the organization refused to cooperate with the hearing.

15. *Asahi Shinbun*, August 4, 1993, p. 2.

16. *Asahi Shinbun*, August 4, 1993, p. 2.

17. Yoshiaki Yoshimi, *Jugun Ianfu* (The War Comfort Women) (Tokyo: Iwanamishoten, 1995), 7–9.

18. Akira Maeda, *Senso Hanzai to Jinken: Nihongun "Ianfu" Mondai wo Kangaeru* (War Crimes and Human Rights: Thinking of Sexual Slavery by the Japanese Army) (Tokyo: Akashishoten, 1998), 24–25.

19. Haruo Sasayama et al., *Chugaku Shakai: Rekishi* (Junior High Social Studies: History) (Tokyo: Kyoikushuppan, 1997), 261.

20. Shozo Sakamoto et al., *Koto Gakko Nihonshi B* (Senior High Japanese History: B) (Tokyo: Daiichigakushusha, 1995), 322.

21. The LDP itself gained more seats, but the party had become smaller before the election because some core members had left to form new parties.

22. For a detailed account, see Haruki Wada, Koichi Ishizaki, and Sengo Goju-nen Kokkai Ketsugi o Motomeru-kai (The Group Requesting the Diet Resolution on Japan's War Responsibility), eds., *Nihon wa Shokuminchi-shihai o do Kangaete Kitaka* (How Japan Has Thought about Its Colonial Rule) (Tokyo: Nashinokisha, 1996).

23. Fujioka had been a progressive scholar of social studies education for decades, but he became a leader of right-wing scholars after studying at Rutgers University as a visiting scholar, around the time of the Gulf war.

24. Yoshinori Kobayashi, "Shin Gomanism Sengen, Dai Niju-yon Sho: Jugun Ianfu Kamatoto Masukomi o Utsu" (A New Arrogance Manifesto, chapter 24: Targeting the Feigned Innocence of the Mass Media on the Issue of Comfort Women), *SAPIO*, vol. 8, no. 15 (1996): 87.

25. Yoshifumi Tawara, "Ianfu" Mondai to Kyokasho Kogeki. From *The "Comfort Women" Issue and Attacks on Textbooks* (Tokyo: Kobunken, 1997), 10–24.

26. After completing this manuscript, the Japanese media reported that several junior high social studies textbooks eliminated the reference to comfort women in their latest editions. Although the exact causes were unknown, it seems that the publishers "voluntarily" removed it in order to avoid controversy.

27. *Asahi News*, March 31, 1997, 16.

28. Nihonno Zento to Rekishi Kyoiku wo Kangaeru Wakate Giin no Kai (A Group of Younger Diet Members Thinking about Japan's Future and History Textbooks), ed., *Rekishi Kyokasho heno Gimon* (A Question of History Textbooks) (Tokyo: Nihonno Zento to Rekishi Kyoiku wo Kangaeru Wakate Giin no Kai, 1998), 446–47.

29. The journal has been the primary progressive—or leftist—social studies education journal in Japan since its inception in 1953.

30. For example, as of 1998, approximately 31,500 teachers teach social studies at junior high schools (grades 7–9), and approximately 82 percent of them are men. See Mombusho (Ministry of Education, Japan), "Heisei 10-nendo Gakko

Kyoin Tokei Chose Hokokusho," in *Report on Statistical Research of Schoolteachers in the 1998–1999 Fiscal Year* (Tokyo: Okurasho Insatsukyoku, 1999), 8, 90.

31. Kiyoko Ihara, "Jugonen Senso: Jugun Ianfu wo Toriagete" (The Fifteen-Year War: Teaching about the War Comfort Women), *Rekishi Chiri Kyoiku*, no. 506 (1993): 89.

32. Fumiko Kawada, "Jyo: Chugakusei ni koso Oshietai 'Ianfu' Mondai" (Introduction: The Comfort Women We Would Like to Teach Especially to Junior High School Students), in Fumiko Kawada, ed., *Jyugyo "Jugun Ianfu": Rekishi Kyoiku to Sei Kyoiku karano Apurochi* (Teaching about "War Comfort Women": Approaches from History Education and Sex Education) (Tokyo: Kyoikushiryo Shuppankai, 1998), 10–11.

33. Hajime Sato, "'Ai, Jugun Ianfu' Hi no Sakebi" (The Cry of the Monument of Grief for "War Comfort Women"), *Rekishi Chiri Kyoiku*, no. 524 (1994): 120.

34. Mikoko Katsuji, "Ianfu Mondai wa Josei no Jinken Mondai" (The Issue of "Comfort Women" Is the Issue of Women's Human Rights), in Kawada, *Jyugyo "Jugun Ianfu*," 18.

35. Sumie Tsuzuki, "Heiwa Gakushu to Sei Kyoiku no Tsumikasane no nakade" (Through the Accumulation of Peace Education and Sex Education), in Kawada, *Jyugyo "Jugun Ianfu*," 48.

36. In many cases, the victims do not report the fact to the police. In some cases the girls continued to earn money through support dating.

37. Rumiko Harada, "Seiteki Jinken wo Oshieru Tema toshite" (As a Theme for Teaching about Human Sexual Rights), in Kawada, *Jyugyo "Jugun Ianfu*," 35.

38. Tsuzuki, "Heiwa Gakushu to Sei Kyoiku," 48–49.

39. Tsuzuki, "Heiwa Gakushu to Sei Kyoiku," 50–59.

40. Tadaaki Suzuki, "Junanasai no Haru o Kaeshite: Jugonen Senso to 'Jugun Ianfu' Mondai" (Return the Spring of Life of Seventeen-Year-Olds: The Fifteen-Year War and the Issue of "War Comfort Women"), in Kawada, *Jyugyo "Jugun Ianfu*," 63–70.

41. Takuji Yoshida, "Kokosei ga Tsukuru 'Jugun Ianfu' Gakushu" (Learning of "War Comfort Women" Developed by High School Students), in Kawata, *Jyugyo "Jugun Ianfu*," 146–55.

42. Masao Yamada, "Sei Kyoiku wo Dodai nisuete" (Based on Sex Education), in Norio Ishide et al., eds., *"Nihongun Ianfu" wo do Oshieruka* (How to Teach about "Japanese Military Comfort Women") (Tokyo: Nashinokisha, 1997), 35.

43. Suzuki, "Junanasai no Haru o Kaeshite," 77.

44. Joan Wallach Scott, *Gender and the Politics of History* (New York: Columbia University Press, 1988), 5.

PART III

*Coalitions at Work: Transgressive,*
*Transracial, Transnational*

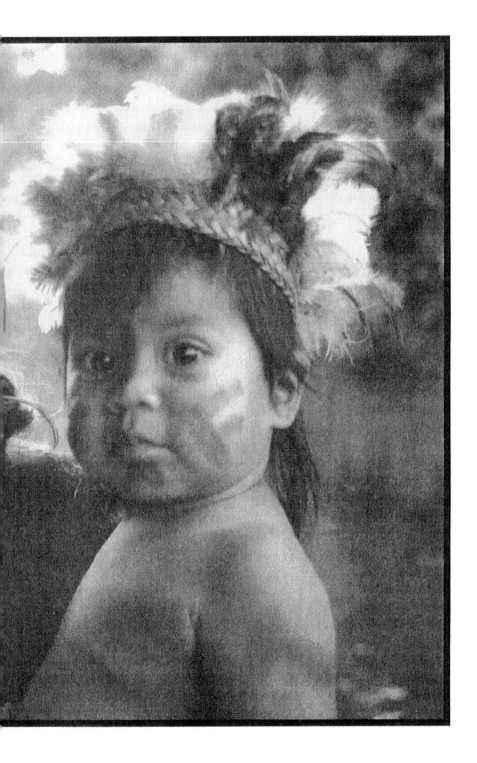

# Chapter 9

# Coalition Politics in Organizing for Mumia Abu-Jamal

## *Sohera Syeda and Becky Thompson*

Mumia Abu-Jamal, a journalist, radio commentator, author of *Death Blossoms: Reflections from a Prisoner of Conscience*, and a political prisoner is on death row in Pennsylvania.[1] We write as two people—a South Asian Muslim woman and a white professor of Sociology and African American Studies—who were members of a multiracial coalition at Wesleyan University in Middletown, Connecticut, that organized an all-Connecticut rally in support of Mumia Abu-Jamal in April 1996.[2] Our interest in community organizing for Mumia Abu-Jamal is based on our knowledge that protests outside the courtroom are significantly influencing the case. Without this work, the execution may well already have taken place. Mumia Abu-Jamal's eventual freedom will depend on a continually expanding national and international coalition of people who take this issue on as their own.

In this article we also examine the relationship between supporting Mumia Abu-Jamal and feminism. We write as women of different generations both of whom are interested in what it means to do coalition work from a multiracial feminist perspective. We are asking: Why are so many women leading the drive for a new trial, in local settings, such as the rally at Wesleyan University, as well as nationally and internationally? What makes using the term "feminism" in relation to this organizing tricky and yet, as we will argue, necessary? How is feminism involved (and not involved) in the campaign for a new trial and why is this a particularly relevant question in the 1990s? We suggest that feminists, among others, need to claim this issue—because the prison system is antiwoman, because political prisoners include men and women; because the escalation of the punishment industry ends up backfiring on people needing publicly funded education—including working-class people. And we need to find ways for women who do not identify as feminists and those who do to push each other forward, analytically and politically.

### Multiracial Organizing among Generation X: When Seeking Justice Is a Process

In the spring of 1996, a multiracial coalition of students at Wesleyan University organized a statewide rally in support of a new trial for Mumia Abu-Jamal. For most of the coalition members, this rally was their first chance to do multiracial organizing. Although many, if not most, had studied Bernice Johnson Reagon's now classic work, "Coalition Politics: Turning the Century," and many had worked interracially on campus, few had been able to see, in practice, why organizing across difference is crucial for building progressive political organizations.[3]

The origins of the rally at Wesleyan University began in a 1995 African American Studies Critical Race Theory Law Seminar, a course that chronicles race-conscious, progressive legal theory that has emerged since the civil rights movement.[4] A multiracial group of five students spent the semester researching the case of Mumia Abu-Jamal and analyzing how his case reflects larger issues about the U.S. prison system, police brutality, and class and race oppression. Through their research—an educational process made possible largely through the incorporation of methodologies developed by critical race theorists—the students became increasingly outraged by what they learned. As a relatively new field within legal thought, critical race theory emerged in the late 1970s in response to the backlash against the gains of the civil rights movement.[5] The goals of critical race theory include accounting for the impact of racism in American law, illuminating the intersection between race, class, and gender in law, and working toward what Mari Matsuda has termed a "principle of anti-subordination." For Matsuda, this principle is as fundamental to the U.S. constitutional legacy as are the ideas of property, equality, and due process.[6] Among critical race theory's many contributions is its use of "stories from the bottom," based on the understanding that these stories change what you see, how you analyze what you see, and the conclusions you can therefore reach.[7] Critical race theorists have published in a much wider range of publications than has been typical for legal scholars and they have brought to public consciousness legal debates historically left on library shelves and tied up in technical, esoteric language.

The students in the 1995 critical race theory seminar drew on approaches they saw modeled by the theorists they were studying. For example, to get to the "stories from the bottom" they drew on personal narratives by Mumia Abu-Jamal, Leonard Peltier, Assata Shakur, Angela Davis, and other political prisoners and used the Internet extensively to access first-hand accounts of those who witnessed and reported on daily trial proceedings. The students attended teach-ins and protest rallies and developed personal contacts with former Black Panthers, former political prisoners, investigative journalists, and others who support Mumia Abu-Jamal. By employing a historical and contextual analysis of legal doctrine, they became increasingly skeptical of the legal and academic principles of neutrality, objectivity, and color-blindness. Their research methodology and vision for the project was geared to resist the widespread misinformation and silence of the mainstream media regarding Mumia Abu-Jamal's case.

The students learned that Mumia Abu-Jamal had not received anything approximating a fair trial after being charged with the murder of a police officer, Daniel Faulkner, in 1981. During the trial, the police intimidated key witnesses for the prosecution and crucial evidence was mishandled and/or deliberately excluded from trial proceedings. Since his conviction for murder and death sentence in 1982, Abu-Jamal's lawyers and supporters have been working for a new and fair trial based on the fact that he did not receive adequate representation and that his political beliefs were used against him during the sentencing phase of the trial. In fact, they see Abu-Jamal's conviction as part of a long pattern of surveillance and harassment by the police. As an adolescent Abu-Jamal was a founding member and Minister of Information of the Philadelphia Chapter of the Black Panther Party. As a highly respected radio journalist, Abu-Jamal exposed police brutality against MOVE, a spiritual community and activist organization in west Philadelphia led by John Africa that is working for racial justice.[8] As a result of these activities, Abu-Jamal was deemed a "threat" to national security by the Philadelphia police department and the FBI. Like many other Black Panthers, he was placed on the FBI Security/ADEX Index.

Since his conviction, Mumia Abu-Jamal's work as a journalist and author, the movement-building efforts of MOVE, and the support of other prisoners' rights activists have helped keep his case alive. Several MOVE members established The International Concerned Family and Friends of Mumia Abu-Jamal, an organization that is at the center of the worldwide movement to free him. On June 2, 1995, however, Governor Thomas Ridge signed a death warrant setting an execution date for August 17, 1995.[9] Several heads of state (including Nelson Mandela, a former political prisoner himself), hundreds of well-known organizations, and nationally and internationally known activists, artists, and intellectuals have campaigned for a new trial for Abu-Jamal. In August 1995, Philadelphia trial court judge Albert Sabo issued an indefinite stay of execution without granting Abu-Jamal a new trial. During Post-Conviction Relief Act hearings before Judge Sabo between 1995 and 1997, Abu-Jamal's defense team systematically established a case of police misconduct, witness coercion, and fabrication of evidence during the original trial in Philadelphia in 1981. On October 29, 1998, however, the Pennsylvania Supreme Court denied Abu-Jamal's appeal for a new trial by negating the credibility of all new evidence while simultaneously upholding flawed prosecutory evidence as entirely truthful. Subsequent motions by the defense team to rehear aspects of the case were also denied. After defeat at the state level, Abu-Jamal's defense team has focused on changing the factual record to incorporate the extensive body of new evidence which sheds serious doubt on Abu-Jamal's guilt.[10, 11] On October 13, 1999, Governor Ridge signed a second death warrant setting an execution date for December 2, 1999.[12] On October 26, 1999, newly assigned Judge William Yohn granted a stay of execution on the basis of Abu-Jamal's recently filed habeas corpus appeal. The stay of execution is a temporary one and is valid until the Federal District Court in Philadelphia completes its review. Written arguments by prosecution and defense attorneys were filed in the district court in February 2000 and oral arguments began between March and May 2000. Abu-Jamal's defense team requested an evidentiary hearing to enter new evidence into the existing factual record.[13] According to defense attorneys and supporters, Abu-Jamal's case is now progressing on a "federal fast track" in which the appeals process narrows step by step just as the international movement mobilizes to obtain a new trial.

Why is Mumia Abu-Jamal the subject of massive national and international protest? Is there something unique to this case or to the city of Philadelphia itself that warrants such global attention to the workings of the American judicial system? Since the U.S. Supreme Court reinstated the death penalty in 1976, opponents have objected to the consistent pattern across the nation of racial bias inherent in this method of punishment. Studies reveal that for similar crimes, the odds of African Americans receiving the death penalty are four times greater than for any other defendant. Furthermore, decision-making power within the judicial system is held along starkly racial lines: 98 percent of district attorneys are white and predominantly male while only 1 percent is African American.[14]

Studies examining the racial politics of the death penalty in Philadelphia support the national trends of racial bias while highlighting some glaring inequities unique to the city itself. While Philadelphia holds only 14 percent of the state's population, more than half of the death sentences issued in Pennsylvania are from this city. Furthermore, 83 percent of death row inmates in the state are African American citizens from Philadelphia.[15] An exhaustive statistical study of death penalty cases in Philadelphia conducted by the Death Penalty Information Center in Washington, D.C., reveals,

> The race of the defendant is not supposed to influence whether a person is sentenced to death but in Philadelphia, it clearly does. Murders by blacks are treated as more severe and "deserving" of the death penalty because of the defendants' race. . . . Stated differently, in Philadelphia, the capital sentencing statute has operated as though being black was not merely a physical attribute, but as if it were one of the most important aggravating factors actually justifying the death penalty.[16]

The political atmosphere is so charged that Governor Ridge has signed seven times more death warrants between 1995 and October 2000 (208 warrants—63 white, 128 black, 16 Hispanic, and 1 Asian) than were signed by the three governors who preceded him (who, in total, signed 29 death warrants). All this while the Philadelphia and Pennsylvania bar associations called for a halting of executions until the state's death penalty system could be proven fair.

As the students at Wesleyan realized the urgency of the case and saw how much original material they had amassed, they decided to host a panel presentation that would be open to the entire Wesleyan community. The presentation, attended by over a hundred students, was the first substantial educational forum for the Wesleyan community about Mumia Abu-Jamal. As in critical race theory, the students saw it as their responsibility not only to examine the relationship between the law and racial power, but also to take steps to change it. Their forum, coupled with a research paper they completed and subsequently sent to several lawyers and activists, provided the first step—both in terms of substance and method—for further organizing on campus. The forum educated people in the community while illustrating ways in which research skills can be politically and ethically relevant.

When students and community activists at Yale University asked people at Wesleyan to participate in a rally in support of Mumia Abu-Jamal, many Wesleyan students already had some knowledge about the case. This background enabled us to quickly organize 125 students and caravan by car to the New Haven rally. When Wesleyan students arrived at Yale and realized we had brought most of the rally's participants, we knew that there was real potential to sponsor a rally ourselves. From that day forward, we began dreaming of a rally that would draw people from community organizations, churches, synagogues, universities, and high schools throughout Connecticut as well as from New York and Massachusetts.

Our hope was to establish a coalition which cut across race, class, occupation, religion, and sexuality. Such a goal meant publicizing how the campaign to free Mumia Abu-Jamal was everyone's issue. As an issue involving the prison system, we saw it as relevant to all taxpayers and their children since tax dollars finance the buildup of the prison system. As an issue involving political prisoners, we saw it as relevant to all people concerned with freedom of speech, creed, and association. Therefore, we saw Mumia Abu-Jamal's case as particularly pertinent to those who have been denied these freedoms—gay men and lesbians, Jews, Muslims, atheists, and people of color. From the outset, we were clear that the racial, ethnic, religious, and sexual makeup of the rally itself would reflect the coalition of people organizing it. We knew that what Ian Haney Lopez refers to as people's "community ties" would have a direct relation to those they network with and eventually have success in bringing to the rally.[17] It was crucial, then, that diversity be embedded in the very structure of our organization.

We envisioned the organizing at Wesleyan as requiring three interrelated stages: outreach, in-reach, and the rally itself. During the outreach stage, the multiracial coalition created committees (publicity, speakers, million-letter campaign, fund-raising, and the like) as a way of incorporating everyone present. The coalition intentionally took steps to ensure that people of color, working-class people, lesbians, and gay men were in key positions on each of the committees. At each meeting, we also noted which communities were and were not well represented. We then made one-on-one contacts with individuals and groups who were not yet at the meetings. We were especially encouraged when the Wesleyan-Middletown Coalition for Police Accountability and Racial Justice, an organization that had been formed in response to the illegal harassment and detainment of four African American students by Middletown police in the fall of 1995, decided to join with the Wesleyan Coalition in Support of Mumia Abu-Jamal to organize the rally. At the end of our organizing effort, our coalition had grown to approximately sixty students who were African American, Asian, Latino/a, white, male, female, Jewish, Muslim, Bahai, Christian, secular, gay, bisexual, lesbian, and heterosexual.

As we put much of our energy into building a multiracial coalition from within, we also began contacting people throughout New England to encourage them to attend the coalition meetings and the rally. We wanted a real cross section of the Wesleyan community to attend the rally—sorority sisters as well as athletes, economics majors as well as African American Studies students, cafeteria workers as well as library administrators. In our networking outside Wesleyan, we planned a similar course, emphasizing how freedom for Mumia Abu-Jamal was everyone's issue—the mechanic at the Middletown Valvoline oil change center, the owner of the local Italian-owned pizza shop, and the students at community and four-year colleges. To do this outreach, Wesleyan coalition members spoke on several radio programs and cable TV programs, at individual community meetings, and to many individuals one-on-one. Retrospectively, however, we believe our outreach beyond Middletown and Wesleyan was our greatest weakness. Most of the six hundred people who attended the rally (with the exception of the speakers and their supporters) were from the local area. This reality speaks to the difficulty of mobilizing people in general in the 1990s. It also reflects minimal transcollegial networks, a long history of strained town-gown relations between people in Middletown and nearby towns, and the very limited involvement of Wesleyan faculty who might have helped us do regional outreach.

What we did do well, however, was to spread the word about the event to individual communities that might not have heard about it otherwise. This step was made possible as coalition members incorporated their organizing into their personal lives. One white South African student coalition member, for example, convinced her journalist mother to write an extended editorial in her widely circulated hometown Rochester newspaper. Two African American women students convinced their high school youth groups and churches to hold educational forums on Mumia Abu-Jamal. Two Puerto Rican nationalist students solicited the support of the New York Congress of Puerto Rican rights.

While we worked to spread the word about the rally, we began the "in-reach" stage of the organizing. This included sponsoring a number of teach-ins on campus. We used a variety of teaching tools (films, discussions, dorm meetings, informational tables) and sponsored a workshop designed to allow coalition members to reflect upon their individual motivations for working on the issue and how they came to consider the issue their own. An African American woman explained how, when she was growing up, "survival" for her Bedford-Stuyvesant family meant putting all its energy into finding a way for her to attain an elite college education. In the process, her family sheltered her from many of life's harsh realities, including the depth of racism and classism. When four of her African American Wesleyan classmates were falsely arrested by Middletown police in the fall of 1995 she realized that, in her words, "I've been sleep walking for a long time." Awakened to the realities of survival beyond her own struggle, she began to understand Abu-Jamal's struggle as related to her own.

A Chinese American woman related the story of her brother's struggles in the Minneapolis public education system. Explaining that the principal at her brother's school wanted to transfer her brother to an "alternative" high school which was really a detention center, she noted, "They keep removing them until they don't exist in society any more." With young men of color comprising 90 percent of the high school dropouts in Minneapolis, the attempts by high school administrators to transfer her brother to a juvenile corrections facility were directly related to the escalation of the prison industry. Another coalition member, a white woman who grew up in Philadelphia, explained how the case of Mumia Abu-Jamal had served as a backdrop for her adolescent years. As the case was publicized around her—in newspapers, on television, and in conversations with teachers—she had been oblivious to the reality of racism. Although she went to school with Mumia Abu-Jamal's son, she had never registered the connections between his reality and her privilege. Working to free Mumia Abu-Jamal was a way to counteract what she termed her "willing and unwilling forgetting."

The connections people made between their personal lives and their political struggles went to the heart of our coalition work. It was through these narratives that we were able to know each other—and see each other eye to eye—in ways we might not have without the "in-reach" work. These connections helped us remember that justice has a face and that social movements derive from people connecting with each other across difference, one person at a time. Our attempts to see ourselves as embodied people—as people with life stories that had brought us to do justice work—paralleled the need to see Mumia Abu-Jamal as embodied. He is a man—not a symbol—a husband, father, grandfather, writer, and activist.

Our "in-reach" work also included making room to deal with conflict within the rapidly growing coalition by setting aside self-reflexive time during coalition meetings. This structure gave us a way to explore how organizing on behalf of a single cause effectively requires refusing to minimize or sideline differences in methods of communication and approaches to organizing. One particularly complicated and crucial conflict that we weathered during an early coalition meeting centered around ways of incorporating spirituality into the meetings and rally without making this spirituality Christian-based. At one of the meetings, an atheist Jewish student, Amanda Shurgin, voiced her frustration that we had held a prayer together delivered by an African American Methodist minister, Ian Straker, prior to departing for a Mumia Abu-Jamal rally in New Haven. Amanda was angry about the prayer because, even though the minister did not use phrases like "in Christ's name" or "as we pray to one God," the prayer still felt Christian-centered. After she raised her concern, the coalition held a lengthy discussion (that continued in various contexts for several weeks afterward as well). At issue was anti-Semitism and how leading a Christian prayer at a Christian-dominated university inevitably marginalized Jewish students (whose visibility at Wesleyan has historically required struggle). This reality was especially problematic because several committed coalition members were Jewish.

At the same time, some coalition members were concerned about ways to avoid anti-Semitism while maintaining a commitment to a spiritual focus in the organizing effort. Because Mumia Abu-Jamal is African American and a spiritual man, and black people have spearheaded much of the support for his freedom, some coalition members emphasized the need to keep the organizing, including the spiritual foundation, black-centered. Further, one of the coalition members (Becky) had recently returned from South Africa where prayer and singing were the heartbeat of people's everyday life—before and after meals, when people arrived at and departed from houses, in the morning and the late night hours.[18] Becky brought back from South Africa an organizing commitment to treat music, prayer, and drumming as equally important as speech, verbal protest, and legal writing. Another coalition member, Sohera, who is Muslim, explained that while at first she saw the Jewish woman's protest as divisive and irrelevant to the coalition's purpose, further thinking helped her realize that her reaction reflected a long history of having to keep quiet about her own faith. For all her life, Sohera had protected herself against Western stereotypical notions of Muslims as terrorists and fanatics by deemphasizing her own religious beliefs. When the Jewish student, Amanda, raised issues about the exclusivity of a Christian prayer, Sohera felt that this student should have simply coped with the prayer, despite her Jewishness, just as Sohera always had. Over time, Sohera realized that neither she nor Amanda should have had to silently accept the exclusivity of the prayer. A painful combination of anti-Semitism and internalized oppression on Sohera's part made it both difficult and necessary to sort this issue out.

The coalition members' many-layered reactions to the prayer specifically and issues of spirituality in general encouraged us to devise rituals at each meeting (and at the rally) that included input from the coalition members. These rituals included reading an excerpt from one of Mumia Abu-Jamal's essays, playing an audiotape of one of his interviews, reading an inspirational quote from an activist, teaching each other and then leading the group in chants, and opening and closing the rally with drumming. During one of our meetings following the rally, we talked about the time and energy we spent on "the prayer incident" and decided that concentrating on that conflict made room for other conflicts that had occurred throughout the planning for the rally. To hope that a coalition is multiracial and multicultural is one thing. To teach each other how to learn from and be accountable to each other is quite another. Throughout, we attempted to treat justice not only as swift and singular acts, evidenced in rallies and massive letter-writing campaigns, but also as a process sustained in the daily and small ways we see and treat each other.

As we worked to get to know each other as a coalition, we also got a chance to work closely with seasoned activists including George Edwards, Pam Africa, Susan Burnett, Ali Bey Hassan, Kathleen Cleaver, and others. The first time some of these activists attended one of our coalition meetings was a turning point in our organizing as their encouragement and suggestions buoyed our confidence considerably. As former Black Panther members, antiracist white activists, the editor of *Prison Legal News*, and other veteran activists applauded our efforts and took time out of their lives to come to our meetings, we knew we were on the right track. The intergenerational connections and our growing links with other student and community organizations situated our local effort within a larger historical context. It was through our connections with them that we were able to gain written statements of support from Sundiata Acoli and Mumia Abu-Jamal, whose generous letter was faxed to us before the rally. In his statement Mumia Abu-Jamal wrote:

> To the students and people at Wesleyan University on April 13, 1996. My deepest thanks and appreciation to the students of Wesleyan University and all those other people who have helped organize this wonderful all-state rally. I thank you all for your support and solidarity on my behalf and against the American way of Death. I am energized and deeply moved by this wonderful work on my behalf. You are the future and it seems we are in good hands. Ona Move! Long Live John Africa. Mumia.

Three of the African American Wesleyan students who had been falsely arrested in Middletown read Abu-Jamal's statement at the rally to draw links between those fighting police brutality, both inside and outside prison.

The actual rally, ten weeks in the making, was bittersweet. It was bitter because Mumia Abu-Jamal's statement had to be read by others, not himself. His absence was the hole at the heart of the rally. The rally was bitter too, as we realized that despite our best efforts, our coalition work had remained largely campus bound. The sweet parts of the rally, however, were many. The rally was, to our knowledge, one of the largest university-led efforts up to that point and the first to attempt to organize statewide. It was cosponsored by fifty-three organizations (at Wesleyan and in New England). Most of the speakers had driven from out of town and donated their time.[19] We held receptions before and after the rally for all the speakers so that they could meet each other and celebrate our presence together. The rally itself lasted two and a half hours, and included African drumming, twenty three-to-five minute speeches, chants, singing, and a fund-raising session. We set up tables to garner letters for the Free Mumia Coalition Million Letter Campaign (culminating in five hundred letters) and other progressive causes. In an effort to honor and appreciate those who had worked alongside us in our organizing, Ajua Campos, the Latino organization at Wesleyan, sponsored a feast after the rally. From the reading of personal statements written from within prison by Mumia Abu-Jamal and Sundiata Acoli, to the group sing-along of Bob Marley's Redemption Song at the postrally party, the coalition celebrated the work done and began to look forward to the work ahead of us.

One month later, several of us traveled to Washington, D.C., to be part of the community of people who delivered tens of thousands of letters to

Janet Reno to urge her to support a new and fair trial. As we embarked on this trip, we thought about how to ensure that organizing at Wesleyan would continue next year and how to avoid the fallout, inertia, and historical amnesia that is endemic to a nine-month-a-year college schedule. It was a challenge to keep the fire burning when so many of the organizers of the rally were seniors, and when the key faculty involved in the rally held temporary appointments at Wesleyan and left at the end of the academic year. The fragility of campus organizing caused by graduation and summers off is coupled by a dearth of classes that make room for research which spurs direct political action. Myths of intellectual objectivity continue to guard against praxis—theory and action. And yet, as several coalition members have said, after four years of reading about coalition politics in many of their classes, it was about time that they got a chance to see it actually happen, and to be a part of that process.

From the rally we learned many lessons about multiracial organizing. We learned that one-on-one communication is vital to create and sustain a multiracial coalition. Second, after we had done much of the groundwork for the rally, we began to feel that it had developed a life of its own. We, of course, had to follow through with the details before the rally. But many of us felt that a power much larger than the individual coalition members was helping us as we raised much more money that we had originally thought possible, found people who willingly traveled long distances to attend and/or speak at the rally, and received tremendous support from seasoned activists. There was something quite liberating about working to free Mumia Abu-Jamal. Third, it was vital for us to find ways to chronicle the work that goes into making rallies and marches possible. So often, the effort required to organize an event leaves little time or energy to document the process. But without this documentation, we run the risk of isolation, a reinvention of organizing wheels, and the draining feeling of working in a vacuum. As Mari Matsuda, Charles Lawrence, Kimberlé Crenshaw, and Richard Delgado explain,

> group identity forms in a way similar to individual identity. Its potential exists long before consciousness catches up with it. It is often only upon backward reflection that some kind of beginning is acknowledged, . . . often it is not until one engages in a conscious reconstruction, asking what led to what else, that a history is revealed, or perhaps more accurately, chosen.[20]

Most college students in the 1990s have grown up at a time when they have had little or no direct experience with organizing around national issues. None have had the privilege of working as part of the civil rights or Black Power movement. Those students who are part of Act Up and feminist organizing may have some knowledge they can apply to organizing in support of Mumia Abu-Jamal and other political prisoners. However, even these students tend not to have experience with multiracial organizing. It is for this reason that we need to pass on the lessons we have learned as we hope others will pass on the lessons they have learned to us.

### *The Politics of Naming: Feminists and/or Revolutionaries*

At no time in the above chronicling of the Wesleyan rally did we label our work "feminist," an omission reflective of the Coalition's mostly unspoken decision not to use the term explicitly during the organizing process itself. What makes this decision theoretically and politically interesting, however, is that many of the organizers see themselves as feminists, including the professor most involved in the process.

Retrospectively, we see a number of reasons for this silence. First, in our attempt to organize a multiracial coalition of men and women, some of us believed that using the term "feminist" would deter some men and women of color from becoming involved. At Wesleyan, and on many U.S. college campuses, feminism is identified exclusively with white women. This equation partly reflects the history of white women who run women's studies programs that privilege white women's scholarship in the curriculum. Racism within the feminist movement at the national level has also contributed to the equation of feminism with white women. A quintessential example of this occurred during the Anita Hill-Clarence Thomas hearings. When white feminists spoke to the media in support of Hill, they did so on the basis of gender and their opposition to sexual harassment, as if race and racism did not frame the entire spectacle as well.[21] Given this and many other examples in recent history, many of the coalition members knew that the association between "feminism" and "whiteness" might hinder interest by people of color. Second, since there were many lesbians in leadership positions within the Coalition, we were also wary of using the term "feminist," given the history of feminism being conflated with lesbians. Our silence about the term "feminist" suggested an unspoken concern that straight men and women might hesitate to become involved.

While the Coalition never used the term "feminism" explicitly, it

would be accurate to say that the way we organized was significantly influenced by feminism. This reality became most clear to us through conversations about organizing with Julia Wright, a writer and an organizer
in France in support of Mumia Abu-Jamal (and Richard Wright's daughter), and Susan Burnett, a key member of the International Concerned
Family and Friends of Mumia Abu-Jamal. As self-identified "children of
Malcolm X" and as a former Black Panther (Julia), they both see themselves as "revolutionaries" but not explicitly as feminists.

For Susan, who is white, in her fifties, and married to a former political
prisoner and Black Panther, "feminism" is what Betty Friedan espoused in
the 1960s, a politics based on attempts to be part of the "white man's system." For Julia, "feminism" is too narrow. For her, the term "revolutionary"
includes feminism but is not limited to it. Both women began using the
word "revolutionary" in the 1960s and have continued to aspire to it since.
For Becky, who came of age in the late 1970s and whose consciousness of
race and class developed alongside that of feminism, feminism has been at
the core of her understanding of political organizing all her adult life. From
the writing of Barbara Smith, the Combahee River Collective, Cherríe Moraga, Gloria Anzaldúa, Audre Lorde, and other writer/activists, Becky was
taught that calling oneself a feminist and not dealing with race, is to not be
a feminist. "Revolutionary" is not a term widely used among her generation
of activists. For Sohera, who is twenty-four, the term "revolutionary" seems
ancient. While feminism has informed her approach to organizing, the term
has been problematic for her. The struggles she had with the white-centered
curriculum in some university women's studies programs, the media representations of feminism nationally, and the colonialist ideology of much
Western feminism have made her cautious about how and when she uses
the term "feminist."

But then, what does it mean when women who came of age during the
civil rights and Black Power movement don't think of themselves as feminists while organizing for political prisoners, and younger women either
avoid the term for fear that it will limit coalition politics or because of the
racist connotations associated with the term? When women with a race
analysis abandon the term "feminism," then who claims it and what are
the consequences of such ownership?

Why have the class and race dynamics of the Mumia case been widely
examined in the literature, on the Internet, and at rallies while the way
that gender informs race and class has largely been unnamed?[22] What are
the consequences of unnaming feminism as key to this coalition work?

What does it mean that the Wesleyan Coalition did not name itself as "feminist" even though most of the key organizers were women of color and much of the organizing relied upon feminist principles? For example, the "in-reach" aspect of the organizing was based on the feminist commitment to the principle that "the personal is political" (a commitment also upheld in the Student Nonviolent Coordinating Committee [SNCC] and other civil rights grassroots organizing as well as in critical race theory's respect for personal narrative as a source of theory). The Coalition's decision to institute a "self-reflexive" time during the meetings stemmed from a feminist attempt to consider process as important as content. The Coalition also upheld gender equity at each step—within committee work, among the rally speakers, and in outreach. Further, the Coalition's attempt to understand the "prayer incident" and anti-Semitism was informed by the writing and activism of Jewish and black feminists who have, for many years, sought to take racism and anti-Semitism seriously without pitting the two groups against each other.[23] In our attempt to make the Coalition inclusive—to avoid alienating people of color, heterosexual people, and white men—were we, in fact, doing an injustice to some of our activist roots?

More importantly, what does it mean that many if not most of the key organizers for Mumia Abu-Jamal nationally and internationally are women, and yet that reality has largely been unnamed? As Julia Wright has said,

> The State still thinks that the men are the dangerous ones and they keep putting them in prison. Meanwhile, the ones on the outside, the women, are the ones the State should really be worrying about.[24]

The organizing in support of Mumia Abu-Jamal is no different than the work in support of Angela Davis and other political prisoners since the 1970s. Historically, women have assumed pivotal leadership positions in the organizing to free Angela Davis, Leonard Peltier, and other American Indian Movement members, many male Black Panthers, and other political prisoners.[25]

What may be different in the 1990s, however, is that women are less likely to step into the background, or to be pushed there, when it comes to assuming the most visible responsibilities (in the media, speeches at rallies, being the lead contact person for an organization, and the like). Ella Baker, bell hooks, Audre Lorde, Manning Marable, and others have chronicled the ways in which black women were expected to support but not lead men during the civil rights and Black Power movements.[26] In her 1982 article "Black Women and the Church," Jacquelyn Grant wrote that while it is often said that women are the backbone of the church, the telling portion of the word "backbone" is "back." "In many churches, women are consistently given responsibilities in the kitchen while men are elected or appointed to the important boards and leadership positions."[27]

In the 1980s and 1990s, women have increasingly refused such relegation as they are becoming the ministers and deacons, professors and administrators, and the lead organizers for progressive political change. A multiracial feminist perspective regarding the struggle for Mumia Abu-Jamal highlights the fact that women are doing much of the work. They are not being sidestepped by men. Some of women's presence is the result of their taking charge while men have been imprisoned; Winnie Mandela, Aung San Suu Kyi, and many other women leaders first gained national visibility as leaders precisely because the men were in prison (or had been murdered). But women's visibility also reflects the 1990s and thirty years of the visible women's movement. In the 1990s, Ramona Africa, a black woman, former political prisoner and MOVE member, won a suit against the city of Philadelphia for the bombing of the MOVE compound in the Osage neighborhood in 1985. Safiya Bukhari-Alston, a former political prisoner and Black Panther Party Member, now serves as the cochair of the New York Coalition to Free Mumia Abu-Jamal. Pam Africa, Chair of the International Concerned Friends and Family of Mumia Abu-Jamal, is a member of MOVE and a paralegal for Abu-Jamal's defense. Susan Burnett has been the National Coordinator of the campaign to free political prisoner Sundiati Acoli. Lawyers and legal theorists Patricia Williams and Kathleen Cleaver have contributed to the national and international media representation of the case. Whether explicitly stated or not, these women are the backbone of the campaign, and, unlike in the past, they are not at the back of the organizations they have built and sustained.

Ultimately, it may be less important what specific terms people use in relation to their approaches to organizing than that the work gets done. Historically, the various perspectives on the term "feminism" among black, Latina, and Native American women are themselves indicators that no one vocabulary will do. For example, while bell hooks and Barbara Smith refer to themselves as feminists, and have traced a long history of feminism among black women in the United States, other black women, most notably Alice Walker and Katie Cannon, use the term "womanist" instead, believing that it avoids the pitfalls associated with the term feminist.[28] For a host of reasons many independently minded women of color opt to use neither term to describe themselves.[29] It is important however, that we find ways to name the intersecting relationships between race, class, gender, and sexuality as they play themselves out in organizing for Mumia Abu-Jamal and all political prisoners. This is crucial if we are to avoid a rerun of the divisiveness that has historically kept people of color and white people from working together on these issues. In 1970, for example, at the beginning of the contemporary feminist movement, members of the Third World Women's Alliance planned to carry a sign at a rally reading "Hands Off Angela Davis" to protest her arrest on trumped-up murder, kidnapping, and conspiracy charges. White feminist organizers blocked the sign, claiming that "Angela Davis has nothing to do with women's liberation." African American Frances Beal responded, "It has nothing to do with the kind of liberation you're talking about but it has everything to do with the kind of liberation we're talking about."[30]

While no such racially inflammatory scene has reached national attention with regard to Mumia Abu-Jamal, the fact that the National Organization for Women, the National Women's Studies Association, and the Feminist Majority are not among the hundreds of organizations which have endorsed a new trial is a telling indicator of the work that still needs to be done. If coalition politics is about ever widening the circle of people who will consider work on behalf of Mumia Abu-Jamal their issue, we will need to work harder to understand what that commitment will take, for both those who do, and do not, use the term "feminist."

### Coalition Politics: Toward Multiracial Feminist Consciousness

Given the varying ideological perspectives of people in support of Mumia Abu-Jamal, building coalitions depends upon an expansive analysis. An issue should not have to deal with women specifically for feminists to consider it their own. In her quest for a spacious understanding of sisterhood, June Jordan writes,

> As a female member of our endangered species, I am searching for a relevant proof of sisterhood: I am searching for relevant proof of brotherhood hinged to that sisterhood. I want to pursue the collective, and the creative, securement of all of our legitimate names for all of our, finally, legitimate lives. I need to establish my legitimate name inside the consciousness of strangers.[31]

June Jordan's liberatory ethics urge us to find ways to establish our "legitimate names inside the consciousness of strangers." The truth is that all people, including feminists, need to support a new trial for Mumia Abu-Jamal simply because it is an issue of justice.

Making explicit how support for Mumia Abu-Jamal is a feminist issue—one that demands an analysis of race, class, and gender—can only expand the opportunities for coalition building. For example, the death penalty and its extralegal counterpart, lynching, have historically been used to uphold white supremacy based on purist notions of white womanhood. Both the death penalty and lynching have centered on the dichotomous construction of white women as needing legal protection from black men while black women have been treated as fair game to men across race. In this construction, white men have not been held accountable from either vantage point.[32] When people oppose the death penalty, as applied to Abu-Jamal and across the board, they counter its historic justification on the basis of skewed notions of black and white womanhood.

The escalation of the prison system in the 1990s is also a multiracial feminist issue. When states spend more money on their prisons than on education, those most in need of publicly funded education will be most affected in the long run—single mothers, working-class people, people of color, recent immigrants, and returning students (the majority of whom are women). The buildup of the prison system has other race and gender implications as well. A disproportionate percentage of women in prison are women of color. The number of women in prison is rising sharply. Between 1986 and 1991, the number of women in state prisons for drug offenses increased by 433 percent (compared to 283 percent for men).[33] Nearly seventy thousand women are currently in state prisons.[34] Approximately 80 percent of female inmates have two or more children under eighteen years old. Because there are fewer prisons specifically for women, female inmates are removed farther away from home and family than the average male prisoner. When men are imprisoned, children lose direct contact with their fathers. When mothers are incarcerated, children lose their homes.[35]

A gender- and race-conscious analysis also broadens what constitutes a "political prisoner." Over 80 percent of women in prison have a history of being sexually abused at home, in the streets, and/or in prison.[36] For many women inmates, their initial entanglements with the law result from their attempts to escape sexual abuse. Given this reality, a multiracial feminist analysis of the prison system supports political prisoners, both male and female, who fit the classic definition of the term—those who receive an unfair trail based on their political beliefs.[37] However, the term "political prisoner" should also include women whose incarceration results from attempts to protect themselves and/or their children from sexual and/or racial abuse.[38] In addition, "political prisoner" should include the estimated 63 percent of young men between the ages of eleven and twenty who are imprisoned for homicide after having killed their mothers' batterers.[39]

A race-conscious feminist analysis recognizes that patriarchy is endemic to the state. This framework treats women who have killed their batterers, the young men who killed their mothers' batterers, as well as Mumia Abu-Jamal, as political prisoners—all of whom deserve justice that has not yet been served. We need an understanding of political prisoners that expands the individuals and groups who may call Mumia Abu-Jamal's case their own. This will, inevitably, add to the organizing on his behalf.

## Conclusion: Brick by Brick, Wall by Wall,
## Free Mumia Abu-Jamal!

We should never lose sight of the fact that the campaign to obtain a new trial for Mumia Abu-Jamal is about one particular human being. At the same time, the urgency of his case, his experience as a journalist and commentator, and the decades-long support he has received from seasoned activists provides tremendous possibilities for coalition building. Activists are well aware that it is easier and more effective to organize on behalf of prisoners' rights and against the prison system when specific people's lives are involved rather generally.

Regardless of who we are and what we call ourselves—feminists, nonfeminists, revolutionaries, or otherwise—the difference between life and death for Mumia Abu-Jamal and hundreds of incarcerated political prisoners is our common denominator. Coalition work in support of Mumia Abu-Jamal challenged us to stretch our skins and unname ourselves as feminists even as we mobilized at Wesleyan using multiracial feminist principles. Brick by brick or one person at a time, coalition politics requires us to converse—without bars—about our ideological, political, and spiritual disagreements. This was the decision of Queers United in Support of Political

Prisoners, who stated that despite Mumia Abu-Jamal's heterosexually-centered ideas about love and marriage, "we must struggle with Mumia over gay issues but we cannot struggle with him if he is dead."[40] It is the enormity of Mumia Abu-Jamal's case and our passion for justice that drives us to work together in ways previously unimaginable.

### ACKNOWLEDGMENTS

For Susan Burnett, 1939–1999, whose tremendous spirit and energy guided us as we worked to free Mumia Abu-Jamal and whose generosity and love helped us as we wrote about our work for justice. We echo the sentiments of Mumia Abu-Jamal, when he writes (September 26, 1999), "To think of Susan is like thinking of a powerful force of nature; for her love was as wild and wonderful as her rage. This dear sister had a profound love for people—poor people, black people, any who rebelled against injustice. She simply loved real people. But phonies beware! She could read you like a script and blast you with the heat of the summer sun. And like the force of nature her great and terrible gifts left many of us in awe and wonder. . . . She lived life boldly, with a fierce and wonderful spirit that one recognized as Family from the first moment of meeting. She will be missed, or more important, she will be remembered with love.

### APPENDIX

The following is a list of some of the significant actions that illustrate the energy and international nature of the movement in support of Mumia Abu-Jamal. Additional information and day-to-day updates of actions can be obtained from http://www.mumia.org (homepage of The International Concerned Family and Friends of Mumia Abu-Jamal) and http://mojo.calyx.net/~refuse/altindex.html (homepage of Refuse and Resist, a U.S.-based nonpartisan organization in support of Mumia Abu-Jamal).

AFRICA
*South Africa*
- November 1995. President Nelson Mandela and Archbishop Desmond Tutu advocate a fair and new trial for Mumia Abu-Jamal.
- Azania, September 24–26, 1999. Azanian People's Organization (AZAPO), Azanian Students' Convention (AZASCO), and Azanian Youth Organization (AZAYO) hold a joint National Congress in Bloemfontein, Free State Province, South Africa (Azania). Petitions demonstrating support for Mumia Abu-Jamal are sent to U.S. Embassy in Pretoria.

EUROPE
*Germany*
- Hamburg, February 20, 1999. More than five thousand supporters demonstrate against the planned execution of Mumia Abu-Jamal. Participants include members of various political parties, families of German political prisoners, members of Kurd communities, the Green Party, and IG Medien (Media Union).
- Leipzig, June 19, 1999. Demonstration outside U.S. Consulate organized by Party for Democratic Socialism.
- Berlin, October 1999. "Aktionsbündnis für Mumia Abu-Jamal" (Action Coalition for Mumia Abu-Jamal). A multinational demonstration of one thousand people from German, Turkish, Kurdish, Iranian, and African communities demonstrate at the U.S. Embassy.

*France*
- Paris, various dates. Seventy members of the French Communist Youth movement conduct a peaceful sit-in at French newspaper, *Le Monde*, headquarters. Expanding mobilization of the youth movement includes one thousand protesters in downtown Paris on April 17, 1999; sit-in at the American Library in Paris by international citizens on June 16, 1999; demonstration disrupting gala opening of the American Film Festival in Deauville on September 3, 1999; two thousand protesters in downtown Paris for the "100 Cities for Mumia" campaign on September 25, 1999; and weekly picketing for Mumia Abu-Jamal outside the U.S. Consulate.
- Paris, July 25, 1999. Five hundred writers from the International PEN-club issue a statement for a new trial. Writers include Gunther Grass (Germany), Peter Handke (Austria), Jorge Amado (Brazil), Harold Pinter (U.K.), and Salman Rushdie (U.K.).
- Paris, October 15, 1999. Indoor rally supporting the Open World Conference in Defense of Trade Union Independence and Democratic Rights to be held in San Francisco, California, on February 11–14, 2000. Ten thousand trade unionists and activists initiate an Open Letter Campaign to Bill Clinton and Janet Reno demanding intervention and an immediate investigation into the violation of Mumia Abu-Jamal's civil rights.
- Villejuif, November 9, 1999. Town Council of Villejuif, a southern suburb of Paris, declares Mumia Abu-Jamal second citizen of honor of the commune. Villejuif Mayor Claudine Cordillot contacts Pennsylvania Governor Tom Ridge to inform him of her intention to visit Mumia Abu-Jamal on death row.
- Paris, November 12, 1999. Comité de Soutien International à Mumia Abu-Jamal et aux Prisonniers Politiques aux Etats-Unis (COSIMAPP). Civil disobedience takeover of the Paris offices of the *International Herald Tribune* to protest the absence of regular reports of Mumia Abu-Jamal's case despite massive interest and support on his behalf across Europe.

*Norway*
- Oslo, February 8, 1999. Forty-seven members of the Norwegian Parliament, including leaders from the Christian Democratic Party, Labour Party, Socialist Left Party, Labour Youth League, and Workers' Communist Party endorse a new trial for Mumia Abu-Jamal.

## NORTH AMERICA
*Canada*
- Halifax, Nova Scotia; Calgary, Alberta; and Victoria, British Columbia, Canada, August 1999. Supporters sponsor protests at U.S. Consulate and deliver signed petitions to government officials demanding a new trial.
- Montreal, September 25, 1999. Members from the Comité des sans-emploi de Montreal-Center (Committee of the Unemployed People in Downtown Montreal), Concordia Student Union, Filipino Workers' Support Group, Migrante International (organization for Filipino expatriates) and The Red Flag demonstrate for "100 Cities for Mumia."

*U.S.A.*
- Nationwide, February 26, 1999. National Student/Youth Day for Mumia Abu-Jamal. High school and college students participate in a national demonstration of support including teach-ins, rallies, leafleting, performance art, and concerts.
- Philadelphia, Pennsylvania, April 24, 1999. Twenty thousand demonstrate at a "Millions for Mumia" rally to demand a new trial for Mumia Abu-Jamal and to celebrate his fortieth birthday. Simultaneous actions took place in San Francisco and Los Angeles, California, Eugene, Oregon, Edmonton, Halifax, Toronto, Vancouver, Barcelona, Berlin, Cork, Dublin, Karlsrue, Lisbon, London, Lucerne, Madrid, Montreal, Nuremburg, Oslo, Stockholm, Saarbrucken, Stuttgart, Vienna, Zurich, and Melbourne.
- San Francisco and Oakland, California, April 24, 1999. Twenty-eight local unions of the International Long Shore and Warehouse Union (ILWU) hold stop work meetings which close down west coast ports from San Diego to Bellingham, Washington, for "Millions for Mumia" campaign.
- San Francisco, California, June 26, 1999. "Torchlight Protest" at UN Plaza in support of Mumia Abu-Jamal leads to the arrest of over two hundred people. Protesters were released later without charges.
- Philadelphia, Pennsylvania, July 4, 1999. International delegation including U.S. Congress members; Reverend Jesse Jackson, President, Rainbow-PUSH Coalition; Aline Pailler, elected representative, European Parliament; and Danielle Mitterand, widow of late president of France, François Mitterrand, meet to support Mumia Abu-Jamal.
- Nationwide, September 19–25, 1999. Demonstrations in eighty cities, thirty-

five high schools, sixty colleges and international events in Toronto, Montreal, Paris, and Azania (South Africa) in support of "Mumia Awareness Week."

• Washington, D.C., January 12, 2000. International delegation of trade unionists from Europe and Africa are scheduled to arrive to advocate a fair and new trial for Mumia Abu-Jamal.

## SOUTH AMERICA
### Brazil

• Volta Redonda, November 1998. Liga Quarta Internacionalist do Brasil (LQB), League for the Fourth International Workers, demonstrate in coalition with the Construction Workers' Union in front of a steel plant demanding freedom for Mumia Abu-Jamal.

• Rio de Janeiro, March 13, 1999 and April 23, 1999. The State-Wide Assembly of the Union of Education Workers of the State of Rio de Janeiro approve a resolution for education workers of Rio de Janeiro state schools to stop work on April 23, 1999 for one hour to meet and demand freedom for Mumia Abu-Jamal.

NOTES

1. Mumia Abu-Jamal, *Death Blossoms: Reflections from a Prisoner of Conscience* (Farmington, Pa.: Plough Publishing House, 1997); *Mumia Abu-Jamal, Live from Death Row* (New York: Avon Press, 1996).

2. The authors thank Kathleen Cleaver, Julia Wright, Margaret Washington, and Susan Burnett for their careful and insightful reading of earlier drafts of this article. We also thank France Winddance Twine and Kathleen Blee for their vision and thoughtful work as editors.

3. Bernice Johnson Reagon, "Coalition Politics: Turning the Century," in *Home Girls: A Black Feminist Anthology* (New York: Kitchen Table Women of Color Press, 1983).

4. The law seminar chronicles critical race theory as an intellectual field developed in response to dominant race and legal constructions in the post–civil rights era. The course examines how critical race theory's genre-busting, interdisciplinary approach to legal theory challenges basic legal categories that subsume and rationalize power differentials. The foundational critical race scholarship—by Derrick Bell, Kimberlé Crenshaw, Richard Delgado, Charles Lawrence, Mari Matsuda, and others—spells out relations between the law and inequality, punishment and social control, socialization and the legal profession, and law and social ethics. Particular attention is given to key contemporary legal and political conflicts about affirmative action, assaultive speech, indigenous land rights, violence against women, and multicultural education.

5. For histories of critical race theory and its methodologies, see Charles

Lawrence, Richard Delgado, Mari Matsuda, and Kimberlé Crenshaw, *Words That Wound: Critical Race Theory, Assaultive Speech, and the First Amendment* (Boulder, Colo.: Westview Press, 1993); Kimberlé Crenshaw, Neil Gotanda, Gary Peller, and Kendall Thomas, "Introduction," in *Critical Race Theory: The Key Writings That Formed the Movement* (New York: Free Press, 1995).

6. In describing a principle of antisubordination as both fundamental and expansive, Matsuda writes, "a jurisprudence of anti-subordination is an attempt to bring home the lost ones, to make them part of the center, to end the soul-killing tyranny of inside/outside thinking. I want to bring home the women who hate their own bodies so much that they would let a surgeon's hand cut fat from it, or a man's hand batter and bruise it. I want to bring home the hungry ones eating from the trashbins; the angry ones who call me names; the little ones in foster care." Mari Matsuda, "Voices of America: Accent, Antidiscrimination Law, and a Jurisprudence for the Last Reconstruction," *Yale Law Journal*, vol. 11, no. 5 (1991): 1405.

7. Mari Matsuda, "Looking to the Bottom: Critical Legal Studies and Reparations," 22 *Harvard Civil Rights–Civil Liberties Law Review* 323 (1987).

8. The arrest and conviction of Mumia Abu-Jamal came at the end of the late 1960s and 1970s when the government declared war on the Black Panther Party and black radicals in general. The war against black radicalism in Philadelphia focused on MOVE, which was dubbed a militant and subversive organization. This war reached a head in 1985 when police bombed the MOVE residence, killing eleven residents and burning sixty homes in Philadelphia's Osage neighborhood. Abu-Jamal's coverage of the city's treatment of MOVE and his support for the organization earned him the title of subversive as well.

9. In 1995 Leonard Weinglass, lead counsel for Abu-Jamal's defense, wrote, "consigning [Abu-] Jamal to death with a stroke of his pen was a particularly vindictive act as Governor Ridge is well aware that Jamal's attorneys are set to file a Petition for Post-conviction Relief seeking a new trial and the setting aside of Jamal's death sentence on June 5, 1995 in the Court of Common Pleas of Philadelphia, Pennsylvania. The previous Governor's policy was to not sign warrants for prisoners whose cases were under appeal. By his actions, Governor Tom Ridge has shown his policy to be a vengeful race to death with an alarming indifference to the judicial process." *Statement of Counsel* by Leonard Weinglass, esq. June 2, 1995. From *The Committee to Save Mumia Abu-Jamal*, 163 Amsterdam Ave., no. 115, New York, N.Y. 212-580-1022.

10. Updates and analysis of Abu-Jamal's case were obtained from C. Clark Kissinger, *Refuse and Resist*, 305 Madison Avenue, Suite 1166, New York, N.Y. 212–713–5657. http: //mojo.calyx.net/~refuse/altindex.html "What's Next in the Courts for Mumia Abu-Jamal," May 1998; "Justice Denied: Analysis of the Pennsylvania Supreme Court Decision on Mumia Abu-Jamal," November 5, 1998; "More Complete Update on Mumia's Case," October 28, 1999; "Report on Na-

tional Planning Meeting," November 25, 1999; "Summary of the Constitutional Claims in Mumia's Petition for a Writ of Habeas Corpus," December 4, 1999.

11. The Federal Effective Death Penalty Act of 1996 requires federal courts to accept the findings of state courts regarding factual issues as true and correct. In other words, federal courts must assume a "presumption of correctness" with respect to the existing evidence. This law severely curtails the appeals process for defendants and gives state courts new powers to prevent effective review of the record at later stages. For Abu-Jamal, then, progressively higher courts in the appeals process will make more narrow examinations of his case. Therefore, Abu-Jamal's defense team has reached a crucial juncture before advancing to courts higher than the Pennsylvania Supreme Court. Any changes in the factual record can only be made at the district court level. To ensure that new evidence favoring Abu-Jamal is included within the purview of the higher courts, Abu-Jamal's defense team must succeed at the district level.

12. In a move reminiscent of his August 1995 order for execution, Governor Ridge issued a death warrant two days before Abu-Jamal's lawyers were set to file a Petition for Writ of Habeas Corpus in the Federal District Court in Philadelphia, Pennsylvania. This is a 160-page appeal citing 29 claims to constitutional violations at the trial, sentencing, and postconviction proceedings, and 600 instances of witness intimidation, suppression of evidence, and police misconduct.

13. While Judge Yohn is expected to presume the correctness of the existing factual record, he is entitled by Article III of the U.S. Constitution to fully review all aspects of the lower state court decisions. In other words, Judge Yohn may reexamine all original evidence dating back to 1981 and new evidence presented in the Post-Conviction Relief Act hearings between 1995 and 1997. A favorable ruling will give Abu-Jamal a new trial or even freedom, while a defeat at the district court will result in higher level appeals to the U.S. Circuit Court of Appeals under tighter restrictions.

14. "Death Penalty in 1998: Year End Report," Death Penalty Information Center, December 1998, 1320 18th Street, N.W., 5th floor, Washington, D.C. 202-293-6970.

15. "Death Penalty in Black and White: Who Lives, Who Dies, Who Decides," Richard C. Dieter, Esq., Executive Director, Death Penalty Information Center, June 1998.

16. "Death Penalty in Black and White."

17. Ian Haney Lopez, "Community Ties and Law School Hiring: The Case for Professors Who Don't Think White," in *Beyond a Dream Deferred: Multicultural Education and the Politics of Excellence*, ed. Becky Thompson and Sangeeta Tyagi (Minneapolis: University of Minnesota Press, 1993).

18. A most thrilling example of this could be seen on CNN during their coverage of the South African parliamentary proceedings after the Constitution was passed in May 1996. After Mandela's speech, many members of the parliament sang a lengthy call-and-response traditional South African song within the

parliamentary room itself. Imagine U.S. senators and congressmen breaking into song after an important piece of legislation was passed.

19. The activists attending and/or speaking at the rally included George Edwards, former political prisoner, former Black Panther and member of the New Haven Ad Hoc Justice Committee in Support of All Political Prisoners; Susan Burnett, former National Coordinator of the Campaign to Free Sundiata Acoli; Pam Africa, member of MOVE and lead organizer for International Concerned Family and Friends of Mumia Abu-Jamal; Nahn Thang Ngo, Committee against Anti-Asian Violence and Asians for Mumia Abu-Jamal; Paul Winter of the Bruderhoff Community; Safiyah Bukhari-Alston, Co-Chair of the New York Coalition to Free Mumia Abu-Jamal, former political prisoner and former Black Panther; David Rudovsky, counsel for Mumia and Professor at the University of Pennsylvania; Mark McClain Taylor, Professor of Theology at Princeton; Imani Perry, graduate student at Harvard in American Civilization; Ali Bey Hassan, former political prisoner and member of the New York Panther 21; Richard Jonova, Partisan Defense Committee, and many others. The Wesleyan speakers included Sumayya Ahmed, Ian Straker, Francisco Tezen, Sohera Syeda, Becky Thompson, Tiffany Corley, and Josh Guild.

20. Lawrence, Matsuda, Crenshaw, and Delgado, *Words That Wound*.

21. Elly Bulkin and Becky Thompson, "The Spectacle of Race in the O. J. Simpson Case," *Sojourner: The Women's Forum*, vol. 9–10 (September 1994).

22. For example, *In Defense of Mumia* is a stunning collection of essays, poems, cartoons, and speeches in support of Mumia. Many underscore the racial and class dynamics of the case. None spell out how gender is involved. See S. E. Anderson and Tony Medina, *In Defense of Mumia* (New York: Writers and Readers Publishing, 1996).

23. See, for example, Elly Bulkin, Minnie Bruce Pratt, and Barbara Smith, *Yours in Struggle: Three Feminist Perspectives on Anti-Semitism and Racism* (Ithaca, N.Y.: Firebrand, 1996). See also the journals *Conditions and Bridges: A Journal of Jewish Feminists and Our Friends*.

24. Personal conversation with Julia Wright, May 20, 1996.

25. See Bettina Aptheker, *The Morning Breaks: The Trial of Angela Davis* (Ithaca, N.Y.: Cornell University Press, 1975); Angela Davis, *Angela Davis: An Autobiography* (New York: Random House, 1974); M. Annette Jaimes, with Theresa Halsey, "American Indian Women: At the Center of Indigenous Resistance in Contemporary North America," in *The State of Native America: Genocide, Colonization, and Resistance*, ed. Annette Jaimes (Boston: South End Press, 1992), 311–44.

26. Joanne Grant and Ella Baker: *Freedom Bound* (New York: John Wiley, 1998); bell hooks, *Talking Back: Thinking Feminist, Thinking Black* (Boston: South End Press, 1989); Manning Marable, *How Capitalism Underdeveloped Black America* (Boston: South End Press, 1983); Audre Lorde, *Sister/Outsider* (New York: Crossing Press, 1983).

27. Jacquelyn Grant, "Black Women and the Church," in *But Some of Us Are Brave: Black Women's Studies*, ed. Gloria T. Hull, Patricia Bell Scott, and Barbara Smith (Old Westbury, N.Y.: Feminist Press, 1982), 141.

28. Barbara Smith, *Home Girls: A Black Feminist Anthology* (New York: Kitchen Table Women of Color Press, 1983); bell hooks, *Feminist Theory: From Margin to Center* (Boston: South End Press, 1984); bell hooks, *Talking Back: Thinking Feminist, Thinking Black* (Boston: South End Press, 1989); Alice Walker, *In Search of Our Mothers' Gardens: Womanist Prose by Alice Walker* (New York: Harcourt Brace Jovanovich, 1983); Katie Geneva Cannon, *Katie's Canon: Womanism and the Soul of the Black Community* (New York: Continuum, 1995).

29. See Gloria Anzaldúa and Cherríe Moraga, *This Bridge Called My Back: Writings by Radical Women of Color* (New York: Kitchen Table Women of Color Press, 1983); Chandra Mohanty, "Cartographies of Struggle: Third World Women and the Politics of Feminism," in *Third World Women and the Politics of Feminism*, ed. Chandra Mohanty, Ann Russo, and Lourdes Torres (Bloomington, Ind.: University of Indiana Press, 1991); Coco Fusco, *English Is Broken Here: Notes on Cultural Fusion in the Americas* (New York: New Press, 1995); Jaimes, with Halsey, "American Indian Women," 311–44.

30. Midge Wilson and Kathy Russell, *Divided Sisters: Bridging the Gap between Black Women and White Women* (New York: Anchor Books, 1996), 200.

31. June Jordan, "Where Is the Sisterhood?" *The Progressive*, June 1996, 21.

32. See, for example, Angela Y. Davis, *Women, Race and Class* (New York: Vintage, 1981); Marable, *How Capitalism Underdeveloped Black America*; Evelyn C. White, *The Black Women's Health Book: Speaking for Ourselves* (Seattle, Wash.: Seal Press, 1994).

33. Adrian Nicole LeBlanc, "A Woman behind Bars Is Not a Dangerous Man," *New York Times Magazine*, June 2, 1995, 35.

34. LeBlanc, "Woman behind Bars," 35.

35. LeBlanc, "Woman behind Bars," 35.

36. See Mary Gilfus, "Seasoned by Violence, Tempered by Love: A Qualitative Study of Women and Crime," Ph.D. dissertation, Brandeis University, 1987, and Mary Gilfus, *From Victims to Survivors to Offenders: Women's Roots of Entry and Immersion into Street Crime, Women and Criminal Justice*, vol. 4, no. 1 (1992): 1–30.

37. Cornel West, "Free Mumia," in *In Defense of Mumia*, 7.

38. Mary Gilfus, "Our Sister Survivors: A Portrait of Women in Prison." Paper delivered at the First National Conference on Battered Women and Justice, St. Louis, Missouri, May 1988.

39. Statistic cited in Kimberlé Crenshaw, "Mapping the Margins: Intersectionality, Identity Politics and Violence against Women of Color," in *Critical Race Theory*, 361.

40. Anderson and Medina, *In Defense of Mumia*, 20.

# Chapter 10

# Extraordinary Alliances in Crisis Situations
## *Women against Hindu Nationalism in India*

### *Paola Bacchetta*

This chapter explores women's alliances across religions, classes, castes, and sexualities against Hindu nationalism during two significant events: a Hindu-Muslim riot in Ahmedabad, Gujarat, in 1985 and Hindu nationalist attacks against lesbianism in 1998. In my analysis of the way these alliances crystalized during moments of crisis, I draw on primary documents by women's and anticommunal organizations,[1] data from interviews with women activists, observations from my own experiences with women's, lesbian, and anti-Hindu nationalist groups, as well as internal and public documents by Hindu nationalist groups.

India has a long history of women's allied organizing, and currently an extremely vibrant all-India Women's Movement (hereafter IWM).[2] Some direct precursors are nineteenth-century struggles against *sati* (in which a wife throws herself, or is thrown, onto the funeral pyre of her husband), harsh treatment of widows, and child marriage (Mani 1989; Chatterjee 1994). At the turn of the century, women's struggles for education, political representation, and legal equality in areas such as marriage and inheritance were orchestrated by mass organizations such as Indian Women's Association, National Council of Women, and All India Women's Conference, founded in 1917, 1925, and 1927 respectively (Kumar 1993, 1995; Omvedt 1979). Other precedents are women's activism in the Gandhian, mass leftist, and revolutionary "terrorist" wings of India's independence movement, won in 1947 (Jayawardena 1994:73–108).

The current wave of the IWM emerged in the early 1970s from a fractured left and other mixed-gender movements (Kumar 1993, 1995; Basu 1992). The early groups espoused a mass-based politics wherein gender concerns intersected with class analysis, and included activists from all sectors of society. For example, Self-Employed Women's Association (hereafter SEWA), a trade union for poor, informal-sector women, was founded in 1972 in Ahmedabad, Gujarat. Women of the Sharmik Sangathana (Toilers' Organization), which emerged from an earlier (1960s) landless laborers' movement in Maharashtra, fought men's physical violence (associated with alcoholism) against women. The United Women's Anti-Price Rise Front, also in Maharashtra, involved housewives who protested inflation in street demonstrations (housebound women beat metal plates and rolling pins in support as they walked by), storming government offices, or raiding warehouses. The Progressive Organization of Women (POW) in Hyderabad, composed of middle-class Maoists, inspired similar groups in other cities. Socialist and communist women created women's wings to their parties, while women workers formed wings in mixed-gender trade unions.

Organizing around women's issues was given national attention as the Indian government's 1974 report on the status of women was publicized, as the United Nations designated 1975 as International Women's Year (Ray 1999:4), and during the International Women's Decade. Women's organizations, however, were among those outlawed when, in 1975, Prime Minister Indira Gandhi, threatened by opposition to her regime, called a national state of Emergency. After the Emergency ended in 1977, new types of women's groups mushroomed across the country, parallel to the old.

The post-1977 IWM is highly heterogeneous, decentralized, and concerned with a wide range of issues in both urban and rural settings (for two excellent analyses of the geopolitical specificities of IWM issues, see Ray 1999 and Basu 1992). Although there are no statistics on the number and size of groups currently operative, the fact that annual IWM conferences draw between four thousand and ten thousand women gives some idea of their enormous scope. This is in spite of the fact that many groups cannot afford to send representatives, and that most women are unable to spare the time to attend.

The post-1977 groups include long-term projects such as women's centers (providing counseling and legal aid), health programs, and income-generating projects. Others are organized around specific issues: dowry murders (wife burning with the goal of keeping the dowry), rape, husbands' alcohol abuse, domestic violence, child prostitution, environmental degradation, Christian women's inheritance rights, Muslim women's rights to maintenance after divorce, working women's hostels, equal wages, and maternity leave. Their organizational forms range from nonhierarchical collectives, to board-run groups, to organizations modeled after traditional left groups and unions.

IWM organizations have a history of working to forge solidarities across classes, faiths, and castes. For example, Jagori, a feminist documentation center in Delhi, with a middle-to-lower-class membership, also works on women's health care autonomy in *bastis* (urban slums) and in villages. Ankur, founded by middle-class women, with largely lower-class membership, also in Delhi, works on access to education, water, electricity, and income-generating projects in *bastis*. In such groups, women struggle together toward common goals, but in the process they also confront each other, critique each other, and form new modalities of political and personal trust with each other. As Kumar points out (1995), building vertical solidarity has been aided by site-specific notions of friendship between women, as reflected in some projects' names, such as Saheli ("woman best friend of another woman"), a women's center in Delhi, and Sakhi Kendra ("center for women friends") in Kanpur. Since the 1980s, women's studies have entered research institutes and universities; the intersection of academics and activists is strong, as evidenced by their joint participation in groups and national conferences.

By 1988, in urban sites such as Delhi lesbians linked increasingly to form submerged networks (Melucci 1998) and organized discussion groups. At that point relations between lesbian and other women's groups were not always cooperative (see, for example, Thadani 1996:88–90). By 1998, with the national controversy around Deepa Mehta's feature film *Fire* (1996) the situation changed dramatically, and many women's groups joined lesbian activists to fight lesbophobic attacks (see below).

## Hindu Nationalism as/and Racism

In India, anti-Other discourses and praxes that correspond more or less in their form, content, underlying logic, and effect to those classified in the West as contemporary racist ones, and that rely on arguments ranging from the biological/hereditary to the racialized cultural, are constructed around axes such as religious-politics, caste, language, or region. Indeed, as Gates (1986:4–13) points out, "race," though "long recognized to be a fiction," continues to function as a trope used to construct, naturalize, and signify "ultimate, irreducible difference" in a range of forms. Hindu nationalism is one of those forms; it is a manifestation of the wider phenomenon of *communalism*. Communalism is based not in biological arguments about race, but rather in arguments about racialized, cultural-religious inferiority and superiority. In Chandra's (1984:1) concise and widely accepted definition, communalism is

> the belief that because a group of people follow a particular religion they have, as a result, common social, political and economic interests. It is the belief that in India Hindus, Muslims, Christians and Sikhs form different and distinct communities which are independently and separately structured and consolidated; that all the followers of a religion share not only a community of religious interests but also common secular interests, that is, common economic, political, social and cultural interests.

Communalists, then, divide India's heterogeneous population of almost 1 billion, composed of people of many faiths (Hindus 80 percent, Muslims 12 percent, Christians 2.5 percent, Sikhs 2 percent, and other groups, such as Buddhists, Jains, Parsis, animists, and others, comprising less than 1 percent each; Premi 1991) into distinct religious communities. They posit each so-called community in a binary mode as mutually exclusive, internally homogeneous, and antagonistic to the others. The mechanisms involved are both *auto-referential*, which involves fabricating "one's own" religious community, and *allo-referential*, which involves erecting an "Othered" religious community (Taguieff 1987). Communalists hold up a particular form of their own religion as truly representative, and designate themselves as its leaders, while negating all the other belief systems and practices that would otherwise fall under that rubric. Communalists similarly homogenize the multiple varieties of the Othered religion into one fantasmic version, designate its leaders, and delegitimize them. This classificatory system and homogenization process negates divergent interests internal to each so-called religious community, based in class, caste (among Hindus, though the structure seeps into other religions as well),[3] gender, and sexual hierarchies, while negating and displacing potential intra- and interpositional solidarities across religions.

Class contradictions traverse every religion in India. Since independence, India has been trying to recover, through a series of five-year plans, from the devastating economic effects of colonialism. Yet in 1991, 332,000,000 people still lived below the poverty level,[4] 300,000,000 were middle class, 10,000,000 were upper class, and the rest fell between the poverty level and the middle class (USG 1995). Low- and outcaste peoples comprise about 25 percent of the total Indian population (GOI 1990:15). In addition to these categories some state governments have identified other classes of people, mainly in rural areas, as "Backward Castes and Classes." They comprise another 27 percent of the total population (GOI 1990:15).[5] Indian women, across all faiths, are located at the negative end of the sex ratio (in 1991, 929 females to 1,000 males), largely due to "the neglect of females" in food consumption and healthcare (Premi 1991:41), and more recently, amniocentesis abuse. Women have a lower literacy rate than men, 39 percent compared to 64 percent (Premi 1991:65).

As in nearly every other country in the world, only heterosexual kinship systems are legally recognized in India, whether these be joint, nuclear, or polygamous families.[6] Sexual hierarchies, too, permeate each faith. British-imposed legislation against sodomy (in 1865), which targets heterosexual and gay male sexual behavior deemed unacceptable while negating the existence of lesbianism, remains integral to the Indian Penal Code (in article 377), despite Indian gay and lesbian activist attempts to remove it (ABVA 1991; CLR 1999:6). As in most of the world, in India same-sex partners are denied domestic partnership and related rights (inheritance, adoption, and the like).

## Arguments and Archive

Herein I consider two forms of women's oppositional action against Hindu nationalism: (1) *indirect*, constructed in everyday acts of vertical and horizontal solidarity among women within and across faiths, classes, castes, political allegiances, and in some cases sexualities, and not necessarily specifically aimed toward combating communalism, and (2) *direct*, site-specific interventions based on these intra- and interpositional alliances, which surface in crisis situations. The two are linked, in that the second form is dependent on the first. The everyday praxis of trust and solidarity formation in common struggles lays the groundwork for extraordinary alliances, which can be called upon in crisis situations and extended into new domains. I deem these alliances extraordinary in the sense that they defy, and move beyond, the normative social order in which the actors are otherwise interpolated (Althusser 1972:170–77). Indeed, the everyday practice of forming unconventional and socially unsanctioned alliances often implies withdrawing solidarity from expected, socially sanctioned alliances, be they rationalized as supposed complementarity (such as between wife and husband), or supposed sameness (such as intracaste, intraclass, and intrafaith). Finally, crisis situations radicalize this process by provoking the extraordinarily allied women to directly challenge some otherwise expected alliances. In the next section I provide background information on Hindu nationalism and its targets. Then I discuss two sporadic crisis situations in which women actors extended their day-to-day solidarities in order to resist Hindu nationalist violence.

## Hindu Nationalism and Its Targets

Hindu nationalism has its roots in upper-caste movements in the later nineteenth century during the colonial period. Hindu nationalism eventually consolidated itself in opposition to secular nationalist forces, especially the Indian National Congress, the largest mass-based, Indian nationalist organization, founded in 1885. Hindu nationalism emerged as a distinct ideology in 1923 with the publication of Vinayak Damodar Savarkar's political treatise, *Hindutva* ("Hinduness"). *Hindutva* proposed that Hindus were the sole legitimate citizens of India; it became a major ideological source for several early twentieth century groups, including the most enduring—the Rashtriya Swayamsevak Sangh (hereafter RSS), founded in 1925, in Nagpur, Maharashtra (called the Central Provinces at the time, under colonially designed boundaries).

Today the RSS has 2.5 million members, and over two hundred additional, related "family organizations." The latter aim to organize every sector of society (into workers' unions, professional organizations, issue-oriented organizations, or identitary groups such as women, forest-dwellers, and the like) and to intervene in every domain of life (Andersen and Damle 1987; Seshadri 1988). Perhaps the most internationally renowned of these is the Bharatiya Janata Party (hereafter BJP), established in 1980, the political party currently at the head of government. Yet another highly visible family organization is the Vishwa Hindu Parishad (World Hindu Council, hereafter VHP), founded in 1964, a churchlike entity destined to unify diverse Hindu belief systems for political (generally anti-Muslim) ends.

Though many analysts have understood the RSS as a reaction primarily against Muslims (Curran 1951; Andersen and Damle 1987; Jaffrolot

1996; Jayaprasad 1991), a detailed examination of the local site where it emerged reveals that, from the beginning, RSS leaders simultaneously targeted low-caste and Muslim forces. Maharashtra has a long history of low-caste struggles; throughout the 1920s they centered on access to educational institutions, employment, and water sources and temples controlled by upper-caste Hindus. At the time, Muslims in Nagpur, unlike elsewhere in India, had gained substantial entry into civil service employment, especially the police forces. The RSS saw the upward mobility of both groups as a threat to upper-caste Hindu hegemony. RSS ideology and practice has always reflected the original anti-low-caste and anti-Muslim stance, albeit with modifications.

The RSS constructed its ideology through a process of selectivity from various sources, such as sanskrit texts, Western orientalist discourse, colonial and nationalist historiography, notions of racial categories constructed in scientific doctrine developed from the eighteenth century onward in Europe, the British colonial administrative practice of *divide and rule*, and colonial military notions of gender and sexuality.

Before analyzing Hindu nationalist reworkings of these sources, I will recall that, as Albert Memmi (1991), Franz Fanon (1974), and Gyan Prakash (1992:353–88) have pointed out, a major tenet of colonialism is the colonizers' imposition of their own cognitive grid, value system, and mode of perception onto the colonized population. Memmi (1991) argues that there are three possible responses to this imposition: the colonized may accept the discourse of the colonizer and attempt to imitate him; the colonized may internalize the discourse of the colonizer only to refute its value system (the colonized attaches positive meanings to the traits the colonizer identifies as essential, deplorable characteristics of the colonized); the colonized may revolt against the colonizer altogether (in political struggle). In India, the bilingual elite, which was most directly exposed to colonial discourse, had an array of responses, from revolt to internalization to imitation. Hindu nationalists, part of that bilingual elite, differed quite a bit from their anticolonial counterparts.

Hindu nationalists drew heavily from orientalist discourse, reworking the selected elements. As Gyan Prakash (1992) has remarked, orientalism was from its inception a European enterprise, as Western scholars entered India, attempted to make sense of Indian religions, selected certain sacred texts for translation, and left others by the wayside. This process, which included pulling Indian sacred texts into a Western cognitive grid, reinterpreting the texts through translation, and dispersing this newly created body of knowledge in the West and in India itself, certainly constituted a form of cognitive violence. Orientalists divided the diversity of faiths now arranged under the rubric of Hinduism into two categories: a Great Tradition comprised mainly of Brahmanical texts, and a Little Tradition, comprised mainly of lower-caste practices. They homogenized the Great Tradition texts, and held that category up as the ultimate representation of Hinduism. Orientalists, embedded in the intellectual universe of scientific race doctrine developed in Europe (Gould 1996), equated *varna* ("caste," see below) with race, placed racialized caste divisions within yet another European theory, that of the superiority of the Aryan race, and formulated the theory of an Aryan invasion of the subcontinent.

According to the Aryan invasion theory, in ancient times Aryans (conceptualized as ancestors of today's Brahmins) entered India, colonized the local population (conceptualized as ancestors of low-caste people and "tribals"), and set up the *varna* system, placing themselves at the top of the hierarchy.[7] *Varna* was indeed present in the mainly Brahmanic texts that orientalists selected to represent Hinduism. But, in their efforts to represent India as "just the opposite of the West," as the ultimate Other, European scholars displaced agency onto an essentialized version of caste, and interpreted it as the central feature of all Indian religious and social organization (Inden 1986:402–3). British colonial interests used the Aryan invasion theory to argue that the British had only done what the Brahmins had done before them: entered India and set up their regime. Colonial administrative interests would rework the place of *varna*, point to caste atrocities, essentializing and generalizing them, to justify colonialism as a "civilizing mission" against "Indian barbarism."

Early Hindu nationalists reproduced the Aryan invasion theory in full (see Savarkar 1923). But the RSS, while retaining the notion of Aryans as Hindus, rejected the invasion portion, because it implied that Brahmins were not indigenous to India (see Golwalkar 1939:6–9). However, the RSS would use the notion of an Aryan (now Hindu) race to formulate its ideas about caste and Muslims.

## Caste

The term "caste" has no origins in Indian languages; it is an English adaptation from the Portuguese term *casta* (meaning breed, race, kind). (The Portuguese had colonized a portion of western India.) The term "untouchable" too, has no Indian equivalent, but was devised by the British to designate those outside what they called the caste system. Historically, the groups the British named "untouchable" have self-identified, like other Indian groups, according to names which reflect their occupations: weaver, leather worker, and so on. Mahatma Gandhi designated the same people Harijans ("sons of God") according to religious criteria, while they themselves increasingly self-designate as Dalits ("oppressed") according to political criteria (Omvedt 1995).

The social divisions within Indian society that are commonly called caste in English are extremely complicated and varied. At a theoretical level, many ancient Sanskrit texts posit *varna* as a fourfold division of society: *brahmins* (priests and intellectuals), *kshatriyas* (warriors, rulers), *vaishyas* (agriculturists, businesspeople), and *sudras* (servants of the other categories). These Sanskrit sources, however, vary as to whether or not *varna* is hereditary or acquired, and also dispute the place of people of mixed *varna* origin. In practice, at the local level there are hundreds of different configurations of *jati* (castes or subcastes), defined in terms of economic occupation and continuums of purity and pollution, to which are attached a wide range of practices. Some of these practices are, indeed, very oppressive, even murderous, and low-caste groups and their allies across the board have fought them for centuries.[8]

The Indian National Congress led by Mahatma Gandhi took a strong stand against caste oppression, and independent India's first Constitution (of January 26, 1950), which was written under the direction of "untouchable" leader Dr. Ambedkar, contains provisions for eradicating caste discrimination. Article 335 provides for *reservation* (affirmative action, or positive discrimination effected by reserving places) in institutions of higher education and in government employment for Scheduled Castes ("untouchables") and Scheduled Tribes, while Article 330 provides for the reservation of seats in the Lok Sabha (lower house of Parliament).

Notwithstanding legal stipulations against caste oppression, it continues to exist (much as racist oppression exists in the United States). Caste oppression is manifested in occupational segregation, hiring practices, hostility toward intercaste marriage, denial of access to (upper-caste controlled) common water sources and temples, as well as residential segregation. Upper-caste supremacists commit acts of violence against low-caste people on the pretext that they have committed caste "transgressions" (use of above-mentioned water sources, intercaste marriage, and so on), but also without recourse to any pretext (such as in upper-caste male rapes of low-caste women). Unlike racisms based in biological arguments, such as antiblack racism in the United States, caste supremacy relies not on selected physical traits, but rather on cultural criteria (pollution stigma [Goffman 1963] mainly related to occupation). There are no clear-cut physical distinctions between upper- and lower-caste people; a South Indian Brahmin may have the same skin color as an "untouchable." However, regional and individual differences in skin color, even within the same family, tend to be differently valorized (lighter skin is more valued, especially in women).

In its first publication, *We Or Our Nation Defined* (Golwalkar 1939: 55–56), the RSS directly reproduced, in the sense of Memmi (1991), orientalist notions of a Great Tradition—Great Tradition superiority and *varna* as an essential and fixed feature of Hindu society (now the Hindu nation)—and used these notions to imply low-caste illegitimacy. Indeed, the RSS deployed the terms Hindu, Aryan, and Brahmin interchangeably (Golwalkar 1939:56), with the Western racialized notion of Aryan intact. In its next major text, *Bunch of Thoughts* (1968) by M. S. Golwalkar, the RSS reiterated its pro-*varna* stance (1968:107–8), but also superimposed biological racial characteristics imported from the West. That is, the RSS accused low-caste Hindus who had converted to Islam (to escape caste oppression in Hinduism) of being mentally inferior (1968:152).

After 1948, the RSS began to revise its biological language, when, following the implication of the RSS in the murder of Mahatma Gandhi, non-Brahminists in Maharashtra trashed the homes of RSS members. In the 1960s the RSS claimed that caste status should be based on talent, not on heredity. In the early 1980s, realizing that its political party, the BJP, needed non-Brahmin votes to gain a place in government, the RSS took a clear stand against untouchability and caste atrocities, and attempted to recruit, organize, and *sanskritize* (assimilate into upper-caste Hinduism) low-caste Hindus. RSS ideologues retained the term Aryan, but redefined Aryan consistent with its earlier usage in many sanskrit texts to mean simply "respectable, learned, one who does one's duties properly" regardless of his or her *varna* (Chakravorty 1995:105). Still, the RSS continued to oppose reservation, arguing, much like opponents of affirmative action in the United States, that access to higher education and to employment should be based on merit, thereby negating the history of caste oppression altogether.

## Indian Muslims and Islam

The primary targets of Hindu nationalist anti-Other discourse and most violent practices are Indian Muslims. For the RSS there are three types of Muslims (Bacchetta 1994b): *Muslims-as-Foreign-Invaders*, identified as upper-class orthodox Muslim leaders; *Muslims-as-ex-Hindu-Converts*, or lower-class Muslims who were once Hindus; and, more recently, *Hindu-Muslims*, a post-1970s designation applied to nonreligious Indian Muslims in an effort to facilitate their reconversion back to Hinduism. In each category, the defining criterion is closeness to or distance from Islam, with those constructed to embody Islam (Muslim leaders) assigned the most negative connotations.[9] Hindu nationalists hold Islam responsible for the downfall of the Hindu nation, which they propose to revive.[10]

In a hyperhomogenizing and ahistoricizing gesture, Hindu nationalists claim that since the twelfth century, when Muslims ruled portions of India, they have uniformly acted to destroy Hindu culture by converting low-caste people to Islam and by demolishing Hindu sacred spaces. Indian historians have countered by pointing to the fact that Hindu nationalists uncritically reproduce British discourse designed to divide and rule Hindus and Muslims; by rendering visible the heterogeneity of Islamic governments in India, especially the most peaceful ones; by reiterating the reasons why low-caste conversion took place; and by reaffirming that Indian Muslims are as Indian as Hindus (see, for example, the many excellent articles in Gopal 1991).

For the RSS, Islam and Muslims are inherently inferior to Hinduism and Hindus. The RSS rationale for this inferiorization is based in (Western) Aryan race theory, Nazi ideology, and going further back, in scientific racist doctrine developed from the eighteenth to early twentieth centuries in Europe (see Gould 1996). As Nancy Leys Stepan (1991) points out, scientific race doctrine, whether it comes in the form of cranology, polygeny, or monogeny, is indeed endowed with remarkable plasticity, and has had very different trajectories across the globe. For example, in Latin America, as Leys Stepan (1991) demonstrates, elements of the doctrine were imposed with their biological component intact and then reworked locally to construct a particular form of eugenics. In contrast, Hindu nationalists, notwithstanding a brief biological moment (complete with monogenist/polygenist assumptions), retained the notion of racial *categories*, but transformed the racializing criteria from biological to cultural. Thus, for the RSS, Muslims are non-Aryans (as invaders and as nonsanskritized, low-caste, former Hindu converts), barbaric, and like Hitler's Jews, a threat to the moral, cultural, and territorial integrity of the Hindu nation.

## *Gender, Sexuality, and Hindu Nationalism*

From its inception Hindu nationalism has been a gendered and sexuated project in both its symbolic and material dimensions. Indian feminists have denounced it as such (see, for example, Chhachhi 1989; contributions in Hasan 1994; Bhasin, Menon, and Khan 1994; articles in Jayawardena and de Alwis 1996; and Butalia and Sarkar 1996). Early membership in Hindu nationalist organizations was confined to males, and the ideal Hindu woman was said to be a chaste, devoted mother of Hindu nationalist sons. By 1936, fearing that upper-caste women might join pro-woman movements (for women's rights, the Gandhi-led independence movement, or leftist movements), the RSS allowed the creation of a women's wing, the Rashtriya Sevika Samiti (hereafter Samiti). Since then, other RSS family organizations have followed suit.[11]

RSS conceptions of its Others are embedded in complicated notions of gender and sexuality. As in colonial contexts elsewhere (McClintock 1995; Lane 1995), reconstructions of gender and sexuality were integral to British rule in India.[12] Holding themselves up as the ideal model for virile masculinity and rulership, the British attempted to discredit both the Muslim political elite (as potential rivals for political power) and Brahmin men (whose leadership positions were in the spiritual domain), thereby ridding themselves of competition. To this end they constructed Muslim men as hypermasculine-aggressive, and Brahmins as hypereffeminate (see Nandy 1983; Sinha 1997). Because India was an administrative rather than a settler colony, there was an insufficient number of British men in India to serve in the army and to occupy low-level civil servant jobs. For military purposes, then, the British constructed, in opposition to the "effeminate" Brahmins, a category of Indian "martial races" (note the racialized notion of caste), designating *kshatriyas* as the ideal, virile Indian men (Nandy 1983). They also instructed a certain portion of the population, especially Brahmins, who (as priests and intellectuals) had a strong historical relation with education, in the anglicist tradition for civil servant positions. Hindu nationalists directly reproduce the values attached to the category of martial races: they propose that ideal Hindu nationalist men should be physically invincible, militarily prepared, and capable of leadership, while accusing their Hindu political opponents in the Congress Party of effeminacy (Bacchetta 1996).

Further, as McClintock (1995) has observed, the British imagined their colonies as a "pornotropics," thereby metaphorically transforming the Indian population into a screen upon which to project rejected British sexual fantasies. They assigned Indians forms of anormative sexuality in relation to British-designed normativity (Ballhatchet 1980). Hindu nationalists, however, turned the notion of India as the pornotropics back onto the British through claims of upper-caste Hindu chastity and morality, and designated the British perverted. But Hindu nationalists also extended the accusation of perversion to those they identified as internal enemies, thereby reproducing the British notion of Muslim men as sexually aggressive, especially toward Hindu women.

The RSS's notions of gender and sexuality are integral to its cultural-racialized constructions of Muslims, and they present parallels with racisms elsewhere. For example, the notion of Muslim-Hindu intermarriage as miscegenation coincides with U.S. white supremacist, South African white supremacist, Nazi, and other prescriptions against interracial marriage.[13] The assignment of hyperaggressive sexuality to the Muslim male as Other parallels white supremacist pretexts for lynching Black men in the United States, as well as French National Front leader Jean-Marie Le Pen's claim that immigrant men disproportionately rape French women (Lesselier 1991:104). And the notion that Muslim women would like to seduce Hindu men and that Hindu men are too chaste and dedicated to the nation to respond (Bacchetta 1994b) recalls white supremacist constructions of U.S. Black women as Jezebels (Collins 1991:67–90).

### Extraordinary Alliances in Crisis Situations: Ending Riots in Ahmedabad

From the 1980s onward, men's (and women's) Hindu nationalist activism increased and radicalized, posing a challenge to the IWM. One such challenge is the crisis situation upper-caste Hindu supremacists instigated and Hindu nationalists consolidated in early 1985, in Ahmedabad, the site of extensive textile mills, and the largest city in the western state of Gujarat. The crisis began in February 1985, following government announcements concerning increased reservation quotas for oppressed groups, a move which, as Upendra Baxi (1990:217) remarks, would have changed very little, insofar as the previously reserved places were rarely filled and went instead to upper-caste Hindus. Notwithstanding this, some upper-caste medical and engineering students organized a massive protest to demand an end to reservation altogether. They threw *kakadas* (lit rags) at people, burned public buses and government offices, boycotted classes, organized illegal rallies, and held public fasts. As Baxi (1990:215–16) argues, this outburst must be understood in context: Gujarat, albeit associated in the public mind with Mahatma Gandhi (who was born, raised, and later based there), is a major site of everyday caste-based discrimination and institutionalized tolerance for caste violence, and the 1985 eruption had other precedents.[14] After about one month of antireservation violence, after curfew had been imposed and lifted, antireservation leaders called for an all-Gujarat *bandh* (closing down, cessation of activities) on March 18. Hindu nationalists then intervened to divert attention from reservation (which they feared would divide Hindus by caste) onto anti-Muslim conflict.

Hindu nationalists allegedly organized attacks on Muslims, targeting not their own neighborhoods but rather the most economically depressed areas of Ahmedabad: the highly congested center, and the industrialized eastern *bastis*. In the center, protagonists burned 115 shops, and in both areas, they used knives, pipes, cycle chains, stones, and special cement balls with protruding nails to kill and maim (Baxi 1990:229). While the majority of the provocateurs were upper-caste Hindu nationalist men (and some female counterparts), they had sparked mainly low-caste Hindu men to perpetuate the violence.

Women's organizations in Ahmedabad denounced the violence, but during the rioting and curfews they were unable to take much action. The headquarters of the largest women's organization in the city, SEWA, mentioned above, was situated in the east, in the midst of the rioting, and had to cease activities there, though leaders and members continued their work in the western part of the city.

SEWA had been founded at the initiative of Ela Bhatt, a middle-class, upper-caste member of the women's section of the (Gandhian socialist) Ahmedabad Textile Labour Association. SEWA currently has 220,000 members throughout India (Alam 1998:117), and approximately 30,000 members in Ahmedabad alone (Rose 1995:47). Of the members in Ahmedabad, 93 percent are illiterate, and 97 percent are slum dwellers (Rose 1995:47), with a high concentration living in the areas affected by the 1985 riots.

SEWA members are self-employed in jobs located outside the formal sector of the economy, such as home-based garment production for middlemen, street vending of edibles, rag picking, and sweeping and cleaning for middle-class households. These jobs are badly remunerated, stigmatized (among Hindus primarily) by their association with impurity, and associated with low-caste status. Historically, the jobs have not been recognized as work at all, but rather have been (erroneously) seen as pass-times to add extra income to the husband's salary (Alam 1998:114). Self-employed, economically depressed women are from all faiths, and this diversity is reflected in the ranks of SEWA membership, although SEWA's administrative leadership, like its founder, tends to be middle-class.

On an ongoing basis, SEWA provides a self-managed support structure to members. One of the major problems that SEWA has solved is high interest rates women informal sector workers must pay to local moneylenders. They are at approximately 10 percent per day and 25 percent per month, while banks, which deny credit and loans to poor women on the grounds that they have no means to repay, normally charge 9 to 17 percent per year (Sreenivasan 2000:64–77). Such loans are vital to women who must borrow to buy the goods used to make their products or the goods they will sell. To remedy this situation, SEWA started its own bank, which today has 54,000 depositors throughout India (Alam 1998:19). SEWA also intervenes in price regulation or in women's relations with middlemen. The headquarters has a self-run child care center and members are trained in health matters. SEWA also works to empower women through self-representation; in an ongoing video project members make documentary films about their lives, which are used in court cases and to encourage other self-employed women across the country to organize. Thus, SEWA is a space where women learn to struggle on their own terms to improve their financial situations, to demand recognition of their work as work, and to demand recognition for their own dignity as persons.

The 1985 riots had a devastating impact on women survivors, including SEWA members: family members were murdered and/or maimed, and their homes were burned. Self-employed women are the sole earners for about 30 percent of poor families (Rose 1995:18), and riots and curfews invariably have extreme, lasting effects. As Mirai Chatterjee (1994: 109–10) of SEWA maintains:

> With curfew everywhere, the women neither go to their work places nor deliver finished products made at home—*bidis* (rolled tobacco cigarettes),

ready-made garments, incense sticks and other articles—to the merchants. In addition, there is no way of receiving fresh supplies of raw materials. Sometimes, with great difficulty and considerable risk, workers manage to deliver finished goods to their employers but later, when curfew is lifted and normalcy restored, they are told by the merchants that all records of goods received and even the goods themselves were destroyed in the violence, so how can they possibly be paid? Further, in some areas which suffer regularly during communal violence, merchants, contractors, and others refuse to give women any work.

In late March 1985, with their neighborhoods under curfew, at great risk some SEWA members from the eastern *bastis*, both Hindu and Muslim, escaped together to the west to speak to SEWA leaders about the violence and to try to find solutions. In doing so, they defied their husbands and sons, as well as the heavily armed police and army who were enforcing the curfew. The women requested that SEWA representatives contact the police and the army to demand that they be allowed to organize a meeting of Hindu and Muslim women in the area under curfew. After much discussion, the officials consented, and local women organized the meeting by word of mouth.

According to Renana Jhabwala, one of the SEWA representatives who helped to arrange and attended the meeting, the first dialogues were in the form of disputes, with Hindu and Muslim participants accusing each others' male family members of starting the riots.[15] But as the discussion wore on, the women, both Hindu and Muslim, realized that the riots had been orchestrated by outsiders to their neighborhood. Their male family members had been told that men of the other religion would attack them at 6 P.M. on the day the riots began, so each had prepared for the riots in advance. Then rumors had spread that Hindus and Muslims were already rioting elsewhere in the city, so men, both Hindu and Muslim, attacked each other imagining that they were protecting their families and avenging their fallen brethren. By the end of the meeting, the women vowed that if such a situation should occur in the future, they would come out into the streets to prevent their male family members from fighting. Afterward, SEWA organized meetings with young men, and then with elderly men. For the most part, wherever they were held the meetings spelled the end of the violence and built ties of stronger solidarity among those who participated. However, in one area, Raipur, local SEWA members wanting peace were perceived as traitors to their religions.

Notwithstanding what happened in Raipur, the SEWA action demonstrates how alliances among same-classed women of different religions at war and among women across classes (the SEWA leadership and membership) allow women to use their positionalities, with all the strengths that each implies, toward a common goal. The SEWA members' initial united act (by Hindu and Muslim women) of defiance against their husbands, the police, and army, which involved risking their lives, had only been possible because the women had forged solidarity and trust in common struggles within the organization. Hindu and Muslim members held some of the same jobs, had struggled together to better their financial situations, and so on, and could now draw on these links in the crisis. The fact that members took risks to involve the middle-class SEWA leadership demonstrates the operability of vertical alliances based in mutual trust and responsibility.

### Combating Hindu Nationalist Xenophobic Lesbophobia

A recent struggle, beginning in 1998, extended women's cross-positional alliances against Hindu nationalism for the first time to a highly controversial, issue: lesbian (and by extension gay) rights. Lesbians and gays had long been active in anticommunalist groups, generally without being visible as such, and Hindu nationalists had long held a homophobic stance in their internal publications (Bacchetta 1999b). But until 1998 Hindu nationalists had not targeted homosexuals in public actions, and the issue of homosexuality had not been discussed in anticommunalist groups.

The point of departure for the 1998 struggle was the Hindu nationalist attack against Deepa Mehta's feature film *Fire* (1996). *Fire* portrays the story of Radha and Sita, two sisters-in-law married to brothers living in a middle-class, Hindu, joint family in New Delhi, who develop a lesbian relationship, and leave the family to live their lives together. After winning awards internationally, the film opened on November 13, 1998 in forty-two theaters in urban India, and, for the first few weeks, though it played to wide audiences, it caused no great uproar. After the initial peace, Hindu nationalists stepped in, and organized protests, damaging several theaters.

In statements to the press, Hindu nationalists, the RSS, and the Hindu Shiv Sena (hereafter HSS) alike argued that the film was an assault on Hindu civilization and Hindu "tradition" (Goyal interview 1999; Unsigned

1999; Sinha 1999:22). They claimed that Mehta should not have used the revered Hindu names Radha (heterosexually associated with the male god Krishna) and Sita (wife of the god Rama)—though at one point India's Censor Board had changed Sita to Nita in a preemptive move to avoid Hindu nationalist protest—because lesbianism is not a part of Hindu culture but was imported from the West (Sinha 1999:17; Bhatia 1998:13).

Elsewhere, I have discussed this in terms of *xenophobic queerphobia*, meaning the strikingly widespread claim across many cultures that nonnormative sexualities and genders originate outside the self-same collectivity (here, for Hindu nationalists, outside the Hindu nation), generally in some enemy camp (Bacchetta 1999b). This notion exiles queers from their own societies. This particular Hindu nationalist claim reverberates with yet another xenophobic queerphobic discourse, that of the colonial British who designated homosexuality as the *oriental vice* they maintained some Britishers had adopted due to excessive immersion in Indian culture. Much current research demonstrates the antiquity and historical continuity of lesbianism, and other alternate sexualities, in Hindu (and other faith) contexts in India, as recorded in ancient sacred texts, in iconography such as at the temple of Khajuraho or the Tara-Taratini temple of Orissa, and in currently surviving practices such as *maitri karar* (friendship agreement between two women, a type of lesbian marriage) in villages in Gujarat (Kanchana 1986; ABVA 1991; Thadani 1996; Ratti 1993:21–33).

While Hindu nationalist action against *Fire* was clearly motivated by lesbophobia, as Geeta Patel (1999) has argued, it was also a convenient way to divert attention from recent Hindu nationalist political and economic failures. The anti-*Fire* protest began only after the ruling BJP lost in several key states in the November 28 state elections, largely because of discontent with its economic policies which had led to soaring prices of basic consumer items such as onions. Moreover, the BJP faced internal Hindu nationalist opposition: the BJP favored opening key state-controlled sectors, such as insurance, to foreign investment, while hard-core RSS leaders favored the status quo (state control). In the past, when Hindu nationalists have felt defeated or divided they have embarked on new issues to re-create unity. Accordingly, following the state elections, on December 3, BJP Home Minister L. K. Advani announced that his government had arranged to protect a shrine disputed by Hindus and Muslims in the southern state of Karnataka, following the VHP claim that it would form suicide squads to take possession of the structure.

The same day, December 3, newspapers reported that on December 2, approximately two hundred members of the HSS had trashed two theaters in Mumbai while *Fire* was being viewed, breaking window glass, destroying a ticket counter, and burning posters of the film. This action, combined with the shrine announcement noted above meant that Hindu nationalists had set off two different diversionary tactics at once. The HSS repeated its attacks on theaters in Delhi on December 3, and on December 6 in Calcutta.

As news about the cinema trashings spread, they aroused widespread protest, some of which was aimed against censorship (mainly from the film industry), and some against the exiling of lesbians (by lesbian, women's, left, and anticommunal groups). Renowned film star Dilip Kumar, along with five others, filed a Supreme Court case calling for the right to create art without censorship, and to have *Fire*'s screening protected under articles of the Constitution relating to freedom of speech, expression, assembly, life and liberty, conscience, and so on. Enraged HSS activists assembled in front of Dilip Kumar's home in their underwear to protest "the exhibition of perverse acts," sarcastically claiming that he "should not be offended when we too behave as is our right—in an obscene manner" (Patel 1999).

As news of the cinema trashings spread, lesbian and women's groups mobilized energetically against them. On December 7, lesbians, artists, and women's groups, along with *Fire* producer Deepa Mehta, held a candlelight vigil in front of a previously trashed theater in Delhi (Regal Cinema), photos of which appeared throughout the press, including the Hindu nationalist press. One of the most visible vigil banners read "Indian and Lesbian" (thereby countering the HSS claim that lesbianism is not Indian).

At times, the objectives of the protestors actually clashed. Ashwini Sukthankar (1999: xi) notes that certain anticensorship segments of the media accused lesbian demonstrators carrying signs outing themselves as Indian lesbians of "hijacking" the movement against censorship. Lesbians critiqued those segments for circumventing the issue of the homophobia that had inspired the attacks in the first place. During this struggle *Fire* was taken out of all cinemas and resubmitted to the Censor Board which had earlier passed it (all films in India must go through the Censor Board before being publicly shown). It then became an object of dispute within the Parliament. Politicians, mainly from the Congress Party and Communist Party, took legal action to get the film reinstated. A host of other politicians denounced the film, including J. Jayalitha of the All India

Anna Dravida Munnetra Kazhagam, who has long been publicly suspected of being a lesbian herself.[16]

Lesbian action was further complicated by the shifting discourse of the filmmaker. Initially, on December 7, the press reported that Deepa Mehta had affirmed: "lesbian relationship is part of Indian heritage, and the film brings into the public domain the hypocrisy and tyranny of the patriarchal family, the issue of women's sexuality, and makes a strong statement about women-women relationships" (CLR 1999:15). Indeed, the film's notoriety had initially come from awards it had won in lesbian and gay film festivals throughout the West. By January 2, however, Mehta stated that she did not "believe in lesbianism," and denied that the film was about lesbians, claiming it was about loneliness instead (CLR 1999:18). In one interview she claimed that "should her daughter ever tell her that she was a lesbian she would be dismayed" (CLR 1999:18).

Some lesbians, in order to defend lesbian rights, found themselves supporting a film they were critical of, by a director whom they feel used them for commercial purposes.[17] Some lesbians have critiqued the film (CLR 1999:6–7) on the grounds that it constructs lesbianism as due to individually bad experiences with exceptionally horrible men instead of as a positive choice by women who love women; it is made for a Western audience, not for Indians, and exoticizes India through the idealization of colorful streets, the spreading of colorful saris, shots of monuments familiar to tourists such as the Taj Mahal, and the insertion of simplistic fragments of the highly complicated epic Ramayana throughout). Furthermore, they argue, the film does not deal with most of the problems lesbians face in India, from the lack of space in which to interact in privacy to issues of identity.

One of the most remarkable features of the struggle around *Fire* is the wide alliance that formed to defend lesbian rights. Eventually, over forty groups (lesbian, women's, trade union, left, anticommunal, and others) united to form a coalition called The Campaign for Lesbian Rights (aka Caleri). The Campaign activists organized demonstrations and candlelight vigils, distributed over seven thousand copies of a leaflet entitled *Myths and Reality—Lesbianism* which gives a contact number for isolated lesbians (reproduced in CLR 1999:36) in public spaces throughout Delhi (universities, cinema halls, and the like) for three months, held public discussions, spoke to the press, and wrote reports and articles. The Campaign continues to exist, to educate the population at large and to press for lesbian rights.

Individual feminists, supportive of the Campaign, also responded sharply and publicly. For example, in a particularly pertinent article in the mainstream press, Ritu Menon of Kali for Women (the first feminist publishing company in South Asia, based in Delhi), countered the Hindu nationalist claim that they were protesting *Fire* to protect Hindu womanhood and civilization. Menon (1998) pointed out that Hindu nationalists have never denounced any form of women's oppression, be it wife battering, dowry murder, rape, or women's economic exploitation, instead opposing women's right to resist oppression and to form bonds with each other. An issue of the anticommunal journal *Communalism Combat*, featured a prolesbian and anticensorship special report on *Fire* (Ghosh 1999:16–19; Madhavi Kapur 1999:20; Ratna Kapur 1999:19). In Delhi, for the first time ever the anticommunalist group Sampradayikta Virodhi Andolan added homosexuals to its list of groups persecuted by Hindu nationalists.

The Campaign for Lesbian Rights and related allied activities mark a concrete shift in lesbian and gay struggles in India. When lesbian and gay issues had surfaced in the press in the 1980s, largely through reporting on lesbian marriages (which often resulted in the partners being separated), lesbian suicides (often due to the threat of separation), and the formation of gay groups in India, the IWM did not openly support them (Naseem 1991:5–6; Thadani 1994:5), with some notable exceptions (such as Jagori, Joint Women's Program, Kali for Women, all in Delhi, and Forum against Women's Oppression in Mumbai). Nor did these issues draw much support from academics, left activists, or anyone else. When at the end of 1991 the group AIDS Bhedbhav Virodhi Andolan (ABVA, AIDS Anti-Discrimination Movement) presented *Less than Gay*, the first citizens' report on the status of homosexuality in India, at a press conference in Delhi, the event and the book were virtually ignored. Why, then, did this situation change?

The shift took place in the context of major sociopolitical changes and the increasing assertion of lesbian and gay political subjectivities. Hindu nationalism arose throughout the late 1980s and 1990s to attain national governmental power in April 1998, and in the process it polarized visions of India's future: Hindu nationalists proposed anti-Other exclusivity, while the IWM, lesbians, gays, leftists, and anticommunalists of all sorts proposed inclusivity. During that period, lesbians and gays organized within India and the diaspora: through organizations (for a list, see any issue of *Trikone Magazine*, published in San Jose, California), publications (Ratti 1993; and, again, *Trikone*), and web sites. They began to represent themselves in films such as Pratibha Parmar's documentary *Khush*. IWM and anticommunalist groups had already been sites for alliances across classes and faiths and had already forged personal trust. When it came down to it, one could either side with Hindu nationalist hate or with a wide vision of inclusivity.

## Concluding Remarks

In the two cases discussed above, women's alliances that emerged in the crisis situations were based in previously formed cross-positional networks. They involved the strategic collective use of differential positionings for common ends, ultimately to undo the normative *divisions* that such positionings otherwise imply. The alliances required differential efforts from each participant. Women on the subordinated end of the normative order's hierarchies had to overcome the distrust that ideologically structures the divisions, to establish trust with those dominantly positioned. Those positioned dominantly, in contrast, had to separate from their dominant positions and from the dominantly positioned collectivity of which they are a part; in most cases this entailed a loss of at least some privilege. This realignment of solidarities sometimes came at a high cost: consider, for example, how *basti* women took control of the situation in Ahmedabad initially against their husbands' will, and the fact that lesbians who came out publicly in the pro-*Fire* actions risked familial alienation or reprisal. In both cases, the women inadvertently exposed the fragility of the positional divisions, and thus the potentially impermanent nature of the normative order itself.

Elsewhere across the globe too, extraordinary vertical and horizontal alliances have often been most threatening to the normative order. Consider, for example, the cross-positionally composed (by race, ethnicity, class, and religion) lesbian collective called DYKETACTICS! in the mid-1970s in Philadelphia. One of hundreds of such collectives in the United States, it was not perceived as threatening until it publicly supported antiwar activists Susan Saxe and Cathy Power, united with elements of the black movement by raising funds for Assata Shakur and attending her trial, organized neighborhood women to struggle against their slum landlord, and explained through alternative media such as *Hera Feminist Newspaper* (Philadelphia) and *Off Our Backs* (Washington) why all lesbians should oppose imperialism, racism, and the class system as pillars of the heteropatriarchy.

In an early period (the 1970s) of the women's liberation movement in France too, *groupes de quartiers* ("neighborhood groups," generally in low-income neighborhoods) allied with the more bourgeois-positioned, albeit Marxist-informed, wing of the university-based women's movement (Rosenfeld 1988:457–66). From the early 1980s in Paris, the Maison des femmes ("women's center") housed fifteen women's groups working on single issues such as employment, immigration rights, abortion, racism, and lesbian rights. Members were diversely positioned (by class, race, national origin, and sexuality). Having a common space, and frequent interactions, allowed each group to call upon others to mobilize massively in crisis situations around their issues (Rosenfeld 1988:457–66).

In all these cases, women's capacities to form alliances are informed by analyses of positional oppressions inclusive of, and beyond, gender. And the activists who have actually formed the alliances, wherever they might be positioned in the matrix of oppressions in their contexts, are women who have actively sought to work across positional divisions toward a higher common goal, both on a day-to-day basis and in crisis situations. This is a lesson from which all women might learn.

### ACKNOWLEDGMENTS

I would like to thank Karen Tice, Seeta Veeraghanta, France Winddance Twine, and Kathleen Blee for invaluable feedback on this essay. I am also greatly indebted to the following friends and colleagues for all our conversations on or related to the subject of this essay: Sheba Chhachhi, Geeta Patel, Sandhya Luther, Ashwini Sukthankar, Abha Bhaiya, Ritu Menon, Gauri Chowdhary, Kamla Bhasin, Gita Shah, Sangeeta Schroff, Rita Mallik, and Tanushri Gangopadhayay.

### NOTES

1. The women's and anticommunal organizations in question are Jagori, SEWA, Ankur, Sampradayikta Virodhi Andolan, among others. The interviews with anticommunal activists have been nondirective and ongoing from 1986 to 1998. The Hindu nationalist organizations in question are the Rastriya Swayamsevak Sangh, the Vishwa Hindu Parishad, the Bharatiya Janata Party, and the Hind Shiv Sena.

2. I employ the term "Indian Women's Movement" because it is the self-des-

ignation of those who comprise it. The category is extremely wide, including individuals, groups, and organizations that struggle to improve women's lives in a variety of ways. I refer to individuals and groups as feminist only in cases where they self-identify as such.

3. See, for example, Imtiaz Ahmad, ed., *Caste and Social Stratification among Muslims in India* (New Delhi: Manohar, 1978).

4. The Indian government defines poverty as being without income sufficient to ensure access to minimal nutritional standards. Middle-class occupations include owning a small business, being a corporate executive, lawyer, physician, white-collar worker, or landowning farmer.

5. "Untouchables" number 130 million.

6. Joint families are composed of aging parents and the families of their married sons, and can also include the families of their married grandsons. Nuclear families are composed of parents and children only. Polygamous families include a husband, his wives, and their unmarried children.

7. For an excellent overview and insightful critique of this theory, see Thapar 1996.

8. On the history of some of these struggles, see O'Hanlon 1985; also Gore 1989; Kavlekar 1979; Schinde 1985. On current Dalit movements, see Murugkar 1991; Omvedt 1995; the vast work of Eleanore Zelliot, and the literature produced by Dalit activists and academics published by the Dalit Sahitya Akademy, such as *Dalit Voice* (fortnightly newspaper from Bangalore, India); V. T. Rajshekar, *Why Godse Killed Gandhi?* (Bangalore: Dalit Sahitya Akademy, 1986); Rajshekar, *Ambedkar and His Conversion*, 1983. The last few decades have witnessed many violent struggles around caste. Among the most highly publicized have been the rapes of low-caste women by upper-caste men (Phulan Devi, on whose life the film *The Bandit Queen* is based, did much to bring this to international attention). Another high-profile struggle is upper-caste protest against the government's 1990 implementation and the 1992 increase of the *reservation* quotas, which culminated in self-immolation by fire by upper-caste students in Delhi, Bombay, and several other major cities. Today low-caste people are more organized, in groups such as the Dalit Panthers, in think tanks (such as the Dalit Sahitya Akademy), as cultural producers (in Dalit poetry and literary movements), and as vote banks.

9. Hindu nationalists have argued that Indian Islamist organizations are akin to their counterparts in the Mahgreb or Middle East. This analogy, however, only works by conveniently forgetting that the organizations are differently positioned in power relations in these different societies. That is, in the former, Islam is the faith of a numerical and sociological minority (12 percent of the total Indian population) while in most of the latter it is the faith of the majority. Thus, notwithstanding the obvious difficulty of drawing analogies across sites, Indian Islamist organizations might be more usefully thought of as somewhat akin to

organizations of minorities elsewhere that construct globalizing, antidominant discourses, but in reaction to oppression, also reproduce elements of supremacist logics in inverted form and in highly complicated ways, such as The Nation of Islam in the United States.

10. See Golwalkar 1939; Golwalkar 1968; Golwalkar 1996; Dubashi 1992; Goel 1998.

11. Elsewhere, I have discussed the Samiti's founding, its separate (and linked) ideological and practical development from the RSS, and its members' differential modes of adherence to Hindu nationalism, in terms of *strategic gender fractionalization* of the overall Hindu nationalist project, which ultimately is determined by men (Bacchetta 1994a, 1996, 1999a, 1999b; on Hindu nationalist women's activism, see Jeffrey and Basu 1998; on the link between family and organization, see Sarkar in Butalia and Sarkar 1996.

12. On typologies of colonialism, see McClintock 1994.

13. Golwalkar states: "To keep the purity of the race and its culture, Germany shocked the world by purging the country of the semite Races—the Jews. Race pride at its highest has been maintained here. Germany has also shown how wellnigh impossible it is for Race and cultures, having differences going to the root, to be assimilated into one united whole, a good lesson for those of us in Hindustan to learn by." Golwalkar 1939:35.

14. Baxi cites the fact that 68 percent of Dalits (untouchables) are denied access to potable water from high-caste Hindu wells, there are sporadic outbreaks of urban anti-Muslim violence, daily exploitation of migrant labor, and the like.

15. From the author's interview with Renana Jhabwala, at SEWA headquarters, August 11, 1986 in Ahmedabad, Gujarat.

16. Jayalitha stated: "Personally, as a responsible leader of a mature political party, I would say that it is better such subjects are not depicted on the screen. In my opinion, entertainment should be clean and wholesome, something which can be viewed by the entire family." CLR 1999:14.

17. Conversation with Sandhya Luther, March 4, 2000, Lexington, Kentucky.

## REFERENCES

Ahmad, Imtiaz, ed. 1978. *Caste and Social Stratification among Muslims in India.* New Delhi: Manohar.

AIDS Bhedbhav Virodhi Andolan (ABVA). 1991. *Less than Gay: A Citizen's Report on the Status of Homosexuality in India.* New Delhi: ABVA.

Alam, Jayanti. 1998. "Women at Work: The Responses of Sewa, Sewu and the ILO." In *Contemporary Social Movements in India: Achievements and Hurdles,* ed. Sebasti L. Raj and Arundhati Roy Chaudhury. New Delhi: Indian Social Institute.

Althusser, Louis. 1972. *Lenin and Philosophy and Other Essays*. New York: Monthly Review Press.

Andersen, Walter, and Shridhar Damle. 1987. *The Brotherhood in Saffron: The Rashtriya Swayamsevak Sangh and Hindu Revivalism*. New Delhi: Vistaar Publications.

Anderson, Benedict. 1991. *Imagined Communities: Reflections on the Origin and Spread of Nationalism*. London: Verso.

Bacchetta, Paola. 1994a. "'All Our Goddesses Are Armed': Religion, Resistance and Revenge in the Life of a Militant Hindu Nationalist Woman." In *Against All Odds: Essays on Women, Religion and Development from India and Pakistan*, ed. Ritu Menon, Kamla Bhasin, and Nighat Said Khan. Delhi: Kali for Women.

———. 1994b. "Communal Property/Sexual Property: On Representations of Muslim Women in a Hindu Nationalist Discourse." In *Forging Identities: Gender, Community and the State*, ed. Zoya Hasan. Delhi: Kali for Women.

———. 1996. "Hindu Nationalist Women as Ideologues: The Sangh, the Samiti and Their Differential Concepts of the Hindu Nation." In *Embodied Violence: Communalizing Women's Sexuality in South Asia*, ed. Kumari Jayawardena and Malathi de Alwis. New Delhi: Kali for Women.

———. 1999a. "Militant Hindu Nationalist Women Re-Imagine Themselves: Notes on Mechanisms of Expansion/Adjustment." *Journal of Women's History*, vol. 10, no. 4 (winter): 125–47.

———. 1999b. "When the (Hindu) Nation Exiles Its Queers." *Social Text*, no. 61 (winter): 141–66.

Ballhatchet, Kenneth. 1980. *Race, Sex and Class under the Raj: Imperial Attitudes and Policies and Their Critics, 1793–1905*. London: Weidenfeld and Nicolson.

Basu, Amrita. 1992. *Two Faces of Protest: Contrasting Modes of Women's Activism in India*. Berkeley: University of California Press.

———. 1993. "Feminism Inverted: The Real Women and Gendered Imagery of Hindu Nationalism." *Bulletin of Concerned Asian Scholars*, vol. 25, no. 4 (October–December): 25–37.

Baxi, Upendra. 1990. "Reflections on the Reservation Crisis in Gujarat." In *Mirrors of Violence: Communities, Riots, Survivors*, ed. Veena Das. New Delhi: Oxford University Press.

Bhasin, Kamla, Ritu Menon, and Nighat Said Khan, eds. 1994. *Against All Odds: Essays on Women, Religion and Development from India and Pakistan*. New Delhi: Kali for Women.

Bhatia, V. P. 1998. *Raise Tempers, Lacerate and Raise the Whirlwind: The Philosophy behind Deepa Mehta's Kinky Film Fire*. Organiser, December 27, 13.

Butalia, Urvashi, and Tanika Sarkar. 1996. *Women and the Hindu Right: A Collection of Essays*. New Delhi: Kali for Women.

*Campaign for Lesbian Rights (CLR)*. 1999. *Lesbian Emergence: A Citizen's Report*. New Delhi: Usha Printers.

Chakravorty, Bankabehari. 1995. *Itihasa of Bharatvarsha from the Bharatiya Viewpoint.* Calcutta: New Bharati Press.

Chandra, Bipan. 1984. *Communalism in Modern India.* New Delhi: Vani Educational Books.

Chatterjee, Mirai. 1994. "Religion, Secularism, and Organizing Women Workers." In *Against All Odds: Essays on Women, Religion and Development from India and Pakistan,* ed. Kamla Bhasin, Ritu Menon, and Nighat Said Khan. New Delhi: Kali for Women.

Chatterjee, Partha. 1994. *The Nation and Its Fragments: Colonial and Postcolonial Histories.* Delhi: Oxford University Press.

Chhachhi, Amrita. 1989. "The State, Religious Fundamentalism, and Religion: Trends in South Asia." *Economic and Political Weekly,* March 18, 567–78.

Collins, Patricia Hill. 1991. *Black Feminist Thought: Knowledge, Consciousness, and the Politics of Empowerment.* New York: Routledge.

Curran, J. A. 1951. *Militant Hinduism in Indian Politics: A Study of the R.S.S.* New York: Institute of Pacific Relations.

Dubashi, Jay. 1992. *The Road to Ayodhya.* New Delhi: Voice of India.

Fanon, Frantz. 1974. *Les damnés de la terre.* Paris, France: Maspero.

Farquhar, J. N. 1967. *Modern Religious Movements in India.* Delhi: Munshiram Manoharlal.

Gadkari, Usha. 1996. *Ancient Afro-Hindu Ethos.* Nagpur, India: Surya Offset.

Gates, Henry Louis Jr. 1986. "'Race' as a Trope of the World." In *"Race," Writing and Difference,* ed. H. L. Gates Jr. Chicago: University of Chicago Press.

Ghosh, Shohini. 1999. "From the Frying Pan into the Fire." *Communalism Combat,* no. 50 (January): 16–19.

Goel, Sita Ram, ed. 1998. *Hindu Temples: What Happened to Them,* vol. 1. New Delhi: Voice of India.

Goffman, Erving. 1963. *Stigma: Notes on the Management of Spoiled Identity.* New York: Simon and Schuster.

Golwalkar, M. S. 1939. *We or Our Nation Defined.* Nagpur: Bharat Publications.

———. 1968. *Bunch of Thoughts.* Bangalore: Vikrama Prakashan.

———. 1980. *Bunch of Thoughts.* Bangalore: Jagarana Prakashana.

———. 1996. *Bunch of Thoughts.* Bangalore: Sahitya Sindhu Prakashana.

Gopal, Sarvepalli, ed. 1991. *Anatomy of a Confrontation: The Babri Masjid-Ramjamabhoomi Issue.* New Delhi: Penguin.

Gore, M. S. 1989. *Non-Brahmin Movement in Maharashtra.* New Delhi: Segment Books.

Gould, Stephan Jay. 1996. *The Mismeasure of Man.* New York: W. W. Norton.

Government of India (GOI). 1990. *India 1990: A Reference Annual.* New Delhi: Publications Division of Ministry for Information and Broadcasting.

Goyal, J. B. 1999. Interview on BBC, New Delhi, December 4.

Hall, Stuart. 1994. "Cultural Identity and Diaspora." In *Colonial Discourse and*

*Post-Colonial Theory: A Reader*, ed. Patrick Williams and Laura Chrisman. New York: Columbia University Press.

Hasan, Zoya, ed. 1994. *Forging Identities: Gender, Communities and Nations*. New Delhi: Kali for Women.

Inden, Ronald. 1986. "Orientalist Constructions of India." *Modern Asian Studies*, vol. 20, no. 3: 401–46.

Jaffrolot, Christophe. 1996. *The Hindu Nationalist Movement in India*. New Delhi: Viking.

Jayaprasad, K. 1991. *RSS and Hindu Nationalism*. New Delhi: Deep and Deep Publications.

Jayawardena, Kumari. 1994. *Feminism and Nationalism in the Third World*. London: Zed Press.

Jayawardena, Kumari, and Malathi de Alwis, eds. 1996. *Embodied Violence: Communalizing Women's Sexuality in South Asia*. New Delhi: Kali for Women.

Jeffery, Patricia, and Amrita Basu, eds. 1998. *Appropriating Gender: Women's Activism and Politicized Religion in South Asia*. New York: Routledge.

Kanchana. 1986. Untitled paper on lesbians in ancient Sanskrit texts, circulated among lesbians in Delhi. Author's archives.

Kapur, Madhavi Shahani. 1999. *Fear of Fire. Communalism Combat*, no. 50, January 20.

Kapur, Ratna. 1999. *Is Fire about Free Speech? Sex? Culture? Communalism Combat*, no. 50, January, 19.

Kavlekar, Kashinath. 1979. *Non-Brahmin Movement in Southern India*, 1873–1949. Kolhapur, India: Shivaji University Press.

Kumar, Radha. 1993. *The History of Doing*. New Delhi: Kali for Women.

———. 1995. "From Chipko to Sati: The Contemporary Indian Women's Movement." In *The Challenge of Local Feminisms: Women's Movements in Global Perspective*, ed. Amrita Basu. Boulder, Colo.: Westview Press.

Lallemand, Myriam. 1991. "La Métaphore sexuelle dans le discours de Jean-Marie Le Pen." In *CelciuS*, no. 42, July–August, 3–9.

Lane, Christopher. 1995. *The Ruling Passion: British Colonial Allegory and the Paradox of Homosexual Desire*. Durham: Duke University Press.

Lesselier, Claude. 1991. "De la Vièrge Marie à Jeanne d'Arc: Images de femmes à l'extrême droite." *Homme et société*, no. 99–100: 99–114.

Leys Stepan, Nancy. 1991. *"The Hour of Eugenics": Race, Gender and Nation in Latin America*. Ithaca: Cornell University Press.

Malik, Kenan. 1996. *The Meaning of Race: Race, History and Culture in Western Society*. New York: New York University Press.

Mani, Lata. 1989. "Contentious Traditions: The Debate on Sati in Colonial India." In *Recasting Women*, ed. Kumkum Sangari and Sudesh Vaid. New Delhi: Kali for Women.

McClintock, Anne. 1994. "The Angel of Progress: Pitfalls of the Term 'Post-colonialism.'" In *Colonial Discourse and Post-Colonial Theory: A Reader*, ed. Patrick Williams and Laura Chrisman. New York: Columbia University Press.

McClintock, Anne. 1995. *Imperial Leather: Race, Gender and Sexuality in the Colonial Context*. New York: Routledge.

Melucci, Alberto. 1998. "The Process of Collective Identity." In *Social Movements and Culture*, ed. H. Johnston and B. Klandermans. Minneapolis: University of Minnesota Press.

Memmi, Albert. 1991. *The Colonizer and the Colonized*. Boston: Beacon Press.

Menon, Ritu. 1998. "The Fire Within: Shiv Sainiks, Women and Indian Culture." *Indian Express*, December 9.

Murugkar, Lata. 1991. *Dalit Panther Movement in Maharashtra: A Sociological Appraisal*. Bombay: Popular Prakashan.

Nandy, Ashish. 1983. *The Intimate Enemy: Loss and Recovery of Self under Colonialism*. New Delhi: Oxford University Press.

Naseem. 1991. "Reflections of an Indian Lesbian." *Bombay Dost*, no. 1–2, 5–6.

O'Hanlon, Rosalind. 1985. *Caste, Conflict, and Ideology: Mahatma Jyotirao Phule and Low-Caste Protest in Nineteenth-Century Western India*. London: Cambridge University Press.

Omvedt, Gail. 1979. *We Will Smash This Prison*. Bombay: Orient Longman.

———. 1995. *Dalit Visions: The Anti-Caste Movement and the Construction of an Indian Identity*. Hyderabad: Orient Longman.

Pandey, Gyanendra. 1992. *The Construction of Communalism in Colonial North India*. New Delhi: Oxford University Press.

Patel, Geeta. 1999. "On Fire." Unpublished manuscript presented at the annual meeting of the Modern Languages Association, San Francisco.

Prakash, Gyan. 1992. "Writing Post-Orientalist Histories of the Third World: Indian Historiography Is Good to Think." In *Colonialism and Culture*, ed. Nicholas B. Dirks. Ann Arbor: University of Michigan Press.

Premi, Mahendra K. 1991. *India's Population: Heading towards a Billion. An Analysis of the 1991 Census Provisional Results*. New Delhi: B. R. Publishing Corporation.

Ratti, Rakesh, ed. 1993. *Lotus of Another Color: An Unfolding of the South Asian Gay and Lesbian Experience*. Boston: Alyson.

Ray, Raka. 1999. *Fields of Protest: Women's Movements in India*. Minneapolis: University of Minnesota Press.

Rose, Kalima. 1995. *Where Women Are Leaders: The SEWA Movement in India*. London: Zed Press.

Rosenfeld, Marthe. 1988. "Splits in French Feminism/Lesbianism." In *For Lesbians Only: A Separatist Anthology*, ed. Sarah Lucia Hoagland and Julia Penelope. London: Onlywomen Press.

Said, Edward. 1978. *Orientalism*. London: Routledge and Kegan Paul.

Sarda, Har Bilas. 1984 edition. *Hindu Superiority: An Attempt to Determine the Position of the Hindu Race in the Scale of Nations*. New Delhi: Vedic Hindu Academy.

Savarkar, Vinayak Damodar. [1923] 1969. *Hindutva: Who Is a Hindu?* Bombay: Veer Savarkar Prakashan.

Schinde, J. R. 1985. *Dynamics of Cultural Revolution: Nineteenth Century Maharashtra*. New Delhi: Ajanta.

Selliah, S. 1989. "The Self-Employed Women's Association." Geneva: International Labour Office.

Seshadri, ed. 1988. *The RSS: A Vision in Action*. Bangalore, India: Jagarana Prakashana.

Shanin, Teodor. 1997. "The Idea of Progress." In *The Post-Development Reader*, ed. Majid Rahnema and Victoria Bawtree. London: Zed Press.

Sinha, Mrinalini. 1997. *Colonial Masculinity: The "Manly Englishman" and the "Effeminate Bengali" in the Late Nineteenth Century*. New Delhi: Kali for Women.

Sinha, Rakesh. 1999. "West's Cultural Laboratory." *Organiser*, January 10, 17 and 22.

Smith, Anna Marie. 1994. *New Right Discourse on Race and Sexuality: Britain 1968–1990*. Cambridge: Cambridge University Press.

Somerville, Siobhan. 1997. "Scientific Racism and the Invention of the Homosexual Body." In *The Gender and Sexuality Reader: Culture, History, Political Economy*, ed. Roger N. Lancaster and Micaela di Leonardo. New York: Routledge.

Sreenivasan, Jyotsna. 2000. *Ela Bhatt: Uniting Women in India*. New York: Feminist Press.

Sukthankar, Ashwini, ed. 1999. *Facing the Mirror: Lesbian Writing from India*. New Delhi: Penguin.

Taguieff, Pierre-André. 1987. *La force du préjugé: essai sur le racisme et ses doubles*. Paris: Gallimard.

———. 1991. "Les métamorphoses idéologiques du racisme et la crise de l'antiracisme." In *Face au racisme: analyses, hypothèses, perspectives*, vol. 2, ed. Pierre André Taguieff. Paris: Éditions la Découverte.

Thadani, Giti. 1994. "No Lesbians Please—We Are Indian: Shattering Some Popular Myths." *Trikone Magazine*, April, 5.

———. 1996. *Sakhiyani: Lesbian Desire in Ancient and Modern India*. London: Cassell.

Thapar, Romila. 1996. "The Theory of Aryan Race and India: History and Politics." *Social Scientist*, vol. 24, nos. 1–3 (January–March): 3–29.

Unsigned. 1999. "Shabana's Swear, Rabri's Roar, Teresa's Terror? The Three Which Sustain Secularism." *Organiser*, January 10, 8.

U.S. Government (USG). 1995. *Library of Congress Country Study: India*. Washington, D.C.: Library of Congress.

# Chapter 11

# Working with Feminists in Zimbabwe

## A Black American's Experience of Transnational Alliances

## Carolyn Martin Shaw

In the fall of 1983, I joined with black, white, coloured (mixed race), and Asian women in the Women's Action Group (WAG) to protest Operation Clean-Up, an attempt by the Zimbabwe government to rid the capital city of prostitutes and vagrants. During Operation Clean-Up, thousands of men and women were picked up in urban areas throughout the country by the police, army, and the Youth Brigade of the ruling party as the government sought to contain what it saw as a social and moral blight. Though some report that an equal number of men and women were picked up, the roundup of women was especially indiscriminate: in addition to actual prostitutes, those arrested and detained as prostitutes included women domestic workers, homemakers, teachers, nurses, secretaries, schoolgirls, and factory workers (two hundred women workers at one factory were picked up on their way to work, leading the manager to believe that there was a strike). Most were black women.

In an article without a byline in a Zimbabwean newsmagazine, Zimbabwean sociologist Rudo Gaidzanwa asserts that "Overall, the number of men detained and held probably equalled that of the women." She goes on to describe the conditions in the detention camps—tin huts surrounded by barbed wire with minimal facilities, little clean water, and rampant disease. She also reports that a pregnant woman released from one of the camps "told us that soldiers were sexually abusing women."[1] In this article, Gaidzanwa relates the story of the manager who found his workforce being held in a football stadium. Unaccompanied women in bars, but also women walking down the street, at bus stops, and in movie theaters were arrested. Some women accompanied by men were arrested, and women were even arrested in their homes: coloured women especially complained of this abuse. The headmaster of a primary school told me of going to the aid of one of the teachers from his school when she was being arrested during the intermission at a movie theater. He was successful in preventing her arrest, but when he walked across the lobby to tell his wife of this success, he found that his wife had been arrested.

Once arrested, women were held in police stations or in compounds erected for this purpose in rural areas. Under an emergency powers act which allowed the arrests, detainees had no access to courts or to legal representation. Women put in detention were released only if they presented marriage certificates or proof of employment. The indignity did not stop there: some women were evicted from their homes, lost their jobs, husbands, or children because of the taint of having been arrested as prostitutes. "Marriage Certificates Required for Women's Release from Jail" read the headline of an article in a U.S. newspaper, which explained that under Operation Clean-Up thousands of women from all walks of life who had been arrested as prostitutes were released from detention or imprisonment only if they presented valid marriage licenses or documents certifying that they were employed.

In this chapter I describe the founding of the Zimbabwe WAG, now a strong nongovernmental organization (NGO) with offices throughout Zimbabwe, and highlight problems of international and interracial feminist organizing in Zimbabwe during that period. I also tell my story. The story I tell is, in part, a personal one, recounting what it was like for me as a U.S. black feminist to work with feminists in Zimbabwe.

I did not feel an immediate affinity with Zimbabwean culture. My feminist politics and humanist empathy led me to become active there. I found many women I could identify and seek solidarity with—from the factory workers who worried that the manager would demand that she have sex with him to keep her job, to the new wife smarting under the demands of hostile sisters-in-law, to the young woman who asked me in halting English only minutes after we met, "Is it better to marry the person you love or the one who loves you?" There are many ways to form alliances of feeling with women in other countries, to hold hands across divisions of race, class, education, religious faith, and sexuality. The problem is, how does a reluctant representative of the United States make a contribution without being charged with cultural imperialism? In this I was not successful. But the movement I participated in was successful.

## The Zimbabwean Context

In 1980, Zimbabwe, formerly Rhodesia, achieved black majority rule after a protracted war against a white settler regime, led by Ian Smith, which in 1964 had declared unilateral independence from the British colonial government. Never more than 2 percent of the population, white settlers had the lion's share of the wealth and owned two-thirds of the best agricultural land, with blacks generally confined to overpopulated native reserves on land of low fertility and productivity. Ian Smith called on two different models for his white supremacist regime: the U.S. colonial model in its unilateral declaration of independence from Britain and the South African model in its separate developmental goals for blacks and white. Zimbabwean blacks fought against the renegade regime primarily in two guerilla armies, supported by the neighboring countries of Mozambique, Zambia, and Tanzania, and by China, North Korea, the Soviet Union, and other eastern block countries. The United Nations called for economic sanctions and the United States and other Western countries joined in a not very effective embargo against the Smith regime in Rhodesia.

The Zimbabwean independence movement centered on mobilizing peasants, with the guerillas especially allying with disenfranchised youth and women. As in the first war against the colonialist where spirit medium Ambuya [grandmother] Nehanda became a symbol of leadership, spirit mediums, many of them women, dispensed military and political advice. Political scientist Christine Sylvester characterizes the conjuncture of interests between guerrillas, spirit mediums, youth, and women as follows:

> Women wanted to end domestic violence and spirit mediums asserted traditional wisdom. Both demands are compatible with some guerilla concerns to valorise and not dominate subaltern perspectives, *and* with the nationalist and Rhodesian-British interests in dominating local leaders (the indirect rule tradition). Male youth interest in elevated status resonates with guerilla efforts to articulate local grievances to a larger project and with unprogressive traditions of male dominance.[2]

Women, especially in the rural areas, were central to the war of independence, as suppliers of food and clothing, and in maintaining and protecting lines of communication and places of encampment for "the boys," as the Zimbabwean armed forces were often called. Margaret Viki, a married woman and mother of seven during the war, put it this way:

> I think that if the women had not been there the freedom fighters would not have won the war. Women did a great job. Cooking and providing food for the freedom fighters was a way of fighting on its own.[3]

There were also a number of girls carrying guns and fighting alongside the boys. One estimate is as many as 250,000 young women were active combatants during the war that lasted about fourteen years.[4] Women combatants suffered the hardships of ill-provided for guerilla armies against the well-stocked armory and airplanes of the Rhodesian forces. But for many of the women the war was the first time that they had worked beside men as equals. With this sense of accomplishment they helped build the new Zimbabwe.

Robert Mugabe, president of Zimbabwe from its founding to the present day, established a Ministry of Community and Development and Women's Affairs in his first cabinet and gave the portfolio to Teurai Ropa Nhongo, the female commandant of one of the Zimbabwean liberation forces. The association of women and community development represented in this ministry is not unusual in sub-Saharan Africa, as women are abundant in the rural areas where resources—electricity, water, roads, transportation, schools, clinics, and government offices—are scarce. The Ministry of Community Development and Women's Affairs (CDWA) has a short and unhappy history. Its immediate precursor was the Women's Department during the formation of the Zimbabwe African National Union (ZANU) in 1963.[5] The Ministry of Cooperatives was once joined with CDWA. Christine Sylvester in a study of feminism and cooperatives in Zimbabwe reports that "by 1989 the government had hived Cooperatives, along with Community Development from Women's Affairs, and placed Women's Affairs under the Senior Minister of Political Affairs."[6]

Within the spirit of social transformation that was so pervasive after independence, Zimbabwe passed the Legal Age of Majority Act (LAMA) which made women legal adults at the age of eighteen, giving them, among other rights, the right to vote, to sign legal contracts, and to marry without their parents' permission. The implications of the LAMA were not clear. For example, women did not understand that under LAMA they could be legal guardians of their children after divorce or the death of their husbands. Zimbabwe followed the Legal Age of Majority Act with several other progressive laws aimed at eliminating gender inequality and promoting the well-being of women and children: the Labor Relations Act (1985) abolished sex discrimination in employment and provides maternity leave in

some jobs, the Matrimonial Causes Act (1985) required courts to order equitable distribution of property at divorce, and the Maintenance Amendment Act (1987 and 1989) enabled the courts to garnish income for payment of court-ordered spousal and child support.[7]

## Operation Clean-Up

This is my story. The beginning is quite simple and commonplace: I was
late. Being late is not unusual for me, but this time, my second week in
Harare, the capital of the southern African country Zimbabwe, when I arrived at my faculty apartment, the woman whom I had hired to look after
my house and child was in tears. "I'll try not to be late again," I apologized. I had lost track of time as I walked home from the University of
Zimbabwe where Fulbright had installed me as a Lecturer in Social Anthropology in the Sociology Department of the University of Zimbabwe.
(Anthropology was and is still associated with colonialism, and my being
a black American did not do much to change Zimbabwean perceptions of
the discipline.) Lilas Zimunga, a Shona woman, close to my age at forty,
the mother of seven, was not comforted by my apology. She had limited
command of English, but nonetheless she explained to me that there was
a curfew. If she missed the connecting bus to the high-density suburb
where she lived, she was in danger of being arrested.[8] I scouted around
and found a neighbor who could drive her to a bus stop where she could
get her bus on time.

The next day I found a note slipped under my door at the university
inviting me to join with other women from the university and the community to organize against the government's Operation Clean-Up which
was arresting black and colored women who were away from their homes
after 6 P.M. The year was 1983 and I was about to begin an association
with feminists in Zimbabwe that would be the high point of my career as
an activist anthropologist, but that would leave me second-guessing
those actions over the years.

In the five-week period of Operation Clean-Up, thousands of women
were arrested. The exact number is uncertain. Journalist Ruth Weiss, living
in Zimbabwe at the time, reports that when the issue was addressed in the
legislature the number was put at 6,300 women arrested.[9] Stories of "baby
dumping" regularly appeared in the papers, and painted women as mon-
sters, abandoning or killing newborn infants, but there was little coverage of

the arrests themselves. Zine Chitepo and Elinor Batezat capture the moment on the second page of the booklet, *Women of Zimbabwe Speak Out: Report of the Women's Action Group Workshop* (Harare, May 1984):

> We were operating in an atmosphere of anti-female hysteria which was encouraged by the Press. Leading articles praised the round-ups and urged further sweeps. Cases of baby dumping were given increased prominence, with strong suggestions that prostitution was a causative factor. Allegations were made of baby-dumping on a massive scale in Chitungwiza which later had to be retracted as being totally unfounded.

No newspapers mentioned the deplorable conditions of the detention camps nor the violence the guards perpetrated against the detained women.

## Women's Action Group (WAG)

The Women's Action Group (WAG), a coalition of primarily middle-class women from Zimbabwe, Britain, Australia, and the United States, formed in response to Operation Clean-Up, was only a couple of weeks old when I joined. Ruth Weiss described WAG as "formed, mainly by intellectuals, both Black and White."[10] White expatriate physicians, development officers, and researchers joined with black Zimbabwean lecturers, university students, civil servants, union organizers, and factory workers, with coloured women from government and industry, and one dedicated university staff member of Indian descent. The black factory workers and union organizers had a high school education or less, while the other black, white, and coloured members were university-educated, some at the University of Zimbabwe, others abroad. Most of the expatriate white members had been active in feminist and antiracist movements in their countries.

The white Zimbabweans in WAG had supported the black independence movement that had overthrown the racist regime of Ian Smith's Rhodesia and led Zimbabwe to independence in 1980. In colonial Rhodesia, black and white women seldom had face to face interactions, though black women provided much of the labor on large-scale white farms. Men were the primary domestic servants, and men, black and white, controlled much of women's productive labor and family income. Two well-used tropes capture the self-image of most white settler women: they were pioneers not confined to metropolitan gender roles or they were the civilizing force for rough and ready white men and savage Africans. Most white women had supported the Rhodesian government, and during the liberation struggle white women were active in the police reserves and in the voluntary services, sometimes as the guards who searched black women.[11] White women working with WAG, who had spent time outside Zimbabwe, in identifying as antiracist, feminist, and, in some cases, lesbian, clearly opposed Rhodesian society and culture.

## Asian and Colored Communities: Working across Ethnic Divisions

Months after I became active in WAG, I learned that race had been the cause of a major rift during WAG's first meetings. Nyaradzo Makamure, a dynamic and outspoken university-educated black Zimbabwean, had left the group, complaining of its international and interracial makeup and worrying that it would blunt mass organizing. None of this was evident when I joined WAG after my colleague, a young black woman at the University of Zimbabwe, slipped that note under my office door. At my first meetings, WAG's cause, stopping the roundup and detention of women, was the sole topic of discussion. At that time there were more whites in WAG than blacks, but at the heart of the group black Zimbabwean women from the university and young professionals predominated. Holding the middle ground between white and black, the Asian and coloured communities (neither of which ever amounted to fully 1 percent of the national population) were often, but not always, separate from each other. Members of these communities were able to vote, were better educated, better employed, and better paid than blacks. In an overview of women during the first eight years of independence, Batezat, Mwalo, and Truscott state

> The racial/gender bias was revealed first by the fact that black women comprised only 7 per cent of the total blacks in professional, skilled and semi-skilled categories of employment, while white, coloured and Asian women comprised a third of their respective groups in the same categories. Secondly, the data showed that white, "African," "coloured," and "Asian" women comprised 54, 39, 5 and 2 per cent respectively of the trained female workforce.[12]

Coloured men had fought with the Rhodesian forces against the blacks, and coloured women, not affiliated with WAG, with whom I talked in the early 1980s just after Zimbabwean independence, expressed disdain toward blacks and African culture. More recently a high proportion of both coloured and Asian communities have embraced black identity and an ideology of black unity.[13]

## Feminist Strategies

The plan that WAG devised to end the indiscriminate imprisonment of urban women was to document the women's experiences so that they could be presented to the Prime Minister of the country, to publish reports of the excesses of Operation Clean-Up in the newspapers, and to demand compensation for women who suffered losses and damages due to their arrest. Even though many of us knew that the government action could not have been undertaken without the tacit or explicit agreement of the Minister of Community Development and Women's Affairs, one of three women in the cabinet, we believed that either the government would be moved by the plight of the women as we presented it or that we would embarrass them into ending the roundup. This strategy grew directly from the class positions of most of the members of WAG, from whatever resources WAG could command, and from our personal and political relationships to government. We were unaware of any other organized movement against Operation Clean-Up and, indeed, there was none.

In 1983, WAG members wrote protest letters to the editors of the major newspapers and published analytical articles in an influential newsmagazine. One such statement reveals how basic the rights recently won by women in Zimbabwe were:

> In Zimbabwe the question of women's liberation was first raised in the struggle for independence. And social changes, especially since independence, have meant that some women, particularly in cities, have been able to acquire a measure of freedom denied to them traditionally (but granted to men)—such as the right to live where they like, rights to work, to walk unaccompanied, to choose their own associates and to go about their daily lives without interference. These freedoms and rights have all been challenged by the "clean-up" campaign.[14]

WAG sustained its protests against the campaign, enlisting the Minister of Community Development and Women's Affairs to deliver its statement and documentation to the Prime Minister. Eventually the government ended Operation Clean-Up and released most of the women from prison, though neither compensation nor reparation were awarded. No one believed that it was solely because of WAG that the campaign had ended, but, as stated in a booklet published by the Women's Action Group:

> We feel that the combined efforts at protest had significant influence over the decision of the authorities to release some of the suspected prostitutes. It was admitted that mistakes had been made and that the manner in which the exercise had been conducted was undesirable.[15]

The women's release and the apology were covered by the national daily newspaper. Journalist Ruth Weiss reports that a "Cabinet Minister acknowledged privately that the affair had been mishandled, but added that respectable women had supported Operation Clean-Up" and further that letter writers to the national daily newspaper had rejoiced that with prostitutes out of the way, men would spend their Christmas bonuses on their legal families in the countryside.[16] In fact, roundups of "prostitutes" continued to occur in Zimbabwe, especially in preparation for international conferences.

WAG is still active in Zimbabwe today, seventeen years later. Over the years the Women's Action Group has changed and grown: WAG's membership is now overwhelmingly black, with branches throughout the country. Its membership is no longer primarily middle class; most of its members are women in rural areas and high-density suburbs (formerly black townships). Officially a nongovernment organization (NGO) with a well-paid staff of almost two dozen women and governed by an interracial all-Zimbabwean Board of Trustees, including one man,[17] WAG sends delegates to international meetings and UN conferences and garners funds from international charitable and development agencies, including the Carnegie Foundation, Oxfam U.K., the U.S. Embassy, Kellogg Foundation, and Ford Foundation. WAG produces booklets, including its "Getting to Know Our Bodies" series (on aches and pains, the reproductive system, pregnancy and infertility, sexually transmitted infections, menstruation and menopause, and cancer). Its magazine *Speak Out/Taurai/Khulumani*, published in the three primary languages of Zimbabwe—English, Shona, and Ndebele—is sold at newsstands throughout the country and presents self-help information on economics, law, health and the family, and deals with controversial issues such as AIDS, sexual harassment, domestic violence, and the sexual abuse of children. WAG also produces radio programs, has translated a video on cancer into

Shona and Ndebele, and holds grassroots workshops on health through-out the country. Outreach and promotions increased the number of women and men coming to WAG offices for counseling and legal advice. WAG still takes up issues in opposition to the government, including ex-plaining to women how the government's Economic Structural Adjust-ment Program (ESAP) negatively affects their lives.

## Women of Zimbabwe Speak Out

To return to the early 1980s and the first accomplishments of WAG: as a group of concerned and dedicated women, WAG had been effective in protesting the government roundup of urban women. With the release of the detained women and its primary goal reached within weeks after its inception, the Women's Action Group captured the momentum and turned to addressing the hegemonic representation of black women as parasitic city women versus the virtuous, long-suffering rural wives. This discourse, well established in colonial and postcolonial African countries where long-term male migrant labor is a common pattern, had framed popular discussions of the government campaign against women in towns and cities: city women were thought to be responsible for taking money away from the rural women's husbands who worked in town. With the support of government agencies, nongovernmental organiza-tions, the university, a religious commission, and, especially, financial backing from the Ford Foundation, WAG held a workshop intended to bring together rural and urban women from four provinces around the capital city to address their common and conflicting problems. Govern-ment community development officers, many of them men in the Min-istry of Community Development and Women's Affairs, introduced WAG members and its agenda at meetings in rural areas and funneled funds for women to travel to the capital city. The workshop, held in the spring of 1984, was attended by over five hundred women, one hundred more than expected. Women came from all over the country. Some rural women, not directly contacted by any official source, had walked miles and spent long hours on buses and lorries to get to the workshop.

The workshop—the first of several over the years—used feminist processes to ensure that there was maximum participation, that the women's voices would be heard, and that their suggestions would be for-warded to official sources.[18] Strategies devised by Zimbabwean women activists, from political rallies to "conscientizing" dramatic skits, dances, and songs, proved effective in helping women to address the problems urban and rural women had in common. One participant remarked, "All this time we were crying at home on our own, not knowing that others share the same problems."[19]

*Women of Zimbabwe Speak Out* was the title of the report on the WAG workshop which was distributed widely to government offices and women's groups. The report, published as a booklet, told the history of WAG, evaluated the workshop, and reported on the experiences and suggestions of the women and men attending the workshop.[20] Many of the problems that concerned the women are widespread on the continent and persistent: family life—child support and family maintenance, marriage rights, and bride wealth (*lobola/roora*)—property-related issues—land rights, income, and inheritance—and sexuality—sex education and contraception. One of the women participants' major fears was that they could lose their children and access to productive and real property if their husbands died or if they were divorced. We worked to inform women that the 1982 Legal Age of Majority Act made women legal adults at the age of eighteen and thereby qualified women to enter into contracts and to be guardians of their own children after divorce or the death of a husband. As we understood it then, these civil laws superseded customary laws (as codified under the colonial regime), but many women were not aware of these changes.[21] (Today, the Zimbabwe Women Lawyers' Association argues that the Supreme Court rulings which diminish the domain of the Legal Age of Majority Act are based on imperfect findings of customary law made by colonial researchers.)[22] As I noted above, Zimbabwe has passed many laws to redress gender imbalances; that is not the problem. Rather, the problem is that local chiefs' courts do not enforce the new laws, fearing they would thereby lose control of women and young men.[23] Competing vested interests are also a problem. Some women in their positions as mothers of adult, marriageable, and employed children have spoken out against the act for giving their children legal independence.[24] Entrenched ideologies of male dominance and discourses which naturalize differences of power and privilege as being about "the nature" of males and females are the problem.

Zimbabwean women activists often use workshops and small groups to identify and speak out against gender inequities and social problems. In 1996–97, WAG organized workshops around themes of recognition of women's work—getting women to value their unsalaried contributions to the home and their rights in family property, marriage, and inheritance—explaining the protections of registering marriages and the limits of customary law, and the issue of women and land—exploring women's access to land as encompassing women's control over the returns from land and from their own labor.

Another project was the Zimbabwe Women Writers Project, started in 1990. The Writers Project addressed issues related to a woman's control of her body and protection of her children by promoting women's literacy, developing writing skills, encouraging the reading of women's writing, and promoting positive images of women in writing.[25] It published its first English volume in 1994, holds writing craft workshops throughout the country, and organizes women into small writing groups. Its anthology consists of poems and short stories, some by professionals but mostly by amateurs, both blacks and whites, including pieces by long-term residents who are not Zimbabwean citizens. Norma Kitson, editor of the volume, included one of her poems inspired—rather, provoked—by the negative reaction of men at an Unsafe Issues Workshop. The unsafe issues often defeat the characters in this moving anthology, but in naming the issues dangerous to women and in daring to speak aloud, women claim their own power. The unsafe issues in Zimbabwe are rape, child abuse, sexual harassment, unwanted pregnancies, abortion, wife and child battering, birth control, baby dumping, and sexist attitudes and practices.

## Feminism in Zimbabwe

In 1984, riding the wave of WAG's success, I felt that I had something to give to Zimbabwe, even if it was mostly my understanding of feminist process honed in long hours of meetings with women students at the University of California, Santa Cruz, in antiracism workshops, mostly with feminist community groups, and in the San Francisco Bay Area Women's Anthropology Caucus. I had something to give and I was everywhere giving it: guest lectures, radio interviews, talks at high school, and a televised debate on the subject: "Resolved: Feminism is the force for change in the world today."[26] WAG was controversial. Students I talked to at the university were concerned about the high proportion of white women active in the group and about whether feminism itself is antimale.

Feminism in Zimbabwe emerged from overlapping discourses of national liberation, scientific socialism, the one-party state, modernity and tradition, and "Western feminism." Each discourse arises from and generates particular emanations of power, social and cultural contradictions, hegemonic and alternative tropes, and images, attitudes, and practices. In Zimbabwe, evoking national liberation brings forth men and women's fight against a racist, capitalist, colonial regime. The active role of female armed combatants during the liberation struggle, their strength and their commitment to change, are presented as evidence both of their not needing feminism *and* as their already being feminists. Scientific socialism as an ideology and methodology for change reigned during the first few years of Zimbabwean independence. To be seen as legitimate, feminism had to take account of the material conditions productive of social relations and to link positive changes in women's condition to improving the lot of all workers.

As independent Zimbabwe defined its political culture, it looked back to its past, to what Zimbabwean Anthony Chennells calls its "classic" culture, and it looked forward to a progressive, modern culture and society.[27] Having shaken off British colonial rule, which British cultural mores do they want to retain? Does freedom mean the chance to finally return to what you were doing before the imposition of colonialism? Or, more to the point in view of the discourses immediately following independence, how do you honor tradition while moving into the modern world? Too often, honoring tradition has meant limiting women's choices. Feminists had to walk a tightrope between balancing tradition and change, deciding for themselves whether the payment of money and goods by the groom to the bride's parents (bride wealth/*lobola*/*roora*) was consistent with women's liberation, and whether to risk removing children from the spiritual protection of their father's ancestors by claiming a woman's legal right to be the guardian of her children after divorce or widowhood.

Despite any protestations as to the diversity of feminism in Europe and the United States, in Zimbabwe's jangly mesh of signifiers, Western feminists were represented as man-hating harridans. The discourse of U.S. feminism, originally called women's liberation, intersected all the other discourses on political culture, pitting Africa against the West, black against white, liberal democracy against scientific socialism, multivocal positions against a unified single party, and African tradition against Western cultural imperialism.

In Zimbabwe, Rudo Gaidzanwa, a WAG founder and outspoken feminist, in a review of women's fiction from the colonial period to independence, risked being labeled an exponent of liberal democracy when she argued that liberated women are ones who exercise choice, act creatively, exploit opportunities, and maximize options.[28] She did agree, however, that drastic changes are needed to take place in society and culture to free women's options, so that choice creatively exercised would not condemn women to reproduce a cultural system that devalues them. Olivia Muchena, whose *Report on the Situation of Women in Zimbabwe* is the definitive survey of Zimbabwean women, engaged the tradition versus change discourse in a panel discussion on feminism in Zimbabwe. She countered men who argued that feminism should be rejected because it came from the outside, by pointing out that men do not reject clothes, cars, and other conveniences that likewise come from outside. In effect, Muchena asserted that culture is not static and that women must not be made to represent "tradition."

Aside from concerns about the biases of feminism, some rural and urban women, including university students, feared that the ruling party would look askance at them for associating with the Women's Action Group. A strong minority of the women we contacted felt that any women's group that worked outside the party's Women's League would be seen by those in power as being in opposition to the party. The government asked one WAG member who was a government worker in rural areas not to talk to two or more women without a party official present. In fact, one of the major discordant notes at the WAG workshop came from a representative of the Women's League who said that the issues raised by the workshop had already been addressed in a party congress. The workshop was "airing dirty linen in public." That criticism received front page coverage in a newspaper report on the WAG conference.

Members of WAG were questioned by the Zimbabwe central intelligence agency: since it was obvious that we were stirring up trouble in Zimbabwe, were we working with dissident groups to destabilize the country?[29] The ideas propounded by WAG were not new, neither were the findings of that first workshop. Since independence women had said that Zimbabwe was not won for men alone and that independence was not only for one sex. Rural women active as armed combatants and supporters during the war were key to Zimbabwean independence. The final verse in a poem, which starts with "Women of Zimbabwe/rise up!" by one of the former combatants captures women's sense of possibilities in newly independent Zimbabwe:

> Let's use our experience
> of the liberation struggle
> to build a new generation.
> Long ago we were like slaves,
> carrying big logs
> but LIFE is now available.[30]

What was new was this joint action, in the new country of Zimbabwe, of feminists from inside and outside the country and the insistence that now was the time for the women's struggle.

### Outside Influences and Socialist Feminism

Even my housemates, friends who had come to live with me from the United States, were critical of WAG. One of my housemates, a black American feminist, had thrown herself into work for WAG, administering surveys in the high-density suburbs, providing technical support with audio and video equipment at the workshop, and editing the audio recordings. She never had a high profile, and over the years has come to think that WAG should have been run solely by black Zimbabwean women. One of my other housemates, a white American feminist, attended some WAG meetings when she arrived in Zimbabwe a few months after WAG's founding, but dropped out quickly. The group did not feel like a Zimbabwean phenomenon to her—it reminded her too much of women's groups back in California. Sold on the notion that feminism had to be antiracist and anticapitalist and personally antinationalist, their disapproval did not deter me. I was stung, however, when a newspaper editorial blasted WAG and me.

I learned through one very negative, vituperative reaction to an interview with me published in a local newsmagazine about the earlier rift in the Women's Action Group. In a guest editorial, Nyaradzo Makamure criticized WAG, naming me specifically as a reactionary *American* social scientist who should not have come "trouble shooting" for the women of Zimbabwe. Makamure explained that she had left WAG within the first week when its international makeup became clear. WAG was an unstructured, nonaccountable group, composed largely of middle-class, men-hating, South African and Western European white women whose actions in the "clean-up" campaign and in putting together the workshop patronized black women and did not recognize their long history of grassroots organizing and of struggle for the motherland. As she saw it, women in WAG were the negative side of expatriate women:

> We do not put all Western expatriate women in the same category. We are aware that there are some genuine scientific socialists and progressives among them. These have a different approach from WAG. They respect Zimbabwean women and trust their capability to lead their own struggle. They offer genuine support and solidarity. The majority of them dropped out of WAG as soon as they realised its true nature.[31]

Makamure's main argument was that the Women's Action Group was a middle-class organization which patronized black women and neutralized mass participation.

Letters to the editor from WAG supporters and members and a rebuttal in the opinion column followed immediately. A committee from WAG recounted its history, methods, associations, and achievements, and defended me as an individual member:

> We may be a relatively small, relatively privileged group of black and white women but we do not believe in keeping our education, our skills, our socialist ideas and hopes for a better society locked up in [an] academic ivory tower.

> To dismiss us as a "middle-class" group is an insult to all of us, whether from middle-class or working-class backgrounds. To us, class interests are what you serve, not what you are. The interests of WAG lie in sharing and participating with all oppressed women in laying the basis for a just, equal, socialist society, as our constitution (which does exist!) shows a spirit of internationalism is indispensable in any struggle, as Zimbabwe's struggle for independence showed. We hope that Nyaradzo will appreciate this point from her present position in the UK.

> We condemn the way Nyaradzo makes our member, Carolyn Clark, a black anthropologist (whom she has never met) the target of her attack.[32]

Among other things, the Women's Action Group countered the attack by letting the writer and the world know that I was black. My race was not obvious in the interview that Nyaradzo Makamure cited. Many WAG members assumed that if she had known it, she would not have published such an attack. WAG pointedly noted that Makarume was herself engaged in a sort of international movement. But the strongest rebuttal was that we too are good socialists. The group's socialist stance had not been clearly articulated until that moment, nor had the constitution. In fact, WAG did begin without a constitution. In recounting the history of the group, founding members Zine Chitepo and Petronella Marambe note:

> Because of the urgent nature of our tasks, the question of formalising ourselves as a legally constituted organisation with a constitution and a formal leadership structure was not considered a priority at that stage.[33]

Part of my influence was to keep our process informal, moving toward consensus decision making and feminist process.

The question of what it means to act as a socialist feminist, for Zimbabwean nationals and for women from outside the country, was the most vexing. Alongside the WAG rebuttal, which I believe was an effective answer to the charges of being antisocialist, disrespectful of government channels, and against grassroots organizing, the newspaper ran an editorial cartoon that blunted any victory we might have been allowed. The cartoon showed a woman, spiderlike around the edges, mired in a pit of male chauvinism, discrimination, and oppression. She is being pulled out by socialism in the guise of a man. Her left arm, on which is written "Women's Lib," joins the "Socialism" of his right arm as he pulls her toward the surface and "Women's Rights." The caption reads, "Wait till I get out of here—then you'll see who's the boss!" Two small cartoon characters—one black, one white—looking at the scene say, "Forewarned is forearmed."

The discourse on socialism is what has been most blunted in the past decade and not just because of the "collapse of communism." In the 1970s, during its war against the renegade white supremacist regime of Ian Smith, the competing armies of the Zimbabwean freedom fighters were allied with the socialist block. After the war, the communist influence was only symbolic and the capitalist economy little changed. A contemporary cartoon in a popular newsmagazine captured the moment by picturing men with the hammer and sickle emblazoned on their T-shirts lifting their shirts to reveal the dollar sign. The Zimbabwean government's economic policy from the center encouraged grassroots cooperatives, established agricultural resettlement projects, and courted private enterprise. On the university campus, an ideological war raged. Highly visible lecturers taught scientific socialism in the classrooms and over the airwaves. Even while Zimbabwe was making changes that would take it further and further away from its socialist ideals, we intellectuals were fighting for control of the discourse of social change. In the press Women's Action Group members were demanding socialist feminism and trying to understand the present moment as a transition to socialism. The biting criticism lodged by Tsitsi Dangarembga and a coauthor in a popular political magazine presages the archfeminism of her novel, *Nervous Conditions*:

> The problem is: women are oppressed in ways that do not seem to be economic, so this oppression will be the last to be destroyed. But if it combines with the new socialist jargon it can lead to worse oppression.

> For example, since socialisation of the means of production is a basic aim of scientific socialism, socialist men in the transitional stages, who still regard women as mean-objects, will happily subscribe to the notion of socialisation of women—joyfully and lustily throwing to the capitalist any shreds of decency and self-discipline they might have had in this respect. So we see a married man, enjoying an evening out with his "sugar mummy," who claims that this is an aspect of traditional socialism that was stifled by the present capitalist system.[34]

The solution Dangarembga and coauthor Juliet Baah propose: revolutionary consciousness and solidarity among women, with women recognizing that they are as good as, as intelligent as, and as useful as men in the home and throughout society. The authors tell men that if they value women in society, appreciate their contributions, join forces with them, then "We promise you, you will not regret it."[35] According to Dangarembga and Baah, the economic and political changes of socialism are necessary to women's liberation, but dignity and respect for women cannot be accomplished without focusing our energies directly on changing social and cultural evaluations of women and ideas associated with what it means to be male or female.

## *Helping Others: The Dilemma of "Western Feminists"*

I was a reluctant representative of the United States and "the West," all my disavowals notwithstanding. Vainly trying to control my own image and representation, I had wanted to dissociate myself from my country's politics and economic policies. I had argued in public debate on feminism that true liberation of women depends on radical changes in structures that promote the exploitation of men by other men, one class of people by another, one nation by another, and one sex by another. To mark how "the West" disavowed me, after that performance, a woman from the British embassy chastised me, saying "You did not speak well." The deconstruction of the category "women" that in the West is linked in part to the protests of women of color against a white, middle-class mainstream, was played out in Zimbabwe in relation to the nation, imperialism, and party politics.

As a North American and U.S. citizen I was suspect. By actively participating in the Zimbabwean women's movement I had not shown proper respect for Zimbabwean women, especially because as a noncitizen I could leave and not be held accountable for my actions. (It took me some time to realize that because I could commit hit and run attacks I was seen by some Zimbabwean feminists as especially useful.) How women from the outside should show solidarity with women in struggle was never made clear. Should they write checks? Petition their male counterparts? Type? Host fund-raisers? Work in their home countries? Repatriate?

### Transnational Funding and Transnational Feminist Alliances

In looking back on my participation now, I believe I did the right thing. International coalitions and international support were crucial to Zimbabwe's independence. Should such coalitions not continue to be a part of the internal struggle? This does not raise the question of whether we *should*, but *how* we support African nations. Recognizing that Zimbabwean feminists exist as a part of larger feminist networks, and that transnational funding supports nongovernmental organizations, the relevant question is: how can individual women best participate?[36] My experience in Zimbabwe demonstrated to me that North American feminists can work directly with women in other countries to promote change, but that these coalitions will encounter obstacles. Outside our home territories, Western women can be scapegoats or lightning rods—but that way we get burned. We can be fairy godmothers, providing finances and resources; or we can be Cinderella, hidden away and working selflessly. I am not sure that my approach to working with feminists in Zimbabwe provides any real guidelines about what made it possible for me to contribute and to feel good about my contribution to the Zimbabwean women's struggle. However, writing this and looking back on that experience, I can identify attitudes or predispositions that helped me and might be of use to others in similar situations:

- I came to the group wanting to get to know women as individuals and to learn about their country from them. I did not join in as an expert.
- I trusted that Zimbabwean women knew how to maneuver in their own political landscape. Only they could make things happen.
- I pragmatically assessed my own talents and skills, confidently offered them, and took pride in my abilities. I was not selfless.
- I was willing to work hard and to follow.
- I had no guilt nor any sense of responsibility for the position of women in Zimbabwe. I felt compassion and identification.

Many women in Western countries feel powerless in the face of national and international politics and multinational corporations. Though the term fails to distinguish most of our efforts as it once did, we are still interested in "empowering" ourselves as women and feminists. Many of us feel that we are subalterns in relation to overwhelmingly male power structures. The successes of the now-threatened affirmative action programs in increasing the presence of women in midlevel positions in the government, corporate, and academic worlds notwithstanding, women still earn less than men, fill the ranks of the poor, and do not determine the quality of life in their countries. Yet in other countries, especially in "developing countries," we are seen as "the powerful," associated with exploitative economic practices and impudent and lascivious media images of women. Women in African countries are rightly confused and justifiably angry when we try to speak for them or to set the terms of discourse. But we can amplify their voices.

Is the authenticity of women's voices muted when men help articulate their position, when women of a different class do, when women of a different race do, when women of a different country do? Surely the effect of an outsider's voice is dependent on what they say, how they acquire knowledge, and the context of power in which that knowledge is used.

In developing countries, Western feminist ideas and practices are part of the social and political landscape, whose contributions can be good or bad, shading and sustaining new growth or like a prickly thornbush, forcing women to stand in particular positions. Women create new discourses from existing ones and appropriate resources and tools from other domains. In Zimbabwe, the participation of Western feminists was positive, but the negative perception of "women's lib" demanded a response, shaping the discourse. Exploitative transnational relations, negative perceptions of Western women, and defensive nationalism pushed women away from particular discourses and practices of liberation.

The Women's Action Group is situated at the intersection of the state and civil society in Zimbabwe, with its beginnings in opposition to a state's action against a segment of its population. WAG's success as an NGO whose members are mostly poor black women in rural and urban areas throughout the country is a product of the courage, diligence, and vision of its current staff and trustees and it is also a testament to a transnational feminist coalition that began when women, coresident for the moment, saw an injustice against women and spoke out against it.

## Conclusion

Current newspaper headlines about women in Zimbabwe scream of the rollback in women's rights, the whittling away of women's status as legal adults, the circumscription of their rights as wives and mothers.[37] A new wave of protests against legal and customary restrictions on women is rising in Zimbabwe. I was a part of one of the last waves—or was it an eddy, localized in Harare?

In 1991 Zimbabwe signed the Convention on Elimination of All Forms of Discrimination against Women, agreeing to ban all forms of discrimination in its laws and constitution. But this arsenal of equity laws has not prevented Zimbabwean courts from ruling that a widowed woman who is the eldest child of a senior wife cannot inherit family land on her father's death and that women who are married through customary law cannot sue for adultery damages. Some interpret these Zimbabwe Supreme Court rulings as legitimating women's subordination to men. There are many problems in the enforcement of laws governing gender equity, not the least of which is the colonial legacy of a bifurcated legal system which pits civil law against customary law as codified under colonial rule. A low literacy rate for women, underdeveloped communication systems, concern about their own and their children's spiritual well-being, fear of social and economic repercussions, and unaccommodating male village councils and lower courts make women unlikely to know the laws and their rights and, when they do know their rights, reluctant to press their cases.

While the social and political situation for women is bleak, the economic situation is even worse. The hopes of Zimbabweans fell as inflation rose and the International Monetary Fund (IMF) and World Bank's Economic Structural Adjustment Programs (ESAP) left the country with high budget deficits and high interest rates, resulting in instability in the macro-economy as the government and business retrenched. Most Zimbabweans live and work on small-scale farms in rural areas, many in large areas of low soil fertility and productivity. The unemployment rate is as high as 50 percent and women and girls, being primarily semi-skilled and unskilled workers, are often targeted when jobs are cut back. The goal of ESAP was to create incentives for investment in manufacturing, reduce government spending, and encourage economic growth and development through increased exports. Riphenburg succinctly captures the result of ESAP in Zimbabwe:

> Since the introduction of the ESAP, Zimbabwe's economy has shown signs of a deepening crisis that is characterized by higher inflation, intensified deindustrialization, increased unemployment, stagnant salaries, and an inability by vulnerable groups to meet basic needs. In Zimbabwe, the signs of social disintegration as a result of economic decline and growing poverty are becoming more visible, resulting in the sacrifice of people's lives or the quality of their lives to the ESAP.[38]

In response to continued government overspending, corruption, and a politically motivated appropriation of land from white commercial farmers for redistribution to landless blacks, the IMF and World Bank pulled many of their programs and credit facilities out of Zimbabwe in the late 1990s. Since that time Zimbabwe has been in the grips of political violence and economic freefall.

In additon to a disastrous political and economic situation, women in Zimbabwe suffer greatly from a scourge devastating their country: HIV/AIDS. In the country, almost one in four adults in their prime reproductive years are HIV positive. NGOs and civil society took the lead in combating AIDS through education, counseling, research, community programs, and support for families and caregivers. In the 1980s, the Zimbabwean government denied the presence of AIDS in the country, calling the report of AIDS in Zimbabwe "western propaganda." Today it must contend with the massive effects of this disease. When I first lived in Zimbabwe in the early 1980s, few could have predicted the AIDS pandemic, the collapse of socialist rhetoric, the decline in the Zimbabwean economy, the spread of political violence, or the precarious ups and downs of women's legal and human rights. Some women's rights groups in Zimbabwe resist racial polarization, work to alleviate poverty, and strive for political change. But the mood of the country has changed. Things were bad that first week I was in Zimbabwe, but the Zimbabwean people had a new country and were very hopeful.

### ACKNOWLEDGMENTS

This paper has gone through several transformations over the years, but no one other than France Winddance Twine and Kathleen Blee has read it in its present incarnation. I thank them for raising provocative questions which prompted me to rethink my experience. Thanks go to University of California, Santa Cruz, graduate students Kristen Cheney and Michelle Rosenthal who helped bring my research up-to-date and to undergraduate Sian Hale who in 1991 brought me copies of *Speak Out* that she had found in Harare. Students in my African Women and Africa Today classes helped convince me I should tell my story. Marge Frantz's students in Women's Studies have, over the years, found their way to my office to hear about my work with women in sociopolitical movements. Their queries helped shape my story. Colleagues in the Anthropology Department at UCSC have been generous in listening to me work through this material. Philosophers Joe Waterhouse and Bill Shaw and anthropologist Naomi Katz read and gave detailed comments on earlier drafts. In writing this, I give tribute to the valiant founders of the Women's Action Group, especially to Peggy Watson and Devi Pakkiri, who now serve on its Board of Trustees.

### NOTES

1. Rudo Gaidzanwa, "'Operation Clean-Up' Takes Women's Lib One Step Back," *Moto Magazine* (1984): 19/20: 5.

2. Christine Sylvester, "Simultaneous Revolutions: The Zimbabwe Case," *Journal of Southern African Studies*, vol. 16, no. 3 (1990): 473. Emphasis in the original.

3. Irene Staunton, *Mothers of the Revolution: The War Experiences of Thirty Zimbabwean Women* (London: James Currey, and Bloomington: University of Indiana Press, 1990), 156.

4. This figure is quoted by Elinor Batezat, Margaret Mwalo, and Kate Truscott, based on a report by the Ministry of Community Development and Women's Affairs, *Women in Construction and Reconstruction in Post-Independence Zimbabwe* (Harare: UNICEF, 1985), 12.

5. From an unpublished interview with CDWA Minister Teurai Ropa Nhongo conducted in Zimbabwe by University of California, Santa Cruz, student Casey Kelso in the early 1980s.

6. Christine Sylvester, "'Urban Women Cooperatives,' 'Progress,' and 'African Feminism,'" in *differences: A Journal of Feminist Cultural Studies*, vol. 3, no. 1 (1991): 43.

7. Carol Riphenburg, "Women's Status and Cultural Expression: Changing Gender Relations and Structural Adjustment in Zimbabwe," *Africa Today*, vol. 44, no. 1 (January–March 1997): 36.

8. "High-density suburb" is a Zimbabwean euphemism for the former black townships.

9. Ruth Weiss, *The Women of Zimbabwe* (London: Kesho Publishers, 1986), 124.

10. Weiss, *Women of Zimbabwe*, 124.

11. Weiss, *Women of Zimbabwe*, 57.

12. Elinor Batezat, Margaret Mwalo, and Kate Truscott, "Women and Independence: The Heritage and the Struggle," in *Zimbabwe's Prospects: Issues of Race, Class, State and Capital in Southern Africa*, ed. Colin Stoneman (London: Macmillan, 1988), 160.

13. Susie Jacobs, "Gender Division and the Formation of Ethnicities in Zimbabwe," in *Unsettling Settler Societies*, ed. Davia Stasiulis and Nira Yuval-Davis, Sage Series on Race and Ethnic Relations, vol. 11 (London: Sage, 1995).

14. This is taken from an article by WAG founders Rudo Gaidzanwa and Petronella Marambe, "Operation Clean-Up," *Connexions: An International Women's Quarterly*, no. 12 (Spring 1984): 18.

15. Zine Chitepo and Elinor Batezat in the WAG booklet, *Women of Zimbabwe Speak Out: Report of the Women's Action Group Workshop* (Harare: May 1984).

16. Weiss, *Women of Zimbabwe*, 124.

17. A personal communication in October 1997 from one of the trustees discusses the presence of men on the Board of Trustees and on the staff: "I suppose the biggest change is that we now have two men trustees (as from last June) and a male editor of Speak Out (as of 14 months ago). We decided that we didn't want to appear to be widening the communication gap between men and women in an already polarised society."

18. Attendees were randomly divided into small discussion groups led by a facilitator from WAG with translators and note takers from the group and the university. Noted women politicians opened the workshop with rousing speeches and the women participants responded with dances and songs. Trade union members of WAG effectively shaped the discourse of the workshop through a play which showed the intersection between the lives of a dependent rural woman and an urban prostitute. The play was performed primarily in Shona, the

language of the majority population in Zimbabwe and the majority of the women attending the workshop. Zimbabwe's history is steeped in drama: during the liberation war, a major tactic of the freedom fighters was to "conscientize" a village through all-night meetings that often included skits dramatizing the relationship between the colonial government and the indigenous people. The report on the workshop was covered in the national Sunday and daily papers, copies were delivered to government agencies, and WAG members consulted with government officers about the workshop and its findings.

19. This statement was taken from the notes in a small group discussion at the workshop. WAG booklet, *Women of Zimbabwe Speak Out*, 10.

20. About twenty of the participants were men from in and around Harare. These men, ranging from university lecturer to the facility janitor, differed widely in their attitudes toward women, their willingness to change, and their ideas of what the problems were. In summarizing their positions in the WAG booklet, I divided the group into "progressives" and "traditionalists," categories that were mildly ridiculed in the newspapers.

21. The Matrimonial Causes Act was customary law codified under colonial rule. According to this law, Ndebele and Shona women were not granted custody of their children at divorce or the death of the husband; women did not have access to land in their own right, but only through a husband, father, or male guardian, and women did not inherit property accumulated by their husbands during marriage. The Legal Age of Majority Act of 1982 overrode aspects of this law. When WAG saw that dissemination of information was one of its major jobs, it joined with other organizations in creating pamphlets to be used in literacy training, dealing with issues raised in its workshops. Important in reaching women about their legal rights were Joan May at the University of Zimbabwe, its Centre for Applied Social Sciences, and the Women and Law in Southern African Research Project.

22. See the online computer article from the All Africa News Agency, "Supreme Court Judgement on Marriage Sparks Debate." www.africanews.org/south/zimbabwe/stories/19990419_feat3.html

23. Nancy Folbre, "Patriarchal Social Formations in Zimbabwe," in *Patriarchy and Class: African Women in the Home and the Workforce*, ed. Sharon B. Stichter and Jane L. Parpart (Boulder, Colo.: Westview Press, 1988), 75.

24. A headline in *Speak Out/Taurai/Khulumani* reads, "We Do Not Want This Law!" and includes the following quotations from women: "We are angry with the government. How could they pass a law which tells our children to do what they want when they are 18?" and "Our Women's League branch has already passed a resolution that we do not want the Legal Age of Majority Act. So do not even talk about it." Vol. 18 (1992): 8. The article following this one argues in favor of the law.

25. Norma Kitson, *Anthology: Over 100 Works by Zimbabwe Women Writers*,

no. 1—English—1994. Collected and presented by Zimbabwe Women Writers, 78 Kaguvi Street, Harare, Zimbabwe.

26. It was impossible to get any of the outspoken black Zimbabwean feminists to support this proposition in debate, though they encouraged me to do so and one of them served as the moderator of the debate. Despite jokes making light of the issues, skillfully delivered by a male newspaper editor, and the allusions to the Bible by a male lecturer in Religious Studies who stood against the proposition, a white male physician and I overwhelmingly won the debate by the vote of an audience filled with our friends and supporters.

27. White Zimbabwean literary critic Anthony Chennells explains: "By using classic instead of traditional or pre-colonial I have tried to indicate the beauty, dignity but finally the inability of pre-colonial Shona culture to deal with a world colonialism has transformed." Anthony Chennells, "Authorizing Women, Women Authoring: Tsitsi Dangarembga's *Nervous Conditions,*" in *New Writing from Southern Africa: Authors Who Have Become Prominent since 1980,* ed. Emmanuel Ngara (London: Heineman, 1996), 75, footnote 8.

28. Rudo Gaidzanwa, *Images of Women in Zimbabwean Literature* (Harare: College Press, 1985).

29. More than one black Zimbabwean party and army fought to liberate Zimbabwe. In the first years after independence, the Ndebele party and army were accused of fomenting discord. Indeed, physicians I spoke with told me that there were many more victims of violence, perpetrated by the government and dissidents, than were reported in the newspapers.

30. Miriam Makore, "The New Zimbabwean Women," in *Young Women in the Liberation Struggle: Stories and Poems from Zimbabwe,* ed. Kathy Bond-Stewart, assisted by Leocardia Chimbandi Mudimu, photographs by Biddy Partridge (Harare: Zimbabwe Publishing House, 1984), 63.

31. Nyaradzo Makamure, "Women's Group—The Failings," guest editorial, *Sunday Mail,* Harare, Zimbabwe, November 11, 1984.

32. This was drafted by a committee of the Women's Action Group. The byline read, "By Peggy Watson, secretary of the Women's Action Group."

33. WAG booklet, *Women of Zimbabwe Speak Out,* 1.

34. Tsitsi Dangarembga and Juliet Baah, "Seizing Power," *Social Change and Development,* vol. 1, no. 9 (1984): 23.

35. Dangarembga and Baah, "Seizing Power."

36. See the introduction of my book, *Colonial Inscriptions: Race, Sex, and Class in Kenya* (Minneapolis: University of Minnesota Press, 1995), for a discussion of overlapping discourses and part societies which I characterize as "interculturality."

37. Two examples of recent news stories on women's rights in Zimbabwe from the computer web site at www.africanews.org are as follows: "Zimbabwe Women Protest a Loss of Rights," May 21, 1999, *Mail and Guardian* (Johannesburg), and "Supreme Court Judgement on Marriage Sparks Debate," April 19, 1999, *All Africa*

*News Agency.* International media coverage has also been given to Zimbabwe's President Robert Mugabe's vicious homophobic remarks. See Margrete Aarmo, "How Homosexuality Became 'Un-African': The Case of Zimbabwe," in *Female Desires: Transgender Practices across Cultures,* ed. Evelyn Blackwood and Saskia E. Wieringa (New York: Columbia University Press, 1999), 255–80. Mugabe's antigay stance certainly contributes to hostility toward feminism.

38. Riphenburg, "Women's Status and Cultural Expression," 40.

*Chapter 12*

---

# Building Connections between Antiracism and Feminism
## Antiracist Women and Profeminist Men

*Eileen O'Brien and Michael P. Armato*

To overturn the vast inequalities that characterize U.S. society, members of the "dominant" groups, including white American men and women, will have to actively engage in the fight for racial and gender justice. Such actions are not unprecedented in U.S. history. Some men voiced support for women's equality as far back as the late 1800s[1] and in the 1970s radical and socialist feminist men's groups emerged in response to the U.S. women's movement.[2] Moreover, white abolitionists voiced their opposition to the enslavement of black Americans in the nineteenth century.[3] In the early twentieth century when the political and social rights of formerly enslaved blacks were denied, white Americans helped to establish, and financially sponsored, the National Association for the Advancement of Colored People (NAACP), an interracial organization, which has been the leading organization combating racial discrimination in the United States. Whites also played a central role in the black civil rights movement, particularly in freedom schools, civil disobedience, and voter registration drives.[4]

Continuing this tradition of what we call "dominant group activism" today are white antiracist and male profeminist activists in North America who see their involvement as necessary to the struggle for social justice. In recent decades, numerous "men's movements" have appeared throughout the United States, typically as small local grassroots organizations. Although some, like The Promise Keepers and certain strands of Robert Bly's Mythopoetic Men's Movement, are antifeminist, others such as Men's Rape Prevention Project, Men Stopping Violence, Men as Peacemakers, Men Stopping Rape, RAVEN, and many others support feminist goals. Moreover, whites are active in antiracist groups such as Antiracist Action, founded in the 1990s, with over one hundred North American chapters and an estimated two thousand core members, and the People's Institute which has trained thousands in its "Undoing Racism" workshops since 1980.[5]

In this essay, we analyze the similarities and differences in the way white antiracists and male profeminists practice activism, concluding with a consideration of the potential for coalition building across these groups. The data are from Eileen O'Brien's study of white antiracists and Michael Armato's study of male profeminists. The antiracist participants came primarily from two organizations: Antiracist Action (ARA) and the People's Institute (PI) for Survival and Beyond.

Eileen O'Brien used participant-observation methods, including "tabling" (providing information about the group and recruiting members at a concert) and protesting at a Ku Klux Klan rally with ARA, and participating in a two-and-a-half-day Undoing Racism workshop offered by PI. She interviewed twenty-four white antiracists (thirteen women and eleven men) from one Canadian city and a variety of regions in the United States. Nine were under the age of thirty, but the majority were thirty to sixty years old; one was over eighty.

Michael Armato's study included interviews with ten profeminist activists. Seven were affiliated with four profeminist organizations from the East, Southeast, and Midwest of the United States: Men Can Stop Rape (formerly known as Men's Rape Prevention Project) in Washington, D.C., Men Stopping Violence (MSV) in Atlanta, Georgia, Men Stopping Rape (MSR) in Madison, Wisconsin, and Men as Peacemakers (MP) in Duluth, Minnesota. Three were not associated with any organization but actively worked for feminist causes, two as abortion clinic escorts in Florida and one as a feminist campus activist in the state of Washington. The men's ages ranged from twenty-five to fifty, with a relatively equal distribution of men in their twenties, thirties, and forties. Armato also participated in a MRPP weekend training workshop in July 1999. Additionally, both authors analyzed the literature of these groups, including pamphlets, newsletters, and web sites.

## Organizational Frames of Activism

Collective action "frames" have been popular in recent work on social movements.[6] Originally proposed by Snow and Benford, framing refers to the way movement actors develop shared understandings of what their goals are and how to achieve them.[7] The concept is an attempt to incorporate interpretive sociology into social movement theory, a response to its previously highly structural focus.[8] Framing becomes part of a shared organizational culture that is drawn upon regularly by movement members.

Frames are not necessarily shared across an entire movement. Within the feminist movement, debates abound over how to frame feminism. For example, whether U.S. professor Mary Daly's exclusion of men from her feminist seminars is indeed a feminist practice would be debated from the position of radical and liberal feminists because of the different ways the two groups frame what feminism is and what its practices should be. Here we want to examine the frames that dominant group activists use to direct their profeminist and antiracist practices. Those practices flow directly from the way they frame what sexism and racism means for them and their organizations.

## Are All Men (Potential) Rapists?

As suggested by names such as Men's Rape Prevention Project, Men Stopping Violence, and Men Stopping Rape, profeminist groups focus on violence in general and sexual violence in particular. This grows directly out of their theoretical orientation toward gender and culture. In contrast to many "rape prevention" programs, which target women and make use of a risk-reduction model of rape prevention—and therefore inadvertently place the culpability primarily on the victims of sexual assault—these profeminist men's groups target what they call the "rape culture" in the United States.[9] Instead of conceptualizing violence as the behavior of exceptional, dysfunctional individuals, they view cultural expectations of manhood in this society as contributing to sexual violence. Peter, an activist from MRPP, explains:

> All of these behaviors, even if they don't directly lead to rape—that you know, every ten times I call a woman a bitch someone else gets raped, it's not that direct—and if we lived in a society in which it didn't occur to people to think of women as there for my sexual gratification exclusively, then it would be impossible for us to imagine that we were in a society that has a million rapes of women and girls a year, impossible.

Another activist, Rob, when asked about how his organization initially determined where to focus its energies, answered:

> We thought the roles that men play in society have a large part in why men commit most of the violence. So the way they are raised to look out and do things and behave are the major part of the problem.

Peter offered a similar sentiment:

> Our name says rape because we see sexual assault as sort of the touchstone of so many other issues that radiate out from it. But ultimately we see our project as redefining what it means to be a man. And sort of creating less destructive modes of masculinity.

Both Rob's and Peter's comments typify the general goal of most of the profeminist organizations: to develop a new, nonviolent paradigm of masculinity.

The culture of rape approach leads these groups to focus on making men (and women) aware of the relationships between everyday language/practices and sexual violence toward women in the hope that it will make individuals more likely to speak out against behaviors that propagate rape culture. Peter explained it quite succinctly:

> Our particular take on our work is that we need to address the bystander issues. Every rapist has a friend, and if we can reach that friend, whether that friend is male or female, then we can reach the rapist. It's sort of [a] male peer support model. You know [the] MADD [Mothers against Drunk Driving] model, "Friends don't let friends drive drunk." Well, friends don't let friends rape either.

Indeed, a central tenet of the ideologies of these groups is that bystanders need to become more active in challenging those behaviors that support rape culture. Rob echoed this sentiment:

> So the idea is really by training those young men to ask questions, ethical questions, about the appropriateness of their behavior, not their own behavior, but it's really built on looking as a bystander at what's happening and making a decision about whether or not you should step in and do something.

In keeping with the notion of bystander responsibility, the culture of rape approach does not distinguish between "good" and "bad" men, arguing that all men (and women) play a role in the continuance (or cessation) of rape culture. Peter traced the development of his thoughts:

And so I've moved from rapists are all crazy and dangerous and all strangers hiding in the bushes and predominantly black, of course, and on down the line to OK rapists look like me, rapists act like me, rapists talk to me, and so maybe I have a role here. Maybe there's something that I can do.

He continued by recounting the words of an elder of his who was instrumental in the founding of his organization: "We live in a society in which bad men rape, good men do nothing, and I can't tell the difference."

In order to reach their target audience, nearly all these groups conduct discussions with high school and college-aged men (and women) about gender, especially masculinity, and its relationship to violence, using a series of exercises as well as personal anecdotes. MSV, based in Atlanta, runs discussion groups to educate batterers and violent men and teenaged boys. Although most participants are court-ordered, all must agree that they have a problem in order to participate. MSV also pushes for better legislation and law enforcement where men's violence is concerned. MRPP has evolved from a support group for profeminist men to an outreach program that makes presentations in area schools. MSR does similar educational work. MP works with a battered women's shelter to provide emergency transport of women to the shelter and to care for children at the shelter to give women a break. They also run various outreach and education programs with area schools, including the "playbook" program, which gives male college athletes a list of alternatives to sexual violence and sexist banter. In all these groups' practices, careful attention is paid to the message that *all* men participate to some extent in a "rape culture."

## Are All Whites Racist?

In contrast with the profeminist male activists, the white antiracist activists did not agree on where to focus their energies. While the focus of PI members was similar to that of profeminist men—that their own propagation of white racism was of central importance to their activism—ARA members' frame of racism as consisting mostly of overt acts like police brutality and neo-Nazi terrorism meant that their own relationship to white racism was not of primary concern.

PI was founded in New Orleans by two black American men as a training institute for those in social service professions that served communities of color. It has a white subsidiary group called European Dissent ("dissenting what has been done in the European name") of which all the PI respondents here are members. PI is most noted for its Undoing Racism workshops, which serve as transformative experiences for whites confronting racism and are now offered on a national and global scale. Focusing on institutionalized racism as a barrier to community organizing and activism, the workshops delve into historical and contemporary race relations and rely on a Malcolm X-like philosophy that whites should be doing separate work in their own communities. PI defines racism as "race prejudice plus power" and states that all whites are racist under this definition. A PI member, Pam, described what it was like to accept this frame of antiracism and incorporate it into her own self-concept:

> That was tough for me to swallow at the training, that [I'm a racist] . . . because I don't wanna believe that of myself. But if you look at the true historical definition of it then yes, I'm a racist. I'm white. I take advantage of the privileges that I have as a white person.

For white PI members, the antagonist is themselves and other whites. As in the "rape culture" frame of the profeminist men, there are no "good whites" and "bad whites" in the framework of PI.

After members complete the Undoing Racism training, they are encouraged to create antiracist change in the white-dominated organizations and groups in which they participate. Such practices include Pam's successful implementation of a "multicultural arts" program at the elementary school where she teaches predominantly impoverished students of color and Kendra's work to get her religious denomination (Unitarian Universalists) to adopt an antiracist agenda at the national level. Kendra described how she used her position as a religious educator at her church to educate children about whites' involvement in racism:

> I was teaching a Sunday school class to ten-year-olds last week and they said to me, "Everyone's a racist. Everyone's a little bit racist." And I said, "No, everyone's *not* a little bit racist. Everyone has some racial prejudice, because of racism. But really, not everybody is a racist." I said, "Racism is something that is when the whole society is set up for one group." I said, "Which [group] is this?" and they could *tell me* that it was white people. . . . *They know* that society is set up by and for white people, they can see it in their experience. And so we talked about some of those things. We talked about who it is that runs the government, who it is that owns most of the banks, who it is that runs the schools, and who it is that makes up standardized tests, and we talked about testing and things like that—things

that are in their experience—and they *can* understand the difference, that it is white people who've been given power in this nation.

Kendra's method of practicing antiracism here is not to point out "good whites" and "bad whites," but rather to emphasize whites' position in the system. PI trainers point out that many whites are "gatekeepers" of white-dominated institutions. Rather than saying whites are "bad" by virtue of their positions in these institutions, PI trainers encourage whites to use those positions to usher in institutional change.

The "all whites are racist" frame of antiracism used by PI differs considerably from that used by ARA, and their practices clearly reflect this difference. ARA was started in the cities of Columbus, Minneapolis, and Toronto by mostly white individuals to counteract Ku Klux Klan and neo-Nazi activity in their communities.[10] Counterdemonstrations at Klan rallies drew initial memberships, and youths wanting to protest right-wing hate groups that were forming at their schools followed suit. ARA focuses predominantly on front-line activism. Its newest project is Copwatch, a system of videotaping and police misconduct litigation to "police the police" in urban neighborhoods.

ARA's frames target overt acts of racism such as neo-Nazi atrocities, police brutality, and, as their mission statement reads, "hate in any form." Members do not generally see themselves as "hateful" human beings. When asked about successes in their antiracist work, most talked about a victory over the Nazis (driving them out of a "territory" such as a concert or a street), or successful cases in which perpetrators of police brutality were convicted. ARA member Tim, for instance, was one of the leaders of the outspoken opposition to the white supremacist "White Power Hour" TV show on his local cable access station. He narrowly escaped arrest when he and some others staged a protest outside the apartment of the host of the show. He credits the actions of ARA with raising awareness about the presence of racist hate and violence in his community. These kind of antiracist practices, which focus on extremists, are typical of ARA members.

The only exception to this pattern within ARA was veteran organizer and key informant Steve who saw himself within the definition of racism:

> So I started trying to be not racist, and was totally unsuccessful at it, and still I am not skilled at it, because you get programmed at an early age and then deprogramming your uncontrollable mental processes as a white person that grew up in this culture—or as a male, for that matter—is not that easy! So this is why it's a lifelong kind of evolution.

While Steve understood himself to be a part of "racism," the practices of ARA do not include the notion of "deprogramming" ordinary whites. Similarly, although members of PI at one time banded together to protest the overtly racist flyers posted by a local fraternity, this is not a regularly occurring practice of the whites in the group. PI members' frame of "all whites are racist" and its related practices of targeting the white-dominated institutions of which they are a part most closely mirrors the profeminist men's "rape culture" frame, while ARA members frame racism as overt acts of hostility in which they cannot imagine themselves participating.

## Dominant Group Activists and Privilege

Dominant group activists face the issue of how to deal with privilege in their organizing efforts. This issue arose in three ways in the profeminist men's groups and the white antiracist groups: in the definition of privilege, the cost of privilege to dominant group members, and the price of dominant group activism.

### The Question of Privilege

First, profeminist men and white antiracists had to decide how they understood gender and racial privilege. While feminist discourse tends to use a language of oppression, power, and privilege, most profeminist men's discourse, surprisingly, is not one of male privilege and female oppression. Although they are sensitive to the notion of gendered oppression, they avoid language that might seem accusatory or offensive to men or ineffective for communicating their message to a wider audience. Consider the following statements made by Rob about his organization's (MRPP's) approach to social change:

> I think it's a very positive kind of a thing. It's not finger pointing. We have been very clear in our organization that we are not going to point fingers at men, which is one of the things that sometimes profeminist groups get into is the finger pointing. We say very clearly, men commit 90 percent of the violence—that's why we're in this. They commit a lot of that violence against women, but they also commit an incredible amount against other men.

One notable exception to this pattern was Andy from MSV who explained that one of his biggest challenges was recognizing and giving up his privilege as a white male in U.S. society. When asked what he meant by that, he offered the following anecdote:

> I remember like when I was really pretty young in [an activist organization for the homeless and poor]. I was probably maybe there for like two months at this point, and I was really getting comfortable and there was one of the women who had helped start it. This was her last meeting and she was sort of giving her final thoughts. And she was leaving and she just said, "You know, I think this organization has a lot to learn and think about as far as like internal sexism and how men handle themselves during group conversations. I feel that men are dominating group conversations. They don't give women a chance to speak or listen to women when they do." And that was like falling on virgin ears for me. Like I was just like blown away by that. And feel like I didn't talk for like the next year, until I learned that was not the way to respond because then that is leaving most of the responsibility and organizational work to women. And so, and just like that process. Figuring out, you know, first of all identifying your privilege. I mean I know like one of, and I don't know if this necessarily came from MSV, but it's like the metaphor that's used a lot there talking about men and privilege is like talking about fish in a fish tank and the water around them. I mean it's just what you live in.

More typical is the position of Robert Jensen who argues that feminism is more compelling to men if it focuses on how it can improve *their* lives. His emphasis is *not* on how sexism privileges men, but rather on how it makes men "miserable," with careful attention to the idea that "being miserable, however, is not the same as being oppressed."[11] Drawing upon personal experience, Jensen believes that bringing men to feminist politics requires a "self-interest" argument rather than a "justice" argument, since "a justice argument does not always persuade people in power to give up some of that power."[12]

Steve, a member of ARA, made an argument similar to Jensen's when he argued that emphasizing the negative effects of racism on whites was an effective antiracist organizing tactic. He was careful, however, to argue that although whites were "victims" of racism, they were not themselves oppressed by racism:

> Racism is not good for most white people. It's good for a few people, most of whom are white, but it could theoretically be better for some nonwhite people as well. . . . It's a benefit we'd be better off without by far. Still doesn't mean that white people on average don't do better than black people in almost every circumstance [because] they do, 'cause of this institution that's

put on everybody. But seeing most white people as victims of it as well is more accurate than to emphasize the privilege element of white racism in the United States.

Steve's position was unusual among white antiracist activists. Most white antiracists subscribed to the notion of privilege as a means of conceptualizing their position in the movement. In fact, ARA members Kristin and Claire both recognized that whites in their group could take more risks at marches and demonstrations than could people of color and were less likely to be arrested. Lori, a nonorganizational activist, concurred and remarked that "if a person of color expresses an antiracist opinion, they're just being overly sensitive," yet, as a white person with privilege, people would "listen to [her] more" because she is a member of the dominant group.

PI members also were also well-versed in the concept of white privilege. Their definition of racism (race prejudice plus power equals racism) recognizes power and privilege as central. To "undo" racism in their own lives and in their positions as "gatekeepers," they believe they must be aware of their racial privilege.

## Costs of Privilege

Second, antiracist whites and profeminist men had to decide how to assess whether there were costs to dominant groups of racial and gender privilege. Profeminist men's organizations see both women and men as casualties of contemporary gender arrangements. Although they do not claim that men are as oppressed as women, profeminist men devote a significant amount of time to exploring the challenges they face as men. In so doing, they seek to address what Michael A. Messner terms the "costs of masculinity" to men who try to live up to a masculine norm, such as shallow relationships, poor health, and early death.[13] Indeed, the desire to mitigate these costs strongly motivates their involvement in profeminist organizations. Their activism is not merely selfless devotion to ending gender inequality, but rather a search for a less harmful version of manhood. One member, Jim, explained that he felt totally liberated when he finally got involved with the profeminist organization in his town because it provided him with close male friendships that were unlike any he had ever had, suggesting that one benefit of profeminist men's groups for their members is a sense of community.

Although white antiracists generally emphasize the *power* inherent in privilege rather than its costs, PI expresses concern about the lack of awareness of community and culture among whites. Included in its Undoing Racism workshop is an evening of "cultural sharing" in which everyone brings a show-and-tell object representing his or her culture. Relative to people of color, whites have a harder time recognizing their racial culture. In one exercise, participants are asked to say what they like about being white or black. Typically, almost all answers by whites are about power (for example, "I like that I am represented adequately in history books, that people don't look past me because of my race," and so on) and nearly all answers by black Americans are about culture (for example, "I like our music, feeling like a family/sense of unity," and so on). PI trainers claim that one barrier to building a multiracial movement is this lack of a sense of belonging to a larger collective among whites. This lack of cultural identity among whites is also seen as a barrier to change, leading some antiracist whites to dissociate themselves from racist whites in their lives rather than working for change.

However, white antiracists do not refer to this sense of community as a major motivation for their antiracist activism in the way that profeminist men do. Although losing an individualistic orientation is one step on the path of "undoing racism" for whites, it does not seem to provide the lasting inspiration and staying power for white antiracists that it does for male profeminists. Rather, white antiracists cite the oppression of people of color and their privileged racial position as their reason for remaining in the struggle. For example, Mike had previously signed up to teach elementary school in an inner city community for a limited number of years, but his involvement with antiracism in the community motivated him to make a lifetime commitment to the city. Thus, after his mandatory contract was over, he chose a life of antiracist activism despite having a "hundred choices" of working in communities that would have been more financially beneficial to him. PI member Lisa concurred with Mike's sentiments:

> Every single day I have to recommit myself to that process. . . . just being very aware of that privilege that I *can*, I can leave this city, I can leave this process, and so, every single day, just making that recommitment that this is something that I believe in and this is something that I want to work for.

Rather than relying on a sense of community that she feels with other whites to keep her motivated, Lisa compared her situation with that of the impoverished people of color in her community and the privilege that she has relative to them. Although there might be costs to being privileged, recognizing them is not what sustains white antiracists.

## Paying the Price

Third, dominant group activists struggle with the costs of their activist practices. Profeminist men often cited their frustration with the work that remains to be done, as did Peter, despite the few serious negative consequences of being profeminist for men:

> On a personal level, I don't sleep any more. I'm so full with the experience of frustration that I'm seeing in men and women about this work, about the ravages that masculinity has committed against our society that I don't sleep. It just keeps going over and over again in my mind. I feel I'm not doing enough, and so I'm exhausted most of the time. . . . I often feel like I can't do any more and then I get the next phone call and I can do more; I have to. So, I think the sign of an old activist, right, are the bags under the eyes [laughs], and I see myself heading there; I'm only thirty!

In contrast, the activist practices of white antiracists often had serious costs, particularly for those not affiliated with any organization. For challenging a fraternity's racist paraphernalia, Lori ended up receiving death threats and eventually had to change schools to finish her degree.

> We were going to hang signs that said . . . "The Confederate Flag: Four Hundred Years of Oppression or a [fraternity name] Tradition? You Decide." And we hung them up all over campus one night when everyone was asleep. . . . like an idiot, I wrote, "For more information, contact [Lori]" [laughs]. And I wrote my number on it, right?! And my PO Box, so of course, what do I get? Millions of harassing phone calls, and [frat name]'s telling me they're going to sue me for defamation! And I'm like, well, it's true, it was their symbol! I don't know what they thought they were going to sue me for, but so I had all these people like calling me up, and all these people leaving me notes in my mailbox telling me I was going to die and I started getting death threats and stuff, whatever, people saying they were going to burn a cross and shoot me.

Some white antiracists have lost jobs by performing acts of antiracism in isolation. Before joining PI, Paul was fired from his job as a teacher when he took his students on a field trip to a civil rights march. Betty's career as a journalist ended when she exposed local incidents of racism:

I wrote a story about healthcare, what the blacks were getting and not getting in [the] county, and I included the fact that the local hospital wasn't
serving any black people. Because we also complained to Washington after
that happened and they sent somebody in, and the hospital straightened
up. But anyway, I got fired. [Interviewer: You got fired? For what?] It
turned out the publisher was on the hospital board.

## Possibilities for Coalition Building

This study suggests three lessons about dominant group activism. First, it
is important to conceptualize *all* dominant group members as implicated
in oppression, not to settle for targeting only extremists. In this study, the
similarity between the male profeminists' "rape culture" frame and the PI
white antiracists' "all whites are racist" frame was striking. Both viewed
dominant group members as part of the structure of oppression they
were seeking to abolish. Because this frame was not shared by ARA white
antiracists, it may be hard to build coalitions across the two dominant
antiracist movements. We argue that ARA needs to broaden its focus to
incorporate antiracist practices focused on everyday racism, rather than
just on overt acts of racism.

Second, we conclude that for dominant group activists, approaches to
privilege should vary based on whether racism or sexism is the issue.
Male profeminists tend to emphasize the cost of men's participation in
hegemonic masculinity rather than the privileges that sexism affords
them. Some white antiracists (particularly PI members) also see the costs
that whites pay in a racist society, but it is not a central aspect of their
movement, which is more focused on racial privileges. This difference
may reflect a difference in the way racism and sexism operate in North
American societies and, therefore, it may not be to the two movements'
advantage to become more alike on this dimension. Profeminist men's
emphasis on costs can help build a stronger sense of community among
men as well as improve relationships between men and women. In contrast, because of the fear of intimate interracial relationships in North
American society, whites are less likely to experience a cost in their relationships with people of color. The possibility of heightened intimacy
with people of color is not likely to attract more whites to antiracism.

Finally, the question of the costs of antiracist and profeminist activism
for dominant group members needs further exploration. Our data suggest

290 EILEEN O'BRIEN AND MICHAEL P. ARMATO

that while profeminist men are occasionally accused of being gay, for the most part they are lauded for being profeminist. White antiracists, on the other hand, are commonly stigmatized as "race traitors." However, we find that being affiliated with an organization can be a buffer against serious repercussions. Many of our sample of profeminist men worked in organizations, which may explain their decreased sense of the costs of activism.

It is also important to note that although our interviews focused on individuals' own "dominant" status, activists often linked racism and sexism. For example, MRPP explicitly points out how race plays into common myths of rape in the United States and therefore bolsters both gender and race oppression. One of ARA's principles is that members should address many other "isms" besides racism (among which sexism is included). Yet the organizations varied in how explicit they were in addressing the connection between racism and sexism. PI prefers not to have its attention diverted to other issues of oppression unless they are addressed specifically in an antiracist framework. As PI member Lisa put it: "Too often we focus on other issues as escapism, like trying to get out of [focusing on] racism." Such sentiments may prove an additional challenge to coalition building across dominant group activist organizations.

## ACKNOWLEDGMENTS

The authors would like to thank all the wonderful activists who shared their time and energy with us for this project, and Kathleen Blee and France Winddance Twine for their helpful comments and editing of our essay. Michael Armato is also grateful to his life partner Amanda for enriching his understanding of feminism.

## NOTES

1. Michael S. Kimmel, "From 'Conscience and Common Sense' to 'Feminism' for Men," in *Feminism and Men*, ed. Steven P. Schacht and Doris W. Ewing (New York: New York University Press, 1998), 21–42.

2. Michael A. Messner, "Radical Feminist and Socialist Feminist Men's Movements in the United States," in *Feminism and Men*, ed. Steven P. Schacht and Doris W. Ewing (New York: New York University Press, 1998), 67–85; Michael A. Messner, *Politics of Masculinities: Men in Movements* (Thousand Oaks, Calif.: Sage, 1997).

3. Herbert Aptheker, *Antiracism in U.S. History: The First Two Hundred Years* (New York: Greenwood Press, 1992).

4. Doug McAdam, *Freedom Summer* (New York: Oxford University Press, 1988).

5. Michael Novick, "Antiracist Action on the Move," *Turning the Tide: Journal of Antiracist Activism Research and Education*, vol. 10, no. 2 (1997): 1–2; Ronald Chisom and Michael Washington, *Undoing Racism: A Philosophy of International Social Change* (New Orleans: People's Institute Press, 1997).

6. Hank Johnston and Bert Klandermans, *Social Movements and Culture* (Minneapolis: University of Minnesota Press, 1995); Enrique Larana, Hank Johnston, and Joseph R. Gusfield, *New Social Movements: From Ideology to Identity* (Philadelphia: Temple University Press, 1994).

7. Scott A. Hunt, Robert D. Benford, and David A. Snow, "Identity Fields: Framing Processes and the Construction of Social Identities," in *New Social Movements: From Ideology to Identity,* ed. Enrique Larana, Hank Johnston, and Joseph R. Gusfield (Philadelphia: Temple University Press, 1994), 185–208; David A. Snow and Robert D. Benford, "Master Frames and Cycles of Protest," in *Frontiers in Social Movement Theory,* ed. Aldon D. Morris and Carol McClurg Mueller (New Haven: Yale University Press, 1992), 133–55.

8. Johnston and Klandermans, *Social Movements and Culture.*

9. Emilie Buchwald, Pamela Fletcher, and Martha Roth, *Transforming a Rape Culture* (Minneapolis: Milkweed, 1993).

10. Novick, "Antiracist Action on the Move," 1–2. Jonathan Franklin, "Skinnin' Heads," *Vibe* (June–July 1998): 84–85.

11. Robert Jensen, "Men's Lives and Feminist Theory," *Race, Class and Gender*, vol. 2 (1995): 114.

12. Jensen, "Men's Lives and Feminist Theory," 115.

13. Messner, *Politics of Masculinities*, 5–6.

# PART IV

*Faith and Other
Unfinished Feminisms*

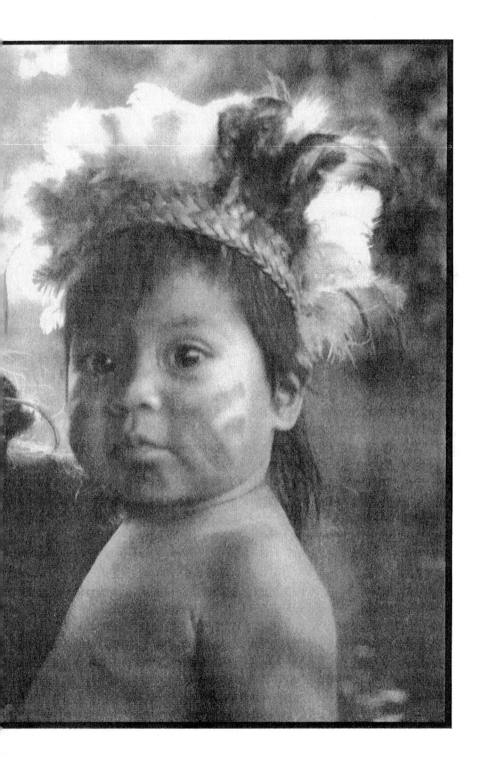

# Chapter 13

# "L'affaire des Foulards"

*Problems of Defining a Feminist Antiracist Strategy in French Schools*

## Jane Freedman

This chapter deals with the interactions of feminisms and antiracisms in French schools, in particular in relation to the debate surrounding the *foulard islamique* (Islamic headscarf) worn by some girls of mainly Maghrebi (North African) origin. This highly politicized debate has involved all the major feminist and antiracist associations in France, highlighting the previous lack of interaction between organized feminist and antiracist movements and leading to questions about how feminists can best engage in antiracist practices. It may be argued that an important effect of the *affaire des foulards* has been to expose the previously unquestioned universalist base of French feminisms: a universalism structured by traditional French ideologies of nation and citizenship which have led feminists to ignore the multiple and multitiered nature of women's identities in contemporary French society. At the same time, feminists have criticized antiracist movements for undervaluing domination based on gender, in particular, in the case of the *affaire des foulards*, for refusing to acknowledge the patriarchal structures present within Muslim communities in France. The issues surrounding the *affaire des foulards* can thus be seen as a salutary reminder of the need for feminists and antiracists to consider the crosscutting nature of dominations and oppressions within all modern societies, not just in France, and to fight against all types of exclusion.

The *affaire des foulards* must also be placed in an international context. France's ambivalent relationship to her former colonies, particularly Algeria,[1] and her fear of the spread of Islamic fundamentalism or *intégrisme*, has created tensions within French society, with immigrants of Islamic origin at risk of being stereotyped as "fundamentalists" or "terrorists." As Nancy Venel notes, the global political context—which has witnessed events such as the Gulf war, the rise of fundamentalisms in Iran, Algeria, and elsewhere, and the Rushdie affair—only adds to the fears of the French.[2] Indeed, the girls at the center of the *affaire des foulards* were often represented by the French media as tools of Islamic organizations aiming to infiltrate France.

This type of racist stereotyping clearly hampers the integration of immigrant communities and attempts to build a feminist antiracist strategy, as the voices of Muslim women themselves are often ignored. However, this fear of Islam is not unique to France, and the lessons of the *affaire des foulards* are relevant for feminists in a global context, in which fear and mistrust of Islam and particularly Islamic "fundamentalism" leads to ignorance of the true nature of Muslim women's identities and situations. We must remember that gender is constructed within a set of global power relations and, as Avtar Brah comments: "Our insertion into these global relations of power is realised through a myriad of economic, political and ideological processes."[3] In asserting the superiority of French culture over patriarchal Muslim culture, many French feminists fell into the trap of ignoring their positioning as white women within a set of postcolonial power relations. This is a trap which it seems only too difficult for feminists of all nationalities to avoid.

The *affaire des foulards* must thus be understood within a set of postcolonial power relations and within the context of French debates over immigration, nationality, and citizenship. These questions have been at the heart of French politics for the past decade, particularly with the introduction of new laws restricting the entry and residence of foreigners in France and making the conditions for obtaining French nationality more difficult.[4] France has a long history of immigration, with a shortage of manpower leading government and industrial leaders to encourage the influx of foreign workers. Before 1945 these immigrants came mainly from Europe, but after World War II, as the process of decolonization[5] began, more and more immigrants began to arrive from France's colonies and former colonies in Africa and Asia, and particularly from the countries of the Maghreb: Algeria, Morocco, and Tunisia.

Algeria in particular, which had been heavily colonized by France and was regarded as an integral part of France itself, was a prime site for the recruitment of workers. The legal status of Algeria established in 1947 allowed for the free movement of the population between that country and France.

Even the protracted and bloodthirsty war of independence did not stop the flow of immigrants from Algeria to France. Indeed, it added to it when, after Algerian independence in 1962, the *"harkis,"* those Algerians who had fought on the side of the French, were forced to flee to France.

The French authorities originally imagined that the workers who came to France from her former colonies would eventually return to their countries of origin. But in fact the arrival of male immigrant labor from the former French colonies in Africa and Asia in the period of rapid industrial expansion following the end of World War II was succeeded from the late 1960s onward by the arrival of families and a movement of sedenterization of the immigrant populations. After the French government officially suspended immigration in 1974 in response to the economic depression caused by the oil crisis of 1973, immigration for family regroupment became the principal form of immigration. There was a subsequent feminization of immigrant populations so that women now make up almost 50 percent of communities of immigrant origin in France.[6] Whilst successive governments have attempted to reach a target of "zero immigration" they have not been able to halt immigration totally, among other reasons because of the protection under international law of immigration for family reunification. But very strict conditions have been applied to those wishing to enter France and subsequent changes in the law have made it even harder for immigrants already resident in France to gain work permits or be eligible for French citizenship.

The question of immigration, particularly from the former colonies, thus continues to be a highly sensitive one in France, made even more so by the rise of the extreme right in the French political arena. The extreme right Front National (National Front), led by Jean-Marie Le Pen, has met with growing electoral success since the early 1980s, campaigning on a racist, antiimmigrant program.[7] Meanwhile other political parties, bowing to pressure from the right, have adopted a harsher stance on immigration and have passed laws to try and stem the flow of "illegal" immigrants into France, and to repatriate those "clandestine" immigrants already present on French territory, while at the same time fully assimilating those of immigrant origin who have the right to stay in France.[8] Those particularly targeted are immigrants of African and Asian origin, who make up 35.9 percent and 11.4 percent respectively of the population of immigrant origin in France.[9]

In this context of limited tolerance toward immigrants, one of the key issues to have arisen has been the creation of a Muslim community in France and the perceived difficulty in "integrating" this community into

French society. In conjunction with the rise of Islamic fundamentalism in an international context, the fear of Islam has blossomed. As Nancy Venel comments:

> The questions posed by the practice of Islam in France create a wave of perturbance in French society closely linked to the unfavourable perception of this religion (due to colonial imagery), but also to current international events which are not likely to calm the spirits.[10]

It is estimated that there are about 4 million Muslims in France,[11] of different origins and differing levels of religious observance. But although the Muslim population in France is far from homogeneous, the dominant French representations tend to treat Islam and Muslims in a reductionist and essentialist fashion, failing to note the important variations and cleavages within the Muslim community. A significant essentialism present in dominant French representations, and one to which I will return later in this chapter, is that concerning the oppression of women by men in Muslim culture. In this situation, Muslims, even those who were born in France and have French nationality, are often reminded of their foreign origins through discrimination and racism, and many describe themselves as second-class citizens. In these circumstances, as Venel remarks, Islam becomes for some a manner of self-affirmation and resistance to the outside world.[12] The young girls who wear their headscarves to school are in many ways making a strong and brave statement about their identity as Muslim women, in the face of much hostility and racism.

While French politicians have paid much attention in recent years to the "problem" of immigration, less concern has been focused on combating racism. There is a law of July 1972 which forbids discriminatory acts or expressions based on race. And a law of August 1989, concerning the conditions of entry and residence of foreigners in France, includes a reminder that:

> Discriminatory acts by holders of public authority, groups or private individuals, incitement to discrimination, hatred or violence, defamation and abuse, for reasons of belonging or not belonging to an ethnic group, a nation or a religion, are forbidden.[13]

In practice, however, as Philippe Bataille maintains, both individual and institutional racism are evident[14] and antiracist organizations have met with limited success.

The largest and most well-known antiracist organizations in France are the Mouvement contre le Racisme pour l'Amitié entre les Peuples (Movement against Racism and for Friendship between Peoples), or MRAP, set up in the 1960s, and SOS-Racisme, a more recent movement which made antiracism fashionable among young people in the 1980s. The founding of SOS-Racisme followed the so-called Marche des Beurs[15] of 1983, when a group of young, mainly Maghrebi, second-generation immigrants marched from Marseille to Paris to protest about the racism that they encountered in their daily lives and to demand equality. Young people of immigrant origin had been mobilizing since the early 1980s against the discrimination they encountered. They performed a series of concerts in 1980 and 1981 entitled Rock against the Police. These were followed by the Marche des Beurs or Marche pour l'égalité et contre le racisme (March for Equality and against Racism) in 1983, and a series of similar marches and demonstrations in subsequent years.

In 1984 SOS-Racisme was founded, led by Harlém Désir, a young man of French-Caribbean origin. Although it succeeded in gaining widespread media attention for its antiracist message in the 1980s, SOS-Racisme declined in influence in the 1990s, in part because of its close links with the Socialist Party which itself lost popularity at the end of the 1980s and early 1990s. SOS-Racisme has also been criticized by commentators like Pierre-André Taguieff for its overly media-centered approach and its preference for large, spectacular events over local, small-scale militant actions.[16]

The style and focus of these antiracist movements, together with the largely male-dominated leadership, has meant that, as Cathie Lloyd points out, the concerns of women of immigrant origin and the particular ways in which they are affected by racism are often overlooked.[17] In some cases this has led such women to form their own associations. One of the most well-known of these is the Nanas Beurs (now known as Meufs Rebeus or Voix d'Elles Rebelles), an association of young women of Maghrebi origin. Souad Benani, one of the founding members, describes how she and other young women from the Maghrebi community set up this association to defend their interests, as

> Women's concerns were often overlooked in the ideological battle for equal opportunities for immigrants. None of the slogans or campaigns showed how young women of North African origin were the victims of discrimination or oppression.[18]

Their association helps women having trouble with their residence or nationality papers, refugees, unmarried mothers, and battered wives, among others. The existence of the Nanas Beurs and similar organizations is symptomatic not only of the failure of antiracist associations to address women's concerns, but also of the way in which mainstream feminist organizations have often overlooked the problems of women of immigrant origin in France.

The question of the Islamic headscarf is just one of those raised by the presence of a settled immigrant population almost half of whom are women. And as Albert Nicollet points out with regard to African women, the sedenterization of the immigrant community and the greater presence of women and children in the immigrant population have heightened the importance of gender relations.[19] However, the issues raised are often ignored both by feminists and antiracists. As with other issues, that of the *foulard* poses important questions both for feminists and antiracists. But in most of these debates it is fair to say that the crucial importance of the interactions of gender and ethnicity has been ignored. In effect, in both academic studies and militant action in France, feminists and antiracists have experienced a series of what Lloyd terms *rendez-vous manqués*,[20] both sides ignoring the connection between sexist and racist dominations.

While feminist research has focused on questions of gender and discrimination in the workplace, family, politics, and the like, more often than not this research has been based on the experience of white women which has been generalized to nonwhite women. Although feminists such as Geneviève Fraisse[21] have theorized about women's domination and have criticized Republican Universalism for its exclusion of women from full citizenship, many feminists—with some notable exceptions, such as Colette Guillaimin[22]—have failed to address exclusions based on racist domination. Similarly, as Nadia Bentichou has shown, research on immigration and ethnicity in France has often ignored the gendered element present in migratory movements, considering women, if at all, only in their roles as wives of immigrant workers and as mothers of the "second generation" of immigration.[23] In fact, as Noelle Barison and Catherine Catarino argue:

> Not realizing or not wishing to realize that immigrant women are situated in a strategic position at the intersection of the social relations of domination which exist between sexes, classes, and ethnic groups, the corpus of research on migration and feminist research which has focused on general themes (work, family . . .) have for years neglected, respectively, women and immigrants.[24]

As well as this failure to take account of the experience of women immigrants in academic studies, there has also been a failure to fully consider the problems of women immigrants by militant organizations, both feminist and antiracist. Halima Boumédienne points to the way in which the Mouvement de Libération des Femmes (MLF), the major feminist movement of the 1960s and 1970s, failed to take account of the material conditions of immigrant women: "The MLF ignored immigrants' specificities as they did those of women from the suburbs."[25] This lack of coordination between feminists and antiracists can be seen as a specific product of French Republicanism, in that both feminists and antiracists challenge the universalism of the Republican model and argue for a national identity which comprehends difference. But in concentrating on one specific difference (either gender or race) they neglect the multiplicity of identities and exclusions.

Having briefly considered the context in which the *affaire des foulards* occurred we can now move on to a more detailed analysis of the affair itself and of the problems it has posed for feminists wishing to define an antiracist strategy in French schools.

## *The* affaire des Foulards

The question of the *foulard* or *voile* (the Islamic headscarf)[26] first hit the headlines in France in October 1989 when Ernest Chennière,[27] a headmaster in Creil, a suburb of Paris, refused to allow three Maghrebi girls to come to school wearing their headscarves on the grounds that this would contravene the Republican principle of secularism. It is difficult to understand the importance of this seemingly minor event for French society without grasping the importance of secularism in French national identity and without understanding the ways in which immigration, particularly from France's former colonies, has brought this national identity into question.

*Laïcité* or secularism has a long history in France, and a key place in French national identity. It is a principle closely connected with Republican universalism and with the doctrine of *liberté, égalité, fraternité* elaborated at the time of the French Revolution. It is perhaps no coincidence that the *affaire des foulards* exploded as France was celebrating the bicentennial of the Revolution and the principles it expounded. In effect, the founding project of the French Republic was the disappearance of difference through the assimilation of all to one "legitimate" culture. Republican ideology seeks to overcome all types of specific identities and belongings and create equality through sameness. Secularism seeks to enforce this equality in the public sector with regard to religion: by removing all religious observance from public institutions the private religious divisions that exist in society can be overcome. This principle has been a key part of the French state education system since the end of the nineteenth century when a series of laws known as the *lois laïques* decreed the secular nature of French schools. As Kay Chadwick reminds us, this secularism in education was reinforced by the formal separation of church and state in 1905.[28]

The French Republican idea of nation places education at the heart of a project of integration into universal French citizenship: through a uniform, secular education children are brought up to be equal citizens. School has always been conceived as the prime site of integration. State schools have always played a role as both instrument and expression of a politics of national identity which aims to detach individuals from their particular community or group of belonging and to assimilate them to the vast collective community which is the French nation. It is impossible to understand the importance of the *affaire des foulards* and the way in which antiracisms and feminisms have operated in France without grasping the importance of this Republican conception of national identity and the place that secular education is seen to have in preserving this identity. However, the principle of secularism has been challenged—particularly within the French education system—by the growing religious diversity of the French population due to an increasingly settled immigrant population.

Creil, the town where the issue of Islamic headscarves first hit the headlines, was like many other suburbs built in the postwar economic boom to house migrants from rural areas and immigrant workers from France's former colonies. Its school was founded to educate the children of these new housing settlements or *cités*. In 1989 when the *affaire des foulards* began it had almost nine hundred pupils of twenty-five different nationalities, and five hundred of these pupils came from Muslim families. Chennière's action in excluding the three girls for wearing their headscarf could thus be seen as an act of racist provocation[29] against the Muslim community served by his school. Many in France, however, saw him as a hero taking a stand to defend the secularism of a French school against the rising tide of a multiracial society.

The *affaire* was first reported in the daily newspaper *Libération*[30] and the story was quickly taken up by other newspapers. The majority of the reports focused on the *affaire* as a challenge to secularism in the French education system and a sign of the failure to integrate immigrants into the system. Although the dispute in Creil was seemingly resolved through a compromise whereby the girls were allowed to wear their headscarves in the school playground and corridors but agreed to let them drop around their shoulders in the classrooms,[31] the affair did not die down, as the media searched for similar incidents elsewhere and launched a debate over the position of Islam in French society. As Chahla Beski remarks:

> The majority of journalists drew attention to the fact that this affair far surpassed the simple story of "three veiled young women in Creil," and presented itself as revelatory of serious questions and anxieties amongst the French concerning the subject of the integration of Muslim immigrants into French society.[32]

The violent reactions this subject provoked attested to its importance for French national identity. An article by five intellectuals in the *Nouvel Observateur* magazine likened the acceptance of the headscarf in schools to the appeasement of Hitler in the 1930s[33] and argued that the end of strict secularism in schools could signal the downfall of the Republic itself.

While the reaction to the *affaire* in the press was rapid, political parties were divided and took longer to comment on the issue. The only party which had a clear line on this question was the extreme right Front National for whom the fact that Muslim girls wished to wear a headscarf to school was a clear sign of an Islamic "invasion" of France. Their spokesman, Bruno Mégret announced that:

> A Muslim civilization has arrived in France. After its installation on French soil, it is now implanting itself symbolically by the wearing of the headscarf in schools. We must ask ourselves the question: Should France adapt her principles to those of immigrants, or should immigrants adapt their customs to the laws of our country? You can imagine our reply.[34]

It is clear that the sentiments voiced by the Front National were not without an echo in public opinion,[35] and other parties were more reluctant to take a stance on the issue.

The Socialist Party was particularly divided, torn as it was between its long-standing loyalty to the Republican principle of secularism and its desire to integrate immigrants into French society. In the end, the Socialist Minister for Education, Lionel Jospin, turned to the Conseil d'Etat

(France's highest administrative court) who ruled that wearing a religious sign to school was not in itself sufficient reason for exclusion from school. This perhaps ought to have been the end of the *affaire*, and it did indeed die down for a bit. But in 1994, the *affaire des foulards* was relaunched when François Bayrou, the Minister for Education in a right-wing government, responding to growing fears about the influence of Islam in French schools, published a circular affirming that "ostentatious" religious symbols should not be allowed in schools. Although he did not name the *foulard* as such, it was clear that this was the "ostentatious" symbol he was referring to as he specifically excluded the wearing of a crucifix or a Jewish *kippa*, which he declared to be "unostentatious."

The timing of this ruling by the minister is significant. It was made as the political situation in Algeria was deteriorating and the *Front Islamique de Salut* (FIS), an Islamic fundamentalist organization, was gaining in power. This demonstrates once again the clear influence of international affairs on domestic political decisions, an influence which feminists must be aware of if they are to devise a comprehensive antiracist strategy within their own countries. Those who believed that the *affaire des foulards* was nothing but an internal debate concerned with the principles of French Republicanism and the integration of immigrants, neglected the global context within which all women are positioned.

Since Bayrou's rekindling of the *affaire des foulards* in 1994, the debate has rumbled on, with regular incidents of exclusion of girls from schools for wearing headscarves and industrial action by teachers in schools where girls are allowed to attend wearing their *foulard*. French society seems to be unable to come to terms with the issue, and neither feminists nor antiracists have found a convincing solution.

## Reactions to the affaire

One striking feature of reactions to the *affaire des foulards* and its aftermath has been the lack of media attention to the gendered element of the question, and the fact that few women were called upon to express their opinions. As Rachel Bloul remarks:

> These debates were also monopolized by men, notwithstanding their apparent concern with the question of women's rights in Islam. French men, Muslim men, male intellectuals and politicians, male personalities gave their opinion ad nauseam over the wearing of the scarves and its sociopo-

litical and cultural consequences. Women, on the other hand, whether Muslim, Maghrebi or French, were hardly heard.[36]

The young women who chose to wear headscarves to school were portrayed in many media reports as mere passive agents: either victims of dominating fathers who insisted on them wearing headscarves, or unwitting tools of Islamic organizations which manipulated them for their own purposes. Those who opposed the wearing of headscarves argued that they were protecting Muslim girls from a patriarchal order which restricted their freedom. Even those who supported these girls' right to attend school wearing headscarves argued that the French school system would help integrate them into French society and "liberate" them from Islamic pressure within their families and communities, implying a superiority of French society over patriarchal Islamic society while ignoring the presence of male domination within their own social order. As Etienne Balibar remarked in an article for the newspaper *Libération*, the argument that the headscarf demonstrates the institutionalized oppression of women is one which Western societies (themselves male-dominated) have used to try and prove their superiority over Muslim societies.[37]

This type of response is typical of a postcolonial discourse which divides women of Muslim (mainly North African) origin into two types: those who have assimilated into French society and adopted French modes of dress, behavior, and the like, and those who remain faithful to their traditional, Islamic cultures. This binary division is a crude and oversimplistic representation of Muslim/Maghrebi women in France whose lives bear witness to a much more complex series of social positionings. As Chahla Beski points out:

> The stereotypical images of women immigrants of Maghrebi origin which categorize them according to certain traits either as "traditional women," "women as objects," or as "Westernized women," "women as subjects," prevent the understanding of the diversity and the complexity of the reality lived by these women.[38]

It is also interesting to note that those who opposed Muslim girls' right to wear a headscarf in school on the grounds that this represented the oppression of women, had little to say about the fact that the girls' mothers also wore a headscarf. It seems that for many the problem lay not in the patriarchal domination of women signified by the wearing of a headscarf as such, but in the decision by young, supposedly "integrated" and "Westernized" women to don a *foulard*. As Sonia Dayan-Herzbrun comments, it is the conjunction between the headscarf and modernity which seems unbearable to many French citizens,[39] a sign of the failure of the French Republican system to fully assimilate second- and third-generation immigrants into French society, or a challenge by these second- and third-generation immigrants to the integrity of French national identity.

This type of confusion over the problem of the Islamic headscarf has also characterized feminist responses to the *affaire*. In fact, many feminists have adopted the position that the headscarf is a symbol of male domination and should, therefore, be deplored. This type of knee-jerk response, taken without listening to the voices of the girls involved, only served to further distance feminists from antiracists. Gisèle Halimi, for example, a leading feminist lawyer and former deputy, resigned from SOS-Racisme when this organization first defended the girls who had been excluded from school in Creil in 1989. She argued, "There cannot be integration without respect for the laws of the receiving country. There cannot be a change in mentalities without women's dignity equalling that of men."[40] Yvette Roudy, a former Minister of Women's Rights, took a similar position, claiming that accepting the wearing of Islamic headscarves would be "equivalent to saying yes to the inequality of women in French Muslim society."[41] Well-known feminist academics such as Dominique Schnapper and Elisabeth Badinter also came out in support of secularism in schools and argued for the exclusion of girls wearing headscarves.[42]

On the ground, many of the teachers who had initiated the conflict by excluding the girls wearing headscarves from their classes or by taking industrial action and striking in protest at the girls being allowed to wear headscarves, did so out of supposedly feminist sensibilities. Elisabeth Altschull, a teacher who has published a book recounting her experience in a school hit by the *affaire des foulards* and has argued strongly against the wearing of the headscarf, recalls how she asked one of her pupils, a thirteen-year-old girl named Aïcha, to take off her headscarf because she felt it her duty to do so as a feminist. She recounts that her reaction to the headscarf was: "More feminist than secular to tell the truth: a thirteen-year-old girl wearing a headscarf seemed evidently unacceptable to me."[43]

While these types of feminist reactions are well-meaning in that they believe themselves to be fighting against the oppression of women, they also demonstrate a failure to understand the situations of Muslim women in France, and the complex reasons why women choose to wear headscarves. This failure to understand leads to easy condemnation of Islamic society as sexist, a condemnation which does nothing for the cause of antiracism, and indeed plays into the hands of racists. The Front National and their supporters are only too happy to see Muslim immigrants being described as sexist oppressors.

This feminist condemnation of the *foulard* as oppressive of women also assumes a homogeneity within the Islamic community, with all Muslim women being similarly positioned. In fact, there are vast differences of opinion among Muslim women themselves concerning the headscarf: those who wear a headscarf do so for various reasons, while others oppose the wearing of a headscarf. Among those Muslim women who opposed it were those who belonged to an organization called Expressions Maghrébiennes au Féminin (EMAF) which organized a demonstration at the time of the original *affaire des foulards* in 1989. These women opposed the exclusion of Muslim girls from school but also planned to tear up a headscarf in public to demonstrate their belief that this was oppressive of women and counter to individual liberties. Similarly, Saoud Benani, a founder member of the Nanas Beurs, an association of young Maghrebi women, argued that: "To legitimize the wearing of the headscarf is to put under pressure all those who are fighting for their emancipation and their liberty."[44] The voices of these Muslim women were seized upon by French feminists wishing to justify their position. However, they represent only a segment of Muslim women in France. For others, the wearing of the headscarf is an autonomous decision, a key part of their identity.

One of the few feminists who took the time to listen to Muslim women before passing judgment on the *affaire des foulards* was Françoise Gaspard, a former Socialist deputy and keen antiracist who had previously fought against the Front National in the town of Dreux. Together with the sociologist Farhad Khosrokhavar, she undertook a series of interviews with Muslim women to discover what meaning the *foulard* had for them. Their findings contradict the dominant representations in the French media which portrayed the girls at the center of the *affaire des foulards* as lacking the capacity to make their own choices. They indicate that the girls' decision to wear headscarves was an expression of their own particular identity, and not a result of pressure from a patriarchal social order. In fact, they report that for many young Muslim women, often those most "integrated" into French society, the choice to wear a headscarf was an autonomous one taken not for militant religious or political reasons, but as an affirmation of identity, an attempt to open up a new space where French and Islamic identity could be combined without conflict:

> It is not a question of conquering society (nor even the Islamic community in France), but of opening up a personal space. In the great majority of cases, there is no such thing as "veiled militancy," but rather a tendency to reconcile the multiple demands of an identity which feels a need to distinguish itself with respect to the outside.[45]

I would argue that this is the key to a feminist antiracist strategy in French schools. Like Gaspard, feminists must listen to the voices of Muslim women and accept that faced with a sometimes hostile host society, they have developed their own coping strategies and their own particular identities. This lesson must also be learned by women in antiracist organizations. These organizations have also had a weak response to the *affaire des foulards* because they have concentrated on the aspect of the debate concerned with the integration of second-generation immigrants, and have forgotten that those at the center of the *affaire* are women. Thus a true feminist antiracist strategy must overcome the divide between feminist and antiracist action, and must, as only Gaspard seems to have done so far, examine the specificity of immigrant Muslim women's position, acknowledging at the same time that this position is in no way homogeneous. Only when feminists persuade teachers to listen to the voices of the Muslim girls they teach and to fully include them in lessons, whether or not they are wearing a headscarf, will a successful feminist antiracist strategy have been achieved.

What the *affaire des foulards* seems to have demonstrated is that feminist antiracist strategies must go beyond an essentialist view of "the other," in this case the Islamic "other," and must consider the intersections of different oppressions and dominations. To develop an adequate feminist antiracist strategy, feminists must accept the multiplicity of identities and positionings within modern societies and white feminists must realize that their positioning depends on a postcolonial global order. In France this entails realizing that immigrant women want and need to find their own identities and that these identities will not necessarily emulate those of white women. And if the affirmation of these new identities involves the wearing of an Islamic headscarf, then feminists should be prepared to support them in this decision and to oppose any attempt to exclude these women, seeing such exclusion as the form of racism it clearly is.

The situation in France is particular in that French national identity depends on a very specific notion of equality: a Republican equality which demands assimilation of all citizens to a norm. Perhaps it is time for French feminist antiracists to stop trying to work within the framework of this Republican model and to challenge the Republican notion of equality. This would entail the realization that equality for Muslim women immigrants in France does not necessarily have the same meaning as for white women. A truly feminist antiracist strategy in French schools would encourage the inclusion of young Muslim women by giving them the space for choice, allowing them to negotiate their own path between their Muslim origins and the dominant culture of French society. In this way these women would develop their own citizenship and be truly included in French society.

## Conclusions

Although the *affaire des foulards* is specific to France, the lessons learned must also be applied internationally by feminists fighting to establish antiracist strategies both within educational establishments and in other walks of life. Within the education system, the affair highlights the dangers of imposing dominant models of gender equality which ignore the ways in which women of immigrant and ethnic minority communities live their identities and in which they themselves fight against the racism they encounter. Feminist antiracists must fight instead for inclusive systems of education that allow space for the development of multiple identities and different models of gender identity. At the same time they must be aware of international pressures such as the fear of Islamic fundamentalism, which have led to Muslim women's voices being ignored, and must place their fight within the context of the postcolonial societies in which they live.

### NOTES

1. The long and bloody decolonization of Algeria has left deep scars in the French psyche. This has not been helped by the current civil war in Algeria and the threat of terrorist action in mainland France by Algerian Islamic organizations.

2. Nancy Venel, *Musulmanes françaises: Des pratiquantes voilées à l'université* (Paris: L'Harmattan, 1999), 12.

3. Avtar Brah, "Difference, Diversity, Differentiation: Processes of Racialisation and Gender," in *Racism and Migration in Western Europe*, ed. John Wrench and John Solomos (Oxford: Berg, 1993), 201.

4. The Pasqua and Debré laws of 1986, 1993, and 1997. For more information on these laws, see D. Fassin, A. Morice, and C. Quiminal, eds., *Les lois de l'inhospitalité* (Paris: La Découverte, 1977, and J. Freedman and C. Tarr, eds., *Women, Immigration and Identities in France* (Oxford: Berg, 2000).

5. The process of decolonization began with the independence of France's colonies in South-East Asia. The independence of Morocco and Tunisia followed in 1958, and that of Algeria in 1962.

6. Institut nationale de la statistique (INSEE) 1990.

7. For more information on the Front National and its program see, for example, G. Birenbaum, *Le Front National en politique* (Paris: Balland, 1992), and J. Marcus, *The National Front and French Politics: The Resistible Rise of Jean-Marie Le Pen* (Basingstoke: Macmillan, 1995).

8. There may be some confusion over the use of the term immigrant. In fact the French often still refer to those who have been born in France and have French citizenship as "*immigrés.*"

9. INSEE 1990.

10. Venel, *Musulmanes françaises*, 17.

11. It is impossible to give a more precise figure, as census data do not include information on religion.

12. Venel, *Musulmanes françaises*.

13. Cited in Sonia Dayan-Herzbrun, "The issue of the Islamic Headscarf," in *Women, Immigration and Identities in France*, ed. Jane Freedman and Carrie Tarr (Oxford: Berg, 2000), 98.

14. Philippe Bataille, "Racisme institutionnel, racisme culturel et discriminations," in *Immigration et intégration: l'état des savoirs*, ed. Philippe Dewitte (Paris: La Découverte, 1999), 285–93.

15. The word Beur signifies the children of Maghrebi immigrants to France. It originates in Arabic slang and was at first a term of positive self-identification adopted by young people of Maghrebi origin. However, it has since taken on more negative connotations as it has been adopted into dominant discourse.

16. Pierre-André Taguieff, "L'antiracisme en crise: Eléments d'une critique réformiste," in *Racisme et modernité*, ed. Michel Wieviorka (Paris: La Découverte, 1993), 357–92.

17. Cathie Lloyd, "*Rendez-vous manqués*: Feminisms and Antiracisms in France," *Modern and Contemporary France*, vol. 6, no. 1 (February 1998): 61–74.

18. Souad Benani, "Les Nanas Beurs," in *Immigrant Women and Integration,* ed. Jacqueline Costa-Lascoux (Strasbourg: Council of Europe Publications, 1995), 79.

19. Albert Nicollet, *Femmes d'Afrique noire en France* (Paris: L'Harmattan, 1993).

20. Lloyd, *"Rendez-vous manqués."*

21. Geneviève Fraisse, *Muse de la Raison: Démocratie et exclusion des femmes en France* (Paris: Gallimard, 1995).

22. Colette Guillaimin, *Sexe, Race et Pratique du pouvoir* (Paris: Côté-femmes, 1992).

23. Nadia Bentichou, *Les femmes de l'immigration au quotidien* (Paris: L'Harmattan, 1997).

24. Noelle Barison and Catherine Catarino, "Les femmes immigrées en France et en Europe," *Migrations Société*, vol. 9, no. 52 (1997): 17–19.

25. Interview in *Courant alternatif*, March 1986, quoted in Lloyd, *Rendez-vous manqués.*

26. The terms *foulard* or *voile* are widely used in dominant French discourse to describe all the different types of headscarf worn by Muslim women. The refusal of the French to use Arabic terms such as *hijab* can be seen as another indication of their opposition to multiculturalism in France.

27. Chennière has since been elected to the French National Assembly as a deputy for the center right RPR.

28. Kay Chadwick, "Education in Secular France: (Re)defining laïcité," *Modern and Contemporary France*, vol. 5, no.1 (February 1997): 47–60.

29. It is interesting to note that at the time of the *affaire* the media argued that Ernest Chennière could not be accused of racism since he himself was of French West Indian origin.

30. "Le port du voile heurte la laïcité du collège du Creil" (The wearing of the headscarf is in conflict with the secularism of the secondary school in Creil), *Libération*, October 4, 1989.

31. This agreement was short-lived, however. As the *foulard* became a national affair the girls changed their minds and refused to remove their headscarves in class.

32. Chahla Beski, "Les femmes immigrées maghrébines: Objet ou sujet?" *Migrations Société*, vol. 9, no. 52 (1996): 44.

33. *Le Nouvel Observateur*, November 2, 1989.

34. *Le Quotidien de Paris*, October 18, 1989.

35. An opinion poll published in *Le Monde* showed that 75 percent of French opinion was hostile to the wearing of the *foulard* in schools. *Le Monde*, November 20, 1989.

36. Rachel Bloul, "Victims or Offenders? 'Other' Women in French Sexual Politics," *European Journal of Women's Studies*, vol. 3, no. 3 (1996): 259.

37. *Libération*, November 3, 1989.

38. Beski, "Les femmes immigrées maghrébines," 46.

39. Dayan-Herzbrun, "The issue of the Islamic Headscarf."

40. *Le Quotidien de Paris*, November 2, 1989.

41. *Le Quotidien de Paris*, November 6, 1989.

42. *Libération*, November 24, 1989.

43. Elisabeth Altschull, *Le voile contre l'école* (Paris: Seuil, 1995), 11.

44. Souad Benani, "Le voile et la citoyenneté," in *Démocratie et Représentation*, ed. Michele Riot-Sarcey (Paris: Kimé, 1995), 86.

45. Françoise Gaspard and Farhad Khosrokhavar, *Le Foulard et la République* (Paris: Seuil, 1995), 51.

# Chapter 14

# Memorializing Racist Massacres
## *Faith versus Feminism in Florida*

## *Cathleen L. Armstead*

This essay examines the Democracy Forum, a small multiracial, faith-based social activist group that was committed to "challenging multiple oppressions."[1] Democracy Forum, in which I was a participant, was organized in the late 1990s in Apopka, a small town in central Florida in the U.S. South. I focus on lessons for feminist antiracists that can be learned from the first project of Democracy Forum, an effort to involve the local community in developing a more accurate history of a racial massacre that occurred in the community of Ocoee, about six miles from Apopka, in 1920. Through this project, we hoped to encourage reflection on how history shapes our day-to-day circumstances and to initiate a public discussion about contemporary forms of oppression. We hoped to create a memorial to the massacre modeled after Holocaust memorials or a permanent exhibit at the Orange County Regional Historical Museum, or to have this history included in the Orange County public school curriculum. In this essay, I reflect on why these hopes were not realized and what this suggests for feminist antiracist organizing. I first review the history of Ocoee to delineate the problems of researching and educating communities about a "hidden" massacre. I then analyze the role of Democracy Forum and discuss the possibilities and limitations of faith-based organizations for progressive political work.

### *The Ocoee Context*

Ocoee, a small rural town in central Florida, was the site of one of the worst eruptions of racial violence in the United States. In 1920, Ocoee was an unincorporated city of approximately eleven hundred people. Almost half its citizens were black, residentially segregated into the town's Northern and Southern quarters. There are multiple versions of what happened on November 2, election night, but what is uncontested is that blacks had attempted to vote. One in particular, Mose Norman, was refused the right to vote. A struggle ensued, he was beaten, and disappeared. At dusk, a mob of whites went to the home of another prominent black, July Perry, where rifle shots were exchanged and two white men died. There was a call to Orlando, the county seat, for reinforcements and over two hundred white men with army-issued rifles descended upon Ocoee. Perry was captured and lynched that night and the black Northern quarters, including twenty-six homes, two churches, and a community lodge, was incinerated. The NAACP's research indicated that between thirty and sixty blacks were killed that night. Shortly thereafter, the citizens of the Southern quarters fled Ocoee. Between November 3 and 28, 1920, over 496 black citizens had disappeared from Ocoee.

The massacre in Ocoee sent very powerful messages to blacks, warning against being too prosperous or exercising citizenship rights. Mose Norman, who was attacked at the polls, owned his own farm, while July Perry, who was lynched, was the overseer of a large citrus grove. A federal report concluded that neither the lynching of July Perry nor the destruction of the town would "constitute a violation of rights secured to the Negroes under the federal constitution or laws as distinguished from the constitution and laws of the state involved."[2] For seventeen years after the massacre, no blacks voted in Orange County, Florida.[3]

During the Civil War (1861–65), slavery was abolished by President Lincoln. On April 9, 1866, the Civil Rights Act was enacted in defiance of a veto by President Andrew Johnson (Republican) and was based on the Thirteenth Amendment of the Constitution. This Act was aimed against the "Black Codes" being enacted by former slave states such as Florida, which sought to restrict the liberties of former slaves. The Black Codes were designed to reestablish white supremacy and resegregate public life by rolling back the political, economic, and social gains made by black people as a consequence of the Fourteenth and Fifteenth amendments to the Constitution. In Florida, as elsewhere in the southern United States, white supremacy was reestablished by racial terrorism. In 1877 federal troops were withdrawn from the former slave states, leaving black Americans unprotected in the face of white racial terrorism.

The violence in Ocoee mirrored the racial violence across the United

States in the late nineteenth and early twentieth centuries. Race riots and white terrorism swept through the northern and southern states during this period. The period between April to October 1917 was known as "Red Summer" by the National Association for the Advancement of Colored People (NAACP) because there were race riots in twenty-five towns and cities in the United States. Organized antiblack violence by the Ku Klux Klan, law enforcement groups, and white mobs caused a wave of lynchings and assaults on black Americans that left more than six thousand dead across the nation and widespread destruction of property held by black Americans. Such racial terror made it clear that, even with the abolition of slavery, law would serve the interest of whites and few blacks would have the financial resources or access to political power to mount successful challenges to a system of white supremacism. In the United States, black Americans lived in segregated communities until court-ordered desegregation of public schools began in 1954, usually over the vocal, even violent, opposition of local whites.[4] Many of the black American members of Democracy Forum came of age in the period of school desegregation in the South and remember the fear they felt as they entered previously all-white schools.

After the mass exodus of blacks from Ocoee in 1920, no blacks returned to the town until the 1980s. Even today, Ocoee is virtually all white, with blacks constituting less than 3 percent of the total population of 22,000. This is in contrast with bordering towns such as Apopka (where Democracy Forum was located) whose black population is 12 percent, or Winter Garden where blacks constitute 14 percent of the population. Ocoee has few blacks in official positions and racial issues are rarely addressed in local elections. Local racial struggles are shouldered by faith-based organizations, particularly the predominantly black Baptist and African Methodist Episcopalian (AME) churches, and by quasi-official committees such as Orlando Mayor Glenda Hood's dialogue on racial relations.

## Democracy Forum

Democracy Forum had its beginnings as a faith-based organization, Dismantling Racism Action Group (DRAG), centered in the Unitarian Church. The Unitarian Church is a nondenominational church that has a reputation for social and political activism. Initially an all-white group,

DRAG met and read an excerpt from *Uprooting Racism*[5] and Peggy McIntosh's article, "White Privilege,"[6] and decided to become active in racial issues in the local community. Its activities included tutoring young black students and adopting a "sister," predominantly black, church. DRAG members then asked Alana,[7] a black woman who was a trained diversity facilitator, to lead the group through a series of focused discussions. Alana, a descendent of a survivor from the Ocoee massacre and herself a survivor of the desegregation of Florida's high schools, was active in local black women's social and political groups and identified as a socialist-feminist. Despite her initial reservations, she began to facilitate DRAG discussions and urged participants to reexamine the assumptions behind their "tutoring" and "adoption" models of social activism. She argued that DRAG would need a better understanding of local history in order to challenge contemporary white privilege and she encouraged alliances with other local groups, including black women working in the Orange County Historical Museum and the NAACP. Moreover, Alana consistently pointed out the connections between racism and other forms of oppression, including sexism and homophobia.

With Alana's help and leadership, DRAG developed a proposal to research and educate the public about the Ocoee massacre and its aftermath. A key element of this project was the decision to reinsert the stories of the women who suffered through the massacre and kept the history alive while rebuilding their lives. Traditionally, the history of Ocoee in the 1920s was told as a heroic narrative focusing on July Perry, although Perry's wife and daughter had remained at his side and defended their home with their rifles. Moreover, it was women's networks through the Baptist and AME churches to which the fleeing families turned for survival. In November 1997, the DRAG proposal was funded by the Burt and Mary Meyer Foundation, a progressive agency committed to grassroots education and organization. Meanwhile the Unitarian Church withdrew its support for unstated reasons. The group reformed as Democracy Forum, an explicitly feminist antiracist group, recruited new members, and held biweekly meetings to plan research and community forums.

To build Democracy Forum, Alana recruited women who were politically active as well as other descendants of survivors of the massacre. She recruited three other women who identified as socialist-feminists. In all there were four socialist-feminists, two middle-aged professional women (one black, one white), and two college students (one black, one white). I was one of the white socialist-feminists recruited by Alana through our mutual involvement in antipoverty organizations. The founding DRAG members also recruited others to Democracy Forum, including members of local black churches. Thus, Democracy Forum came to be composed of three distinct groups, two of which were faith-based—the white Unitarians and the black church members—and a socialist-feminist group that was not faith-based. Members were diverse in age—ranging from nineteen to seventy-two—and in education, but almost all regarded themselves as middle class.

The initial meetings of Democracy Forum were devoted to discussing values, ground rules, and communication, and to creating a nonhierarchical structure. All our key decisions were to be reached by consensus. During discussion we would listen, pause, consider, and question assumptions. We wanted to be a nonhierarchical group that did not mimic societal patterns of race and gender. We argued that if we were to challenge white supremacy we could not have a white man be a leader or spokesman. Thus we deliberately chose pairs of leaders for each team: co-coordinators, membership, media and community outreach, and research. Choices were based partially on individual interest and ability, and partially on race and gender. This strategy would later become problematic when white men charged us with "reverse racism."

Given their emphasis on the ideals of community and universal humanity, faith-based organizations like Democracy Forum are fertile grounds for activism and hold promise for cross-class and antiracist movements. Still, abstract notions of community do not always translate into cooperative, mutually respectful actions. The white members of Democracy Forum (both men and women) who identified themselves as faith-based progressives included feminist, antiracist, and pro–gay rights positions among their core beliefs. A few white women were openly lesbian. The women from this group were able to discuss white male privilege but were not able to see their own racial privilege. The white men from this group agreed in principle with the critique of white male privilege but felt slighted and ignored as individuals when asked to step down from leadership positions. Both men and women from the faith-based group often reacted to conflict, anger, and disagreements over political strategy with a plea to "agree to disagree," defining their reaction as one of "tolerance."

Many of the black members of Democracy Forum were members of the AME or Baptist churches. Although black churches have historically been central to struggles for black equality and civil rights, many have a strong patriarchal tradition and oppose reproductive freedom, divorce, and homosexuality.[8] Some black women in Democracy Forum criticized the male leadership of black churches or identified as feminists, but other black women were ambivalent or negative about feminism. The nonfeminist black members of Democracy Forum were also hostile to gay rights.

Members of Democracy Forum thus had different goals for the group, according to their race, gender, and politics. Most black members were committed to understanding the Ocoee massacre and memorializing the victims. In contrast, most white members wanted to educate the white citizens of central Florida about our disastrous and violent history. It was only the socialist-feminist minority who were explicitly dedicated to memorializing the victims, educating the community, and changing the racial conditions of the present.

Gendered racial differences appeared when white men seemed more interested in dismantling the racism of those they termed "other whites," than in dealing with their own privileges. At public presentations, especially those with press coverage, some white men routinely engaged in shouting matches with public officials or other prominent white citizens. White women were less vocal about dismantling racism, but focused instead on the importance of oral histories and the necessity of hearing "silenced voices." They assumed that having white women listen to oral histories by blacks was the route to "finding voice," when, in fact, many survivors and descendants of the massacre had not been silent but merely unheard. As Alana frequently noted, "Black folk have been talking about this for a *long* while." The socialist-feminists were explicit that their political commitments shaped their decision to join Democracy Forum. As one explained, "For me [I joined because of] the possibility of progressive social change with the opportunity to work with a diverse multicultural group."

Thus, although our intent was to work together as a progressive group with shared leadership and equality in participation, many of the black men and women who were recruited by Alana left after the first few meetings. They were disturbed by what they noted as the "hypocrisy of white folks" who were reluctant to make the connections between oppressions and chose to concentrate on the historical legacy of racism. The factors that made our working together difficult were an anti-intellectualism, an obsession with locating the "authentic black community" in a manner that dismissed the perspective of black members of Democracy Forum, internal conflicts of race and gender, and tensions between faith-based and feminist agendas.

## *Anti-Intellectualism*

Anti-intellectualism was a strong undercurrent in Democracy Forum, as well as among our audiences. For example, Meridian, a black woman descendent of survivors of the massacre and a prominent member of Democracy Forum, was vocal about her distrust of academics and "white knowledge." She did not believe in questioning oral history accounts or comparing these with official documents, insisting that "Black people won't talk with a tape recorder" and that newspaper reports, census data, and federal files were "all lies."

It is difficult to discount her concerns. Academic writing and knowledge have often distorted the experiences of blacks, especially women. Many official records of racial incidents are incomplete or fabricated. Local newspaper accounts were racially biased. However, these sources were also helpful in the reconstruction of the massacre of Ocoee. Accounts from the national press included observations by Walter White, then field secretary of the NAACP and chief investigator of the Ocoee massacre. Official documents enabled us to locate the unmarked graves of July Perry and Robbie Robertson, two black men who were killed that night.

The Ocoee massacre as a personal tragedy is one form of understanding. But understanding the Ocoee massacre through multiple sources and through theorizing can be politically important. As feminist theorist bell hooks notes:

> Support of anti-intellectualism in [the] feminist movement is a good example of ideology that undermines and impedes progress. . . . Most women are deprived of access to modes of thought that promote the kind of critical and analytical understanding necessary for liberation struggle.[9]

If theorizing about race and gender has been biased, inaccurate, and harmful, important and powerful insights have also emerged from intellectual work. Thus the tendency toward anti-intellectualism in political action needs to be addressed by feminist antiracists. We need to popularize, disseminate, and actually teach theories for empowerment. We need to make the reading accessible and provide spaces for people to connect their reading to their lived experience. Democracy Forum's failure to address this was a major factor in its ultimate failure.

## Defining the Community

Additionally, members of Democracy Forum had different definitions of the "community" they wanted to educate or change. Some defined the community as the original residents of Ocoee and their descendants, which would include descendants both of survivors and of those who participated in the mob. Prominent white citizens of Ocoee maintained that the wholesale burning of the town was accomplished by "outsiders" and they saw themselves as equally victimized by the massacre, arguing that "it doesn't make sense for an outsider to come in here and rename things." However, defining the community geographically did not do justice to the significance of the massacre. Prominent white citizens of Ocoee had participated in the violence, as did local, state, and federal government officials who armed whites with rifles and refused to prosecute the offenders.

In contrast, the majority of Democracy Forum members, of both races, defined *the community* as the "black community," arguing that the massacre happened to blacks, therefore whites should not "speak for them." Yet defining the community as the black community meant accepting the racial divisions imposed by the dominant white society. According to feminist scholar Peggy Weiss, "The very division of people into distinct communities (the gay community, the black community, etc.) can be caused by a dominant group's enforcement of particular identities and can impose great costs."[10] It was important for Democracy Forum to achieve a clear understanding of the power of white supremacy, but focusing on the "black community" in isolation made the larger "white community" appear to be the normative one.

The socialist-feminists in Democracy Forum had a different vision of the community. They argued that since the Ocoee massacre was an attack on the citizenship rights of blacks, it was an attack on everyone who valued the idea of citizenship. They argued that the idea of community needed to rest on firmer ground than either "ethnicity" or "shared victimhood," that it should involve a notion of shared histories and a shared future. However, this socialist-feminist position did not prevail in Democracy Forum.

## Conflicts of Race and Gender

Contemporary relations between white women and black women rest upon a brutally oppressive legacy of slavery, sexual violence directed at black women, enforced segregation, and exploitative domestic work. Women must explore the impact of this history on their perceptions of each other in order to work together. To this end, the socialist-feminist members of Democracy Forum instituted a reading and discussion circle focusing on the relationships between black and white women. Yet discussion remained centered on "other" black and white women rather than on the divisions within Democracy Forum itself. Although both black and white members denied that there were racial differences or hostility between the women in Democracy Forum, many actions signaled a deep distrust. For example, Meridian was reluctant to tell her own history (her mother survived the massacre), to share photos of her relatives, or even to disclose her address and telephone number. White women saw Meridian's distrust as an idiosyncratic quirk instead of examining the role of race and power in shaping her distrust. White women also found it difficult to understand how they contributed to racial oppression or how they experienced white privilege. As bell hooks has noted elsewhere about white women:

> Identifying as "victims," they [white women] could abdicate responsibility for their role in the maintenance and perpetuation of sexism, racism, and classism, which they did by insisting that only men were the enemy. They did not acknowledge and confront the enemy within.[11]

Within Democracy Forum, most white women did not participate in the tasks of organization. They were noticeably absent from the planning meetings, although quick to show up at public presentations. Alana gave the following example:

> Jennifer committed to being the person doing grant writing. Then she sent word that she would not be able to do that, she had other commitments. But then she showed up again and made some inclinations that she wanted to do that still. She is someone I only see at major events like retreats and training. And in between we have missed some major grant cycles.

Another source of conflict occurred when some black women expressed dismay at what they termed the "pettiness" of feminists, especially black feminist women. For example, when Alana said that she was disturbed that some of the younger black women were being ignored in the group, other black women claimed that Alana was being too sensitive. Also, some black women defended the racist and sexist practices of particular men in Democracy Forum, because "it was how they were brought up."

Moreover, there were sharp differences in the way black women were treated in Democracy Forum, especially by white men. For example, Meridian had stature among the whites as the descendant of a survivor in ways that Alana, although also the descendant of a survivor, did not. Meridian, who was less educated and less articulate than Alana, was perceived as an authentic black woman who was outspoken in her opinions, perhaps because her opinions—she didn't hate anybody, she didn't "see color," and we were "all equal in the eyes of the lord"—were compatible with the beliefs of most white members.[12] In contrast, Alana was described by white members as petty and tyrannical, perhaps because she had a more systematic critique of interlocking systems of oppression. Alana's principled insistence that we all participate in a racist and sexist society and that we all need to confront "our issues" before presuming to educate the public pushed the group to accepting a very high standard for itself but left more than one person angry.

Finally, it was not surprising that the four women who identified as socialist-feminist would be marginalized and perceived by some in Democracy Forum as a "power-hungry clique." Other white women did not share their commitment to antiracism as an essential component of feminism. Black men and women did not share their commitment to feminism. And white men were threatened by their anger.

Tensions among members of Democracy Forum became clear in the effort to conduct an oral history project of the 1920 massacre. We began by reading academic materials on oral histories, and then practiced among ourselves by interviewing group members who were consistently not heard: three black women and one white woman. The majority of white women attended the oral history training, many because of their eagerness to later conduct interviews of "the community." However, some white women were not eager to interview black women members of Democracy Forum and were dismayed when these interviews revealed the mistrust and hostility in the group.

There were marked racial differences in the way people responded to strife in the group. Rachel, a young black socialist-feminist, talked about "Things that aren't stated in the meetings. Male/female things. Age things, um, that we haven't like verbalized." Sara, a white woman, responded by asking Rachel, "Do you think getting together for dinner or a potluck dinner or a picnic or whatever would help?" Rachel answered, "I don't think interaction alone really solves much, and that you can interact with people that you still do not trust. I don't think that's very effective."

White men in Democracy Forum exhibited a similar desire for harmony. This was evidenced in an exchange between a white man and Alana when she was discussing the difficulties she had in being heard as a black woman. Alana described being dismissed as a "troublemaker" at work and having her family criticize her for "getting too far away from her beginnings," and said that she did not also want to be ignored in a progressive organization. In Democracy Forum, she stated, "my proposals are blocked. Until a white woman suggests them. [Sighs]. I'm thinking we live in really different worlds." At one point, Alana stated,

> One of the white men in Democracy Forum was interested in some information about antipoverty programs. . . . I agreed to be interviewed for his research if he would not state my name. That could jeopardize my job. He agreed and we had a nice interview. However, in his paper that he submitted to a journal he identifies me by my real name AND my position. . . . I was very clear about anonymity. However, it gave him credibility to use my name. That is both racism and sexism. Can you see him doing that to a white man?

The interviewer defended himself simply by saying that this was a mistake—as if race and gender do not also shape mistakes. He then attempted to recover the fellowship he thought the group had by telling Alana, "You're being a little harsh on us this morning. I would like to have some contrast. I would want you to talk about the positive."

Despite these tensions, the oral history training was somewhat successful in forcing white members to listen to black women members. However, it ultimately failed because all the white members didn't like what they heard and three white women and two white men left the group. In a revealing and contradictory moment, Jennifer, a white woman, frankly confessed that she was leaving because of the group's insistence that each one confront his or her own racism. She explained that "All of this antiracism stuff. I'm not racist. I'm in an interracial marriage. And all of that antiracist stuff, I've done all that. And it's too painful." Other whites withdrew from the group feeling criticized and blamed. One white man even suggested that Democracy Forum engaged in "reverse racism":

I can report that what I have felt since this group so hopefully began has been a steady process of dehumanization. . . . Why was I not surprised that at the May 14th meeting certain positions were to be offered seemingly exclusively to women of color? Is it our purpose to mildly replicate the evil racism and sexism we are investigating?

In the most surprising move, Alana also left the group, saying she was tired of teaching white people, tired of explaining to white people, and tired of assuaging white people's guilt.

## Faith versus Feminism

There was also an uneasy relationship in Democracy Forum between religion and progressive political action which was further complicated by race and gender. This conflict became most obvious when a black male minister, Reverend Manley, joined the group. Reverend Manley was progressive on antiracism issues but was not a feminist. His goal in joining the group was to "embrace the cause of justice, regardless of how difficult it may seem at first." Manley's definition of "the community" was broad and inclusive, ironically resembling the socialist-feminist position. He wrote:

> The citizens of the state of Florida, county of Orange and city of Ocoee are inseparable and indistinguishable as it relates to the past, present and future. We are one Florida, one Orange County, and one Ocoee. Therefore we must face the misdeeds of *our* past. (Emphasis in the original)

Reverend Manley was not only interested in this particular attack or its history, but he was also a resident in Ocoee and very concerned with the ongoing racism his children encountered. His analysis of the event as damaging to an entire community and his insistence on connecting history to the present should have proved helpful to Democracy Forum. Yet Reverend Manley's participation revealed the many contradictions and rifts in our group and he quickly became a lightening rod for disagreements.

Most black women members of Democracy Forum were appreciative and respectful toward Reverend Manley. At his very first meeting, Celia, a black woman, deferred to him as "more knowledgeable" about the 1920 massacre despite her own yearlong work researching this history. At his third meeting Celia invited him to an interview with the *Wall Street Journal* and, at the end of the interview, remarked that the Reverend was a "godsend."

However, Reverend Manley disagreed with some of the processes and goals of Democracy Forum. In particular, he was impatient with dialogue and decisions by consensus, and insisted that "there are always natural leaders in groups." He did not accept the idea of different types and styles of leadership, nor did he support gay rights or feminism, commenting that:

> My people expect certain things of me and frankly I expect certain things of myself. Homosexuality is a sin. I don't agree with the right wing's approach to homosexuality, but it's a sin.

and

> My wife knows that I get kicked around in the community all day. I expect that. But when I come home, I don't expect to take anything from my partner. I can't fight on two fronts at the same time. We have that understanding. We are in this together.

Not everyone in the group embraced Reverend Manley. Two black members, a man and woman, both younger than twenty-one, were uncomfortable because he continually ignored their contributions. The two white socialist-feminists were also uncomfortable with Manley's commitment to patriarchy and the idea of "natural leaders."

Despite the reservations of some members, Manley came to be seen as the "leader" of Democracy Forum. For example, the *Wall Street Journal*[13] described Democracy Forum as "Mr. Manley and some activists" and concluded its report with Manley's goal to establish a black church in Ocoee (the first since 1920). Within one week of this national coverage, Reverend Manley left Democracy Forum and formed his own group, using the names and telephone numbers of the descendants that we had gathered. His group, the Ocoee Restoration Project, is currently negotiating with the mayor for land upon which to build a black church. Celia no longer described the reverend as a "godsend" but said, "he took a ride off our backs so he could go off and do his own thing."

## Conclusion

Black history is like a palimpsest, a tablet upon which violence and repression have been written, rewritten, and then erased from view. But like a palimpsest, these erasures are never fully complete, they continue to shape our lives. This was clear in our efforts to reconstruct the Ocoee massacre, a piece of history that is not documented in textbooks and remains unknown to the vast majority of whites. The official records are lost, inaccurate, or incomplete. The few remaining survivors are elderly and the descendants of survivors are difficult to locate and some are reluctant to discuss the trauma. More importantly, the Ocoee massacre has become mythologized among blacks in Central Florida. Many believed that the massacre was due to attempted rape. Others had grown up with the myth that it wasn't the whites of Ocoee who had burned down the town, but "riffraff" from neighboring communities (a comforting version for white descendants who repeatedly claim, "My daddy protected our blacks," when discussing these events).

The complications that we faced in our efforts to reconstruct the events of 1920 suggest lessons about feminist antiracist work with faith-based organizations. In order to be successful in such coalition work, it is necessary to build group consensus on the core values of feminism and antiracism; to decline to "agree to disagree" at the expense of core values; to tolerate conflict and build supportive procedures for dealing with it; to refuse to accept denial as an adequate stance toward issues of privilege; to create achievable steps toward our shared vision of an inclusive community; and to consciously confront anti-intellectualism in our work.

Ultimately, Democracy Forum, which began its work with such high hopes for political change, accomplished much less. The goal of educating the community remained at the level of a history lesson, failing to draw connections to the current reality of racial inequities in central Florida. Issues of race, gender, sexual orientation, and anti-intellectualism continually surfaced in the group and were not resolved. Our partial success in rewriting and publicizing the history of the Ocoee massacre was achieved at the expense of attacking the multiple and intersecting nature of racial, gender, class, and sexual oppression. To go further, feminist antiracist community educating and organizing projects need to create forums for critical dialogue and reflection among citizens while simultaneously paying attention to the complicated ways in which the systems of domination and oppression based on race, gender, sexuality, or class that are the focus of our organizing efforts can also constrain the process of working toward those goals.

## NOTES

1. "Democracy Forum Brochure: Vision and Values Statement," January 1998.
2. "Letter from the Attorney General in "Lynching—Ocoee Florida," Part 7, Se-

ries A Reel 9, Group 1, Series C, Administration Files, Box C-353. Papers of the National Association for the Advancement of Colored People (Microfilm edition).

3. "Living Down Image of Riots," *Orlando Sentinel*, September 7, 1986.

4. David Colburn and Jane Landers, *The African-American Heritage of Florida* (Gainesville, Fla.: University of Florida Press, 1995).

5. Paul Kivel, *Uprooting Racism: How White People Can Work for Social Justice* (Gabriola Island, British Columbia: New Society Publishers, 1995).

6. Peggy McIntosh, "White Privilege and Male Privilege: A Personal Account of Coming to See Correspondences through Work in Women's Studies," in *Race, Class and Gender: An Anthology*, ed. Margaret Anderson and Patricia Hill Collins (Belmont, Calif.: Wadsworth Publishing, 1994).

7. Following sociological convention, I have kept my informants anonymous by assigning a pseudonym to each.

8. Patricia Hill Collins, *Black Feminist Thought* (New York: Routledge, 1990).

9. bell hooks, *Feminist Theory from Margin to Center* (Boston: South End Press, 1984), 113.

10. Penny A. Weiss, "Feminist Reflections on Community" in *Feminist and Community*, ed. Penny Weiss and Marilyn Friedman (Philadelphia: Temple University Press, 1995).

11. hooks, *Feminist Theory*, 46.

12. Patricia Williams, *Seeing a Color-Blind Future: The Paradox of Race* (New York: Noonday Press, 1997).

13. Roger Thurow, "Race Relations Come Late to a Florida Town That Exiled Its Blacks," *Wall Street Journal*, November 1, 1998.

# Chapter 15

# Casting Off Servitude
## Assessing Caste and Gender Inequality in India

## Ashwini Deshpande

In 1991, the government of India introduced a proposal to reserve 33 percent of electorates for women in the local self-governments (the municipality and the metropolitan council levels). After much debate, the measure was passed in 1993. Three years later, a bill for extending such reservation to the parliamentary and state legislative councils was introduced; in 2000 this was still pending in parliament. While the novelty of the move lies in a version of affirmative action having been formulated for roughly half the country's population, the debate over its passage has been complicated by the fact that India already has in place caste-based schemes of compensatory discrimination. This latest move generated a vitriolic upsurge of anti–affirmative action and anti-low-caste sentiment, in addition to intense antiwomen tirades.

When India became independent from British rule in 1947, the current affirmative action policy (reservation of 22.5 percent of seats in educational institutions, government employment, and electoral constituencies) was enacted to target jatis and tribes, economically the weakest and historically subjected to discrimination and deprivation. Since these were identified in a government schedule, they are called the Scheduled Castes (SCs, roughly 16–17 percent of the national population, but with substantial regional variation) and Scheduled Tribes (STs, roughly 6–7 percent of the population and again with a distinct geographic distribution). The former untouchable castes often identify themselves by the Marathi word Dalit (meaning "the oppressed"), employed as a term of pride. While the SC/ST nomenclature has grown out of government policy, Dalit is a more loosely defined social category.

The states in contemporary India are the result of linguistic reorganization of former princely states, each culturally and historically distinct, in the early 1960s. This preexisting diversity was further complicated by two factors. First, the impact of British rule was lopsided as was the consequent "modernization" of different states. Second, several states witnessed major social reform movements that shaped the sociocultural contours of the region in subsequent years. With this kind of diversity, it is useful to think of India as comparable to Europe if the latter were one country. Thus, mapping the regional variation in gender and caste inequality is important. Given that the regional differences are products of specific historic conditions, they can provide clues to the differential impact of alternative policies.

Quantitative research into intergroup disparity in India is in its infancy. In response to this gap, this chapter undertakes an economic inquiry into the interaction of the caste and status of women in postindependence India. As an economist I seek to contribute to the efforts of feminist activists concerned with development and economic empowerment in India by providing data that can be read in conjunction with the vast pool of existing qualitative research from other disciplines for a more comprehensive understanding of the problems that low-caste women encounter in India.

## The Indian Caste System

The institution of caste has intrigued and fascinated Western scholars, who often attempt to build a straight parallel with racial divisions. Although both provide crucial descriptions of intergroup disparity in their respective societies, caste and race are distinct, not mirror images of each other. One major distinction between race and caste is that in India caste and gender discrimination are inextricably linked through the religious ideology of Brahminic Hinduism. However, the economic situation of the lower castes in India often resembles that of American Indians (also referred to as Native Americans) and blacks in the United States. Thus racism and casteism have similar outcomes for members of these groups.

Caste divisions in India are not dichotomous, and indeed, there is considerable debate over the exact hierarchy between the different castes. This is further compounded by the fact that the word "caste" in English is used to describe both the varna and jati systems. Briefly, the varna system is the ancient division (believed to be roughly three thousand years old) of the Hindus into mutually exclusive, endogamous, hereditary occupation groups: Brahmins (the priests and teachers), Kshatriyas (warriors and royalty), Vaisyas (traders, merchants, and businessmen), and Sudras (all manual jobs) at the bottom. Over the years, another tier got added to this system, the Ati Sudras, the lowest of the low (those who do the menial jobs). While I report the occupational division here, the varna system in its entirety is meticulously detailed, with rules for social interaction, food consumption and production, ceremonies and rites, and so forth—in short, all aspects of life in its various constituents are covered. The hierarchy here is clearly defined, the top three varnas also being called the "twice born," and the bottom two subject to exploitation, humiliation, and deprivation, with the lowest subjected to the most degrading practice of untouchability.

This occupational division suggests that it corresponded to a rudimentary economy. Over time, there developed a jati system with the same properties as the varna system, but a much more complex occupational structure and rules of living. It is tempting to think of the jatis as mere subsets of varnas, but the correspondence between a given jati and its varna counterpart is not always clear. The jati is the real operative category at the present time; as there are between two and three thousand jatis in existence, it is necessary to define the phrase "caste inequality" precisely in order to ensure that it does not become a vacuous generalization.

Distinct from the caste hierarchy, more than 50 million Indians belong to tribal communities outside the fold of the Hindu religion (Hindus constitute roughly 85 percent of India's population, estimated to be 1 billion at the time of writing). These are the Adivasis (aborigines) whose origins precede the Aryans and even the Dravidians of the South. Many have lifestyles and languages that are distinct from any of the known religions in India.

In general, available data allow for a three-way division of the population, thereby dictating how caste inequality can be defined (by comparing SCs and STs together with the Others). The latter category, essentially a residual one, is very large and heterogeneous, comprising castes that are not necessarily socially and economically very distinct from the SCs. This three-way division thus *understates* the relative disadvantage of the SCs.

## Women and the Caste Hierarchy

From the varna to the jati, from the ancient colonial to the contemporary, the common theme underlying the various manifestations of the caste system is that it is inegalitarian and oppressive toward Dalits and women. Thus, the caste-religion nexus is strongest among the upper castes, as they view themselves as custodians of the established religious tradition and hence conform strictly to the caste code as part of their religious duties. In contrast, the Dalit castes have historically been relatively egalitarian toward women. It is important to note that the practice of Hinduism varies widely between regions and castes. Constraints on women and a derogatory attitude toward Dalits is inherent in the upper-caste religions code.

Is there a dialectical relationship between caste status and women's status? A lower-caste woman is trapped in relative poverty, deprivation, and sexual abuse but has fewer restrictions on her public visibility than does an upper-caste woman. Among the upper castes, the poverty level varies (although upper castes as a group are economically better off than the lowest castes), but the lives of the women are restricted by a mass of taboos.

Although there appears to be a trade-off between material well-being and constraints on public visibility, for the Dalit women this trade-off is more illusory than real. It is possible that their relative freedom to work outside the home is the result of compelling poverty and not of a radical belief in women's fundamental right to work. Thus, subject as they are to prejudice, deprivation, discrimination, and oppression, Dalit women are the worst off.

Moreover, the distinction between the two caste rungs, based on the public visibility of women, is increasingly redundant. While the actual upward mobility of the Dalits has been negligible (see Deshpande 2000a; 2000b), they have tended to emulate upper-caste traditions perhaps as part of the oft-discussed phenomenon of sanskritization.[1] Since "constraints on women are an essential part of a rise in caste hierarchy" (Liddle and Joshi 1986:59)—the rise could be real or presumed—castes which were known for their relative egalitarianism have adopted practices that undervalue the role of women in the family and in the workplace (such as disinheritance from land, exclusion from the productive economy, removal from public life and seclusion inside the home). This in turn has been responsible for the spread, among other things, of the now ubiquitous practice of dowry. Also, since women are seen as the "custodians of purity of the house and its members" (Srinivas 1976:229), they may be under tremendous pressure to conform to antiquated and conservative traditions that work against their desires. This growing undervaluation of women may have altered the egalitarian nature of marital relationships among the lower castes.

The devaluation of women is explained, at least in part, by their role, both perceived and actual, in productive work. How do we disentangle the effects of gender and caste in shaping women's lives? An examination of several indicators of the standard of living of women in different caste groups begins to illuminate this question from an economic perspective.

## Data

My data are a sample of about 89,000 women from all twenty-five states in India, drawn from the National Family and Health Survey (NFHS) for India done in 1992–93 which includes data on 88,562 heads of household, mostly male. The sample is mainly rural, accurately reflecting the rural-urban divide in the Indian population, only 26 percent of which is urban. Despite the predominantly rural population, the share of agriculture in GDP has declined from 40.5 percent in 1975 to 27.8 percent in 1996. In that year, industry contributed 29.2 percent of GDP, and the services sector contributed 43 percent, also the fastest growing sector of the three (World Bank 1998). With its agroclimatic diversity, India produces almost all the major crops, including cereals—both rice and wheat—pulses, and cash crops. Industrialization, both in its geographical spread and composition, displays marked regional variation. With the IMF-sponsored New Economic Policy (NEP) in place since 1991, liberalization and globalization have been rapidly changing the contours of the Indian economy, replicating several of the disastrous consequences these policies have already had in other parts of the world (AES 1999).

## Indicators of Standard of Living

### EDUCATION

My calculations based on the NFHS data set indicate an appallingly high level of illiteracy among women *and* the presence of intercaste disparity. For India as a whole, 77.3 percent of SC women and 69.7 percent of ST women reported no education, as compared to 51.6 percent of Other women. Moving to the other end of the spectrum, 0.74 percent and 0.88 percent of the SC and ST women respectively had higher education, compared to 5.39 percent of Other women. The distribution of the northern states[2] is worse than the national average, with the exception of Delhi (the capital) and Himachal Pradesh. While Delhi has lower illiteracy across the board, the disparity between castes is the highest. The western states of Goa, Gujarat, and Maharashtra also report lower illiteracy levels. The significant outlier is the coastal southern state of Kerala, which has subsequently achieved full literacy.

ASSET OWNERSHIP

Land, consumer durables, and livestock ownership can be summarized under one heading because the NFHS questionnaire asked the women about the *household* ownership of these assets. In a nutshell, the distribution of ownership reveals substantial intercaste disparity and both SC and ST women are affected by the relative deprivation this disparity entails for their families. The interesting feature here is the divergence in the distribution of these assets as reported by the women and by the household heads. Although the two distributions should be nearly identical, women report larger assets than do heads of household, especially for consumer durables and livestock. It is difficult to interpret the difference.

## Women and Work

The results on women's occupational distribution is an illustration of how a pure quantitative analysis, divorced from a feel for the underlying social structure, can lead to inaccurate conclusions. The all-India calculations reveal that 60.1 percent of SC women, 48.31 percent of ST women, and 70.26 percent of Other women self-reported themselves to be "not working." The majority of the remaining women (those who self-report themselves to be working) are associated with primary activities. Again with the exception of Himachal Pradesh, all the northern states reveal a percentage of women not working that is noticeably greater than the all-India average. The averages of the eastern and northeastern states "not working" are slightly higher than the national average, with the western numbers lower and the southern numbers substantially lower than the national average.

Prima facie, this confirms the widespread notion that Indian women are not engaged in productive work. But my familiarity with India made it difficult for me to accept these results at face value. Also, given the high incidence of landlessness in this predominantly rural sample (61 percent of SCs own no land, for instance), the assertion that women are not working seems untenable. In order to track this anomaly, I first went back to the questionnaire. The section that deals with work starts with a series of questions about the husband's/partner's work. Then follow questions about the woman's work. The first of these is, "Aside from your own housework, are you currently working?" If the response to this is negative, then the entire subsequent section is skipped, thus giving us no information about what kinds of work these women may be engaged in.

Many agricultural tasks are done by women at home and it is highly probable that the respondents may have discounted their own contribution as being no more than a part of normal household chores.[3] It is worth noting that in rural India household enterprise is the predominant form of economic activity (Sundaram and Tendulkar 1988:318). However, women, being part of the household enterprise, may not be paid for their labor, which reinforces the belief that their contribution is nonproductive. Srinivas (1976:225) writes that agriculture is a "familial activity," with "clear and self understood division of labour between the sexes among agriculturists and this includes both activities inside and outside the household. Each set of activities is seen as supportive of the other." Palriwala (1996) discusses the practice of *aaoni-jaaoni* in Rajasthan, in which women move between their natal and marital homes depending upon where their labor is more in demand, and thus their contribution is undervalued in both homes. Thus a closer look at this question indicates that the self-reporting by women as "not working" could well be the result of a combination of several factors: the low worth they attach to their own contribution, reflecting the low worth society attaches to their work, how productive work is defined in their own minds; and the perception that working for wages is a mark of low status.

A number of case studies confirm the suspicion that, certainly in rural areas, far greater numbers of women are engaged in productive work than these numbers indicate.[4] Kanungo (1993), in two decades of observations in Rajasthan and West Bengal, found that

> transplanting is done solely by women, by bare hands . . . planting, weeding and hoeing are done by both men and women . . . major part of processing of paddy, wheat, jowar, bajra etc. are done by women . . . allied agricultural activities like animal husbandry . . . tending the milch cattle, keeping cattle feed ready as well as milking the cattle are done by women. (1993:486)

Mencher (1996) discusses the sexual division of labor in the rice-producing districts of Tamil Nadu and finds that the type of work that the women do differs by region, caste, training, and so on. Among the small landowning households and tenant households, low-caste women work on their own lands and sometimes for others, and are involved in the purchase of inputs, preparing food for laborers, frequently supervising field operations. Kapadia's (1995) study confirms these trends. In her study of low-caste Pallar women of Tamil Nadu, she finds that it is the women who form the major part of the workforce, contributing a far greater share of their incomes to their households than their husbands, and more regularly. Deliege's (1996) case study of a village in Tamil Nadu finds that "among the low castes, the wages of women represent an important part of the household income and therefore basically all the women work as coolies or agricultural labourers" (1996:85).

These case studies also confirm the evidence of intercaste disparity in women's work. Due to greater restrictions on their public visibility and fewer economic compulsions, participation in the labor force differs by caste. Srinivas (1976:229) argues that "[Sanskritization] alters the lifestyle of those who have 'arrived,' and in particular, it has radical effects on the lives of women. It immures them and changes the character of the husband-wife relationship." For this study, the immurement aspect is more relevant. These results, while they may underestimate labor force participation rates, do reflect intercaste disparity correctly, with higher-caste women having lower rates of participation. However, immurement does not imply the luxury of idleness; Mencher's (1996) study finds that among the higher-caste landowning households, although women do not work in the fields they are very closely involved in a variety of day-to-day supervisory operations. Srinivas (1976:226) outlines the variety of tasks that fall into the domain of upper-caste women, including cleaning and processing grain and several food-processing jobs. He points out that these women may also be involved in some economic activity of their own, such as acting as pawnbrokers for needy relatives and neighbors, selling paddy on the sly, or running a *chit fund* (monthly contributions by members paid to a fund that accumulates over time).

Mascarenhas-Keyes's (1990) study of Goa found that women from a few elite Brahmin families that had good incomes from large estates did not work in the fields. However, in most other Brahmin families, women contributed to the sowing, weeding, and harvesting of paddy, cultivation of vegetables, and the rearing of farm animals such as pigs and chickens. But the Brahmin women, unlike the Sudras, did not sell their labor and worked for other households on a reciprocal basis. Desai (1996) reports a study that shows that production work outside the house is considered of secondary importance for women. "The higher the caste status, the more important it becomes for women to remain secluded" (1996:103).

So far we have looked at upper-caste women. Kapadia (1995) finds that among the Muthurajas of Tamil Nadu, an agricultural caste that spans the spectrum of low, low-middle, and upper-middle class, socially aspiring men tend to withdraw their wives or sisters from wage work. "The women themselves are not always happy to withdraw from agricultural wage work, even though it is hard and back breaking, because it is their only source of independent income" (1995:250).

For men and women, women working for wages are seen as an indicator of low status (Srinivas 1976; Epstein 1996), even though few can afford the "luxury" of keeping women at home. Attitudes toward women's work are negative, irrespective of the specialization of their work (Agarwal 1997). Mencher (1996) reports that "when an activity is done by women, it is considered easy work, but when the same activity is done by men, it is regarded as hard work" (1996:61). She also finds that the reason why women are excluded from certain activities, such as applying pesticides, is not out of concern for their health (since they are exposed to pesticides while weeding and transplanting anyway), but due to a reluctance to entrust women with such expensive items.

When we consider urban women, the caste-class interaction has interesting implications for the participation of women in employment. While constraints arising from caste have not disappeared, an upper-class background often enables urban women to break free of traditional caste dictates. This is reflected in their presence in higher education, professional occupations, marriage choices, and so on. However, their absolute numbers can be deceptive, since in proportional terms they remain a small minority (Liddle and Joshi 1986). Even here, with significant exceptions, an urban educated girl is expected to marry within her jati and to be less educated than her husband.

There are other dimensions of women's work that are not captured by these data. Dubé (1996) points out that the continuity of a caste's traditional occupation such as crafts, petty trading, or scavenging may be dependent upon women for it falls upon them, when male members of their caste leave due to low status or low pay, to continue the traditional occupation.

Given the vast qualitative evidence on women's work, it is clear that quantitative estimates reflect an underlying social tendency to underreport and devalue women's work.[5] Moreover, when women are working, they may not enjoy the privileges that are presumed to be associated with economic independence. Our data contain no information on wages or salaries, nor on consumption, but the descriptions of work in the literature suggest that women receive poor earnings for *paid* work, lack control over their meager earnings due to their subordinate status in the family, and face dismal working conditions, occupational hazards, and long working hours when hours are defined at all.

## The Gender-Caste Development Index

This paper follows the methodology of Deshpande (2000b) in constructing the gender-caste development index (GCDI) for four groups—SC women, Other women, SC households, and Other households (household results are based on the information for the head of household, 90 percent of whom are male). This index is based on all five indicators discussed above—education, occupation, landholding, asset (consumer durables) ownership, and livestock ownership. I find that what I term as the *caste effect* dominates for the majority of Indian states, such that Other households are better off than Other women, who in turn are better off than SC households, which are better off than SC women. In other words, Others as a caste group are better off than SCs as a caste group (and within each caste group, household heads are better off than women). The exceptions to this are the states of Himachal Pradesh (north Indian hill state) and Kerala (southwest Indian coastal state), where women in both groups do better than SC households. However, some features of these findings are disturbing. For instance, the highest GCDI in the country is for Other women in the northwestern state of Rajasthan, a conclusion difficult to accept for anyone with some familiarity with India.

Given the discrepancy in responses between household heads and women on the number of consumer durables, I wondered if that was distorting the absolute values of the GCDI. So I decided to calculate a modified GCDI, without the consumer durables. With this calculation, there is a clear and strong gender effect for Delhi, Uttar Pradesh, Rajasthan, Madhya Pradesh, Bihar, Orissa, Assam, Andhra Pradesh, and Karnataka. Other households are better off than SC households, which in turn are better off than Other women, who are better off than SC women. In other words, heads of households for both castes are better off than women for both castes (and within each gender, SCs are worse off than Others). Except for Delhi, all the other states here are in the lower half of the per capita income ranking.

In Jammu, Tripura, Punjab, and Gujarat, there is a weak gender effect, which differs from the strong gender effect only in that SC households and Other women are very close to each other in terms of their GCDI. It is difficult to hypothesize a link between overall income level of the state and this effect, since the former two of the four states are low per capita income states while the latter two have a high per capita income.

In Haryana, Himachal Pradesh, Maharashtra, and Tamil Nadu, we find the caste effect dominating (as explained above). All these states are in the upper half of per capita income, which again highlights the difficulty of postulating any relationship between per capita income level and caste and gender inequality. Note that Himachal Pradesh is a state with low disparity, high GCDI (highest for SC women in the country) and Maharashtra has a high GCDI for all categories. In this scheme, a complete outlier is Kerala, which follows a pattern that defies characterization. In Kerala, SC women are worse off than Other women, but both the women groups are better off than SC households; all the three are worse off than Other households.

The diversity of patterns notwithstanding, SC women are at the bottom of the rung across India, illustrating the double burden of caste and gender borne by this section of Indian society. The worst GCDI for SC women is in the two states with the highest levels of per capita income (Delhi and Punjab), followed by Haryana (number three in per capita ranking) and Bihar (one of the poorest states in the country; also one with shockingly high and gruesome incidents of violence against Dalits in general).

## The Education-Occupation Index

Since education and occupation are the two variables in the GCDI that relate to the respondent as an individual (rather than the household), it is worthwhile to construct an index analogous to the GCDI based on education and occupation alone. These findings show that the general pattern of Other households being the best off and SC women being the worst off exists throughout the country, except in Kerala, which is a consistent outlier for all patterns. Also, with the exception of Himachal Pradesh and Jammu, the gender effect dominates in most of the states. Focusing on the women alone, the index is better for the southern and western states than in the north and the east. The real variation in this index comes from the variation in education; occupation (when applicable) tends to converge toward primary activities.

## Access to Information

Education and access to the media are the two potential sources of information about the world; we have already seen the low levels of education among women and SCs. In light of these facts, I decided to focus on data on television and radio, rather than questions about the readership of newspapers. The question that was asked was, "Do you listen to the radio or watch TV at least once a week?" The following results were interesting: first, the figures are very low (in the country as a whole, 54.35 percent of the SC women replied "no" to the above question); second, intercaste disparity exists (the corresponding figure for Other women is 40.1 percent); third, there is substantial regional variation, comparable to the regional variation in education. The answer "no" is much lower in the southern and western states of the country. The figures for the northern states are next best and those for the eastern states are the worst. These figures should be interpreted with caution as they relate to 1992–93 and the decade of the 1990s has seen the rapid spread of cable television to all parts of India. In the context of poverty, it may appear that the viewership may be low due to low ownership. However, a comparison with ownership figures suggests that viewership figures are higher than ownership ones.

The use of the terms "best" and "worst" implicitly assumes that exposure to electronic media has a favorable effect; that need not always hold. We have no information on the content of programs that the women are watching—if the viewership is devoted exclusively to watching soap operas/movies (movie-based programs) or religious propaganda, then the desirability of this exposure and its information content is questionable. However, I believe that the exposure to media has the *potential* for increasing access to information, and thus broadly speaking I view access to the media as a positive tool, all the caveats about the negative effects of the media notwithstanding.

## Other Indicators of Disparity

The calculation on the data set reveals the existence of intercaste disparity in the type of cooking fuel used by women. This is important because it suggests that poverty, which would dictate access to and choice of cooking fuel, is not caste neutral. The choice of cooking fuel has implications for the health of the women as well as the ease of cooking. For instance, if wood is the primary cooking fuel used, then the women have the added task of collecting the wood first before they start to cook. The results indicate that the overwhelming majority of the SCs and STs rely on wood, cowdung cakes, coal, and the like. To varying degrees, all these cooking fuels pose a health hazard because they expose the women to large volumes of smoke in addition to much longer cooking times. The percentage of women using modern cooking methods is very low for SCs and STs and much higher for the Others. Except for Delhi, which is a city-state, western India is the other region where the shift toward modern methods is most pronounced.

At this point, it is worth reminding ourselves that the preceding numbers reveal only part of the multifaceted tyranny of exploitation, abuse, and discrimination that is an integral part of a Dalit woman's everyday life (see, for instance, Meera 1979 and Human Rights Watch 1999). Despite the abolition of bonded labor in 1976, it continues to exist in several parts of India and the majority of the bonded laborers are Dalits, including women and children.[6] The inhumanity of this modified form of slavery has been well documented and has prompted the legislation for its abolition. Its indifferent implementation and hence the persistence of bonded labor reflects the social and political clout of upper-caste landlord employers.

Although outlawed, large parts of India (both rural and urban) continue to have toilets cleaned by manual scavenging, a practice that is entirely the "preserve" of some of the Dalit castes. Not surprisingly, these castes face greater social discrimination than other Dalits and live in completely segregated colonies. Subject to one of the worst forms of indignity through entire lives, these meagerly paid workers (made up of very large numbers of women) battle with disease and ailments arising from appallingly unhygienic conditions, their condition made worse by virtually nonexistent labor legislation and social ostracism.

Parts of South India, particularly in Andhra Pradesh and Karnataka, also still have the *devdasi* system (literally, female servant of god), whereby prepubertal young women are "married" to the lord. Typically the *devdasis* are Dalit girls from very poor families and the initiation ceremony is performed as if an honor were being bestowed upon the girls. While some of the *devdasis* are excellent artists (performers of classical music and dance, some of whom are highly renowned), most end up being victims of this system of ritualized prostitution in the service of upper-caste patrons. Some are eventually auctioned into urban brothels. Their social position offers them very little protection from the police or the judiciary. "When a *devdasi* is raped, it is not considered rape. She can be had by any man at any time" (Human Rights Watch 1999:150). This system works over and above "regular" prostitution, that is, the degrading compulsions of poverty, illiteracy, ignorance, and abuse push Dalit women into prostitution.

Unarguably at the bottom of the socioeconomic ladder, Dalit women are subject to attacks by upper-caste men with impunity. Terrifying tales of sexual abuse, rape, torture, mutilation, murder, and massacre of Dalit women by upper-caste men have been reported, and police brutality compounds their vulnerability. In general, the combination of caste, class, and gender bias in the police and the judiciary means that these women have minimal protection if at all.

## Resistance or Accommodation?

Far from being mute sufferers, women in India have a long and continuing tradition of resistance and struggle, both in organized movements and in their daily lives (see, for instance, Kumar 1993). The Indian women's movement is large and vibrant, and encompasses a variety of streams—some very similar to Western feminism and some that are culturally and ideologically distinct. In analyzing the Indian women's movement, it is important to avoid the fallacy of equating Indian tradition with patriarchy and oppression, and Western exposure (especially the influence of British colonialism) with modernity and progress. As Liddle and Joshi (1986:49) point out,

> women's resistance to oppression in India neither began nor ended with the British women's intervention, but had its roots in the Indian social structure and cultural heritage. . . . [T]he two movements had very different starting points and developed in different directions.[7]

In fact, the earliest questioning of Aryan or Brahminic dominance is found in women's writing during the Bhakti movement. This medieval movement against religious and caste orthodoxy is not only an indicator of the long-standing resistance to conservative tendencies, but also demonstrates how a struggle against orthodoxy is as much a part of Indian tradition as orthodoxy itself. It was "characterised by the abandonment of the self in devotion and love for a personal God, and by the deprecation of all man-made social and religious distinctions" (O'Hanlon 1985:224). The earliest expression of this was in the eighth century in Tamil Nadu and from there it successively spread to other parts of the present day India, a remarkable achievement for a period that predates the idea of the nation-state and nationalism.

It would be naive to view the Bhakti movement simply as a utopian upsurge, since, like all social movements, it was characterized by considerable complexity. Degrees of radicalism within the movement varied across time and space, and in the ultimate analysis the extent to which this movement succeeded in breaking the dominant orthodox religious-caste mold is a moot point. The earlier phases of the movement, especially in Tamil Nadu, Karnataka, and Maharashtra were more radical in terms both of the number of women who took part and in the rejection or questioning of patriarchy, the caste code, and constraints on sexuality than were the later seventeenth-century movements that developed in the north. These and many other caveats notwithstanding, the movement was an important landmark in the struggle against caste hierarchy and women's oppression. Even if orthodoxy ultimately triumphed, the Bhakti movement succeeded in building a fundamental critique of the Aryan philosophy that was at the root of the subordination of women and Dalits.

The contribution of women to the anticolonial nationalist movement, both as illustrious leaders and as participants in numerous mass movements, is better documented. The particular dimension of the women's movement in this period relevant to the present paper is the renewed attack on the restrictive practices of caste orthodoxy with a demand for a life of dignity for women and low castes. Again, I make no attempt to summarize the efforts of numerous individuals in the struggles, agitations, and movements that either directly attacked religious orthodoxy (and thus advocated Dalit and women's rights) or confronted these issues more tangentially in the course of a wider focus on imperialism and class struggle. However, a few illustrations are useful.

Savitribai Phule (1831–97), wife of Jyotiba Phule, the progressive Dalit social reformer from the western state of Maharashtra, became a "poet, scholar and activist in her own right" (Tharu and Lalita 1991:211) by first educating herself and then going on to become a crusader for the rights of women and Dalits. Together husband and wife founded the Satyashodhak Samaj (loosely translated, society for the quest for truth) in 1873, based on the "desire for a form of social organisation that would reflect the merits and aptitudes of the individual, rather than enforcing birth as the basis both for occupation and for religious status" (O'Hanlon 1985: 223). "By insisting that God was available to all his human creatures and that no intermediary was necessary for the invocation of divine power, the society attempted to remove any justification for the special sanctity of the Brahmans" (O'Hanlon 1985:237). The history of the freedom movement is replete with such instances from all parts of the country (see, for instance, Kumar 1993).

The contemporary Indian women's movement is highly complex both in its ideological leanings and in its method of struggle. Women's organizations span the entire ideological spectrum from extreme left to extreme right, thus indicating an awareness of this issue from all quarters. The extreme right organizations function mainly as mouthpieces of conservative forces and thus their place in the movement for the emancipation of women is questionable. However, it is important to note that their capacity to mobilize women is not insubstantial and they present a serious challenge to the other organizations that question orthodoxy. Also, their presence suggests that the orthodoxy-versus-emancipation dichotomy cannot be equated with a men-versus-women one, since we now see powerful women, with a mass following, advocating the path of conservatism.

I believe that this complicates the task of the women's movement, since the forces on the extreme right claim to be representatives of the Indian tradition they seek to protect. This has a powerful moral and cultural impact and the movement for women's liberation displays a varying level of interest in engaging with this issue. Organizations that work closely with left political parties attempt to link gender and caste oppression with the socioeconomic establishment that seeks to preserve and perpetuate upper-caste, upper-class control over the economy and society in general. These organizations rely largely on an agitational approach to mobilize women and the Dalits. Since land-ownership is a major source of upper-caste economic dominance, land reform is an essential element of the struggle for equality. Some organizations, such as the All India Democratic Women's Association, link this with the demand for more female-headed households, so that the land reforms do not end up worsening gender disparity.

Another section of the women's movement links gender oppression essentially with constraints on women's sexuality and is closer, in some senses, to the feminist movements in the United States and Europe. There is also a relatively depoliticized component of the women's movement that focuses solely on individual support to traumatized women (a component of the earlier two ideological streams as well), while not directly addressing theoretical issues concerned with women's oppression. All these components work simultaneously, sometimes in tandem, and I believe the vigorous ideological debates within the movement lend it a certain vibrancy.

Over the last several years, a consensus has emerged within the women's movement about the need for affirmative action in the political arena for women. Employing arguments similar to those supporting the Scheduled Castes reservations, the Indian women's movement remains optimistic that if given greater political representation, women would increase their ability to reform social and economic policy to better suit their needs. However, there are concerns that some women candidates would be put up as puppets while the real control may lie with their husbands or other male family members. The counterargument is that even if that happens initially, over time the presence of women in decision-making bodies would help alter both their self-perception and their actual position in society.

The normal process of economic development may not, on its own, lead to a reversal of the gender imbalance in the political arena. Thus the current situation almost demands a specific program of affirmative action, as opposed to concentrating on the economic independence of women as a vehicle for greater political participation. India's record of women in mainstream politics—a woman prime minister for nineteen years and several women as chief ministers of state and as ministers in both central and state governments—appears impressive compared to most developed countries where, despite economic independence, women remain underrepresented in government positions and key decision-making positions in business. But the key question that unites the women's movement the world over is the degree of control that women have over the political process.

## Conclusion

Based on the NFHS data, this paper constructs a gender-caste development index and several smaller indices to assess the interaction of gender and caste inequality in postindependence India. It develops the notion of the "caste effect" and the "gender effect" as a preliminary tool for assessing the relative strength of gender-caste status across the different regions of India. This preliminary economic investigation suggests that women in general, and low-caste women in particular, remain at the bottom of the various indicators of development that the paper discusses. There is substantial regional variation, suggesting that different combinations of social policies and histories of social reform could lead to different outcomes. The figures on women's work may underestimate the actual role of women in productive work, indicating the low worth that is attached to their contributions and the taboos surrounding working for wages. The restrictions on women's public domain, initially confined to the upper castes, now transcend almost all the caste groups. However, the vibrant and growing women's movement spans a range of ideological positions, indicating that women in India are not passive.

A segment of the women's movement directly challenges established religious and caste orthodoxy that is bigoted and discriminatory toward women and low castes. There has been a growing demand that women should be involved in decision making that affects their destiny, which has resulted in reserving 33 percent of the local self-government seats for women candidates. But the extension of this to the higher levels of decision making is stalled due to stiff resistance from most legislators. What unites the Indian women's movement with struggles in other parts of the world are concerns related to the participation of women in formulating policies that shape their lives, to a combination of gender and ethnic/racial/caste stereotyping, and to a just and democratic political-economic order.

### ACKNOWLEDGMENTS

I am grateful to France Winddance Twine and Michelle Mendez for their comments on the first draft and to Kalindi Deshpande for information on the Women's Reservation Bill. Thanks also to the Mellon seminar participants for lively discussion at the Carolina Population Center, where a preliminary version of this paper was presented. The CPC library courier service was amazing in its help with reference material.

### NOTES

1. "A low caste was able, in a generation or two, to rise to a higher position in the hierarchy by adopting vegetarianism and teetotalism, and by Sanskritising its

ritual and pantheon. In short, it took over, as far as possible, the customs, rites, and beliefs of the Brahmins, and the adoption of the Brahminic way of life by a low caste seems to have been frequent, although theoretically forbidden." Srinivas 1962:42.

2. The northern states are Jammu, Punjab, Haryana, Delhi, Rajasthan, and Uttar Pradesh.

3. Kapadia (1995) reports that not only do men tend to minimize the contribution of the women in their families toward productive work, but the women are socially conditioned to undervalue and underreport their own work. So even if they are making a major economic contribution, it would not be socially recognized and therefore would not show up in economic surveys.

4. Mencher (1996) argues that the census materials have tended to underreport the involvement of women in agriculture. One of the reasons for this is that the census enumerators are males, who talk mainly to the male members of the households, and that the census is taken at a time in the year when there is relatively little agricultural activity. In the NFHS data that I use, it is not clear whether the enumerators were male or female, but the respondents for this data set were women. So the reasons for underestimation in these data would be different.

5. This excludes the entire range of work (conventional housework) that is not counted as productive, which exclusion is controversial.

6. Bonded labor refers to work in slavelike conditions tied to the landlord/employer (often the same as the moneylender) in order to pay off debt.

7. This perspective on the women's movement is not the starting point of all analyses. Accounts of the women's movement in India often begin with the nineteenth century (for instance, Radha Kumar's analysis [1993]) coincides with the spread of Western education and corresponding ideas of equality.

REFERENCES

AES (Annual Economic Survey). 1999. "The Indian Economy 1998–99: An Alternative Survey," Delhi Science Forum, New Delhi.

Agarwal, Bina. 1997. "'Bargaining' and Gender Relations: Within and Beyond the Household," *Feminist Economics*, vol. 3, no. 1: 1–51.

Deliege, Robert. 1996. "At the Threshold of Untouchability: Pallars and Valaiyars in a Tamil Village." In *Caste Today*, ed. C. J. Fuller. New Delhi: Oxford University Press, 65–92.

Desai, Neera. 1996. "Women's Employment and Their Familial Role in India." In *Social Structure and Change*. Vol. 2, *Women in Indian Society*, ed. A. M. Shah, B. S. Baviskar, and E. A. Ramaswamy. New Delhi: Sage, 98–112.

Deshpande, Ashwini. 2000a. "Recasting Economic Inequality." Manuscript under submission.

———. 2000b. "Caste at Birth? Redefining Disparity in India." Forthcoming in the *Review of Development Economics*.

Dubé, Leela. 1996. "Caste and Women." In *Caste: Its Twentieth Century Avatar*, ed. M. N. Srinivas. New Delhi: Viking, Penguin Books, 1–27.

Epstein, T. Scarlett. 1996. "Culture, Women and India's Development." In *Social Structure and Change*. Vol. 2, *Women in Indian Society*, ed. A. M. Shah, B. S. Baviskar, and E. A. Ramaswamy. New Delhi: Sage, 33–55.

Human Rights Watch. 1999. "Broken People: Caste Violence against India's Untouchables." New York, Washington, London, Brussels; March.

Kanungo, Sukla Deb. 1993. "Dalit Women's Search for Identity," *Social Action*, vol. 43 (October–December): 481–94.

Kapadia, Karin. 1995. *Siva and Her Sisters: Gender, Caste and Class in Rural South India*. Boulder, Colo.: Westview Press.

Kumar, Radha. 1993. *The History of Doing: An Illustrated Account of Movements for Women's Rights and Feminism in India 1800–1990*. London: Verso.

Liddle, Joanna, and Rama Joshi. 1986. *Daughters of Independence: Gender, Caste, and Class in India*. New Delhi: Kali for Women; London: Zed Books; Totowa, N.J.: Biblio Distribution Center, 1986.

Mascarenhas-Keyes, Stella. 1990. "Migration, 'Progressive Motherhood' and Female Autonomy: Catholic Women in Goa." In *Structures and Strategies: Women, Work and Family*, ed. Leela Dubé and Rajni Palriwala. New Delhi: Sage, 103–28.

Meera V. 1979. "Prisoners of Inequality: Sexual Abuse of Dalit Women." *Race and Class*, vol. 20, no. 4 (Spring): 417–21.

Mencher, Joan P. 1996. "South Indian Female Cultivators: Who Are They and What Do They Do?" In *Social Structure and Change*. Vol. 2, *Women in Indian Society*, ed. A. M. Shah, B. S. Baviskar, and E. A. Ramaswamy. New Delhi: Sage, 56–78.

O'Hanlon, Rosalind. 1985. *Caste, Conflict, and Ideology: Mahatma Jyotiba Phule and Low Caste Protest in Nineteenth-Century Western India*. Cambridge: Orient Longman and Cambridge University Press.

Palriwala, Rajni. 1996. "Negotiating Patriliny: Intra-Household Consumption and Authority in Northwest India." In *Shifting Circles of Support: Contextualising Kinship and Gender in South Asia and Sub-Saharan Africa*, ed. Rajni Palriwala and Carla Risseeuw. Walnut Creek, Calif.: Alta Mira, 190–220.

Srinivas, M. N. 1962. *Caste in Modern India and Other Essays*. New York: Asia Publishing House.

———. 1976. "The Changing Position of Indian Women." *Man (N.S.)*, vol. 12: 221–38.

Sundaram, K., and Suresh Tendulkar. 1988. "Toward an Explanation of Interregional Variations in Poverty and Unemployment in Rural India." In *Rural Poverty in South Asia*, ed. T. N. Srinivasan and P. K. Bardhan. New York: Columbia University Press, 316–62.

Tharu, Susie, and K. Lalita. 1991. *Women Writing in India: 600 B.C. to the Present.* Vol. 1, *600 B.C. to the Early Twentieth Century.* New York: Feminist Press at the City University of New York.

United Nations Development Program. 1990. *Human Development Report.*

World Bank, World Development Indicators, WDI-CD ROM, 1998.

# Chapter 16

# Mapping the Meanings of "Racism" and "Feminism" among Women Television Broadcast Journalists in Canada

## Minelle Mahtani

> More women in the [televisual] industry is not enough: there need to be more women with a politicized understanding of the ways in which women's subordination is currently reproduced and with the will to change it.[1]

> All I can say is that the sexism in the newsroom was manageable. The racism was not.
> —a woman journalist of color, 1999

Almost half the people employed by Canada's biggest media corporation are women,[2] and according to a recent UNESCO report on employment patterns in the media, women now make up the majority of journalism students on campuses.[3] However, despite the increase in the representation of women, the everyday culture of Canadian newsrooms remain male controlled and male defined.[4] This led me to question why the increased number of women working in the media has not effectively challenged racist and sexist ideologies in the newsroom. In this chapter I explore the political understandings of "feminism" and "antiracism" among women television news journalists to explore the impact of the North American women's movement on working women's perceptions of feminism and antiracism in the newsroom.

Between 1994 and 1999 I worked at the Canadian Broadcasting Corporation.[5] I am identified as a "woman of color" in Canada. My father is of South Asian descent from India and my mother is from Iran. They met in London, United Kingdom, and then immigrated in the 1960s to Toronto, Canada, where I was born. Broke after completing six months of my Ph.D. in London, I returned to Toronto and was offered a job as an editorial assistant—for all intents and purposes, a "go-for" who delivers newspapers and distributes the news script. Initially I saw the job as a way to solve my cash-flow woes and vowed to return to London as soon as possible to complete the degree. But I fell in love with the craft and was thrilled to be promoted to a weekend researcher position on the national weekend news program. After a year of organizing panels, conducting phone interviews, and shooting stories, I was hired as a researcher/associate producer on the flagship news and information program for the network, "The National"—the daily hourlong show providing a combination of news and current affairs to viewers across the country. As a researcher/producer working for the main network, my job included researching and developing story ideas, interviewing politicians and pundits, going out with the crew to tape stories, and then returning to the edit suite to put that night's story together.

An analysis of women broadcast journalists is important for women working outside broadcast television because television news journalism plays a powerful role in the representation and circulation of racial and gender ideologies. As Tator has noted, "the media holds up a mirror in which society can see itself reflected."[6] The media provides an instrument through which public understandings of feminism and antiracism are communicated. What Canadians think about visible minorities and women is in part influenced by the media to which Canadians are exposed. Thus it becomes crucial to examine the beliefs of the people who are responsible for creating the images of women and minorities that we see every night on the news. In particular, it is important to identify the ways in which bias and discrimination are woven into the policies and practices of media organizations.

Paula Skidmore has argued that most studies on the gendered politics of the newsroom reveal no differences between the sexes within that site. However, she insists that there is much anecdotal evidence to the contrary from the women producing the news themselves.[7] Missing from most studies of news and gender is an analysis of how journalists contemplate terms such as "feminism" and, in Canada, "antiracism"—which has taken on a particular political salience in Canada since the 1980s—

despite the fact that many have emphasized the importance of challenging racism and gender discrimination in the media.

## Toronto: The Canadian Context

Canada is considered one of the most multicultural nations in the world, with 29.4 percent of Canada's population identified as being of "British only" descent and 23.5 percent of the population identified as being of "French only" descent. People defined as "other" come in at 26.9 percent, a figure higher than the "French only" population. The ethnic groups that fall under the rubric of "other," include German, Italian, Polish, Scandinavian, Jewish, Black, Greek, Filipino, and South Asian, among others. Three point nine percent of the population is of "First Nations" or Aboriginal decent. Fifty-three percent of women in Canada identify as being of visible minority descent—a figure that outweighs those who identify as "white."[8] Toronto, where this research was conducted, is Canada's largest city. Its racial diversity is extraordinary: visible minorities make up almost 40 percent of Toronto's population. With a population of over 3 million, four out of every ten nonwhites now living in Canada reside in the greater Toronto area. Among the ethnic population of Toronto, three groups predominate: Chinese (25 percent), South Asian (24.7 percent), and black (20.5 percent).[9] Toronto is also considered Canada's center for media work (in both news and film) and is often compared to Los Angeles and New York as one of the leading cities in the world for media production.

## Canada's Multicultural Policy

Canadian multicultural policy has served not only as a guideline for government policy since 1971, but also as a framework for national discourse on the construction of Canadian society. What distinguishes Canada beyond its status as a multicultural country is that the multicultural project has been enshrined in its constitution and through law in very particular ways, reflecting a salient part of the social and political context of Canada. As a policy, multiculturalism emerged in part because of the challenges posed by the influx of ethnically diverse immigrants into Canada. Canada's immigration policy of 1962 (formalized in 1967) was the first in the world to abolish all quotas or preferences on the basis of race, national origin, religion, or culture. Ethnicity and country of origin were replaced by education and training as the criteria for entry into Canada. Many non-Europeans from developing nations were encouraged to come to Canada. As the demographic shift quickened, the social landscape of the country, especially in the urban areas, began to change.

In view of this increased ethnic diversity and subsequent demands for cultural protection and social equality among ethnic groups, the Canadian government began to reappraise its relationship to ethnic minorities. It established the Royal Commission on Bilingualism and Biculturalism in 1962, originally in response to "growing dissatisfaction and friction between the two founding races: the English and the French,"[10] without specifically setting out to explore ethnic relations in Canada. The Commission was directed to approach its task in terms of one country, two languages (English and French) and two cultures (British and French) with some vaguely defined contribution by the "others."

At this time political debates in Canada were informed by antiracist and anticolonial independence movements in the international arena. Quebec was already caught up in growing nationalism. As the Commission carried out its task, it appeared to the Canadian government that "visible minorities" should also have rights and government funding. The Commission gradually altered its focus as it ran into hostility in the Western provinces where second-, third-, and fourth-generation Ukrainian Canadians emphasized that they continued to be denied equal respect and opportunity because of their cultural heritage. As a result, the Commission's mandate was extended to include the contributions made by the other ethnic groups. These concerns of the Commission were revealed in its report.

After tabulating its responses, the Commission recommended a major extension of bilingualism to help alleviate the disharmony in English-French relations, conceiving of a bilingual framework within which other ethnic groups could prosper. Although the Commission agreed that bilingualism should be a national goal, it modified its own terms of reference from biculturalism and argued for a multicultural policy within a bilingual framework. It attempted to establish an ongoing dialogue between the government and minority groups, launching the participation of those groups into the political agenda. A highly contentious policy emerged, designed to fit minority cultural differences into a workable national framework.

In 1971, Prime Minister Pierre Elliott Trudeau made a speech in Parliament in which he outlined the responses to the "B and B" report. The official promotion of multiculturalism has been heralded as a turning point in Canadian history. The key tenets of multicultural policy included a commitment to assisting

> all Canadian cultural groups that had demonstrated a desire and effort to continue to develop a capacity to grow and contribute to Canada . . . to assist members of all cultural groups to overcome cultural barriers to full participation in Canadian society . . . to promote creative encounters and interchange among all Canadian cultural groups in the interest of national unity.[11]

In an effort to put these principles into practice, the government established several programs during the 1970s. Multicultural grants were issued to support the development of various cultures and languages. Specific initiatives for language and culture maintenance received substantial government funding, reaching nearly 200 million dollars between 1971 and 1990. A Multicultural Directorate was established within the Department for the Secretary of State in 1972. For most Canadians throughout the 1970s and 1980s, multiculturalism became synonymous with tolerance. Since this by now had become central to their self-image, they supported the policy enthusiastically. Canadian nationalists often cited official multiculturalism as one of the characteristics, along with bilingualism, that distinguished Canada from the United States.

Some have called for the abolition of multiculturalism as official government policy, reasoning that it only encourages the ghettoization of ethnics whereby immigrants can indulge their nostalgic love for their mother countries. Others have insisted that it promotes official, largely cosmetic government programs designed to placate the Quebecois, native Canadians, blacks, and Asians. These sorts of critiques reflect public sentiment about the policy. By 1998, the Department of Multiculturalism had merged with the Department of Canadian Heritage, the budget of official multiculturalism having been cut back significantly. Coming under attack for its liberal rhetoric and its lack of analysis of power relations, definitions of multiculturalism remain obscure, ridden with problematic meanings and implications.[12]

## Antiracism: A Response to Multiculturalism

In light of these critiques of multiculturalism, educators in North America began to contemplate forms of "antiracism" instead—a critical form of multiculturalism geared to bringing about more egalitarian changes in society while paying attention to forms of race and class oppression. Marking a radical departure from mainstream multiculturalism, it aimed to unveil the manifestation of institutionalized forms of racism in the policies and practices of large institutions. Antiracism differs from multicultural policies in that it aims to locate schools, corporations, and institutions as part of complex and systematic discrimination in Canada. Insisting that multicultural policy never was, and never could be, a substitute for antiracist legislation, antiracism was promoted as a way of challenging racism rather than solely celebrating difference. Issues of ethnic inequality and racial discrimination were seen as having significant political and economic roots embedded in the history of social institutions in Canada, going far beyond what multicultural policies could address. Thus it was stressed that antiracist tenets, as opposed to multicultural ones, emphasized the eradication of racial inequalities within structural frameworks, including inequalities based on gender and class. Multiculturalism had also been critiqued for failing to recognize the roles of gender and class in the experience of racialized groups. Antiracist education was seen as challenging static multiculturalist conceptions of culture by integrating class and gender into its analysis.[13]

Canadian multicultural policy plays an important role in women's conceptions of antiracism and feminism. Canada has transformed a descriptive fact and normative idea into an official ideology, as reflected in its government policies, programs, and practices. It is taken for granted outside the country that because of such a strongly funded multicultural policy, racism should be on the decline in such a "racially diverse" nation. It is important to challenge this assumption and analyze the beliefs and values surrounding race and gender among women journalists and women journalists of color. Thus, against the backdrop of such a policy, I chose to explore how women journalists in Canada contemplated feminist and antiracist practices in the newsroom.

### Negotiating the Meaning of "Feminism" in the Newsroom

In this section I draw upon interviews I conducted with fourteen women broadcast journalists, of which three identified as women journalists of color.[14] These women had worked for a variety of broadcast radio and television news organizations in Canada, including the Canadian Broadcasting Corporation, City TV, CTV, CBC Newsworld, Global Television, as well as other news gathering organizations in Canada. All were currently located in Toronto, although many of them had worked in other newsrooms across the country at some point in their careers. I explore the ways in which particular ideologies about women and women journalists of color are challenged and negotiated in the newsroom. One ideology which wove through many of my interviews was the continued assertion by women journalists that more women were being hired than ever before in the newsroom. Most of the women insisted that the demographics of the newsroom had changed from when they had first started working as journalists. Many were optimistic about the future of gender dynamics in the newsroom, insisting that gender discrimination was on the decline. Serafina, a thirty-two-year-old South Asian reporter/producer, explained:

> I remember a time when there were very few women working in the newsroom. It was a very macho, male-oriented work environment—basically a "boys club." I remember feeling that I couldn't be too much of a "girl" if I wanted to survive. I even started to change the way I dressed—no more skirts or lipstick—and tried to blend in. But within a few years, there was a great increase in the number of women hired, and the culture changed dramatically. I think it's a good work environment for women now.

However, this perspective was challenged by some women journalists who indicated that while a few women are becoming heads of shows and senior producers, white and middle-class males still hold most positions of power. As Kathy, a forty-four-year-old, self-identified Jewish national television news producer, commented:

> Despite the fact that there are many women who work in this office, the reins of power lie with the men. There are more women executive producers and managers than ever before. But there are still departments where women are still in a distinct minority, and are not encouraged to enter.

Often there was an ambiguity associated with this observation—as if it didn't necessarily qualify as gender discrimination. Lily, a twenty-eight-year-old Asian news producer, suggested,

> Do I think there's equality between men and women in the newsroom? Yes and no. On the one hand we're paid the same, are expected to work as hard and for the most part, work in a harassment-free environment. On the other hand, we don't have enough female managers. I take heart that the

exec. producers of several programs are female, but when we go right up the ladder, the numbers of women drop significantly. When was the last time we had a female V.P. of News and Current Affairs?

It has been suggested that reporters undergo a particular process of socialization which is decidedly masculine when they first learn the skills necessary for their jobs in the newsroom. The taken-for-granted norms of the corporate world that permeate their workplace make it difficult for some women journalists to identify, let alone challenge, these conventions. There was clear anxiety around personally identifying as a "feminist" in and out of the newsroom. Indeed, it seems that although academics have insisted that we can no longer rely on static conceptualizations of feminism, many women journalists had stereotypical and antiquated notions of feminism, reading it less as a personal identity and more as an outwardly politicized lobbyist stance. Sara, a white, self-identified Jewish anchor in her fifties, defined a feminist as: "Someone who actively lobbies for and promotes women, and women's issues. No, I don't define myself as a feminist." At the same time, Sara pointed out that when she first started working as a journalist, she had to deliberately challenge stereotypes of female roles in broadcasting. When I asked if she had ever witnessed a discriminatory act in the newsroom, she offered:

> No, I haven't witnessed it. But when I first started working at a commercial radio station way back in 1970—it was really the beginning of a new era. There had been no broads in broadcasting, except for the obligatory "house-hold hints" dispenser. I was told women's voices were not authoritative enough—and since no one was hearing their voice, it had no authority. I worked my guts out trying to prove the boss wrong. But three years later I left to cover the election for standard broadcast news in Ottawa. I hated the experience and got into television.

Initially I attributed this tendency not to identify as a feminist to a generational particular conception of a traditional feminist. However, I discovered that many of the younger female journalists also shared this definition of feminist. Easton, a twenty-nine-year-old self-identified Ukrainian radio news producer, offered this response when I asked what image came to her mind when I used the word "feminist":

> Gloria Steinem. Somebody very intelligent, and a little bit angry, with biting but humourless wit, and an agenda. A vaguely 60s feel. Feminists seem to me to be people who actively live their feminism full time; it's a title, same as "doctor." I do define myself as a feminist—with qualifications.

That is, if asked "Are you a feminist or not?" I'll say "I am." But if asked to describe myself, it's not a term I'd pull out myself, at least not until we were about fifty adjectives in. I don't associate with my own image of feminists, although I think I maintain some of the same ideals and objectives. The difference is in the practice; I don't exert feminism in the activist protesty way I think of "feminists" as doing.

Clearly, some women journalists do not identify with feminism, perceiving it as an old-fashioned and passé notion. Some women journalists shied away from the idea of working on "feminist stories." Judy Rebick, a well-known self-proclaimed feminist journalist in Canada, has said that

the [Canadian] media has decided that feminism is dead and that the women's movement has two feet in the grave . . . the media in general underestimates activists in general and women's groups in particular.[15]

The views of the women in this study echo Rebick's suggestion. Even the women who identified as "feminists" expressed concerns about developing stories with a "feminist" angle.

Women journalists who were less likely to identify as feminists communicated their reservations about the ways in which they employed their gender with regard to sexuality in the newsroom. Suzanne, a twenty-six-year-old self-identified European national television news producer, explained:

Yes, I guess I do identify as a feminist of sorts. This applies in the newsroom—but only if I apply my own definition. I don't think gender plays a role in the newsroom. But in field stories or interacting with male guests my gender has come into play. I have been hit or I have questioned myself as to whether or not I was using my femininity to get what I needed. I always question myself in these situations. Wondering whether I am being appropriate or perhaps "too feminine."

Easton also expressed some concern about the way she employs her sexuality in the workplace and how that confuses notions of feminism for her:

What role does gender play at work for me? Sometimes I use my femininity as an advantage, appearing more demure, helpless or flirtatious than I am in order to persuade or win a concession. Sometimes people use it against me, making coy flirtatious remarks that I wish they wouldn't. But it doesn't upset me; it's sort of part of how things work. Sometimes I use it, sometimes it's used against me; that seems a fair tradeoff. I've never felt that it was ever seriously used against me, however, in terms of holding me back.

Or in getting me promoted, either. On a larger scale, I do notice a difference when women are running a show, and when it's dominated by men.
The cooperative spirit seems stronger under women, versus a strong sense
of hierarchy and instruction of orders by men. It could be argued that
that's a function of individual styles, and that's true, but I don't think so.

In contrast, women journalists of color actively racialized gender issues. They were clear about identifying as feminists in and out of the
newsroom. All the female journalists of color saw themselves as feminists,
often insisting that antiracism was part of their feminist project (although it is important to note that only three women of color journalists
were interviewed, due to the reality that fewer women of color work in
the newsroom). Serafina explained her definition of feminism as follows:

A strong, independent woman who believes in fairness and equality (racial
equality as well as equality between the sexes). I think my image of feminists has changed in the last few years . . . simply because most of the independent "career women" I knew are now also wives and mothers. Feminists
can look like anything! I consider myself a feminist in all areas of my life
. . . it's not something I leave at home when I head to the office. I'm sure
there are more women working as television current affairs producers now
than men. I think there's an assumption that if you are a woman in our
business, you must be a feminist.

When asked whether or not she described herself as a feminist, Lily explained to me that her interests in antiracism and feminism were intertwined. She went on to say, "I absolutely define myself as a feminist. I feel
sad when women say, 'I'm not a feminist, but I believe men and women
should be paid equally. I mean, what do you think feminism is, exactly,
anyway?'"

### The Meaning of Antiracism in Canadian Newsrooms

The question about antiracism in the newsroom led to a very different set
of responses, in which all the women interviewed readily identified as antiracists. There is a marked difference between the way this term is contemplated within the newsroom and the struggle over the meaning of antiracism as a concept and as a set of contested practices. In Canada,
among antiracist educators the term "antiracist" refers to the production
and reproduction of systematic racial inequality and the importance of

unraveling structural and institutional forms of racism. The women journalists interviewed had very different perceptions of the term "antiracist" as applied to themselves. Indeed, every single one of the women interviewed identified as an "antiracist" with responses ranging from "Yes. I believe in fighting racism at every opportunity" to "I certainly hope so!" However, their definitions of antiracism revealed a distinctly personalized identification with the term rather than a focus upon the eradication of racial inequalities in institutions. The following is a smattering of responses to the question "what is an antiracist?"

> To be antiracist means to be against any kind of action or comment that casts a disparaging light on someone because of their race. To be against unfair treatment of anyone based on their nationality, skin color, or ancestry . . . A person who promotes equality between different ethnic groups, who will not allow any stereotypes or misconceptions to go unchallenged.

There was a split between perceptions of racism in the newsroom as well. Many of the self-identified white journalists carefully explained that they thought people of color were getting opportunities on par with others in the newsroom. However, their responses were cautious, ranging from: "It's starting" to "Yes, I think so" to "I don't know how many people of color are hustling for opportunities in the newsroom." Statements like these indicate that these women experienced anxiety around questions of minority representation in the newsroom and had nagging doubts about their own perception of racial discrimination.

The women cited here expressed outrage against racism, but were unclear as to whether discrimination was actively practiced in their workplace. They had difficulty identifying and dealing with racism, although they alluded to the possibility that racism could well exist in the newsroom—it's just that, as "white women," they wouldn't know about it. The women of color journalists, on the other hand, had a very different perception of racial inequalities in the newsroom, citing several examples of racism in their workplace. Women of color journalists encounter particular racialized gendered ideologies about their ability to perform competently in the newsroom. Here, Serafina explains how many senior editors expected her to work on race stories exclusively and how her perceptions of stories are affected by her own racial identity:

> Race plays a huge role in my day-to-day work. It influences my story selection, and even my interview questions. I am very keenly aware of how different my life experience is [from that of my peers] because I am a visible-

minority woman. It affects how I look at a story—how I judge and interpret news events. I think my supervisors recognize it too—because I'm
often assigned the "immigrant/refugee/race" stories.

Serafina went on to discuss this further:

> All I can say is that the sexism in the newsroom was manageable. The racism
> was not. The women journalists who are now in their forties and fifties have
> made it much easier for those of us who followed. Unfortunately, the same
> can't be said for visible minorities. We still have to fight the image that we're
> nothing more than "unqualified tokens" who were hired because of our skin
> color. There's a lot of work that still has to be done.

Understandings of racial discrimination among white women journalists and women journalists of color were markedly different. Whereas
Serafina described witnessing experiences of racism, journalists like Eu-
ston commented that she didn't "see" or "feel" any gender or racial discrimination in the newsroom:

> Generally, I'm in an environment where I'm not constantly conscious of
> my gender or race and the advantages or disadvantages it causes me. Which
> I think is pretty good.

Many of the white women journalists interviewed told me that they
felt slightly uneasy responding to questions about race, simply because
they had never experienced any racism in the newsroom and had never
heard about any incidents. In contrast, the women of color journalists interviewed revealed many examples of racial discrimination. I was interested in the stark differences between these forms of knowledge. The tension and stress associated with some of the responses to questions of
racism among white women journalists demonstrates that racism is so
firmly embedded and pervasive in the dominant culture of the newsroom
that it is often invisible. Ruth Frankenberg, a U.S.-based white feminist
scholar of British origin, has explored the notion of "whiteness" which I
see as relevant here. Frankenberg sees whiteness as a position of structural advantage, associated with privileges of the most basic kind. Second, she claims it carries with it a set of ways of being in the world, often
not named as white but looked upon as either normal or invisible.[16] In
many of these interviews, I noted how racial denial tends to engender a
disingenuous innocence, reflecting the difficulties of acknowledging the
oppressive constraints (and privileges) of whiteness.

Returning to the problematic nature of multicultural policy may shed some light on the complexity of this perception. These beliefs are in no small part nuanced by the dominant ideological discourse communicated through multicultural policy. The rhetoric of multiculturalism continues to linger in the minds of these women, punctuating the public discourse which encourages Canadians to see their country as an egalitarian and multicultural nation. These women's responses to questions about antiracism are personalized, not framed as an institutionalized and systematic problem. People believe in and support multicultural principles in theory but not necessarily in practice. For example, people believe that if more minorities are hired, a more diverse workplace necessarily means that racial inequality will be eradicated. Many of the white female journalists interviewed noted that more visible minority women were being hired at their media organizations and that this contributed in part to making a workplace more "antiracist." However, greater diversity does not mean that there is less discrimination in the newsroom. In the following excerpt, Serafina suggests that the gender bias in journalism as a profession is changing as the relative power of female journalists improves, although it remains highly problematic with regard to race. She points out that racism in the newsroom is still a common experience among journalists of color, especially in terms of the treatment of minorities in news pieces:

I don't think there has ever been enough of an emphasis on accurate reflection of minorities in news pieces. The way it often works with a news story is that the government will release a report, or pass legislation on something early in the day . . . then researchers and reporters will scramble to find someone (an ordinary Canadian, as we used to call them) who is affected. Most of the time, that "ordinary Canadian" is white. The only time you are guaranteed to see an ethnic face is when the story has to do with immigration, race, or poverty. Stories about healthcare, budget cuts, or the environment seldom include visible minorities. I remember hearing researchers and producers argue that it was too difficult to find minorities for stories on a daily deadline because they didn't have the time to look. It's a very easy out. Instead of spending my time arguing with them about it, I decided to just make sure that I would book a minority whenever possible. So when I was asked to find kids for an arts story, or employees for a labor piece, I made sure they included people of color. A number of times, my supervisors commented on how "diverse" the people in the stories were. I did it under the same deadlines as everyone else. I thought it was valuable to show that it can be done. It knocks a few holes in their argument, don't you think?

Serafina claims that journalistic efforts to portray cultural diversity in Canada often fail to provide enough substantive detail that would enable Canadian viewers to better understand the experience of immigrants beyond the endless ritual references to ethnic groups' "rich cultural heritage." In part, this can be attributed to the nebulous nature of the multicultural policy—a policy whose rubric extends to the Canadian Broadcasting Act. Given the CBC's public service mandate and its journalistic independence as protected by the 1991 Broadcasting Act, it has a set of clear responsibilities to which it must adhere, including the "reflect[ion of] the multicultural and multiracial nature of Canada."[17] However, many women of color journalists pointed to the differences between theory and practice. Although the women journalists explained that they were beginning to witness a greater gender balance in newsrooms in Canada, with regard to race journalism remains one of the most segregated professions in North America.[18] The shift in terminology from "inequality" to "diversity" disguises those very institutional, systematic inequalities embedded in producers' preconceived notions about ethnic communities. Renaming alone is not enough to combat the prejudices which "color" racist perceptions in the newsroom. It masks racial hierarchy and marginalization within newsroom practices.

## Feminism in Canada: A Cautionary Tale?

In 1999, the number of women producers at the Canadian Broadcasting Corporation increased from 36.2 percent in 1988 to 46.1 per cent.[19] Despite the high number of women employed at the CBC, it is impossible to estimate the number of self-identified feminists within the organization, as such figures have never been tabulated. Although there are several major feminist and antiracist organizations in Canada, including the National Action Committee on the Status of Women (NAC), I found it difficult to identify any organization devoted to examining the marginalization of women in broadcast journalism.[20]

In this chapter I have explored how gender and racial ideologies affect workplace practices in Canadian newsrooms. In examining the institutional mechanisms through which racism and sexism are articulated in the day-to-day lives of women journalists in Canada, my interviews suggest that women journalists couch their definitions of "feminism" and "antiracism" in vernacular forms, echoing many of the associations of feminism with the stereotypical images of the 1960s and 1970s. Second, although many women expressed a desire to produce "antiracist" programming, many were unclear or unsure how to go about achieving such a project. Despite the proliferation of texts examining feminism and antiracism in academe, it seems that many professional women in newsrooms remained untouched by these sophisticated analyses. Powerful remedies against sexism and racism should not only be discussed in lecture halls—there is a need for greater understanding of racial and gender bias in the workplace as well.

The situation in Canada also reveals that, despite the increasing number of white women and women of color working in Canadian broadcasting, institutional sexism and racism have not been effectively challenged by women in this field. This can be understood in part by taking a critical look at the official discourse on multiculturalism and antiracism in Canada. As a policy, multiculturalism expresses the ideology of the nation as a unity of human difference, without unraveling how tensions arising from those differences can be managed. This problem was reflected in my interviews, which revealed a contradiction between the desire on the part of women journalists to celebrate antiracism and to be ideologically committed to equality, juxtaposed against the continued persistence of structural racism as a practical reality among journalists of color. Antiracism and multicultural strategies are one and the same for many white women. Multicultural policy as a backdrop for Canadian identity often ensures that forms of institutionalized racism are rendered invisible.

The experience of Canadian broadcast journalism provides a "cautionary tale" to feminists in other national contexts. My research reveals that the women interviewed are not involved in organized social justice movements, but rather in "individual" projects to advance their journalistic careers—a kind of "sink or swim" mentality. Their experiences suggest that women in broadcast journalism have increased their numbers without creating an organized and collective approach that could provide an explicitly feminist and antiracist organization for broadcast journalists in Canada. Although major feminist organizations in Canada like NAC have emphasized the importance of antiracist approaches, there has been no formalized project to examine racist and sexist ideologies in newsrooms across Canada.[21] Broadcast news can be used as a tool for cultural and social change or be employed as a means of reinforcing the status quo.

It is imperative that feminist organizations consider ways to strategically intervene by recruiting women and men working in journalism into feminist antiracist media projects. Women employed in Canadian broad-casting journalism often appear to participate in news production that may sustain racist and misogynistic ideologies in order to advance their careers. My interviews revealed that women journalists of color experi-ence strong feelings of helplessness, fear, and anger toward the institu-tionalized and systematic racism within newsmaking organizations. I suggest we move beyond questioning the male presence and its effect by exploring the racist nature of the news production process.

#### ACKNOWLEDGMENTS

I am grateful to both France Winddance Twine and Kathleen Blee who offered helpful suggestions on various drafts of this chapter. France Winddance Twine in particular asked me some challenging political and intellectual questions, and I thank her warmly for her acute analytical insight and unswerving encourage-ment and enthusiasm. I also owe a debt of gratitude to the women who shared their personal opinions with me during the interview process.

#### NOTES

1. Jane Arthurs, "Women and Television," in *Behind the Screens*, ed. Stuart Hood (London: Lawrence and Wishart, 1994), 100.

2. CBC, *Representation of Members of Visible Minorities at the CBC*. Prepared by Human Resources System Support (Toronto: CBC, 1999). HRIS (1976–95), VIP (1998).

3. Margaret Gallagher, *An Unfinished Story: Gender Patterns in Media Em-ployment* (Paris: UNESCO Reports on Mass Communication, 1995).

4. Cynthia Carter, Gill Branston, and Stuart Allan, eds., *News, Gender and Power* (London: Routledge, 1998).

5. In 1996 the CBC granted me a leave of absence. I returned to London to complete my Ph.D. in Geography. In July 1998, I returned to my job as a re-searcher/associate producer in the newsroom. A year later, I decided to leave the CBC. But my interest in television news, and in gender inequalities and minority representation in the media in particular, continues. I have discussed my experi-ences at the CBC in detail because my history of employment in broadcast jour-nalism provides me with a particular "insider" role. It offered me access to the women I interviewed for this project. I am all too aware that my privilege and power as a journalist of color and an academic creates a particular standpoint from which I examine these issues.

6. Carol Tator, "Taking a Stand against Racism in the Media," a speech by Carol Tator, Urban Alliance on Race Relations. Presented at Racism in the Media, a conference sponsored by the Toronto Community Reference Group on Ethno-Racial and Aboriginal Access to Metropolitan Services, October 1995.

7. Paula Skidmore, "Gender and the Agenda: News Reporting of Child Sexual Abuse," in *News, Gender and Power*, ed. Cynthia Carter, Gill Branston, and Stuart Allan (London: Routledge, 1998).

8. Statistics Canada, *Census: Nation Series, Ethnic Origin* 1996.

9. Statistics Canada, *The Daily: 1996 Census Ethnic Origin, Visible Minorities* (Ottawa: Statistics Canada, February 17, 1998), 11-001E.

10. Canadian Royal Commission on Bilingualism and Biculturalism, *Report of the Royal Commission on Bilingualism and Biculturalism: The Cultural Contribution of the Other Ethnic Groups* (Ottawa: Queen's Printer, 1962).

11. Canada, House of Commons Debates, statement of Pierre Trudeau, October 8, 1971.

12. For more nuanced discussions of multiculturalism, I refer the reader to Marlene Nourbese Philip, *Frontiers* (Stratford, On.: Mercury Press, 1992), and Audrey Kobayashi, "Multiculturalism: Representing a Canadian Institution," in *Place/Culture/Representation*, ed. James Duncan and David Ley (London: Routledge, 1993).

13. For further explorations of the meaning of the term "antiracism," I refer the reader to the following: Goli Reza-Rashti, "Connecting Racism and Sexism: The Dilemma of Working with Minority Female Students," in *Antiracism, Feminism and Critical Approaches to Education*, ed. Roxana Ng, Pat Staton, and Joyce Scane (Westport, Conn.: Bergin and Garvey, 1994), and Roxana Ng, "Racism, Sexism and Nation Building in Canada," in *Race, Identity and Representation in Education*, ed. Cameron McCarthy and Warren Crichlow (London: Routledge, 1993).

14. I limited my scope to those women who worked in either television news or radio news. They worked in a variety of capacities, which included stints as editorial assistants, researchers, producers, show writers, chase producers, and reporters. The youngest of these women was twenty-seven, the oldest in her fifties. I attempted to interview a wide range of ethnic groups as well as women with disabilities. I asked the women a total of twenty questions with regard to their beliefs and values related to race and feminism, including "What does feminism mean to you?" "What does "antiracism" mean to you?" and "What role does gender play in your day-to-day life at work?" In order to protect the women who gave of themselves in these interviews, I have used pseudonyms and have left vague the names of the news organizations that each woman worked for at the time of the interview. The interview segments by no means represent the entire population of the newsroom. Not all women journalists will recognize the descriptions of the newsroom experience or agree with the points of view of the women expressed here.

15. Judy Rebick, "Women's March Overlooked by Media," *London Free Press*, March 10, 2000, A17.

16. Ruth Frankenberg, *White Women: Race Matters: The Social Construction of Whiteness* (Minneapolis: University of Minnesota Press, 1993).

17. Canada, House of Commons, *Broadcasting Act 1991* (Ottawa: June 4, 1991).

18. Farai Chideya, *Don't Believe the Hype* (London: Random House, 1995).

19. Women constituted 41.5 percent of the CBC workforce in 1998 (CBC Statistics, 1999).

20. However, it is important to note that the Canadian Association of Journalists does have a women's caucus and a listserve.

21. I would be remiss, however, if I did not mention that some researchers and organizations have begun to investigate racism in the media more broadly, including the Urban Alliance on Race Relations, the Centre for Research—Action on Race Relations, Media Awareness Network, Toronto Coalition against Racism, and the Antiracism Response Network, among others.

# Chronology of Selected Feminist, Racist, and Antiracist Actions

1825    The Ladies Society for the Relief of Negro Slaves established in Britain.

1830–33    Hundreds of thousands of women in Britain signed antislavery petitions which represented the first large-scale intervention by women in Parliament.

1848    First convention in the world held specifically to discuss women's rights. Attended by 240 people (including 40 men) in Seneca Falls, New York.

1861–65    Civil War in the United States.

1863    The Emancipation Proclamation issued on January 1, 1862, declared "free only those slaves who lived under Confederate rule."

1865    Slavery abolished in the United States by the Thirteenth Amendment to the Constitution by 121 to 124 votes.

1867    Barber-Scotia College founded in Concord, North Carolina, to educate recently emancipated black women in the United States.

1868    Fourteenth Amendment to the Constitution (July 28) affirmed the rights of citizenship to black people born in the United States.

1875    Civil Rights Act of 1875 enacted under President Ulysses S. Grant; the last piece of civil rights legislation in the United States until 1957.

1881    Spelman College, the oldest liberal arts college for black women, founded in Atlanta, Georgia, to provide an education for black women who were excluded from the state-sanctioned racially segregated public universities and private universities.

1883    Aboriginal Protection Board (later Welfare) established by the New South Wales government.

1883    United States Supreme Court rules that the 1875 Civil Rights Act does not apply to "personal acts of social discrimination."

1896   The National Association of Colored Women (NACW), the oldest secular black organization in the United States, was incorporated with the merger of the National Federation of Afro-American women (founded in Boston in 1896) and the National League of Colored Women.

1896   Supreme Court ruled in Plessy v. Ferguson, which legalized systematic race discrimination by introducing the concept of "separate but equal."

1902   White women granted suffrage in Australia.

1909   National Association for the Advancement of Colored People (NAACP) founded by six black Americans and 47 whites on the 100th anniversary of Abraham Lincoln's birth.

1914–18   World War I.

1917   Indian Women's Association founded.

1920   Nineteenth Amendment to the Constitution ratified, granting women suffrage in the United States.

1923   Equal Rights Amendment introduced in the U.S. Congress.

1925   National Council of Women formed in India.

1928   First conference on the Status of Aboriginal Women held in Australia.

1930   White women granted suffrage in South Africa.

1932   Women granted suffrage in Brazil.

1939–45   World War II.

1944   Women granted suffrage in France.

1945   Granting of women's suffrage in Japan.

1947   India gained independence from Britain, its former colonial ruler.

1948   First International Women's Day since Second World War in Japan.

1948   Apartheid established in South Africa.

1948   United Nations adopted the Universal Declaration of Human Rights.

1948   United Nations adopted the Convention on the Prevention and Punishment of the Crime of Genocide.

1948–94   Apartheid (from the Afrikaans word for "apartness") was a social and political policy or racial segregation and discrimination enforced by white minority government in South Africa. After the primarily Afrikaaner Nationalist came to power, the social custom of apartheid was systematized under law.

1949    Women granted suffrage in China.

1950    Women granted suffrage in India.

1950    The Population Registration Act of 1950 put all South Africans into three racial categories: Bantu (black Africans), white, or Colored (of mixed race). A fourth category, Asian (Indians and Pakistanis) was added later.

1956    The Italian government ratified the 1954 Convention on Equal Pay of the International Labour Office.

1957    Women granted suffrage in Nigeria.

1959    Promotion of Bantu Self Government created ten South African homelands administered by reestablished African tribal self governments, pseudo-states within South Africa.

1961    South Africa granted independence from British rule.

1961    Fanny Lou Hamer, Black civil rights leader, was sterilized without her knowledge or consent.

1961    Attendance of Conference of Asian and African women by nine Japanese female representatives.

1962    Equal Pay Act passed in the United States.

1963    United Nations Declaration on the Elimination of All Forms of Racial Discrimination.

1963    *The Feminine Mystique* by Betty Friedan published and became a bestseller in the United States.

1963    Women granted suffrage in Kenya.

1964    1964 Civil Rights Act enacted under President Lyndon B. Johnson (Democrat); the most extensive civil rights legislation since the nineteenth century.

1964    Betty Friedan and her colleagues formed the National Organization for Women (NOW).

1965    1964 Civil Rights Act passed in the United States.

1965    United Nations adopted the International Convention on the Elimination of All Forms of Racism.

1965    Unilateral declaration of independence by Rhodesia (Zimbabwe).

1965–70 Southern Rhodesia (Zimbabwe)—War of Independence from British rule.

1966    Referendum enabling Aboriginal and Torres Strait Islanders to vote.

1967    Yemen established independence from British rule.

1968    Dennis Banks, Clyde Bellecourt, and George Miller organized the American Indian Movement (AIM) in Minneapolis, Minnesota. Like the Black Panther Party, AIM was sparked by discriminatory arrests of American Indians by police in Minneapolis at St. Paul.

1969   Stonewall rebellion in New York City.

1969   The Aborigines Welfare Board established in Australia.

1970   The Bantu Homelands Citizenship Act made every black South African a citizen of one of the homelands, effectively excluding blacks from South African politics.

1970   First women's liberation mass demonstration in Japan.

1971   Black Panther Party, Women's and Gay Liberation organizations held Revolutionary People's Constitutional Convention in Philadelphia, Pennsylvania.

1972   First issue of *Ms.* magazine, the first commercial feminist magazine in the United States arrived at newsstands.

1972   Self-employed Women's Association (SEWA) founded in Gujarat, India.

1972   The Boston Women's Health Collective published the first edition of *Women and Their Bodies* (renamed *Our Bodies, Our Selves*) which launched a national women's health movement in the United States.

1972   Saito Chiyo founded *Agora*, the longest running feminist journal in postwar Japan.

1973   Roe v. Wade (January 22). Striking down a Texas criminal ban on abortions not necessary to save the life of the mother, the United States Supreme Court issues its 7–2 decision, which recognized for the first time that the constitutional right to privacy encompasses a women's right to terminate her pregnancy.

1973   The National Black Feminist Organization founded, held a conference, and launched ten local chapters in the United States.

1973   United Nations adopted the International Convention of the Suppression and Punishment of the Crime of Apartheid.

1973   United Women's Anti-Price Rise Front formed in India.

1973   First woman advisor to the Australian government.

1974   The Mexican American Women's National Association (MANA) founded.

1974   Progressive Organization of Women formed in India.

1975   United Nations declared 1975 as the International Year of the Women.

1975   UN Conference for International Women's Year in Mexico City.

1976   Patriotic Front against white rule formed in Rhodesia (now Zimbabwe) by ZAPU and ZANU.

1977   The Combahee River Collective Statement published by black feminists in the United States.

1977   The National Center for Lesbian Rights established, as a project of Equal Rights Advocates, a feminist based-organization in the United States.

1977   Equal Employment Law passed in Italy.

1978   First World Conference to Combat Racism and Racial Discrimination held in Geneva.

1978   Inauguration of International Women's Studies Association and Japan Women's Studies Association.

1979   Convention on the Elimination of All Forms of Discrimination (CEDAW) passed by the United Nations.

1979   Native Indian women's walk from Oka Reserve (near Montreal) to Parliament in Ottawa, Canada.

1980   Equal Rights Amendment defeated. It failed to be ratified by two-thirds of the states in the United States.

1980   Black majority rule in Zimbabwe.

1981   The Legal Age of Majority passed in Zimbabwe, giving eighteen-year-old women complete independence and adult legal status.

1981   UN Human Rights Committee ruled in favor of Sandra Lovelace (a Native Indian woman), finding Canada in violation of the International Covenant on Civil and Political Rights.

1981   Kitchen Table Press published *This Bridge Called My Back: Writings by Radical Women of Color* (edited by Cherrie Moraga and Gloria Anzaldua) in the United States.

1982   The Feminist Press published the landmark book *All the Women Are White, All the Blacks Are Men, But Some of Us Are Brave: Black Women's Studies* (edited by Gloria T. Hall, Patricia Bell Scott, and Barbara Smith) in the United States.

1983   Kitchen Table Press published *Home Girls: A Black Feminist Anthology* (edited by Barbara Smith).

1983   Second World Conference to Combat Racism and Racial Discrimination held in Geneva.

1983   Colored and Asian women granted suffrage in South Africa.

1983–   United Nations Programme of Action for the Second Decade
2003   to Combat Racial Discrimination.

1984    Translation and publication of the Japanese edition of *Our Bodies, Our Selves.*

1984    Geraldine Ferraro nominated by the Democratic Party as the first women Vice Presidential candidate in a U.S. election.

1985    United Nations Third World Conference on Women in Nairobi, Kenya.

1985    State of emergency declared in South Africa.

1989    Meetings on human rights of illegal Asian female workers cooperatively organized by women's groups in Japan.

1990    Demands made by Korean "comfort women" that Japanese prime minister recognized Japan's responsibility for forced prostitution during World War II.

1990    Japanese women's groups coordinated nationwide protests against beauty pageants in Japan.

1990    Women granted suffrage in Yemen.

1990    Release of Nelson Mandela from prison.

1991    African American Women in Defense of Ourselves published an advertisement in the *New York Times* and a number of national newspapers in the United States in response to the Anita Hill–Clarence Thomas hearings.

1993    Ruth Bader Ginsburg became the first feminist to be appointed to the Supreme Court of the United States.

1993    India established a quota system for women in local elections.

1994    Black women voted in the first democratic elections in South Africa.

1994    Nelson Mandela became the first South African president elected in a democratic vote.

1995    Fourth World Conference on Women in Beijing, China.

1997    European Year against Racism.

1997    Stolen Generation report published in Australia.

1999    The Zimbabwean Supreme Court decided that in instances where customary law clashed with constitutional provisions guaranteeing equality, "the African nature of society dictates that women are not equal to men." Only African women are bound by customary law.

1999    Thirty-four years after it was first submitted for approval, the contraceptive pill was approved by the Health Ministry in Japan.

2000    World Conference against Racism.

2000    World March for Women.

# Selected List of Feminist and Antiracist Organizations

*Australia*

**Aboriginal Centre of Tasmania**
198 Elizabeth Street
Hobart, Australia

**Riawanna Aboriginal Education Centre**
Churchill Avenue
Sandy Bay, Tasmania 7005
Australia

**Council for Aboriginal Reconciliations**
Locked Bay 14
Kingston ACT 2694
Australia
Website: *http://www.austlii.edu.au/car/*

**Office of the Status of Women**
Women Tasmania
Public Buildings, Franklin Square
Hobart, Tasmania 7000
Australia

*Canada*

**MediaWatch**
A nonprofit feminist organization working to eliminate sexism in the media.

517 Wellington Street West, Suite 204
Toronto, Ontario
M5V 1G1
Canada
Phone: (416) 408-2065
FAX: (416) 408-2069
Website: *www.mediawatch.ca*
Email: info@mediawatch.ca

**The National Action Committee on the Status of Women (NAC)**
NAC, a coalition of more than 700 groups, is the largest feminist organization in Canada.

234 Eglinton Avenue East, Suite 203
Toronto, Ontario
M4P 1K5
Canada
Phone: (416) 932-1718
FAX: (416) 932-0646
Website: *www.nac-cca.ca*

**Antiracist Action—Toronto**
P.O. Box 291 Station B
Toronto, Ontario
M5T 2T2
Canada
Website: *web.apac.org/~ara/who/intro.htm*

**Canadian Race Relations Foundation**
Committed to building a national framework to fight racism in Canadian society. Opened in 1997 after an agreement was reached between the Government of Canada and the National Association of Japanese Canadians. Under the terms of the agreement the federal government promised to create a Canadian Race Relations Foundation to "foster racial harmony and cross-cultural understanding."

4576 Yonge Street
Suite 701, Toronto, Ontario
Canada
M2N 6N4
Website: *www.crr.ca*

*France*

**SOS-Racisme**
28 rue des Petites Ecuries
75010 Paris
Website: *http://www.sos-racisme.org*

**Groupe d'Information et de soutien aux travailleurs immigrés (GISTI)**
3 villa Marces
75011 Paris
France
Phone: 01 43 14 84 84

**Maison des femmes**
163 rue de Charenton
75012 Paris
France
Phone: 00 33 1 4 343 4113

**Les Nanas Beurs**
126 rue de Casteja
92100 Boulogne
France

**Women Living under Muslim Law**
Boite Postale 20023
34791 Grabels Cedex
France


*India*

**All India Democratic Women's Association**
121, Vithalbhai Patel House
Rafi Marg
New Delhi 110 001

**National Federation of Indian Women**
1001, Ansal Bhavan
K.G. Marg
New Delhi 100 001

**Sahelia**
85 and 108, Defence Colony Flyover Market
New Delhi 110 024

**Joint Women's Program**
14 Jangpura B
New Delhi 110 014

**All India Women's Conference**
6 Bhagwan Dass Road
New Delhi 110 001

**CREA (Creating Resources for Empowerment in Action)**
CREA believes that every girl and woman should enjoy her inherent right to dignity and therefore must have human rights—a life free from violence, access to health, education, information, and other vital resources. CREA aspires to build national, regional, and international linkages among women in local leadership and increase their capacities to become more effective advocates for women's human rights.

7 Mathura Road, Jangpura B
New Delhi 110 014
Phone: 91-11-4310985
FAX: 91-11-4628753
Email: *creaworld@mail.com*

*Italy*

**Centro Interculturale delle donne**
(The Intercultural Women's Center, Alma Mater)
Via Norberto Rosa 13/1
Torino, Italy
Phone: 011 24.64.330

**Associazione Produrre e Riprodurre**
Via Vanchilia 3
Torino 10125, Italy
Phone: 011 812.25.19

## *Japan*

**Center of Research and Documentation on Japan's War Responsibility**
Website: *http://www.jca.apc.org/JWRC*

**Asia-Japan Women's Resource Center**
Website: *http://www.jca.ax.apc.org/ajwrc/*

**Violence against Women in War—Net Japan**
Website: *http://www.jca.ax.apc.org/vaww-net-japan/*


## *South Africa*

**Gender Equity Unit (GEU)**
University of Western Cape
Private Mail Bag X17, Bellville 7535
Phone: (021) 959-2813
FAX: (021) 951-1766

**Rape Crisis South Africa (RCCT)**
Website: *http://www.rapecrisis.org.za*
Box 7935, Western Cape, South Africa
Phone: (021) 447-1467
Email: carol@rapecrisis.org.za
Director: Carol Bower

**End Racism and Sexism through Education (ERASE)**
P.O. Box 262
Salt River 7924
WCAPE, South Africa
Phone: (021) 448-6934
Website: *http://www.womensnet.org.za*


## *United States*

**Anti-Racist Action**
P.O. Box 82097
Columbus, OH 43202

Phone: (614) 424-9074
Website: *http://www.aranet.org*

**Exotic Dancer's Alliance**
2215 R Market St., Suite 186
San Francisco, CA 94115
Phone: (415) 995-4745

**Black Women for Wages for Housework**
P.O. Box 86681
Los Angeles, CA 90086-0681
Director: Margaret Prescod

**U.S. Prostitutes Collective**
P.O. Box 14512
San Francisco, CA 94114

**Center for Third World Organizing**
1218 E. 21st Street
Oakland, CA 94606
Phone: (510) 533-7583
Email: *ctwo@actwo.org*

**Center for Health and Gender Equity (CHANGE)**
CHANGE works to ensure that the health and population policies of international institutions supported by the U.S. government actively promote women's reproductive and sexual health.

6930 Carroll Ave., Suite 430
Takoma Park, Washington, D.C.
Phone: (301) 270-1182
Website: *www.CHANGE@genderhealth.org*

**Critical Resistance**
Website: *http://www.prisonactivist.org/critical/*

**International Concerned Family and Friends of Mumia Abu-Jamal**
Website: *http://www.mumia.org/index3.html*

**Men's Rape Prevention Project**
P.O. Box 57144
Washington, DC 20037-7144
(202) 265-6530
Website: *http://www.mrpp.org*

**Men Stopping Violence**
1020 DeKalb Ave., #25
Atlanta, GA 30307
Phone: (404) 688-1376
FAX: (404) 688-4021
Email: *mstewart@igc.org*

**Men as Peacemakers**
205 West 2nd St., #424
Duluth, MN 55802
Phone: (218) 727-1939
Email: *peacemakers@computerpro.com*

**Men Stopping Rape**
306 N. Brooks Street
Madison, WI 53715-1090
Phone: (608) 257-4444

**People's Institute for Survival and Beyond**
1444 Johnson Street
New Orleans, LA 70116-1767
Phone: (504) 944-2354
Email: *pisabnola@aol.com*

*Yemen*

**International Cooperation for Development (ICD)**
P.O. Box 1045
Sana'a
Republic of Yemen

**The Empirical Research and Women's Studies Center**
Sana'a University
P.O. Box 1802
Sana'a
Republic of Yemen

**Women's Economic Empowerment Association (WEEA)**
P.O. Box 19175
Sana'a
Republic of Yemen

## *Zimbabwe*

**Women's Action Group**
P.O. Box 135
Harare, Zimbabwe
Email: *wag@wag.org.zw*

# Index